Competition and the State

Competition and the State

Edited by Thomas K. Cheng, Ioannis Lianos, and D. Daniel Sokol

STANFORD LAW BOOKS
An Imprint of Stanford University Press
Stanford, California

Stanford University Press
Stanford, California

Printed in the United States of America on acid-free, archival-quality paper

Library of Congress Cataloging-in-Publication Data

Competition and the state / edited by Thomas K. Cheng, Ioannis Lianos, and D. Daniel Sokol.
pages cm — (Global competition law and economics)
Includes bibliographical references and index.
ISBN 978-0-8047-8939-4 (cloth : alk. paper)
1. Antitrust law. 2. Restraint of trade. 3. Competition—Government policy. I. Cheng, Thomas K., editor of compilation. II. Lianos, Ioannis, editor of compilation. III. Sokol, D. Daniel, editor of compilation. IV. Series: Global competition law and economics.
K3850.C643 2014
343.07′21—dc23

2014002232

ISBN 978-0-8047-9162-5 (electronic)

Typeset by Newgen in 10.5/14 Bembo

Contents

Contributors

Joseph Bauer is a professor of law at Notre Dame Law School.

Thomas K. Cheng is an associate professor at the University of Hong Kong Faculty of Law.

Philippe Gagnepain is an associate member of the Université Paris 1 Panthéon-Sorbonne.

R. Richard Geddes is an associate professor in the Department of Policy Analysis and Management at Cornell University and director of the Cornell Program in Infrastructure Policy.

Leigh Hancher is a professor of European law at the University of Tilburg and is also counsel at Allen & Overy.

Deborah Healey is a senior lecturer and director of the Corporate and Commercial Stream at the University of New South Wales Faculty of Law.

Alberto Heimler is a professor of economics at the Scuola Superiore della pubblica amministrazione (the Italian School of Government).

Dae-Sik Hong is a professor of law at Sogang Law School.

Marc Ivaldi is a professor at the Toulouse School of Economics.

Chantal Latgé-Roucolle is an assistant professor of economics at the Ecole Nationale de l'Aviation Civile.

Ioannis Lianos is a reader (associate professor) in European and competition law and economics at University College London (UCL) and director of the Centre for Law, Economics and Society at UCL. He is also the head of the competition unit of the Laboratory on Law, Development and Innovation at the Higher School of Economics in Moscow.

Francesco Salerno is a senior attorney at Cleary Gottlieb Steen & Hamilton.

D. Daniel Sokol is an associate professor at the University of Florida Levin College of Law and a senior research fellow at the George Washington University Law School Competition Law Center.

Paul Stephan is the John C. Jeffries, Jr., distinguished professor of law at the University of Virginia School of Law.

Alexander "Sasha" Volokh is an assistant professor of Law at Emory University School of Law.

Wentong Zheng is an assistant professor at the University of Florida Levin College of Law.

Competition and the State

Introduction

Thomas K. Cheng, Ioannis Lianos, and D. Daniel Sokol

Governments intervene widely in markets to achieve various policy goals. Sometimes these policy goals align with one another and sometimes they conflict and require various trade-offs in policy responses, such as to pursue efficiency, to correct market failures, or to ensure equity and distributive justice.

In recent years, the interaction of competition law and policy with state (government) activity has attracted considerable interest from the global competition community, both among scholars and within policy circles.[1] Developments around the world have created the need to reconsider the roles of competition and the state. This reconsideration forces competition law to interact, sometimes uneasily, with a broader and somewhat distinct competition policy. The broader competition policy (which includes not only competition law but also other measures to address issues of competition in the economy) interfaces with state activity across many different levels of how government organizes economic behavior.

Government organizes economic activity in part through the shape and nature of regulation and overall state involvement. Understanding the distinction between competition law and policy clarifies competition authorities' capabilities and limitations when it comes to promoting competition in situations of a broader regulatory overlay. Competition law focuses on enforcement, whereas competition authorities also must address issues of nonenforcement such as advocacy and institutional design. When considering the question of institutional design, how countries design optimal competition policy involves three choices: what to leave to the jurisdiction of competition law (and competition agencies and judges), what to assign to noncompetition authorities (such as sector regulators) exclusively as part of their jurisdiction, and how to establish concurrent jurisdiction among the competition authority and two or more regulatory authorities.

The role of competition advocacy on the part of competition authorities is significant in both developed and developing economies. The state sets the rules by shaping how market forces work. A focus on country competitiveness often highlights regulatory barriers to business creation and economic growth. These include rules and regulations that may impact how the market operates. For example, licensing requirements may serve certain important noncompetition purposes, such as ensuring quality of service. However, overly stringent requirements may create significant barriers to entry and reduce competition. Addressing these barriers has been a significant part of competition policy in both young and old competition authorities and has fed into efforts at reform.

Efforts at competition advocacy shape the economic activity that competition law enforces. Depending on the legal system, competition law may directly (or only indirectly) address public restraints, private restraints, and mixed public-private restraints on competition.

A number of factors, some long term and some more immediate, have made the role of the state as it relates to competition an issue of primary importance. Most immediately, the impact of the worldwide financial crisis has led to a fundamental reexamination of the state's role in economic development. Countries that had liberalized various parts of the economy reacted to the financial crisis via direct government intervention through increased government ownership interest in strategically important firms (such as in the financial sector or for firms that had significant employment).

Many countries passed new laws and regulations that fundamentally reorganized the role of the market in a given country. Even though many of the debates surrounding policy decisions centered on "competition" and "competitiveness," competition authorities for the most part played only a minor role in the formulation of these policies.[2] As countries face continued economic crises, the need for effective competition law and policy will only grow. Yet, the various permutations of both the state's and competition law's roles remain vague.

The state's role in the economy is both pervasive and unclear. This is due to problems in measuring state-related activity. There is no definitive measure for state involvement in economic life. One way to measure the degree of government intervention in an economy is usually in terms of public expenditure as a percentage of GDP. In the Organisation for Economic Co-operation and Development (OECD) countries, the degree of government intervention, measured in terms of public expenditure as a percentage of GDP, has on the average increased, although there are marked differences among its members. In 2011, this ranged from around 31.5 percent (Korea) to 56 percent (Denmark), with the OECD countries averaging 43.3 percent.[3]

Another way to measure the impact of the state's role on competition is to measure regulation's role, as the OECD does,[4] across countries based upon competition in the nonmanufacturing economy. This portion of the economy represents two-thirds of economic activity in OECD countries and those parts of the economy that are the most growth oriented. These studies find variation in domestic and foreign direct investment patterns,[5] the labor market,[6] productivity,[7] and their impact on structural reforms.

One can also calculate the number of international trade barriers to determine how much control the state has over how the market operates. Although tariff barriers have declined over time, in developed world countries these have been replaced by nontariff barriers. In short, barriers to trade in goods and services remain significant.[8]

What does the role of the state mean as it relates to competition? This government intervention may take different forms, depending on the policy area and the dimension of government action with the preservation of some form of market competition. For example, governments may intervene as market makers: they might decide to use competitive tendering to introduce competition for goods and services that were previously supplied solely by the public sector; they might introduce more choice in the provision of public services by opening access to private or voluntary sector providers; or they might make tradable permits accessible in such a way as to most efficiently allocate among private providers the costs of engaging in an activity that is harmful to society.

The state may operate to create or facilitate markets, or in some cases to act as a market participant. Governments can affect markets through direct participation as a supplier to provide public goods and services that free markets are unlikely to supply at an adequate level. Governments also act as significant buyers of goods and services from the private sector to deliver public services and perform their normal functions. In dispensing public services the government may establish a state-owned enterprise (SOE) or a public-private partnership (a relatively recent phenomenon, as Chapter 3 discusses), or it may decide to procure services through a competitive tendering process.[9] Alternatively, the state may act as a deregulator in which it removes regulation to unleash market forces within various parts of the economy.

Starting in the late 1970s and early 1980s in the United States and the United Kingdom, the deregulatory/economic liberalization movement spread across the world. This trend became more pronounced in the 1990s. In more recent years, the liberalization road map to economic development has come under fire from both liberal economies and countries that have organized their economies along a more managed path. Countries that managed their economies less, such as the United States and the United Kingdom, suddenly found themselves owners of significant firms and regulators of industries that had been left more to market forces in the past.

The emergence of new global economic powers, where state intervention in the economy remains the norm rather than the exception, particularly China, is another significant factor that forces a reconsideration of the relationship between competition and the state. Because of the export-oriented nature of the Chinese economy, other countries must confront the Chinese competitiveness in ways that the legal system has not been able to do. An important part of the structure of China's managed economy (and to a certain extent of other countries in specific sectors) is its reliance on SOEs.[10] SOEs are present in various economic sectors, from gambling and alcohol sales to utilities, transport, oil, universities, and health care. SOEs have been instrumental in the economic success of some jurisdictions and are important players in global markets. In some cases, SOEs behave much the same way private firms do, with similar capital structures and a profit-maximizing incentive. In other circumstances, profit maximization is less important than revenue maximization, and managerial structures and controls resemble those of government ministries. As the lines separating private and public in the context of SOE incentives become blurred (see Chapters 1 and 13 for further discussion), the way competition law should address potential anticompetitive conduct by SOEs becomes an issue.

Likewise, governments may intervene indirectly by influencing private markets when they create either negative or positive impacts on consumer or total welfare. In this case, command and control regulation or more market-based incentive forms of regulation might be other venues for taxes and subsidies to influence the incentives and behaviors of private firms. Sometimes, governments deliberately try to influence consumer behaviors in a variety of ways—for example, by providing information on hidden costs associated with certain types of consumption (e.g., advertising campaigns against tobacco or alcohol) or by nudging consumers to adopt a behavior that will protect their self-interest. They might also attempt to indirectly influence businesses by coordinating private-sector activities to generate the appropriate amount of information for the adoption of public policies or by promoting self-regulation by business, as this generally saves implementation costs.

In some situations, government intervention may be the by-product of corruption, may be captured by special interests, or it may be following the right objectives but be badly designed—what is called "government failure."[11] In this case it will be, in general, welfare reducing. In other instances, however, government intervention is justified by legitimate public interest objectives. Of course, it is not the aim of competition law to correct any form of government failure if that failure does not impact the competitive process. Competition law may supplement other areas of law in an effort to improve government action and increase efficiency. Yet, the role of competition law is also relevant in the context of legitimate state action, depending on the forms that the latter may take, some of which may affect the competitive process more than others.

This book analyzes the multifaceted role of the state and its impact on competition law and policy. The chapters address various aspects of the tensions and complexities involved in competition and the state's role. Although the book offers different normative approaches, economic analysis remains a unifying theme. The way economic analysis is used in competition law and policy can create problems in other parts of regulation.

Several chapters provide examples of how these factors might impact competition across a number of different areas. For example, airline regulation, covered in Chapter 1, must ensure customer safety, and in some countries, airports are required to provide flights to smaller airports for reasons of fairness. Yet, liberalization that promotes competition by allowing additional domestic carriers to compete, reducing entry and fare restrictions, and reducing barriers to foreign carriers creates significant price deflation. Chapter 2 discusses the various goals regarding the provision of health services. Allowing consumers to choose their own health coverage, physicians, and health care facilities opens the door to intense competition. This competition had to be managed in such a way as to create incentives for hospitals while maintaining the principle of competitive neutrality. Therefore, government intervention in the economy may indeed affect the competitive process and thus be subject to the scope of competition law. This raises the questions of how competition law can apply to government activity and if specific competition rules and principles for public actors must be established. It also questions the scope of competition law as opposed to the role of advocacy to identify and correct anticompetitive legislation and regulation.

The starting point of each competition law regime is obviously different because its evolution largely depends on the role and place of government intervention in the economy. For example, in the United States, the Sherman Act does not have any specific provisions on state restrictions on competition and has mainly targeted privately owned corporations, in view of the few state-owned enterprises in the United States. It has also declared regulations adopted by the federal state or the states to be immune, under certain conditions, from antitrust enforcement.

In Europe, state action was soon subjected to the strict scrutiny of European Union competition law, in view of the important role of state-owned undertakings in the European economy,[12] the need to preserve market integration, and the *effet utile* of EU competition law against the attempt of national governments to protect their national champions or incumbent firms by adopting anticompetitive regulations.[13] Competition law thus operated as a complement to the internal market project. As a result of these broader aims of EU competition law, the legal framework put in place by the constitutive treaties include, in addition to provisions on collusive and unilateral conduct, provisions on the control of state aids and the conduct of state monopolies and undertakings entrusted with special or exclusive rights.

The EU courts have also developed a body of case law on different forms of public restrictions on competition, ranging from SOEs' dominance, to the regulation of state privileges and licenses conferring exclusivity, to state measures that restrict competition or that facilitate private restrictions.[14] The EU is not the only jurisdiction possessing specific competition rules applying to state action. Among other jurisdictions, Russia, Mexico, and China (see Chapter 10) prohibit state and local measures that unduly restrict the free flow of goods in their internal trade. There is also binding international governance of state action across a number of areas within the trade setting, such as telecoms,[15] financial services,[16] and state trading enterprises.[17]

More recently, competition advocacy has risen in importance as one of the major tasks of competition agencies, with a special Advocacy Working Group created in the International Competition Network (ICN).[18] According to the ICN standard definition, competition advocacy "refer[s] to those activities conducted by the competition agency related to the promotion of a competitive environment by means of nonenforcement mechanisms, mainly through its relationships with other governmental entities and by increasing public awareness of the benefits of competition."[19] In performing their competition advocacy functions, competition authorities are interacting increasingly with other parts of government and utilizing an important tool to make their voice for competition heard.

Even if one assumes that competition law (in the broad sense) should apply to various forms of state action, it is still important to ascertain if competition rules applying to government activities should take into account that, contrary to the action of private economic actors who are motivated by the pursuit of their own interests, state actors are presumably motivated by the promotion of the public interest. Certainly, the calls for competitive neutrality are strong,[20] but while SOEs may have some inherent advantages, they can also suffer from certain disabilities due to the variety of tasks and missions of general interest they assume. Hence, one might argue that SOEs should be subject to competition rules, albeit with some adjustments.[21]

This book seeks to fill a void by providing a collection of works that address various aspects of the role of the state across a number of dimensions as it relates to competition law and policy. Part I reconceptualizes the interaction between competition law and government activities, in view of the profound transformation of the conception of state action in recent years, by looking to the challenges of privatization, new public management, and public-private partnerships.

Chapter 1, by Alexander Volokh, focuses on a core issue of the role of the state in competition law. SOEs have been set up in many jurisdictions for a market replacement function. When economies become liberalized, there is the potential for market-based competition. It is in this context that privatization might both raise funds for the government coffers in the near term and create greater efficiencies for the long term. However, in many instances, there have been concerns that privatization's positive effects may have been mitigated as public monopolies were replaced by private ones. Chapter 1 links two themes of privatization to competition law: corporate governance and competition policy. The chapter discusses the impact of privatizations on natural monopolies and explores why competition law may serve as an entry-promoting policy. Using standard public choice methods, the chapter then discusses the limitations on public monopolies (including organs of the government) that create exemptions from competition law. Ultimately Volokh is agnostic on which form of ownership is optimal, as so much of successful economic organization of society is context specific.

In Chapter 2, Ioannis Lianos recasts the law and economics of competition using a socio-legal approach. He argues that the traditional dichotomy of market versus state in competition policy is a false one because it ignores the multifaceted nature of the concept of "state," the evolution of the composition and role of public bureaucracies, and the interaction between politics and scientific (here economic) expertise in policy making. One should take into account that a neoliberal state will require a different approach in the interaction of competition law with government activity from a patrimonial or a neocorporatist one. In a neoliberal state, the value of competition may already be integrated in all forms of state action. The "technology" of professional public bureaucracy has also evolved in parallel toward a more proactive technocracy, assuming tasks of forecast, knowledge gathering, and sharing. Regulators compete with competition authorities in the market for expertise and may sometimes be better placed than the latter in reconciling the different objectives pursued by government action with the principle of competition. Lianos illustrates this new dynamic by focusing on two examples: the competition screening of regulation, including the interaction between the regulatory impact assessment tool and competition assessment, and the way competition and other regulatory values have been balanced in the UK managed-competition health care services sector.

In Chapter 3, R. Richard Geddes analyzes competition issues, where the roles of the private and public sectors have been blurred. He discusses public-private partnerships (PPPs). These are agreements between public and private sectors to design, construct, operate, and finance infrastructure projects. PPPs have a number of potential competitive concerns. The differences in the public's versus the private sector's cost of capital affect their competitive position and call for action. His starting point is that antitrust law may be poorly positioned to address public-private competition issues created by the developing use of public-private partnerships. For example, the private partner in a public-private partnership is typically granted an exclusive concession to operate the transportation facility for a fixed period. These are usually long-term contracts, in view of the sunk costs incurred to develop the infrastructure, and include a noncompete clause insulating the private partner from public-sector competition. Yet, despite their potential to restrict competition, they may benefit from competition law immunity because they result from a concession contract between a public and a private actor and the concession is overseen by the state. Principles borrowed from utility regulation and franchise bidding may provide a better framework for addressing competitive issues posed by PPPs.

Indeed, competitive neutrality principles may be embedded in the public-sector comparator (PSC) test, which is considered one way to increase competition between public and private provision for the benefit of the public. Another mechanism for addressing competitive concerns that is not typically utilized in public utilities is the rebidding of the concession and the adjustment of concession length to increase the frequency of rebidding

The chapters in Part II debate whether a substantive legal framework that addresses competition issues as they relate to the role of the state can be put into place. In Chapter 4, Wentong Zheng examines how competition law might address SOEs' anticompetitive practices, given some of the lessons from trade law. As he notes, unlike private firms, the state may simultaneously be both regulator and market participant via SOEs. While this issue has become increasingly important in antitrust, there is a longer history of addressing such concerns under international trade law. Zheng offers examples from both antidumping and subsidies law to aid competition law in its inquiry into competition concerns regarding SOEs.

Merger control is another area in which both the setup and the function of the legal regime impact how much the state leaves to market forces, and indeed the extent to which the state chooses antitrust over, or concurrent with, other forms of regulation. In Chapter 5, D. Daniel Sokol explores the complexity of these sets of trade-offs. In a sense, the question of whether to have antitrust merger control and the factors that such an analysis considers are, in part, political issues. Sokol explores via theoretical discussion and case studies the extent to which political factors are (and should be) recognized within competition law and policy in merger control. According to Sokol, the first level of politicization occurs in the decision of whether or not to utilize an antitrust merger analysis that exclusively applies an economic welfare standard (total or consumer welfare) or that includes noneconomic factors such as "fairness." The debate over the politicization of antitrust also plays out in the mechanisms by which antitrust merger law interacts with other forms of merger review—for example, in the case of sector regulation when a regulator must consider other noncompetition economics factors as part of the merger analysis, such as "public interest."

What exactly public interest means and how consumer welfare analysis interacts with it is the focus of Chapter 6, by Alberto Heimler. Heimler notes that governments play a significant role in promoting competition and use a variety of policies for this purpose, including, most prominently, property rights rules, regulatory reform, trade liberalization, and antitrust law enforcement. All these policies share the objectives to be achieved (greater competition), but they differ in terms of the instruments they use and the intensity with which they are able to promote market mechanisms. Contrary to the general understanding, regulation is pervasive. Price control of public utilities; concession for the use of public property, including the radio spectrum; pollution control; information requirements of all sorts; accreditation of suppliers of credence goods; and delimitation of exclusivities are all areas where governments intervene directly in our economies, although often disregarding the effects of the imposed regulatory structure on incentives. While antitrust enforcement in the last few decades has thoroughly emphasized the role of incentives in achieving optimal economic outcomes (making sure that the law is interpreted so as not to block welfare-enhancing firm strategies), such an understanding does not seem to have played a similar role in regulation, trade policies, or even in the protection of intellectual property rights. Heimler compares the ideology that inspires antitrust enforcement with that behind other areas of government intervention, concluding that the antitrust approach is the most market friendly and the one that, in consideration of the relevance it provides to innovation and growth, should be widely adopted. A possible strategy in this respect is to have the different communities that inspire competition policies—trade, regulatory reform, intellectual property, and antitrust communities—develop common approaches and strategies, possibly under the auspices of international organizations, such as the OECD or the United Nations Conference on Trade and Development (UNCTAD).

Although Chapters 4, 5, and 6 focus on the domestic implications of various mechanisms to address competition concerns, a number of international law doctrines offer some doctrinal mechanisms to address issues involving competition and the state. Several international law doctrines apply to conflicts that implicate competition among states.

In Chapter 7, Paul Stephan addresses how to achieve optimal international competition policy through an analysis of the concepts of territoriality, sovereign immunity, and act of state under international law as interpreted by U.S. courts. Stephan notes that should optimal global consumer welfare dominate all policy objectives pursued by governments, competition authorities probably would not distinguish between private and governmental restrictions of competition. Yet, in a world where states pursue other objectives and embrace strategic trade objectives, the unilateral pursuit of aggressive pro-consumer competition objectives might lead to trade wars instead of cooperation. This creates interesting institutional questions as to which—the government or the courts—should intervene to mitigate the risks of conflict.

In Chapter 8, Joseph Bauer also examines U.S. courts' focus on international law issues. Bauer confronts how the Foreign Trade Antitrust Improvements Act of 1982 (FTAIA) has created barriers to creating a successful legal claim under U.S. antitrust law through both its enacting legislation and subsequent case law. He argues that as a consequence of case law developments, the FTAIA has reduced consumer welfare by harming U.S. plaintiffs.

In Part III, case studies of national experiences are presented. In Chapter 9, Dae-Sik Hong provides the first English-language analytical description of the Korean competition advocacy system. This system is important because of the scope of the Korean Fair Trade Commission's power (cabinet level and the ability ex post and ex ante to review all new legislation and regulation). This level of competition review of legislation and regulation has evolved over time and reflects issues in Korea's political economy and institutional design. Yet, this form of competition advocacy has particular salience globally as competition authorities try to create more effective mechanisms to limit anticompetitive government economic intervention.

In Chapter 10, Thomas Cheng analyzes administrative monopolies under the Chinese Anti-Monopoly Law (AML). Tied to Volokh's question in Chapter 1, but specifically in the Chinese context, Cheng asks if Chinese SOEs are to be used when there is market failure, when the provision of public goods is at issue, or for some other purposes. These other purposes include situations in which SOEs may serve as an extension of the state to control the political and economic organization of China, as SOEs implicate employment and federalism issues. Cheng notes that abuses of administrative monopolies under the AML emanate from systemic issues in Chinese political and economic organization. Consequently, as long as China promotes SOE national champions and values such champions over competition, the potentially ameliorative effects of the AML for abuses will not be attained.

In addition to ex ante work regarding advocacy, competition law can act ex post to correct for distortions in the market. One mechanism to do so is the EU state aid system. State aid is a form of subsidy in which the state may influence national economic policy through targeted interventions. However, the EU has instituted limits on the types of state aid a country in the EU may offer. Chapter 11, by Leigh Hancher and Francesco Salerno, examines the evolution toward an effects-based approach under state aid law. Their analysis leads to a common framework (and reference to economics and the theory of market failure). At the same time, they examine how the form of state aid and the different priorities of the Commission in certain sectors might challenge this uniform effects-based approach to state aid control. Because there is no real effects-based approach and because other forms of state intervention are not subject to the same stringent requirements, Hancher and Salerno ask whether member states would behave strategically. This in turn raises the need to devise an overall framework that subjects all types of state action to some analysis of the competition distortions they might impose.

Questions of centralization are not relevant merely at the supranational level. In Chapter 12, Deborah Healey describes how state and competition interact within the Australian context. Healey examines how government has acted as a market actor and how Australian competition law has been used in such a context. While there is some immunity under competition law for government action, until relatively recently this provided competitive advantages for immune government bodies. The Australian experience also includes competition-based regulatory reform, which has had tangible benefits for Australian consumers. However, Healey questions whether these reforms have been sufficient.

Chapter 13 examines in a country-specific context the role of the state in sectors that are heavily regulated. Philippe Gagnepain, Marc Ivaldi, and Chantal Latgé-Roucolle discuss the issue of public concessions in the transport sector. They explore how to provide sufficient managerial incentives in a way that improves competition. The particular dynamics of competition in urban transport are related to the form of regulation that shapes the industry via the public service tenders and their regulation. The authors test the implications of their model with data on the French transport sector. The chapter concludes that the regulatory framework of the sector has an impact on costs, regulation creates network effects among operators within the same group through incentive schemes, and the regulatory framework is itself a reflection of the regulator's objectives rather than simply the welfare of urban transport services users.

Part I

Conceptualizing and Re-Conceptualizing the Interaction between Competition Law and Government Activities

Chapter 1

Privatization and Competition Policy

Alexander Volokh

Why are we discussing privatization in a book about competition policy? Because the scope of government and the role of the state are central to broader issues of competition. Privatization of monopolies without sufficient antitrust protection has been a recurring complaint among critics of privatization. So, on the other side, has been anticompetitive behavior by state-owned enterprises that often are not subject to antitrust at all. More theoretically, antitrust law may focus on certain problems and choose to ignore others as being unrealistic because of an assumption that firms behave as profit maximizers. But given the mass of public choice literature exploring what governments supposedly maximize, as well as empirical evidence that privatization often increases productivity and profitability,[1] this may be a bad assumption when firms are owned (or even heavily regulated) by government.

This chapter, therefore, explores the links between privatization and competition policy. First, in Section I, I explain why privatization is even relevant at all—a question economists paid surprisingly little attention to before a quarter-century ago. I survey theoretical models and empirical results, discuss the relevance (if any) of theory to policy, and show how privatization can be a catalyst for various forms of social change. Many policies are complementary to privatization, in the sense that the design of those policies systematically affects the effectiveness of privatization; two of the most important complementary policy areas are corporate governance and competition policy, and most generally, privatization works better when accompanied by liberalization. Moreover, since failures in both of these areas lead to distortions relative to the imaginary "perfectly competitive" outcome, good corporate governance and good competition policy are to some extent substitutes.[2] I briefly address the connection between privatization and corporate governance in Section II and discuss at length the interplay between privatization and competition policy in Section III.

I. Privatization and Its Possible Irrelevance

A. Irrelevance?

Privatization has a long history. Peter Drucker advocated "reprivatization" in 1969,[3] but the term *privatize* and its derivatives were used even earlier to refer to the sell-off of government assets in West Germany in the 1950s and in Nazi Germany in the 1930s and 1940s. Even before that, as far back as the 1920s, the term *denationalization* was used.[4] And asset sales (or giveaways) and contracting out existed even before there was a word for them; vast public lands were privatized in the United States under the preemption and homestead acts of the mid-nineteenth and early twentieth centuries. Jeremy Bentham envisioned privately managed prisons in the late eighteenth century,[5] and contracting out—in tax collection and many other public services—goes back to ancient Greece and the Roman Republic.[6]

The history of the *theory* of privatization, though, is quite short. For much of its history, privatization was "a policy in search of a rationale."[7] Early debates over privatization were unrigorous, and the era of economically sophisticated discussion of privatization probably began in 1987, when David Sappington and Joseph Stiglitz pointed out that, in a simple model, whether assets are owned publicly or privately is irrelevant.[8]

To simplify their model slightly, suppose the government is considering whether it should own an asset. The asset produces a quantity Q, with valuation $V(Q)$ (which could encompass any objectives, including distributional ones). The government could induce private providers to produce the optimal quantity by simply paying a price $P(Q) = V(Q)$. (Many other contracts will do just as well—for instance, "Produce the optimal quantity Q^* in exchange for a price that guarantees you zero economic profits, or we boil you in oil"—but the Sappington-Stiglitz proposal has the advantage that the government doesn't need to know costs.[9]) The private provider would thus get paid the entire social benefit of his production, but the government can extract this rent by auctioning the right to produce among potential noncolluding risk-neutral suppliers with symmetric beliefs about the least-cost technology.[10]

One might add that a government manager can be incentivized the same way with a wage $W(Q) = V(Q)$, so all ownership modes are equivalent. Generalizing still further, Q could be multidimensional and indicate not just quantity but any attribute of how the business is run. Any public-sector rules can be imposed by contract or written into regulations; government enterprise, contracting out, and a regulated market are thus potentially equivalent in every way.

From this perspective, much of the conventional wisdom about privatization appears—if not wrong, at least undertheorized. Private firms may have better capital-market monitoring—but capital-market monitoring has its own problems, and why can't the government retain any advantages of such monitoring by only owning partial shares in firms? Private firms may have harder budget constraints, but why can't the government shut down failing agencies or, alternatively, as recent events remind us, bail out failing private firms?[11] Private firms may have stronger profit-based incentives, but why can't the government simulate these using public-sector compensation schemes with high-powered incentives? (The last two questions combined could be summarized as "Why privatize when one can liberalize instead?") Governments might undermine the investment incentives of public agencies by redirecting their profits to other uses, but can't shareholders do the same? Public agencies may have goals that are hard to specify, but isn't this also a problem when the government regulates private firms? Governments may be subject to interest-group lobbying, but can't that lobbying also affect contracts or regulation of private firms? Governments are better positioned to accomplish social goals, but can't they also accomplish those goals through contract or regulation?[12]

One can easily apply these points to various concrete examples. Why should the U.S. Postal Service be public rather than contracted out to Federal Express or the United Parcel Service, or even left to a regulated private market? The USPS takes all comers and charges uniform postal rates, but that could be written into regulations.[13] The USPS loses money, but FedEx could charge its customers the same as the USPS right now and collect its deficit in contract fees from the government. On the other hand, the government could regulate prices and subsidize entrants in a private market. The quality and speed of postal delivery can be easily checked and made the subject of rewards and punishments by mailing test letters and packages. On this last point, one could make similar arguments about the Transportation Security Administration, the nationalization of which was rushed through post-9/11 with very little appreciation of Sappington-Stiglitz.[14]

Of course, the best way to use any equivalence theorem is as a checklist to see how differences emerge when the assumptions of the theorem do not hold up. One issue is that the rent-extraction auction might not work well because of, say, collusion, asymmetric beliefs, risk aversion, or the winner's curse. To the extent that the winning bidder retains some rents, $P(Q) = V(Q)$ privatization potentially implicates distributional concerns—and requires raising government revenue, with the associated deadweight loss of taxation.

But the literature has mostly focused on the most obvious line of inquiry: $V(Q)$ might be indescribable because of the sheer number of possible contingencies (really, $V(Q)$ is $V(Q, \theta)$, where θ, a parameter describing the state of the world, can take too many values). $V(Q, \theta)$ might even be unknown until θ occurs (after the contracting stage); Q might be unverifiable; the contract $P(Q) = V(Q)$ might be imperfectly enforceable; and so on.

In short, the $P(Q) = V(Q)$ contract is trickier than it seems. This idea has a name—the theory of incomplete contracts—which was pioneered by Sanford Grossman, Oliver Hart, and John Moore[15] in a theory-of-the-firm context and is now the centerpiece of privatization theory as well. It is now second nature to privatization theorists that "any organizational mode can be copied by any other organizational mode through a complete contingent contract. Therefore, if there is any difference, it must be due to the fact that only *incomplete contracts* are feasible at the stage of privatization."[16]

B. Relevance?

Sappington and Stiglitz did not present a theory of government behavior that would allow a comparison of government and private ownership; that is the story of the post-1987 theoretical research. I summarize a few of these models below to give a flavor of the sorts of contractual incompleteness that could support a difference between different modes of ownership.

One possible difference between public and private agents, suggested by Jean-Jacques Laffont and Jean Tirole, is that the private manager has to answer to two principals—the government and the shareholders—while the public manager answers to only one. The disadvantage of private management is that cost-reducing effort is suboptimal: "The multiprincipal situation dilutes incentives and yields low-powered managerial incentive schemes."[17] The advantage is that the private manager has greater investment incentives because the shareholders are less likely to expropriate the manager's investment to secure greater social benefits. So privatization trades off these two types of effort and investment.[18]

Another difference, suggested by Klaus Schmidt, is that the government might have better access to inside information about the agent's finances when the agent is public. Knowing the agent's costs can lead to bad incentives. If costs turn out to be high, it will be ex post optimal to subsidize the enterprise, but this leads to low ex ante incentives to reduce costs. A government ignorant of costs will not subsidize as much and will inefficiently shut down some enterprises, but at least cost-reducing incentives will be improved. The trade-off is between productive and allocative efficiency.[19]

Another strand of the literature, spawned by Hart, Andrei Shleifer, and Robert Vishny (HSV), stresses the importance of residual control rights—that is, the right to do whatever is not prohibited by the contract. A contract to run a government program—say, a prison—only specifies a basic service, but the agent can invest in thinking up various innovations to the service. Some innovations cut costs (and, by assumption, reduce quality); private managers spend too much effort thinking of these because they keep every dollar saved. Other innovations improve quality (and, by assumption, cost more). Private managers will be able to appropriate some of the net benefit by renegotiating the contract with the government. Their incentives to think up such innovations are suboptimal, but at least they are better than those of public managers, who have a more precarious bargaining position. Privatization trades off these two types of innovation.[20]

The HSV model has been quite influential. Hart himself used it in later work on public-private partnerships (PPPs), where he discussed whether the contractor who builds the facility should be the same as the one that runs it.[21] Patrick Schmitz also used an HSV-style model to discuss the advantages of joint ownership,[22] and Timothy Besley and Maitreesh Ghatak used it to discuss privatization in the presence of altruistic providers.[23]

Most models assume a benevolent government. (*Benevolence*, in economists' lingo, invariably means utilitarian social welfare maximization[24] or something like it.[25]) In some models, nonbenevolence makes privatization more desirable, because private ownership limits the scope of politicians' private agendas.[26] But a nonbenevolent government can also transfer resources to its supporters by nonbenevolently regulating private firms, so the superiority of privatization does not necessarily follow. As Shleifer and Vishny point out, "With full corruption the allocation of control rights and cash flow rights between managers and politicians does not affect either the efficiency of the firm or the transfers it receives."[27] Moreover, they say, if the government continues to regulate firms heavily, privatization (the transfer of cash-flow rights) "may actually make things worse. Politicians continue to use their control of regulated firms to pursue political objectives, but it is now less costly for them to do so." Transferring control rights, not just cash-flow rights, to managers—a process that Shleifer and Vishny call "commercialization"—may be necessary for privatization to work.[28] So the costs and benefits of privatization depend on the precise form of nonbenevolence.[29]

C. Empirics and the Uses of Theory for Policy Makers

No serious model unambiguously predicts benefits from privatization, so empirics are a good check. Unfortunately, many empirical studies are less useful than they may appear because the choice of enterprises to privatize is nonrandom. Profitable firms might be privatized first, whether because they're the most likely to restructure,[30] because such restructuring will generate less unemployment and be more politically palatable, because buyers are easier to find for profitable firms, or because the sale of profitable firms generates more money.[31] Alternatively, sometimes it is unprofitable firms that are privatized—for instance, through liquidation.[32] Either way, naive estimates are misleading.

Thus, the best empirical studies are those that use instrumental-variables approaches or otherwise address selection bias.[33] A recent review by Saul Estrin and colleagues, which takes selection bias into account, concludes that in central and eastern Europe, privatization has mostly increased productivity; the effect is much smaller in the countries that belong to the Commonwealth of Independent States (which now includes all former Soviet republics except the Baltic states and Georgia).[34] Privatization also has a nonnegative effect on profitability in central and eastern Europe, the former Soviet countries, and China, though the size and significance of the effect depends on the type of ownership: concentrated domestic private ownership, managerial ownership, and foreign ownership are good.[35]

An earlier review by William Megginson and Jeffry Netter concluded that, for nontransition economies, privatization increases "output, efficiency, profitability, and capital investment spending" and decreases leverage; the studies "are far less unanimous regarding the impact of privatization on employment levels in privatized firms."[36] To prevent the political fallout from investors who lost money after buying shares in privatized firms, governments engaging in their first large share-issue privatizations typically "establish (or augment)" an SEC-like agency, establish regulatory bodies for natural monopolies,[37] improve disclosure rules, and otherwise modernize their corporate governance.[38] Not that all the evidence cuts the same way: where Rafael La Porta and colleagues have found government ownership of banks negatively associated with growth rates,[39] Svetlana Andrianova and colleagues have recently found an association in the opposite direction.[40] (But, consistent with Sappington-Stiglitz, Andrianova does not rule out that the effect may weaken with increased quality of regulation.)

It is apparent from these results that privatization does not exist in a vacuum. The results are different in Russia than in the Czech Republic, or when ownership is foreign versus domestic, because institutional details matter—many more than are apparent from reading the models. Those who are familiar with the reward structure of the economics profession will not be surprised that the theoretical models focus on a few factors. There is no glory or prestigious publication in finding that the case for privatization depends on the competence or public spiritedness of public servants: the point is both obvious and politically charged. Nor is there glory or prestigious publication in finding that the desirability of privatization depends on the quality of corporate governance or antitrust law in the private sector—or on the presence of civil service protections, public-employee unions, APA/FOIA-type statutes, or procurement regulation in the public sector. In principle, any problems along those lines can be fixed by statute (or by constitutional amendment or changes in judicial interpretations), so if those are contractual incompletenesses, surely they are not interesting ones.

This explains the articles locating the key contractual incompleteness in supposedly more "fundamental" differences, like the allocation of residual control rights or the government's loss of accounting information about private entities. This is, of course, interesting, and the trade-offs identified are real. But all the boring differences between sectors are relevant as well, even if not "core." Government employees might indeed be less motivated, or they might be more public spirited. Corporate governance or antitrust or civil service law or public employee unions might be hard to change, or the optimal fix for those policies might be elusive. Unlike theoretical economists, policy makers live in a world where not every policy is politically on the table.

The same is true of various other—perhaps "accidental"—features of the public or private sectors. Private prison firms and public-sector corrections employee unions may have different abilities and incentives to lobby for greater incarceration.[41] Prison privatization may make juries less deferential toward prison officials, since juries are often tougher on corporations than on governments.[42] Soldiers can be imprisoned for disobeying orders, but employees of private military companies cannot.[43]

There is no shame, therefore, in discussing what *isn't* covered in the models. More generally, it is clear that privatization causes institutional change and is also affected by preexisting institutions, notably corporate governance and competition policy. It is to these institutions and policies that I now turn.

D. Privatization as Catalyst

In some ways, privatization can be a catalyst for other forms of social change. Some argue that privatization promotes democracy[44] or broadens the distribution of wealth or stock ownership (thus limiting future left-wing governments).[45] Privatization can also help develop a country's financial markets.[46] For all the talk of the optimal sequencing of privatization—whether it should be antitrust before privatization, corporate governance before privatization, liberalization before privatization—the feasibility of the program depends on political support.[47] Privatization may sometimes be necessary to produce the dispersed class of owners that will become a political force for institutional reform: perhaps privatization in some form is a necessary precondition for liberalization.[48]

For instance, it has not necessarily been all negative that Russian privatization concentrated ownership in the hands of a relatively small number of "oligarchs." Concentrated ownership is often positive for productivity, since it helps overcome the free-rider problem in monitoring management.[49] The oligarchs have been a positive force not only for enterprise restructuring and productivity but also for institutional reform—to say nothing of constituting a big business lobby and funding source that may have played a role in preventing the return of Communists to power.[50] Of course, the experience has also had its strong negatives: the oligarchs have not been keen on competitiveness or free trade; the privatization was far from transparent or egalitarian; and the constituency for privatization in Russia has suffered as a result.[51] The important point, though, is that the development of transparent economic institutions should be judged by what is feasible, not by the optimal textbook approach.

II. Privatization and Corporate Governance

The success of privatization also depends on corporate governance. Most models ignore agency costs, and this is fine where corporate law does a tolerable job of controlling managerial self-dealing, but it is not so fine where the institutions to control self-dealing are underdeveloped. Thus, Bernard Black and colleagues argue that Russian privatization went awry because there was no brake on asset stripping and other forms of managerial looting.[52] The trouble may not have been the oligarchs as such, but a system that let managers maximize their utility without the check of corporate law.

This is perhaps why privatization in the former Soviet republics has enhanced productivity when the new owners were foreign but much less so (if at all) when the new owners were domestic.[53] Perhaps foreign companies had better corporate governance in their home countries, or perhaps they were less vulnerable to political pressure from shady post-Soviet governments.

Not that bad corporate governance is a problem that magically appears when an enterprise is privatized. Governance in public enterprises is also bad. Daniel Sokol documents that the quality of governance in government postal enterprises varies widely; that governance is better where postal enterprises are commercialized, corporatized, and competitive; and that some of the worst offenders are in advanced economies like the United States.[54] Thus, even bad privatization might be more efficient than business-as-usual public enterprise, though a more sophisticated program, whether involving better private corporate governance or a corporatized state-owned enterprise, might be more efficient still.

The regulation of nonprofits is also important. Glaeser and Shleifer show that nonprofit status can be valuable: by weakening the provider's incentives to maximize profits, nonprofit status can signal quality when quality itself is nonverifiable. Moreover, altruistic entrepreneurs will be attracted to the nonprofit form.[55] This matters for privatization, given the role of nonprofits (both secular and religious) in public-private partnerships worldwide and the importance of "faith-based initiatives" in the United States. Besley and Ghatak show that when both a provider and the government can make productive investments in a project and when the provider is altruistic, then the provider should own the project if it values it more than the government does.[56] As a result, nonprofit regulation can play a valuable role in preventing profit-making firms from abusing the nonprofit form.

III. Privatization and Competition

A. Privatization of Natural Monopolies

Hart, Shleifer, and Vishny write that "competition strengthens the case for contracting out," if "consumers can assess quality and have a choice among competitive suppliers."[57] This might describe auto manufacturers but not, say, electric utilities. The distribution of electric power is conventionally considered a "natural monopoly"; that is, cost is minimized when a single firm covers the whole industry, so competition between firms is thought to be wasteful.[58] Electric utilities in the United States are thus conventionally run either as public-sector monopolies or as private-sector monopolies whose prices are regulated by a Public Utility Commission.

In the case of true natural monopolies, consumers are powerless, but even then, competitive bidding—perhaps even between public and private providers[59]—can strengthen the case for privatization. Franchise bidding—where the winner of the auction is the one who commits to offer the lowest prices or (for multidimensional services) the best overall deal—has been proposed to counter monopoly power in utility regulation and has actually been used in cable television regulation.[60] Of course, if the formula for picking the auction winner (for instance, the definition of the "best overall deal") embodies a lot of discretion, the effectiveness of the mechanism depends on a well-run auction.[61] Competition at the bidding stage, contract enforcement difficulties, and reputational concerns matter as well.[62]

Cable television is an example where whatever monopoly exists is purely local. Outside of the traditional natural monopoly context, a similar example is prisons. Prisons are contracted out one at a time, and no state has ever contracted out all its prisons. As of 2010, only 8 percent of prisoners were housed in a private prison, about 7 percent in state systems, and about 16 percent in the federal system. Of the 30 states that contracted out, the median percentage of inmates in private prisons was about 10 percent, and no state's percentage exceeded 45 percent.[63] The result is a fairly concentrated, but not monopolistic, private prison industry. Prison provision thus consists of "the public sector," with a 92 percent "market share" and a few private firms with an 8 percent market share—or, to speak more precisely, a public sector in each state with a share between 55 percent and 100 percent and some firms sharing the rest.

Private provision, combining bidding with strong cost-cutting incentives, has thus increased competition without any special antimonopoly policy. Costs have dropped somewhat, though the magnitude of the drop depends on one's accounting assumptions, with some methods yielding savings around 15 percent and others yielding savings around 3 percent (or even finding sometimes that the public sector is more cost-effective).[64] And while quality studies have been poor, careful comparative studies have not strongly favored either sector.[65] Naturally, whatever success the enterprise has had—and this is hotly disputed[66]—depends on competent monitoring, a working tort and constitutional litigation system, and reputational concerns. Moreover, the full potential of prison privatization is still untested, since tying compensation to performance measures like low recidivism (as opposed to giving flat per diems with penalties for particular incidents) and giving prison companies the flexibility to experiment (as opposed to incorporating the public prison rule book in the contract) are still in their infancy.[67]

Such piecemeal privatization may have also had salutary political economy effects. While public prison guard unions are big pro-incarceration lobbyists, the evidence that private prison firms lobby for incarceration is slim (despite activists' claims to the contrary), perhaps because privatization, by fragmenting the industry, has introduced a collective action problem in lobbying.[68] As I have written elsewhere, "In a roundabout way, . . . privatization is a form of antitrust and antitrust is a form of campaign finance regulation."[69]

These have been examples of how privatization can be pro-competitive even without specific antimonopoly policies. Sometimes, though, if the goal is to prevent monopoly power, specific policies may be necessary. For natural monopolies, those who are pessimistic about the possibilities of successful franchise bidding[70] will want to stick to more traditional modes of public utility regulation, like rate-of-return regulation or price caps.[71]

B. Antitrust and Other Entry-Promoting Policies

Outside natural monopolies, one can restructure enterprises before privatizing them piecemeal for greater competition, or one can rely on antitrust law. Privatization is frequently criticized for proceeding without effective antimonopoly provisions, merely replacing government monopoly with private monopoly[72]—though, as mentioned above, political concerns may sometimes make this unavoidable.[73] The simple fact that selling monopolies raises more revenue than selling competitive companies may also explain the reluctance to restructure.[74]

Aeromexico and Mexicana,[75] the two major airlines in Mexico, were privatized in the late 1980s and de facto merged in 1993. (Their immediate post-privatization history is a good case study in the importance of other policies. Aeromexico restructured more effectively because it was privatized out of bankruptcy and was not tied down by earlier collective bargaining agreements.) Gordon Hanson writes that the merged companies controlled over 70 percent of the domestic air travel market in Mexico. Antitrust could have prevented the consolidation of their market power, perhaps by blocking the de facto merger. But Mexico's antitrust law did not take effect until a few months later.

The existence of robust antitrust law might thus assuage some fears that newly privatized state entities will gain monopoly power. Not that antitrust law is a panacea: in the United States, a company that starts out as a monopoly or that grows to become a monopoly through unobjectionable means can generally price as it likes, certainly including monopoly pricing and perhaps even including limit pricing. Continuing antitrust activity in recently privatized areas like telecom in France and postal service in Germany show that regulation does not magically lead to markets mimicking perfect competition.[76] Robert Feinberg and Mieke Meurs write that in eastern European transition countries, early antimonopoly efforts had little effect: "Many of the largest firms form[ed] a single technological unit, defying efforts of demonopolizers to break them into smaller enterprises." Efforts to split firms along regional lines only resulted in regional monopolies, and existing connections among managers facilitated collusion.[77]

The recently uncovered international air cargo cartel—a conspiracy involving at least 20 airlines—suggests that antitrust may not work perfectly even in its core area of policing price fixing, though its effectiveness would surely increase with higher fines, aggressive leniency programs, and personal sanctions on responsible corporate officers.[78] This particular cartel managed to acquire a surprisingly large number of participants primarily because the alternative to price fixing, for many of the participants, was bankruptcy.[79] Moreover, the implications for privatization policy are ambiguous, since at least two of the participants, China Airlines and Singapore Airlines, are directly or indirectly government owned.

Add to these problems the danger that antitrust will wrongly condemn legitimate business practices[80] and that antitrust enforcement in developing countries is likely to be less competent than in the developed world. Add as well the public choice concern that companies will use antitrust to shield themselves from their too successful competitors.[81] It is not that antitrust is useless as a complement to privatization, but there may be other, perhaps more useful, complementary policies.

Feinberg and Meurs suggest, again for eastern Europe, a privatization-liberalization synergy: entry-facilitating policies can be even more valuable than explicit antimonopoly laws. Mexico is a good case study on the importance of entry. In 1991, it deregulated air travel by first reducing domestic carriers' entry and fare restrictions and then reducing barriers to U.S. carriers.[82] At the time of Hanson's article, a small, low-cost airline had entered the domestic market (several more have entered since then), and fares were already significantly lower for international than for domestic flights, where U.S. carriers provided competition.

In short, free trade and entry liberalization are themselves competition policies that can be effective complements to, or even substitutes for, antimonopoly laws.[83] One might add to the list a liquid capital market, as well as general deregulation, both of which one expects to facilitate entry.

C. Escaping Anticompetitive Public Enterprise Regimes

Antitrust is not merely a form of damage control—a way of reining in firms in the transition from public-spirited but inefficient public ownership to rapacious and anticonsumer private ownership. The reality is that public ownership has anticompetitive dysfunctionalities of its own.

In an early model, Sam Peltzman argued that public enterprises subsidize voter-taxpayers with prices below the profit-maximizing level, using higher prices for nonvoters to cross-subsidize voters and price discriminating less among voters.[84] This was pre-Sappington-Stiglitz, so Peltzman gave insufficient consideration to whether the government could regulate private enterprises to the same effect, but these effects could plausibly emerge from an explicit incomplete contracts model.

In any event, it is empirically observed that municipalities often engage in profit-making activities and "exert[] law-making power to exclude competitive challenges. . . . [M]onopoly profits frequently provide a politically preferable alternative to taxes as a general revenue source."[85]

In light of this, the fact that various legal doctrines (at least in the United States) exempt governments from an otherwise pro-competitive regime is an independent argument for privatization. The most obvious example is the state action exemption from antitrust law. In *Parker v. Brown*, the Supreme Court held that the Sherman Act does not "restrain a state or its officers or agents from activities directed by its legislature."[86] Municipalities do not automatically get this exemption because, unlike states, they are not sovereign. But they nonetheless get a pass if their anticompetitive activities were authorized by a state's "clearly articulated" policy.[87] And in *Town of Hallie v. City of Eau Claire*, the Supreme Court suggested that a state statute can "clearly contemplate" municipal anticompetitive conduct even if such conduct is merely "a foreseeable result" of permitted municipal activity.[88]

Hallie justified this position with a presumption "that the municipality acts in the public interest"—partly because of the public scrutiny, disclosure regulation, and electoral accountability that municipalities have and private firms do not.[89] Electoral accountability, of course, is all well and good, but one way for municipal officials to be faithful agents of their constituents is to make monopoly profits at the expense of outsiders,[90] as in *Hallie* itself. How clear is clear and how foreseeable is foreseeable are continuing areas of ambiguity under antitrust state action doctrine.[91]

The state action doctrine is problematic in other ways as well. The exemption requires active state supervision,[92] but how active is active likewise has never been fully spelled out.[93] Moreover, when the challenged actor is a municipality rather than a private organization, the "requirement" is actually optional and merely serves "an evidentiary function" to ensure "that the actor is engaging in the challenged conduct pursuant to state policy."[94] Between fully private actors and municipalities is a "gray area consisting of hybrid state or local entities" where the vitality of the active supervision requirement is decided case by case.[95]

Couldn't we just fix the doctrine instead of bypassing it through privatization? Perhaps. But suppose there were no state action exemption? Or suppose we required more "clear articulation" and "active supervision," limited the set of entities subject to the exemption, denied the exemption for market participants, and the like?[96] Regular antitrust law may *still* be a bad fit for entities that are not traditional profit maximizers. A predatory pricing claim against the U.S. Postal Service would probably lose if the USPS could not plausibly recoup its lost profits from the predation period.[97] This is a plausible attitude to take against a profit-making firm, but a government-owned enterprise may be maximizing revenues or employment rather than profits, which makes predation more credible in the postal context. Sokol suggests alternative pricing tests that would facilitate the application of antitrust law in these cases, but he grants that constructing an administrable test might be difficult.[98]

The Dormant Commerce Clause is another example where public actors have special privileges. In *C & A Carbone, Inc. v. Town of Clarkstown*, the Supreme Court invalidated a flow control ordinance that required all trash producers in the town to use a particular private trash processing facility. The ordinance, the Court wrote, was protectionist and undermined a national market in garbage.[99] But in *United Haulers Ass'n v. Oneida-Herkimer Solid Waste Management Authority*, which differed only in that the favored facility was publicly owned, the Court upheld the ordinance on the grounds that government, as the protector of health, safety, and welfare, is different.[100] Note how the Court fails to come to terms with Sappington-Stiglitz, and Justice Alito, in dissent, points out as much (though not in those terms). Yes, the facility in *Carbone* was nominally private. But the contractor had agreed to build the facility for free and transfer it to the town five years later for $1. The town guaranteed a minimum waste flow, let the contractor charge an above-market tipping fee, and committed to make up any deficit in tipping fees if the waste flow was less than the guaranteed amount.[101] "[F]or all practical purposes," the facility "was owned by the municipality."[102]

This is a case where nominal privatization, even under conditions of (otherwise) complete contracting, would make a real difference in the state's ability to pursue anticompetitive policies. The case is even clearer when public actors are direct market participants—in which case doctrine gives them complete leeway to favor in-state interests.[103] Privatization would thus directly serve competitive goals, since regulating a private market to achieve the same result would be unconstitutional.

These are all cases where privatization would further competition. Perhaps it would be better to instead just fix the offending doctrines. But Congress has "shown little desire" to meddle with antitrust.[104] Dormant Commerce Clause doctrine is constitutional. More generally, as I have noted, second-best fixes are often practically the first-best option for policy makers.

Moreover, one can say the same of any regime that treats public and private organizations differently, even when the regime has little to do with competitiveness. For instance, the Supreme Court, in *College Savings Bank v. Florida Prepaid Postsecondary Education Expense Board*, has expressly rejected a market participant exception to state sovereign immunity.[105] Sovereign immunity means that a state can violate generally applicable laws with impunity—which, if nothing else, operates as a barrier to entry against private competitors.

Various mini-immunity doctrines, like public prisons' (but not private prisons') immunity from tort law with respect to their discretionary activities,[106] or the rule that grants qualified immunity under § 1983 to public state corrections officers but denies it to private ones,[107] pose similar problems. (Of course, one should also take account of contrary doctrines that treat the *public* sector more onerously, like the procedural requirements of the Freedom of Information Act, the Administrative Procedure Act, or the requirement of voter approval of bond issues.[108])

Nor are these merely contingent quirks of U.S. law. Public enterprises are often treated more leniently under the prevailing regulatory regime, whether by explicit doctrine or by favoritism and nonenforcement.[109] If the underlying regulatory regime (the one that the public enterprises are evading) is itself unjustified, one may think that the more nonenforcement, the better—but it is unlikely that a regime of *selective* nonenforcement, where the sole beneficiaries are public enterprises, is even second-best. Thus, privatization can serve the salutary role of moving exempted public enterprises into the more stringent "default" regime.

None of these are knockdown arguments against government ownership. The standard theoretical arguments discussed earlier still apply, so government ownership can still be more efficient than private ownership in many cases. The foregoing considerations are merely examples of institutional details that, for better or worse, differ as between the public and private sectors. To the extent these details are hard to change, the most efficient ownership structure will differ from the structure that one would otherwise support.

* * *

It is clear, then, that privatization is no cure-all. Liberalization—that is, an economic policy that encourages entry and discourages monopolistic behavior and that emphasizes hard budget constraints, good corporate governance, free trade, and the like—is necessary for privatization to produce the most benefits. In light of this, one might ask why if one liberalizes, privatization is required at all. State-owned enterprises have found unexpected flexibility in various transition countries when faced with economic reform. Hard budget constraints, restrictions on credit, competitive markets (including liberalized trade and currency convertibility), and bankruptcy laws have spurred improvements in their corporate governance and competitiveness.[110] Even in the United States, government enterprises appear to perform better when faced with a more competitive environment. Witness the improvements in public schools in the face of school vouchers or other accountability mechanisms,[111] or the improvements in municipal services when public- and private-sector providers compete with each other under a regime of competitive neutrality.[112]

Certainly, this is better than nothing. Can we do even better by adding privatization? Shleifer says we can. It's true that mere corporatization—shifting control rights from politicians to managers without privatizing—can stimulate restructuring, but this depends on how much de facto control or influence over public firms politicians still retain. "In a country like Russia," he writes, "where the mechanisms of political influence are numerous and the politicians' demand for influence is high, corporatization by itself is a rather weak measure."[113] Privatization—giving managers (or outside shareholders) cash flow rights in addition to control rights—depoliticizes firms still further because it strengthens managers' and shareholders' opposition to government control (both by creating a political class of owners and by adding foregone profits to the managers' costs of following government dictates) and because it weakens the avenues by which government can control firms.[114]

And what is true "[i]n a country like Russia" is no less true in a relatively advanced rule-of-law state like the United States. Recent experience with companies in which the government has recently taken an ownership stake, like GM, shows that government firms are characterized by government control no matter how strenuously the government insists otherwise.[115] Moreover, this is the sort of control that would be much harder to pass through Congress if it were to be imposed regulatorily on an entire private industry. Independent private stakeholders who can selfishly assert their own interests—and demand potentially expensive bribes if they are to do the government's bidding—are necessary not only in Russia but everywhere.

Chapter 2

Toward a Bureaucracy-Centered Theory of the Interaction between Competition Law and State Activities

Ioannis Lianos

Competition law and economics literature has always portrayed the relationship between the principle of competition and government action in antagonistic terms. According to the Chicago school of antitrust economics, state action or government-induced action is considered the most frequent source for restrictions of competition.[1] Public choice theories have also cast doubt on the motivations of state action, thus contributing together with the Chicago school of economic analysis to lay the foundations of a distinct theory of government failure, with the aim to marginalize government, which completes the market failure dominated theories of neoclassical economics.[2] The perception that the state constitutes a monopoly, with the ability to coerce any economic provider operating in its territory to adopt and maintain anticompetitive conduct for an indefinite period of time, without any challenge, has formed the core claim of the deregulation agenda worldwide. The anticompetitive effects of government action can even be felt postliberalization with a number of entrenched dominant positions by former monopoly incumbents being preserved through anticompetitive conduct. Some authors have even characterized public restraints as a global limit to competition law, calling for an enforcement of competition law against government action that benefits special interests.[3] In contrast, others argue that "the democratic process contains many flaws, but curing them is no antitrust's assignment" and that "if Congress wanted to draft anticapture legislation, it could do so, but one would hardly imagine that this legislation would forbid monopoly or combinations in restraint of trade while explicitly saying nothing about abuses of governmental process." Such authors have advanced a more limited role for antitrust in the process of "democratic government."[4]

These different perspectives illustrate the complexity of the matter. It is unclear how and to what extent the many different variables that authors take into account when comparing "competition law" with "state" action—the "democratic process," "private interests," "public" versus "private" restraints, "special" versus "general" interests—are connected or if they are separate issues. For example, in the absence of a proper "democratic process," should antitrust always apply to be able to preserve some form of market competition? This assumes that in the absence of electoral competition, market or "quasi-market" (in the case of an administered economy) competition is the only option left to promote efficiency, with the latter referring to policies that correspond to citizens' (for the purpose of political competition) or consumers' (for the purposes of market competition) preferences.[5] How would one go about addressing the distinction between "public" and "private" restraints when the enforcement mechanism of the state is frequently used to orchestrate "private" restraints of competition?[6] Would the distinction between "public" and "private," or between "political" and "market," competition always hold when restrictions on market competition could be traded for political support (power) and thus limit electoral competition or when governments frequently act through private actors?

An underlying assumption, common to these perspectives, is that the "state" is juxtaposed to the "market," the two forming different conceptual categories, having a defined timeless meaning across different cultures. No efforts are made to explore the black box of the "state" and understand the operations of the different branches of power, the intersection of politics with scientific expertise in policy making, the beliefs of the agents whose actions comprise the phenomena to be explained, or their interaction within a specific polity. If public choice theory applies to political science analysis the conceptual framework of markets, it has not adequately taken into account the input of the political science or political sociology literature on the concept of "state" when this does not share the rational choice model preferred by economists.[7] Yet, this literature may offer useful insights. For example, a predominantly patrimonial state sets very different challenges for competition law enforcement and regulation, more broadly, than a neoliberal or neocorporatist one: one size does not fit all.[8]

At the same time, it is important to acknowledge the different disciplinary and cultural identities of bureaucracies and/or "technocracies" involved in governmental decision making and their evolution, in particular as competition law can also be envisioned as having always been (e.g., Europe) or having evolved to (e.g., the United States) a technocratic discipline.[9] This emphasis on the technocratic dimension of competition law also carries some understanding on the relationships between politics and scientific expertise (in this case economics) in decision making, as will be examined later.

This chapter challenges the traditional antagonistic conception of the interaction between competition law and the state by advancing the need to examine in depth the nature of government bureaucracies involved in decision making and their respective claims for expertise and legitimacy. The analysis focuses on the context of a neoliberal state,[10] since it can provide useful insights on the erosion of the state/markets binarity and the interaction of competition law with government activity. A different analysis may apply to other forms of states, but this is not within the scope of this study.

I. Unveiling the Concept of the State: Government Bureaucracy and the Principle of Competition in the Neoliberal Tradition

In a liberal state, the power of government to regulate market activity is limited by two factors. One is the set of principles *external* to the government, such as the concept of natural law or the theory of the social contract between the sovereign and its subjects, from which basic rights were derived, thus distinguishing "the domain of possible governmentality" from the domain of fundamental freedoms (on the basis of a "juridico-deductive approach"[11]). The other is the emergence of an *internal* rationality of governmental practice, in essence the new discipline of political economy and the philosophy of utilitarianism. These new "technologies of government" set limitations on governmental reason by separating the sphere of intervention of public authorities from that of individual independence or autonomy, the foundations of the market system.

Yet, there is an essential difference between these internal and external limitations:

> Political economy reflects on governmental practices themselves, and it does not question them to determine whether or not they are legitimate in terms of right. It considers them in terms of their effects rather than their origins."[12]

Hence, governmental action is not only subject to the binary distinction of legitimate/illegitimate but also to the distinction of true/false, introduced by political economy, the market becoming a site of "veridiction-falsification" for governmental practice. This is based on the following assumption:

> [I]nasmuch as prices are determined in accordance with the natural mechanisms of the market, they constitute a standard of truth which enables us to discern which governmental practices are correct and which are erroneous.[13]

Classical liberalism conceived the role of the state as supportive of the principle of individual autonomy; its only precept was for the state not to intervene, with the exception of rules guaranteeing some minimum standards for an equitable exchange (e.g., absence of fraud and coercion in contracts). The political consensus on the minimal intervention of the state in the market to preserve market freedoms (sometimes described as the "night watchman" state) curtailed the need to develop an extensive administrative apparatus in addition to courts (adjudicative system). Yet, the gradual building of a welfare state led to some intense governmental intervention in the market. The neoclassical price theory of market failure and Keynesian economics were the intellectual backbones of modern liberalism. But more importantly, the rise of government bureaucracy offered the appropriate tool, the technology, for that expansion to occur. The role of government in markets is thus closely related to the development of the professional project of public bureaucracies.

The "technicization" of the state through bureaucracy gave birth to a different form of legitimacy.[14] Bureaucracy is based on a hierarchical and functional organization, clearly defined areas of expertise, standard operating procedures, and fixed-role descriptions. The essential assumption of the bureaucratic form of organization is that bureaucrats identify their own interest and ideas with the organization of which they are part. Bureaucracy is thus perceived positively, a view profoundly linked to the image of professional expertise and political neutrality to which it is attached. Like all large-scale organizations, the state tends to be bureaucratic in nature. The expansion of bureaucracy is thus inevitable and profoundly linked to the expansion of the state (in a chicken and egg way), because it is the only way of coping with the administrative requirements of large-scale social systems.

One of the main characteristics of bureaucracy is the clear-cut hierarchy of authority, with a chain of command stretching from the top to the bottom, clear rules on the conduct of officials at all levels of government, a clear career path based on seniority, and a separation from politics and ideology, since the focus is on means and procedural rituals rather than policy outcomes. Indeed, the role of bureaucracy is not to design policy but to implement policies decided in the political realm. The concept of bureaucracy presupposes by essence a primacy for politics and a clear dichotomy between politics and scientific expertise.[15] Under this model, the development of procedural rituals reinforces the top-down control of public bureaucracies and avoids the integration of scientific expertise in decision making if it would have challenged the primacy of the political realm.

In conclusion, bureaucracy is seen as an essential step in the reconceptualization of the role of the state, according to the principle of rationality. It is perceived as a form of sophisticated technology, enabling the state to intervene and regulate markets while preserving the primacy of the political realm. In one of his classic texts, Max Weber notes:

> Bureaucracy offers above all the optimum possibility for carrying through the principle of specializing administrative functions according to purely objective considerations. Individual performances are allocated to functionaries who have specialized training and who by constant practice learn more and more. The "objective discharge of business primarily means a discharge of business according to *calculable rules* and without regard for persons."[16]

This positive view of bureaucracy is intrinsically linked to both the expansion of government's role in various areas that until then had been managed by market activity only and the reinforcement of the institutional apparatus of the state. Along with this, and during the same period, comes the establishment of either central ministerial departments or independent administrative agencies. In some jurisdictions, a specialized judiciary is put in place to deal with issues arising from the normative activity of state bureaucracies.[17] In other words, the expansion of government's role in markets would not have been possible in the absence of the "technology" of professional public bureaucracy.

Yet, this positive account of bureaucracy was soon to be challenged by functionalist sociologists such as Merton, Selznick, and Crozier, among others. Merton emphasized the "dysfunctions of bureaucracy" stemming from bureaucratic ritualism and an emphasis on procedures instead of underlying organizational goals on policy outcomes. His emphasis on goals implicitly eroded the primacy of the political realm, as goals are evolving, they can be interpreted, and tensions between different goals should be dealt with before any effective administrative action takes place.[18] Based on the "human relations approach to bureaucracy," Merton acknowledged the limits of Weber's ideal type, since the discipline necessary for obtaining the kind of standardized behavior required in a bureaucratic organization may ultimately lead to a displacement of goals. This inflexibility of bureaucratic organizations and their overspecialization can impede bureaucrats from innovating and responding creatively to new challenges. The "vicious circle" of bureaucratization is further reinforced through a mechanism of cooptation and the diffusion of a special ideology securing the necessary minimum of conformity and loyalty to the organization.[19] Crozier notes how the bureaucratic system of organization "is not only a system that does not correct its behaviour in view of its errors, [but] it is also too rigid to adjust without crisis to the transformations that the accelerated evolution of industrial society makes more and more imperative."[20] The emergence of the field of public policy post–World War II attempted to challenge this ritualistic view of public bureaucracies for an arrangement that would incorporate systematically scientific expertise in policy making and the implementation of policies.[21]

These criticisms of the bureaucratic state became even more pronounced with the emergence of neoliberalism as a new paradigm for economic theory and policy making. Here we can distinguish between two trends in neoliberal thought: first, the development, partly in parallel with the theory of market failure, of the theory of government failure in welfare economics, and second, the emergence in Germany of the ordoliberal model of neoliberalism, which has profoundly marked the intellectual foundations of the European economic integration project.

The first story is well known and is not detailed here. To Ronald Coase's virulent criticism of Pigou's theory of externalities, suggesting that the assessment of the performance of different institutions (firms, markets, regulation) should involve the comparison of alternative institutional arrangements, public choice theorists added the analysis of government from a rational choice perspective: "government, like the market in a pure exchange economy, is viewed simply as an institution for aggregating or balancing individual demands for public policies."[22] The implications of these two standpoints for government intervention in the economy are devastating. Once the supply of government policies is viewed as a proper market, the mechanisms of collective choice are built upon three articulations: voters make political decisions to maximize their utility; lawmakers seek to maximize the votes they obtain and stay in office; and voters are not rational because given that voting and informing oneself about policy are costly and the benefits derived from an individual vote are nil, it makes more sense for them to remain completely uninformed about public policy.[23] In view of the collective action problem for diffused and large group interests, smaller groups are more likely to win rents from the government and to capture policy makers. Consequently, regulation does not promote the public interest but the goals of powerful interest groups. The analysis has been transposed to nondirectly elected regulators, such as the executive (bureaucracy) and judicial branches of government, which, it has been noted, offer a more durable form of protection.[24]

The standard model relies on the fact that the nonmarket nature of government's outputs leads to a measurement problem, since it is not possible to define, as in a market system, the number of units of output produced as such but only to report the level of activities from which output levels may be inferred. This leads to a monitoring problem, where the purchaser of public services—for example, the government operating as the agent of all citizens—cannot observe and thus monitor the bureaucrat's efficiency. Because of the bureaucrat's knowledge about her real costs, she might well exploit this information asymmetry if she operates, as is often the case, as a monopolist supplier. Indeed, the monopoly nature of most public service providers frees them from the competition process and does not enable the government (and ultimately the citizens) to dispose of an alternative source of information over the real costs of the provision of public services. The incentives of the bureaucrat are thus by nature in opposition to the public interest. Since the bureaucrat's salaries are unrelated to improved efficiency, because of the monitoring problem, the bureaucrat does not pursue, as do private business managers, profits but essentially nonpecuniary goals—the maximization of budget size and the expansion of the bureau's personnel and tasks—both leading to organizational slack and wasteful duplication of competencies.[25] Empirical studies have examined the comparative cost structures of private firms operating in a competitive environment and public monopolies or undertakings partly controlled by the state and found that the latter provided the fixed output demanded by the community at a higher cost than necessary.[26]

One may also remark that empirical evidence is inconclusive on the ability of citizens to control effectively government and bureaucracy and the possibility for democratic competition to produce "efficiency levels comparable to those achieved by market competition."[27] Furthermore, most of the empirical backing of the public choice theory relies on correlations between some limited variables indicating capture to infer causation, without a proper falsifiable analysis of the impact of other variables rather than capture on the regulatory outcomes, such as ideology or structural and demographic characteristics.[28]

Finally, public choice theory mostly assumes a monopolistic setting with regard to the provision of public services[29] without taking stock of electoral competition in democratic politics and also competition coming from institutions other than the government, such as the not-for-profit sector, religious organizations, unions, corporations, and families.[30]

The second is the ordoliberal version of neoliberalism, which is particularly influential in Europe. Born in Germany in the 1930s, ordoliberalism was opposed to any variant of planned state interventionism in any form: Bismarckian state socialism, Nazi autarchic planification, or Keynesian-style interventionism. Attacking New Deal programs or the Beveridge plan as symbols of the welfare state, ordoliberal authors emphasized the risks of state management of the economy, thus adhering partly to the government failure theory but also to the idea that the distinction between the "market" and the "state" is intellectually sterile. They advanced instead market economy as the principle and model for the state, which should be organized on the basis of the principle of competition.[31] The ordoliberals' research program has been nicely summarized by Foucault:

> Since it turns out that the state is the bearer of intrinsic defects, let's ask the market economy itself to be the principle, not of the state's limitations [as was the case in the liberal model] but of its internal regulation from start to finish of its existence and action. In other words, instead of accepting a free market defined by the state and kept as it were under state supervision—which was, in a way, the initial formula of liberalism—let us establish a space of economic freedom and let us circumscribe it by a state that will supervise it; the ordoliberals say we should completely turn the formula around and adopt the free market as organizing and regulating principle of the state, from the start of its existence up to the last form of its interventions—in other words, a state under the supervision of the market rather than a market supervised by the state.[32]

According to Foucault, ordoliberalism relied on three major shifts from the old liberal tradition: a shift from the concept of exchange (which limited the role of the state to ensure respect for the freedom of those involved in the exchange on the basis of the principle of laissez-faire) to that of competition (the state actively intervening to prevent a distortion of competition and the creation of monopolies); a shift from the perception of competition as a natural and preexisting given to a view of complete competition as "an historical objective of governmental art" to be actively pursued by the state; and a shift from the view of the relationship between competition and the state as reciprocally delimited areas to that of a "complete superimposition of market mechanisms, indexed to competition and governmental policy," with the market constituting the "general index in which one must place the rule for defining all governmental action."[33] The relationship between competition/markets and the state is thus reversed compared to the classic or modern liberal models without, however, leading to a new form of laissez-faire. It is important to understand here that the ordoliberal version of neoliberalism argues that the competitive market order should be integrated at the constitutional level and not at the subconstitutional level: that of choosing policies. This constitutional dimension requires the institutional framing of market processes: the market being transformed into a constitutional order. Contrary to welfare economics, ordoliberal authors aim to enforce a competitive order in an *indirect* manner, framing the rules of the game rather than seeking to improve the outcomes *directly* by way of specific interventions into the economic process.[34]

II. Implications on the Relationship between Government Activity and the Principle of Competition: Bureaucracy versus Technocracy

These different traditions of neoliberalism may have different implications for the relationship between government activity and competition. If one adopts a public choice perspective, it is possible to argue that any form of state intervention in the marketplace carries the risk of capture and inefficiency. There is a wealth of empirical literature on the inefficiency of sector-specific regulations, but similar claims have also been made with regard to competition law.[35] The burden of proof is on the state to establish the need of its intervention through competition law, and the standard of proof is set high on the assumption that the self-correcting mechanism of the market will take care of any eventual failure in the absence of state interference. Such an approach leads essentially to subject state intervention to a stricter competition assessment than private action, as by essence the monolithic (and monopolistic) nature of government intervention departs more from the optimum of competitive markets (and the standard of perfect competition) than even concentrated private market structures. However, it is also clear that from this perspective the field left to competition law versus other forms of state intervention remains open for negotiation, a negotiation conducted through and according to the rules of the communicating tool of scientific expertise—in this case, economics. As a result of a greater recourse to social sciences in public policy, the erosion of traditional divisions of labor and the emergence of risk society, bureaucracy has also seen its role change, since it has been gradually transformed from a rigid structure performing merely tasks of execution to a more proactive technocracy, assuming tasks of forecast, knowledge gathering/sharing, and communication with the public. Technocracy presupposes the systematic integration of scientific expertise in policy making, not only at the level of the policy conception but also at the implementation level. The assumption is that the realm of politics and that of scientific expertise have convergent logics and that politics and policy making are driven by scientific/expert consensus, thus inversing the primacy of politics approach that characterized the bureaucratic form of organization.[36] The incorporation of specialized scientific personnel (e.g., economists, policy analysts) in public bureaucracies (e.g., ministerial departments, regulatory agencies) exemplifies this new balance of power between the political and the scientific realms.[37]

It is important here to reflect on the implications that each form of state intervention—for example, antitrust versus regulation—entails to the general claims of expertise and "technicization" that have built bureaucratic legitimacy, on which ultimately rests government's authority to intervene in the marketplace. Ministerial departments and regulators often possess superior expertise on the characteristics and problems of the industries they supervise than do competition authorities or courts, which are by essence of generalist nature, dealing ad hoc with a plethora of cases across different sectors. This is due to superior technical skills (for example, a telecom regulator understands interconnection better than an antitrust authority), superior expertise, and more information (as a result of their systematic activity in the sector), but also because of different epistemic communities and values represented by these regulators, thus capturing a more diverse set of citizens' and consumers' preferences (e.g., environmental regulators often value the protection of the environment more than the protection of competition). In principle, the sector-specific regulators should be better placed to assess the welfare effects of their interventions on consumers and citizens, with the exception, of course, of circumstances where they remain "captured" by the specific interests they are supposed to regulate. However, a similar claim can be made to a certain extent also for competition authorities, thus indicating that from a public choice perspective, the two situations constitute, in practice, functional equivalents. Hence, if there is any claim for an antitrust authority to intervene and control some other form of state activity, this can only happen, under this approach of neoliberalism, because of the antitrust authority's superior expertise on matters relating to the regulation of markets and competition—in essence, economic expertise—or their independence from the other sectors of government bureaucracy.[38] This is not the place to expand on the important role and continued presence of economists in government bureaucracies, although there are significant differences across jurisdictions that may justify different approaches in the interaction between competition law and government action.[39] In any case, with the probable exception of public utilities' regulators, competition authorities have been one of the first venues in government bureaucracy, at least in Europe and the United States, where a high level of economic expertise has been progressively developed, either in house or contracted out to the market of professional experts. Competition authorities claim, on average, more expertise than other government departments in competition law analysis. This configuration should lead to an expansion of the scope of competition law and advocacy, with the exception of instances where the specific industry requires some superior form of economic expertise, which antitrust authorities do not possess, in view of the specific characteristics of the industry. In such rare cases, sector-specific regulation may benefit from antitrust immunity.[40]

In contrast, in the ordoliberal model, competition is a value to be preserved as such, whatever the circumstances and outcomes. This comes out of the constitutional dimension of the principle of market economy. Thus, considerations about the superior technical expertise of government departments and regulators have no place in the analysis of the appropriate scope of competition law intervention versus some other regulatory action. The European Treaties constitute an illustration of this constitutional dimension of the competition principle. Article 3(1)g of the former Treaty of European Communities recognized the vital importance of establishing "a system ensuring that competition in the internal market is not distorted." The Court of Justice relied on this provision to apply the principle of competition to state measures in a number of cases.[41] The Court has placed particular emphasis on Article 3(1)g when confronted with a conflict between competition rules and other EU policies and objectives[42] and has pronounced, on the basis of this provision, that competition law constitutes a "fundamental objective of the Community."[43] Finally, the Court referred to this article when it granted to national competition authorities the power to set aside provisions of domestic legislation that jeopardize the *effet utile* of EU competition law.[44]

The existence of a specific provision emphasizing the role of competition law in the text of the "Principles" part of the founding treaties led to specific implications as to the interpretation of this provision and its relationship with other Community activities. This was reinforced by Article 4 of the Treaty on the European Communities, which was introduced by a treaty revision in 1992, adding a new joint action of the Community and the member states: the "adoption of an economic policy, which is based on the close coordination of member states' economic policies . . . and conducted in accordance with the principle of an open market economy with free competition." The scope of the competition principle was thus extended beyond the narrow confines of the competences of the Community (although these were already broadly defined): the member states should also be inspired by this principle in conducting their economic policies. Although Article 3 of the Treaty of the European Union (TEU) does not refer any more to the principle of "undistorted competition" or "free competition," following the suggestions made by former president Sarkozy of France, Article 3(3) TEU provides that the EU shall establish an internal market with the goal to achieve "a highly competitive social market economy, aiming at full employment and social progress." In addition, according to Protocol n. 27, "the Internal market as set out in Article 3 TEU includes a system ensuring that competition is not distorted." It is too early to assess the impact of the textual modifications introduced by the Treaty of Lisbon, but it seems in general that despite the introduction of the concept of "social market economy" and some horizontal clauses in the European Treaties requiring the consideration of environmental and social policy impacts for EU policies, the principle of free competition remains a primary objective governing all action of the EU.[45] This constitutional dimension implies that in the presence of a conflict between regulation enacted by the EU or its member states and the principle of free competition, the latter should take precedence, irrespective of the degree of (economic) expertise of the national or EU bureaucracy implementing the regulation. For example, in subsequent cases, the European Courts have affirmed the absence of any competition law immunity for sector-specific regulation, thus adopting a completely opposite perspective than the U.S. Supreme Court.[46]

The strategy of integrating the value of competition at all levels of government intervention, because of its constitutional status, also had implications on the organization of the provision of public services across the member states of the EU. National approaches and styles diverge and are still exercising a powerful symbolic and rhetorical, if not any more legally binding, influence (because of extensive EU harmonization). For example, the French concept of *service public* has served for a long time as a battle cry against the expansion of the competition law provisions of the European Treaties to the public sphere, as it has been given, at least subliminally, an organic (service public should be provided by public bodies) versus a material (universal service can be dispensed by public and private bodies) meaning. In spite of a slight move toward a less conflicting terminology in the treaties and secondary legislation, with the concept of "services of general economic interest," the tension remains significant.[47] For the proponents of service public, its domain is mutually excludable from that of competition law, as any expansion of the scope of competition law will lead to an automatic restriction of the scope of service public. The introduction of specific competition law provisions for public undertakings or the recognition of the *right* of citizens to receive public services illustrate that the two principles are perceived as antagonistic to each other.[48]

On the contrary, the British experience on the interaction of government with the competition principle has been different. The monolithic welfare state that emerged from the Beveridge plan in the 1950s and 1960s was subject to the neoliberal cure of liberalization and privatization during the Thatcher era in the 1980s and to "third way" management in the 1990s and 2000s. A key objective of New Public Management was to achieve a "postbureaucratic" government, where the introduction of purchaser/provider separation, the creation of quasi-markets, outsourcing, and user control would allow multiple forms of provision to be developed to create more competition among potential providers.[49] The recent white paper "Open Public Services" by the UK coalition government and subsequent legislation that has been adopted or is still in process also aim to introduce consumer choice and competition in the provision of services by opening public services to a range of providers, not only from the public sector but from the voluntary and private sectors as well. "Open Public Services" goes so far as to declare that "[a]part from those public services where the government has a special reason to operate a monopoly (e.g., the military), every public service should be open so that, in line with people's demands, services can be delivered by a diverse range of providers."[50] This will be achieved by having suppliers from the private and voluntary sectors enter the public procurement process; providers competing with one another to deliver services directly to individuals armed with personal budgets and entitlements or the power of choice; and the full development of a voluntary, community, and social enterprise (VCSE) sector, accountable to local communities and thus to democratic electoral competition.[51] Following these proposals, the provision of most government services in the United Kingdom would be organized according to the principle of free competition. While the approach does not share the constitutional dimension of the German ordoliberal perspective and its rules-based approach (it is more outcomes oriented), they both follow a similar direction.

In conclusion, a bureaucracy-centered theory of competition law and the state interaction will be simultaneously more context aware and empirically focused than current approaches. First, at the macro level, it becomes important to analyze the value structure foundations on which competition law enforcement is built by looking at the degree of intrusion of neoliberal values in the design and operation of public institutions. Modern bureaucracy is more knowledge based and outcome oriented (technocracy) than the Weberian description of it as a mere technical, rational, administrative routine–style implementation of public policies decided elsewhere. Second, at the micro level, the knowledge base, the skills, and the disciplinary/professional background of government bureaucracies need to be explored in depth before determining the appropriate method of interaction with authorities entrusted with the implementation of competition law norms (competition authorities and courts). The level of development of the competition law regime and, of course, the intrinsic quality of government bureaucracies, their sources of wisdom, and their ability to produce efficient policies are also among the elements to take into account.

III. Case Studies on the Interaction between the Principle of Competition and Government Action in a Neoliberal State

What are the implications of the transformation of public action in a neoliberal state for the application of competition law to government intervention in markets? To answer this question, I examine two case studies illustrating two possible strategies of interaction between the principle of competition and government action in a neoliberal state. First, the tendency to subject all types of state action to the discipline of competition may be systematized by the establishment of a prophylactic ex ante competition screening of all proposed laws and regulations. Second, competition in the provision of services of general interest should be adequately managed so as to produce the best possible outcomes from a public policy perspective. Hence, competition may only be introduced for some parameters (e.g., quality) but excluded for others (e.g., price). The traditional analytical framework of competition law will in this case need to be adjusted to reflect the proper balance between the different aims pursued by government action. The UK managed-competition system in the health care services sector provides an illustration of how this balancing operates in practice.

A. Introducing Competition Screening in Regulatory Impact Assessments

In recent years many countries have introduced the tool of ex ante competition assessment in the process of evaluating legislative bills, draft regulations, or policies. Sometimes, this competition screening is integrated in the general system of regulatory impact assessments (RIAs), and in other cases it has an autonomous existence.

The OECD has prepared a competition checklist in the context of its "Competition Assessment Toolkit," suggesting a detailed competition analysis of a policy proposal should it have any of the following four effects: setting limits on the number or range of suppliers; limiting the ability of suppliers to compete—for example, by reducing their ability to set prices, advertise, or market their goods, or by raising their costs; reducing their incentive to compete by creating a self-regulatory or coregulatory regime, or increasing transparency over the outputs, prices, sales, or costs of the suppliers by requesting the publication of information; and finally, limiting the choices and information available to consumers.[52] If the proposal affects one of these parameters, a detailed, more comprehensive competition assessment should be undertaken by looking at the regulatory proposal's impact on the main determinants of competitive pressures for the market in question (e.g., the existence of coordinated effects or reduced incentives for innovation). This assessment involves the definition of a relevant market. The proposed regulatory design should be considered in a comparative context in which alternative means of achieving the regulatory objective that are less restrictive of competition are identified and assessed. If these are not found, then a comparison should be made between the costs and benefits of the proposal, the latter being adopted "only if that comparison shows that, after taking into account the costs of the anticompetitive impact the assessment identified, the proposal's enactment will yield a net benefit."[53] A similar approach is also taken in other jurisdictions.[54]

Some jurisdictions have put in place more general RIA procedures to examine the impact of proposed regulation and legislation on a number of variables, including economic, social, environmental, and health effects, the competition screening process being, in some cases, cited as one variable among others. For example, the European Commission's Impact Assessment Guidelines include competition screening as one of the various economic impacts that RIA routinely explores.[55] This integration of the competition assessment tool into the broader RIA analysis raises questions on the possible links between the two procedures. First, the OECD Competition Toolkit notes that RIA takes a more static approach, comparing likely outcomes based on the existing economic and regulatory environment, whereas competition assessments are more future oriented, taking a dynamic efficiency approach and focusing on the effects of the proposal on consumer choice rather than on the economy and public policy in general.[56] However, it is not clear how different these tools are in practice and how much competition assessment has been integrated in RIA analysis (Figure 2.1). Competition authorities and courts have already been using cost-benefit analysis techniques in assessing ex post the competitive impact of various forms of regulation.[57] One could finally argue that competition assessment is based upon competition / industrial organization economics methodologies, whereas RIAs tend to use a broader set of methodologies. Yet, the possibility of cross-fertilization and intensive borrowing between the two techniques should not be underestimated now that RIA procedures have become more systematic at the EU and national levels.

Second, the institutional framework of RIA and that of competition screening might be different. Although it is recognized that the assessment should be performed by the "frontline" government departments developing the proposal, under the review of an external party, most frequently an Impact Assessment Board, these bodies in general lack competition expertise. Competition authorities have a role to play in reviewing any proposal with potential effects on competition (as part of their competition advocacy mission) and making (binding or nonbinding) recommendations,[58] in engaging in ex ante consultations

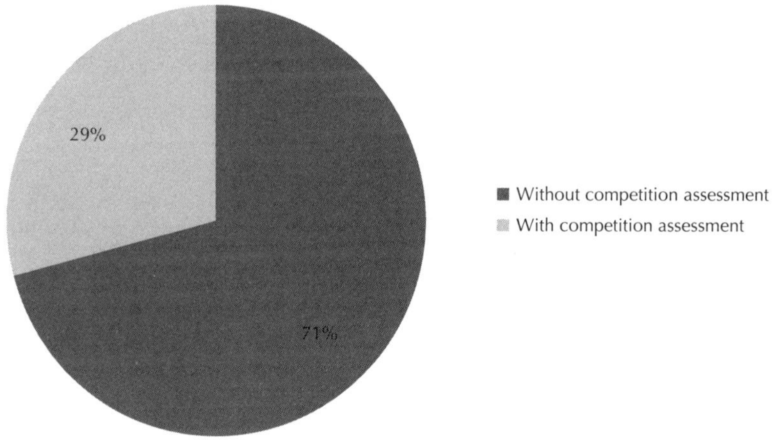

Figure 2.1 The place of competition impact assessments in regulatory impact assessments in the EU, 2006–2012

NOTE: I have analyzed all 659 Regulatory Impact Assessments published at the European Commission website through March 2012.

with the "frontline" government department performing the RIA,[59] in adopting guidelines for policy makers detailing how competition screening should be performed and integrated in RIAs,[60] and in providing advice and training to policy makers at any stage of the process.[61]

Nonetheless, the generalization of competition screening of draft regulations and laws, as part of the RIA procedures, will inevitably erode the differential of expertise that now benefits competition authorities in comparison to "frontline" government departments. Once the "culture" of competition assessment is integrated across government bureaucracies and once internal expertise in the form of departmental specialists (lawyers and mainly economists) gets fully developed, the integration of the competition screening in the RIA tool would be complete. Certainly, there are arguments for maintaining an independent institutional voice for competition inside government bureaucracies, but in a neoliberal state this institutional complexity might not offer much. In some cases, it might even be counterproductive because the independence of competition authorities might make them ineffective competition advocates—especially in crisis situations—so the need to establish also advocates for competition within the core government departments, and not only outside ministerial departments, in competition authorities.[62]

In conclusion, the integration of competition screening in RIA challenges the view that competition and government action are antithetical to each other, and it marks the evolution toward a complete integration and diffusion of the principles of competition across government bureaucracies.

B. The Emergence of a New Style of Competition Law for Government Services: Managed Competition in the Health Care Sector in the United Kingdom

The British National Health Service (NHS) was subject to major reforms since the introduction of quasi-markets into the delivery of public services and the separation of the funding and provision role of the state in the national health system in 1990.[63] This market-oriented approach aimed to reduce costs without public cuts in entitlements. Its main goal was to respond to accusations that NHS bureaucracy was inefficient by introducing an institutional split between purchasers and providers bodies and more competition in the provision of publicly funded health care. When the state contributes funds, it purchases services from a variety of providers of health services, all operating in competition with one another. These "quasi-markets" replace monopolistic state providers with competitive independent ones (initially public providers and, since 2008, private or nonprofit ones). But unlike conventional markets, on the supply side, the providers that are competing with one another are not trying to maximize profits, nor are they privately owned. On the demand side, a third party, not the patients, makes the purchasing decisions.[64] In 2006, the National Health Service Act introduced reforms giving patients a choice of where they received health care and introduced nonprice competition among public hospitals and between public and private (also voluntary sector) providers to deliver secondary care to publicly funded (through taxation) patients.[65] Hence, NHS patients who get referrals from their general practitioners can choose from four or more specialists registered with the Care Quality Commission (CQC) who are qualified to provide medical services for the tariffs set by the NHS or, where it is not covered by the national tariff, the price set by the local commissioners.[66] These are based on a prospective payment system, known as Payment by Results (PbR), where the hospital fee is determined by the government on the basis mainly of patients' diagnoses with some other adjustments. Since the Health and Social Care Act 2012, all public hospitals are to be organized by 2014 to NHS Foundation Trusts, which are independent of the Department of Health and jointly licensed by two independent regulators, Monitor (economic regulator) and the Care Quality Commission (quality standards).

How does competition work in these "quasi-markets" in view of state funding? As funding follows patients around the system, introducing patient choice creates financial incentives for providers to compete for market share.[67] Since a regulator sets the prices, health care providers compete over nonprice dimensions to attract patients. There is empirical evidence that competition on quality, when the administered price is set at the right level, generates significant benefits for the patients and thus provides better value for taxpayers.[68] Because the regulated price is generally set above the providers' marginal costs, the most efficient providers will have the financial incentives to increase the quality of their services until their profits approach zero. But would a public or nonprofit provider respond to these financial incentives at least as much as a private provider would if there is no proper profit to be made? Subsequent reforms were necessary to enable senior management to be responsive to financial incentives:

1. The hospital remuneration was organized in annual block contracts paying for the use of the hospital's facilities for a range of services to predefined populations.
2. Hospitals were progressively allowed to retain surpluses, and their financial situation was subject to central government's control, which

still has the power to remove senior management from hospitals that are in deficit.

3. Patients should be offered an adequate environment to exercise choice and be responsive to quality of care signals.
4. Intermediaries such as the Clinical Commissioning Groups also should be offered financial incentives and autonomy to ensure that patients are elastic to quality and exercise their choice diligently.

With these reforms, NHS bureaucracies became subject to the disciplines of the competitive process.[69] Similar reforms have been initiated in various other EU member states.

The introduction of competition and choice in the mixed market of secondary care (that involved both for-profit and nonprofit providers), in conjunction with the administered price system, raises the question of the application of competition law in this peculiar setting. It is clear that for competition to work, a broad duty of competitive neutrality should be imposed, encompassing the need to clarify if and how competition law may apply in this context.[70] This issue has generated much debate, in view of both EU and UK requirements, that the entity to which competition law applies should be an "undertaking"—that is, an entity exercising an economic activity, the latter concept defining the scope of competition law.[71] Some feel that public hospitals that provide free services and are funded by the state should not be considered undertakings, so competition law should not apply to them. Others, however, believe they are undertakings and that competition law should apply.[72]

From a legal perspective, there are two problems with using competition law in this context. First, the case law of the European Courts provides clearly that if an organization purchases goods it does not intend to offer as part of an economic activity but to use for some other activity, such as an activity of a purely social nature, then it is not acting as an undertaking simply because it is a purchaser of those goods.[73] In this context, the public hospital's services are purchased by the NHS, under the direction of the Department of Health, for the social purpose of providing universal health care, funded by tax revenues (a compulsory way of funding). Second, proponents of the application of competition law advance that, at least for some of the health services, public hospitals can potentially make a profit and still be qualified as undertakings.[74] Yet, transposing the concept of "profit" in a nonprofit setting is a difficult endeavor. As said previously, the financial incentives offered to public hospitals for inducing them to compete do not relate to monetary profits but to mainly bureaucratic-related incentives. These incentives can include, for example, senior management keeping their jobs, the hospitals being granted bigger budgets, or, since the introduction of the Health and Social Care Act 2012 with equal treatment for both public and private providers if they fail, being able to keep their public status, since "failed" and debt-ridden NHS Foundation Trusts may pass to private management.

Thus, it is somewhat ambiguous how competition law can be used—in which case, other principles, public policy, or institutional matters may influence the choice of the adequate interpretative option. From a public policy perspective, if competition law is not used for nonprofit hospitals, whereas private providers are subject to it, it may introduce an anomaly, at least as far as using the competitive neutrality principle, since public and private providers compete for patients and private providers can make profits.[75]

From an institutional perspective, however, enforcing general competition law in this context might be problematic. First, competition authorities and, to a certain degree, courts, with the mandate to enforce competition law, are experts in competition law principles but not on issues relating to the health and safety of patients. Their mission-oriented role—preserving the competitive process—may also influence their setting of priorities between the value of competition and other values, such as integrated care, which might be of importance to patients. As a recent OECD secretariat report reminds us, the competitive process allows an efficient allocation of resources irrespective of the underlying set of preferences. Yet, it might also result in undesirable outcomes as far as the care patients receive.[76] Hence, it should be considered an instrument for the provision of high-quality health care, rather than as an end in itself.

Second, the provision of effective health care requires the cooperation of different providers across—but also at the same level of—the health care chain. To ensure a seamless health service to patients and economies to the taxpayer, providers and commissioners must exchange the necessary information about ways to improve patient safety and joint research and development. Joint purchasing and cooperation may also sometimes be necessary to disseminate and launch innovations faster. In a competitive and segmented health care market, there is always the risk that care will be fragmented and that one provider will not always know what another provider has done, leaving the patients to sort out how and when to deal with different providers for different elements of their care. Cooperation among providers is thus essential for enabling integrated care.

Due to their generalist nature, competition authorities or courts are not, however, well placed to develop the technical expertise and acquire the necessary information to guarantee the preservation of integrated care, nor are they generally ready to accept that cooperation might in some cases be more important than competition. It thus becomes essential to entrust the application of competition law principles to a sector-specific regulator. In the United Kingdom, Monitor has extensive competence in ensuring the right balance between cooperation and competition, with the assistance since 2009 of a new statutory advisory committee, the Competition and Cooperation Panel. The new Health and Social Care Act 2012 makes clear that Monitor's "main duty" is "to protect and promote the interests of health services by promoting the provision of health care services which . . . is economic, efficient, and effective, and . . . maintains or improves the quality of the services," thus ensuring that patient interests always come first.[77] The Health and Social Care Act also requires Monitor to "exercise its functions with a view to preventing anticompetitive behavior in the provision of health care services for the purposes of the NHS which is against the interests of people who use such services," although one should note that promoting competition does not form part of Monitor's main duty, nor is even mentioned as a secondary one.[78] Where an integrated service raises competition concerns, Monitor will focus on *what benefits patients*, its role being to ensure that the benefits to patients outweigh any negative effects to competition and that any negatives are kept to a minimum.[79]

Finally, the concept of "restriction of competition" in the health care quasi-markets and the cost-benefit analysis to be performed differ from those employed in competition law. First, the restriction of competition relates to harm to patients (reduced patient choice for NHS-funded services) and taxpayers from lower-quality services, although in some limited circumstances they might also have some effect on prices for nonroutine elective services.[80] Second, the benefits to be taken into account to outweigh the existence of a "restriction of competition" in this sector do not always take the form of the usual cost and quality efficiency gains of competition law. Certainly, economies of scale and scope lowering short-run variable costs, increases in the number of patients (the "output" to maximize), or procedures reducing transaction costs are benefits to consumers that are usually taken into account in general competition law. But other factors, such as improved recruitment and retention of staff, better information, shared clinical working practices, and seamless patient care, might not be easily transposable in the context of general competition law. It becomes therefore clear that a different institutional and/or, to some extent, substantive law setting is needed to enforce competition law principles in this peculiar setting.

For this reason, before the Health and Social Care Act 2012, the United Kingdom put in place a specific competition law regime that applied to all commissioners and NHS-funded services providers, irrespective of whether they were public, private, or third-sector organizations. These Principles and Rules for Cooperation and Competition (PRCC) were not legally binding provisions enforceable by courts; they were inspired by general competition law but at the same time emphasized a number of other parameters of essence for the promotion of competition in these quasi-markets, such as rules for the commissioning and procurement of health services, the transparency and fairness of the payment regimes, the duty of commissioners and providers to co-operate to deliver seamless and sustainable care to patients, and rules regulating promotional activity. A Competition and Cooperation Panel (CCP) was also set up to provide advice on matters of compliance with the PRCC and has adopted extensive guidelines on the interpretation of the PRCC with regard to conduct and merger cases.[81]

Following the enactment of the Health and Social Care Act 2012, the CCP has been integrated in Monitor, which also has the power to apply general competition law concurrently with the Office of Fair Trading (OFT). Hence, general competition law will also apply to the health care sector, although through a different institutional framework than nonregulated sectors with the concurrent jurisdiction of both the sector economic regulator and the competition authority.[82] How would the interaction between these two competition authorities work in practice? The broad duties of the Monitor will inevitably weigh in the decision-making process and may lead to different outcomes than a situation where the OFT would be involved on its own.[83] As it has been clearly formulated in the recently published interpretative notices on the new regulatory regime, when investigating anticompetitive behavior, Monitor will have to take into account the objective of health commissioners "to secure patients' needs and improve quality and efficiency."[84]

Focusing on the different values, competencies, and methodologies used by the respective bureaucracies and on how these could complement one another in the enforcement of competition law in this sector might offer a better predictive tool of their interaction than a normative theory on the relationships between sector-specific regulators and competition authorities or courts. In a neoliberal state, where competition is a value underpinning any form of state action, the exact place of other values becomes a matter for continuous negotiation between different segments of public technocracy. These rely on their expertise/epistemic competence on the substantive issues of the policy area to which they intervene, rather than on their general bureaucratic competence or procedures and administrative routines, as would have been the case in the traditional (Weberian) view of bureaucracy. For example, the CCP, and now the Monitor, relies in its decision-making process on the input of two groups of experts: the clinical reference group, which consists of experts in public health and medicine who provide advice on health and safety issues, and the economics reference group, which consists of experts in health economics and competition who offer consultations on competition economics and analytical techniques/methodologies. This expertise is more extensive than what competition authorities usually get (who mainly focus on the economics of industrial organization).

In essence, it is necessary to conduct a comparative institutional analysis[85] focusing on the respective expertise, among other criteria, of each bureaucracy (competition authority or sector-specific regulator) before determining the appropriate interaction between these different institutions. Ministerial departments, sector-specific regulators, and competition authorities all constitute imperfect alternatives. The question is which alternative is best (for welfare—the underlying aim of state intervention), given the real world of high information costs and the fragmentation of expertise (over different dimensions of welfare). Comparative institutional analysis makes it possible to choose from these imperfect alternatives.

This is particularly true in the United Kingdom, where sector-specific regulators in charge proceed to a concurrent application of competition law, in addition to their other duties. The efficacy of the competition authority should not be presumed for all regulatory "transactions" aiming to promote competition and welfare, but it should be subject to a comparative analysis of alternative institutions, some of which are sector-specific regulators or self-regulatory bodies. The possibility of capture should, of course, be factored into the comparative institutional analysis, but its impact should not be overestimated in comparison to the possible benefits of regulation. As Oliver Williamson rightly observed, "Even if the benefits of regulation decline over time and go negative, the discounted present value may remain positive."[86] The proximity of the goals of sector-specific regulators to those of government departments (as they are by definition broader than the simple preservation of a competitive market, which is the main task of a competition authority) may facilitate the integration of these different goals within a unified framework of rules or standards for undertakings to comply with. Quite often ministerial departments or sector-specific regulators are not only responsible for regulating market failures or market imperfections (which is what competition authorities do) but also for proceeding to some redistributional transactions (e.g., public service obligations), the latter being a highly politicized area of government activity. One would expect that the information asymmetries, with regard to the political/strategic objectives pursued by the government or legislature, would also be lower for ministerial departments and sector-specific regulators than for competition authorities, thus providing some advantages to the first two in the comparative institutional analysis.

* * *

Current accounts of the interaction between competition law and state activities are based on a clear-cut old liberalism style distinction between "state"/"government" and "market," which do not take into account the emergence of the neoliberal state. By doing so, they also ignore the multifaceted nature of the concept of "state" and the important inputs of political science and sociological literature on the different forms of state and the evolution of the composition and role of public bureaucracies. By advancing a "bureaucracy-centred theory" of the competition law and the state interaction, this chapter offers an alternative interdisciplinary theoretical framework that can be successfully transposed into different institutional and cultural settings. More empirical work needs to be done to explore the hypothesis presented in this chapter in different societal and cultural contexts.

Chapter 3

Competition Issues and Private Infrastructure Investment through Public-Private Partnerships

R. Richard Geddes

In this chapter, we examine competition issues raised by increasing reliance on private infrastructure investment in the United States through the use of public-private partnerships, or PPPs. PPPs are contractual agreements between a public-sector infrastructure project sponsor and a private-sector entity that allow for greater private-sector participation in the design, construction, operation, and financing of infrastructure projects. Because PPP use is growing in the United States, provision of infrastructure through PPPs is often compared with provision under traditional project delivery. In a PPP, private partners are typically granted long-term concessions to operate and maintain infrastructure. This raises a set of competition issues that are relatively new in the U.S. infrastructure sector, while resurrecting old issues, such as the social cost of public- versus private-sector capital.

This chapter discusses competition issues that have arisen as a result of increased use of PPPs, with an emphasis on the transportation infrastructure sector. The issue of differences between the public sector's and the private sector's costs of capital is a particular focus.[1] In Section I, we discuss why PPPs are increasing in importance and why they intensify direct competition between public- versus private-sector provision of infrastructure. In Section II, we show why the relative cost of public- versus private-sector capital is important in this debate. We also compare the risks that taxpayers and private investors absorb by examining the differing nature of their residual claims. Residual claims are the property rights to a firm's net cash flow. We stress one aspect of taxpayer residual claims, which is that they are nontransferable, or nontradable. We discuss several reasons why the lack of transferability inherent in taxpayer residual claims is likely to increase the cost of capital relative to the private sector's transferable claims. We view the cost of capital through the lens of the principal-agent relationship between politicians and firm managers.[2] We note that the nontradability of public-sector residual claims implies that ownership concentration cannot change in response to greater benefit to principles through better monitoring of their appointed agents. In Section III, we discuss how alternative policy approaches via competition policy can help address such issues, including through concession bidding and competitive neutrality policies. We suggest that, in addition to the effects of tax-exempt municipal debt, the nontradability of public-sector residual claims should be taken into account when considering competitive neutrality within the PPP context. In Section IV we conclude.

I. Public-Private Partnerships in the United States

The use of PPPs is rising in the United States due to a confluence of forces that are putting pressure on traditional methods of infrastructure delivery, particularly in the transportation sector. In transportation, those forces include rising traffic demand, aging facilities, declining revenue from fossil fuel taxes, and constrained state and local transportation budgets.[3] For example, total vehicle miles traveled (VMT) in the United States increased by 347 percent between 1957 and 2003, while total highway mileage increased by only 15 percent.[4] Traffic congestion also increased in the country's major urban areas. According to the Texas Transportation Institute's 2010 *Urban Mobility Report*, annual hours of delay per peak-time traveler increased 136 percent between 1982 and 2009 in the nation's 14 largest urban areas. A typical peak-period commuter in the Washington, D.C., metropolitan area, for example, can now expect to experience an average of 70 hours of delay per year, or almost three full days.[5] Vehicle emissions also increase significantly in congested traffic, which further harms the environment. The annual overall cost of traffic congestion to the U.S. economy was recently estimated at $168 billion.[6]

Meanwhile, a disturbingly large portion of the country's transportation infrastructure is in a state of disrepair. As of 2013, about one in nine bridges in the United States were structurally deficient; the average age of U.S. bridges is 42 years.[7] Moreover, traditional funding sources for transportation infrastructure construction and renovation are declining. This is due in part to reliance on gasoline and diesel taxes for that funding. Both inflation and the use of more fuel-efficient vehicles are eroding the purchasing power of fossil fuel tax revenues.

One important response, particularly at the state level, is an increased role for private designers, construction firms, and investors through the use of PPPs. PPPs have been utilized to deliver large infrastructure projects in many other countries, including Australia,[8] Canada,[9] the United Kingdom,[10] France, Italy, Portugal, and Spain.[11] As Table 3.1 shows, since 1985, the United States has lagged behind other major regions and countries in terms of private infrastructure investment per dollar of gross domestic product. Canada, for example, has far more private infrastructure investment per dollar of GDP than the United States, as does Europe.

This low rate of private participation in U.S. infrastructure is surprising given the long history of private investment in other network industries, such as water, railroads, and electricity, as well as the strong U.S. legal institutions underlying both property rights and the enforcement of contracts.[12] Possible reasons include the extensive use of fuel taxes rather than direct user fees to fund infrastructure such as roads, bridges, and tunnels. Additionally, privately financed toll roads declined in the United States after the failure of many wooden plank roads in the nineteenth century.[13]

PPP use in the United States is, however, rising. As Figure 3.1 in the appendix suggests, both the number and size of U.S. PPP projects have gradually increased. This is particularly true for projects that involve a greater degree of private participation than merely designing and constructing a facility (i.e., a "design-build" project). Moreover, competition between private project delivery and traditional delivery is likely to increase in the future given the constraints on state and local budgets. Although the private sector has long

Table 3.1 PPPs worldwide, nominal total costs (in US$ billions), 1985–2011

Country	*PPP activity*	*GDP (2011)*	*PPP activity/2011 GDP (%)*
Asia, Australia	187.2	21,390	0.875
United States	68.4	15,227.074	0.449
Canada	45.2	1,711.473	2.64
Mexico, Latin America, Caribbean	88.5	5,613.501	1.58
Europe	353.3	19,879.574	1.78
Africa, Middle East	31.5	3,966.397	0.794

SOURCE: Public Works Financing (PWF), "2011 Survey of Public-Private Partnerships Worldwide," 264, 2011: 1–24 (for dollar value of PPP investment); GDP estimates by region are from IMF World Economic Outlook (April 2012).

provided design and construction services through design-build projects, direct competition for the provision of facility financing, operation, and maintenance services was relatively rare in the United States until recently.

The growing use of PPPs raises competition issues that are relatively new to the transportation sector. The private partner in a PPP is typically granted an exclusive concession to operate a facility, such as a road, bridge, or tunnel, for a fixed time period.[14] Infrastructure assets are, by their nature, situation-specific, sunk, and largely irreversible. Long-term concession contracts are necessary to protect both the public-sector project sponsor and the private-sector investor. From the private partner's perspective, the concession contract protects irreversible infrastructure assets from expropriation.[15] Contracts typically contain provisions that protect the public by setting initial toll rates and limiting toll increases, while ensuring that the asset is properly operated and maintained.

Concession contracts protect investors by granting them an exclusive franchise for the life of the concession, through clearly defined toll schedules and through noncompete and compensation clauses. A noncompete clause is a guarantee provided by the public partner that it will not build an unplanned, competing transportation facility within a specific distance from the privately operated facility. Such clauses have been controversial in that they may limit the government's ability to undertake projects in contravention of a noncompete clause.[16] Perhaps because of such controversy, noncompete clauses are now unusual, having been replaced with less strict compensation clauses. Under a compensation clause, the public partner is allowed to construct an unplanned facility that competes with the PPP, but it must compensate the private partner for revenues lost due to the additional competition. Conversely, such clauses may also require that the private partner compensate the public partner if an unplanned facility, such as a new interchange, increases revenue to the PPP facility.

Although the private partner is insulated from competition via the concession agreement, it is unlikely to face prosecution under the antitrust laws, since the Parker immunity doctrine may apply.[17] The Parker doctrine applies to private agents when they act at the direction of the state after it creates a regulation that has anticompetitive effects. PPPs by definition are contractual arrangements under which the private partner provides a public service, such as a transportation facility, at the behest of the state. This would seem to meet the requirement that the anticompetitive conduct "must be compelled by direction of the State acting as sovereign."[18]

A two-part test set forth in *California Retail Liquor Dealers Association v. Midcal Aluminum* determines whether or not an act should be treated as state action for the purposes of antitrust immunity: "First, the challenged restraint must be one clearly articulated and affirmatively expressed as state policy; second, the policy must be actively supervised by the State itself."[19] Regarding the first aspect of this test, the state policy must include a public policy goal, such as providing all citizens with access to transportation. This clearly articulated state policy may be inferred "if suppression of competition is the 'foreseeable result' of what the statute authorizes."[20] State-level PPP-enabling laws may be important in creating the clear intent required by the test's first part, since they often state in their preambles their intent to promote the use of PPPs in the state. The test's second part suggests that ongoing monitoring and oversight of the concession contract by the public project sponsor are important.[21]

The exclusivity created in a concession contract, combined with state oversight of the concession, suggests that the private partner may receive immunity from prosecution under the antitrust laws via the state action doctrine. There are, however, other ways in which competition is facilitated in the provision of PPPs, which is through the use of a public-sector comparator.

II. Public-Private Partnership Competition Issues and the Public-Sector Comparator

In jurisdictions where PPPs are used, there is often a formal process for comparing the cost of the two forms of delivery, which is known as the public-sector comparator (PSC). In addition to typical competition among private firms, the PSC allows an additional degree of competition to be introduced in PPP provision by directly comparing the PPP approach with traditional project delivery. The PSC "estimates the hypothetical risk-adjusted cost if a project were to be financed, owned, and implemented by government" in the most efficient manner possible by government.[22] The cost of project provision under the PSC is then compared directly with provision via a PPP to ensure that the PPP approach provides the public with value for money relative to traditional delivery.

Competitive neutrality is a key aspect of the PSC.[23] Competitive neutrality refers to the concept that when firms in the public and private sectors are in direct competition in some business activity, the public firm should not benefit from competitive advantages (or disadvantages) created by virtue of its governmental links.[24] Potential benefits of such a relationship include, among others, preferential tax treatment, explicit or implicit debt guarantees, and exemption from various regulations, such as those affecting the environment. There are also potential competitive disadvantages, or burdens, placed on public-sector firms, sometimes including universal service and common carrier obligations. Common carrier obligations have been imposed in network industries such as railroads, postal services, public airlines, and taxicabs, among others.

Competitive neutrality is particularly relevant in those cases where there is a new private entrant in a market that was previously an exclusive state monopoly. Prior to the use of PPPs, competitive neutrality was less important in the United States as compared to many other countries because the private sector predominated in large industries, such as oil, coal, steel, railroads, and electricity, since they were founded, while state-owned enterprises (SOEs) have played a much larger role in those industries in other countries.[25]

Competitive neutrality becomes more important as the level of competition between an SOE and a private firm increases. Competitive neutrality is typically embedded in a broader national competition policy that attempts to eliminate such competitive advantages and thus ensure a "level playing field" between public- and private-sector firms.[26] Such competition policies are commonplace internationally.[27] A 2009 Organisation for Economic Co-operation and Development report, for example, reviews policies in 27 countries relating to their competitive neutrality rules.[28]

The public-sector comparator explicitly allows for adjustments derived from SOE status to be considered.[29] It ensures that there is no net financial advantage of one form of delivery relative to another stemming strictly from its ownership status. Competitive neutrality policy, as embedded in the PSC, can be thought of as a mechanism to address issues raised by PPPs via increased competition between public- and private-sector provision.

III. Competition Issues and the Cost of Capital

Competitive concerns between public and private provision can arise from several sources, including perceived differences in the cost of capital stemming from softer SOE budget constraints[30] and cheaper SOE financing due to an implicit government guarantee.[31] Both aspects are likely to impact the cost of government versus private-sector capital. Because large infrastructure projects are capital intensive, understanding differences in the relative cost of capital between the two is critical. The cost of capital is also important for the PSC because, as noted, the PSC must estimate the hypothetical, risk-adjusted cost if the project were to be delivered exclusively by government. The cost of debt capital is particularly important because public-sector projects are financed with debt only, although taxpayers still bear residual risk. Projects incorporating equity provided by the private sector also utilize a high degree of leverage.

When the relative cost of capital is discussed within the context of U.S. PPPs, the debate often focuses on the cost of debt capital.[32] In the United States, income from municipally issued debt is exempt from taxation at the federal level, which lowers the interest rate that bondholders are willing to accept to hold that debt. Differential tax treatment reduces the cost of debt to municipal issuers relative to private issuers, artificially lowering the cost of capital to the public relative to the private sector.[33] However, lower interest rates driven by that tax treatment reflect revenue lost to the U.S. Treasury rather than a net social gain associated with government-issued debt. This reduction in interest rates is likely to be substantial and a main driver of yield spreads between taxable and tax-exempt interest rates on bonds.[34] Depending on whether the debt used to fund infrastructure projects is toll-revenue backed or general obligation, interest costs may also be lower because taxpayers provide an implicit guarantee unavailable to most private issuers.[35] That is, taxpayers implicitly absorb some of the risk associated with debt repayment, since the government's taxing power can be used to raise revenue to service debt.[36] Government issuers are unlikely to allow a default on their debt when there is scope for tax increases because the subsequent ratings downgrade increases their future cost of capital. Taxpayers are therefore effectively providing free insurance for government debt.

Although taxpayers are rarely thought of as equity capital providers, there is now wide agreement that they are nevertheless residual risk bearers in public-sector projects financed through government-issued debt.[37] If a project's returns (perhaps through toll revenue from a transportation project) are higher than expected, taxpayers will benefit through lower taxes, greater government expenditures, or the retirement of government debt, and conversely if the project's returns are lower than expected. The risks inherent in a project can be allocated to either taxpayers or to private investors, but overall project risk is generally independent of which party bears it. The fundamental question is whether taxpayers or private investors are more efficient at risk bearing.

A large literature now focuses on the relative efficiency of those groups in bearing risk. In an early paper, Jorgenson and colleagues[38] argue that the marginal return from additional public-sector investment should be evaluated at the risk-free rate. Arrow and Lind[39] formalized that analysis into a theorem and suggested that taxpayers could more efficiently bear the risk associated with public-sector investment because it was spread over a larger number of risk bearers, with each one bearing a smaller fraction of overall project risk. The Arrow-Lind theorem has been summarized as stating that "as the net returns of an investment of a given size are shared by increasingly many individuals, the risk premium for the respective individuals vanishes, and, more importantly and perhaps surprisingly, the aggregate of these premiums for all individuals also approaches zero."[40] According to this theorem, if risk can be spread over a sufficiently large number of taxpayers, the cost of that risk bearing can be eliminated entirely.[41]

Although the Arrow-Lind approach remains influential,[42] the view that the public sector is more efficient at risk spreading and thus that its cost of capital should be evaluated at a lower rate is questionable. Some observers conclude that the public sector's cost of capital is unlikely to be systematically lower,[43] while others argue that the public sector's cost of capital is instead likely to be higher.[44] These commentators generally do not consider distortions in the cost of debt created by implicit taxpayer guarantees, as well as the effects of that debt on taxpayer's balance sheets. Kenneth Small summarizes the uncertain nature of the debate by stating, "The current state of knowledge does not enable us to say whether this extra shadow value of publicly raised capital is as great as the risk premium required by the private sector."[45]

Despite this large literature, researchers have not yet considered carefully how the differing nature of public- versus private-sector residual claims is likely to affect the cost of capital and thus competitive neutrality.[46] Differences in the nature of public- versus private-sector residual claims, however, affect the social cost of risk bearing in important ways. We here focus on the role of *captive equity*. Captive equity stems from the fact that public-sector residual claims are not separable from residency in the jurisdiction in which the taxpayer resides (that is, they are nontradable), while private-sector residual claims are transferable at low cost on an equity market. Taxpayer residual claimants are captive equity holders in the sense that they can only exit their investments in public-sector projects by incurring the cost of changing jurisdictions. Taxpayers are thus required to provide risk-bearing services to the project without compensation.

An analogy to the cost of labor—wages—is illustrative. Suppose the government, under penalty of a fine, required citizens of a certain jurisdiction to construct infrastructure projects without compensation.[47] This policy lowers the amount the government actually pays to labor—that is, its wage bill—to complete the infrastructure projects. Compelling unpaid work on infrastructure is an effective policy for reducing the incurred, but not the social, cost of infrastructure provision. The same is true if capital providers are compelled to bear risk without paying the opportunity cost of those risk-bearing services.

In the case of labor, one aspect of competitive neutrality should be a correction for the opportunity cost of labor when comparing the overall social cost of public-sector provision with its social private-sector cost. The opportunity cost of labor is the wage that the same workers would forego by giving up their next best employment opportunity.

Analogously, when calculating the public sector's social cost of capital for inclusion in the public-sector comparator, a shadow price reflecting the return that private investors would require to voluntarily provide risk capital under the same circumstances should be included. The shadow price should reflect the risk premium that investors would demand to provide capital to a project with the same risk characteristics. If taxpayers are risk averse, then the social cost of bearing debt-financed project risk will exceed the government's direct cost of debt service incurred, and the risk-free rate understates the social cost of risk bearing, just as labor costs to the relevant jurisdiction under a compulsory work law understate the social cost of that labor.[48]

We next consider a second effect of nontransferability on the relative cost of capital. We note that tradability of residual claims impacts ownership concentration. By ownership concentration (or, conversely, ownership dispersion), we mean the fraction of a firm's outstanding equity held by various proportions of its shareholders.[49] More dispersed ownership is critical for competitive neutrality because, *ceteris paribus*, it increases the cost of capital by increasing agency costs. Agency costs stem from the agency (or the principal-agent) problem between a firm's owners and the individuals who manage it. Those costs exist in all organizations where owners and managers are distinct groups and in owner-managed firms with multiple owners. The agency problem stems from the fact that contracts are necessarily incomplete because they cannot be costlessly written and enforced.[50] The agency problem generates social costs through (1) the owner's (i.e., the principal's) efforts to directly monitor managers (the agents); (2) managerial choices that deviate from the interests of firm owners; and (3) bonding expenditures undertaken by managers.[51] In the case of publicly financed infrastructure, taxpayers are principals in their capacity as asset owners, as are shareholders in publicly traded corporations. The question of how to incentivize the firm's managers to operate the infrastructure in the interests of its owners forms the core of any firm's governance problem.

The essence of Arrow and Lind's view of the benefits stemming from public-sector provision is that greater dispersion of project ownership through the tax system offers a lower cost of capital because each taxpayer faces *de minimis* project-related risk. However, this focuses on the benefits of greater dispersion while ignoring its costs. This is odd, since the literature dating back to Berle and Means's famous 1932 book on the corporation[52] view the agency problem that stems from more diffuse ownership as *the* central concern with the modern corporate ownership form. Diffuse ownership results in Berle and Means's classic "separation of ownership and control" that creates tension between firm owners and managers. Under the modern corporate form that allows large amounts of capital to be raised, the firm's owners—its shareholders—have attenuated incentives to monitor managers *because* their ownership stake in the firm is very small. Although the benefits of managerial monitoring here accrue to all shareholders, the costs fall entirely on the owner undertaking the monitoring. Shareholders will thus rationally free ride off the monitoring efforts of others.[53] This creates shareholder shirking.

Ownership concentration is central to corporate governance because greater shirking caused by increased ownership dispersion exacerbates the agency problem between firm owners and their appointed managers. The costs associated with greater dispersion imply that the optimal level of ownership concentration is not zero, as Arrow and Lind suggest. Risk-spreading benefits due to greater dispersion must always be weighed against increased agency costs from that dispersion. Rather than being fixed at a level determined by the number of taxpayers in the jurisdiction, the optimal level of ownership concentration is likely to vary across time, across industries, and to depend on the jurisdiction's institutional arrangements. For publicly traded corporations it has been shown to be endogenous and to vary in predictable ways in response to such factors as firm size, the type of regulation, and industry risk.[54] Although researchers have noted likely differences in agency costs depending on the type of provision,[55] they have not considered how the nontradable nature of SOE residual claims relative to those of private firms will affect those costs.

Variation in ownership concentration is thus an additional, critical mechanism for monitoring managers and for reducing agency costs between firm owners and their appointed managers. That mechanism helps to lower the firm's risk and thus its cost of capital. Such a mechanism does not exist in publicly financed projects, and firm governance is likely to suffer as a result.[56] Empirical evidence indicates that markets assign a higher cost of capital to firms displaying poor governance.[57]

We next consider a third implication of nontransferability on agency costs. Nontransferability, and the absence of the direct voting rights normally associated with the stock of privately owned firms, implies that managers are insulated from the market for corporate control. Because SOE residual claims are not transferable, it is impossible for control over the assets of an SOE to change hands through a hostile takeover if managers are not acting in concert with owners' interests. The market for the control of publicly traded corporations is an important and well-recognized mechanism for disciplining the actions of managers in corporations with tradable residual claims.[58] Empirical evidence indicates that firm value is higher when there is an active market for corporate control. As with ownership concentration, the nontransferability of SOE residual claims implies that taxpayers are absorbing the risk of higher agency costs without an attendant increase in expected returns. This is an additional cost of taxpayer risk bearing inherent in the nature of tradable residual claims that is not accounted for in standard assessments of the relative cost of capital.

There is a further implication of the fact that public-sector residual claims are not separable from residence in the project's jurisdiction, while, depending on their form, private-sector residual claims can be transferred at low cost.[59] The nontradable nature of public-sector residual claims disallows project risk from being priced. For large infrastructure projects, this includes risks such as construction cost risk, demand or revenue risk, and regulatory risks. The tradability of private-sector residual claims creates a price for those claims, which allows asset prices to adjust for risk. The lack of a price for public-sector residual claims implies that the cost of risk bearing to taxpayers is opaque.[60] Researchers have examined cross-country evidence on the effect of regulations intended to enhance transparency. That work suggests that such policies as improved accounting standards, more extensive disclosure requirements, stronger securities regulation, and stricter enforcement mechanisms significantly lower the cost of capital. This is consistent with the view that lower levels of transparency stemming from a lack of residual claim pricing are associated with a higher cost of capital.[61]

The higher cost of capital generated by nontradable SOE residual claims has important implications for competitive neutrality. Because of captive equity, the higher cost of equity capital associated with SOEs is not actually paid out to shareholders in the form of higher expected returns and is not recorded on government balance sheets, while such costs are clearly priced into the equity of an investor-owned firm. Private firms will thus display a higher apparent, but not real, cost of capital. The social cost of SOE capital is instead higher, suggesting that when capital costs for public- and private-sector provision are compared, an adjustment should be included for the cost of equity capital that accounts for the effects of nontransferability of taxpayer equity.[62]

This raises the question of what competition authorities can do to help address competitive concerns when private provision through a PPP is compared with a public incumbent that benefits from captive equity. The above discussion suggests that authorities should require an analysis of the equity cost of capital in the public-sector comparator that includes the unpriced social cost of taxpayer-provided risk-bearing services. Such an imputed cost of public provision, however, must be assessed under the same legal and institutional arrangements faced by taxpayer-owners. The question becomes: what expected return would taxpayers demand to provide risk-bearing services voluntarily under the institutional arrangements that surround that risk bearing? Although we do not attempt to assess the magnitude of the premium that taxpayers might charge to provide capital under public-sector risk-bearing arrangements, our analysis suggests that it is likely to be significant.

IV. Mechanisms to Address Competition Issues

Including competitive neutrality in the public-sector comparator is one mechanism to address competitive concerns brought about by private participation in the provision of infrastructure. Other mechanisms include rebidding the concession to inject additional competition and adjusting concession length to alter rebidding frequency. Regarding rebidding, the importance of competition among firms for the right to serve a particular market—competition for the market rather than competition within the market—has been recognized since at least 1859.[63] It was restated and updated in 1968 by Harold Demsetz and others.[64] The competition created by rebidding, and the threat of it, helps to ameliorate issues of market power when private partners operate infrastructure facilities.

Moreover, concession length can be adjusted to introduce more frequent bidding for the right to operate a particular transportation facility or to serve a particular area, while still providing the concessionaire sufficient time to receive its required risk-adjusted return on investment. With regard to PPPs, concession length adjustment has been formalized and implemented through the modern concept of least-present-value-of-revenue (LPVR) auctions.[65] In this case, the public partner determines the maximum acceptable toll, the service quality standards, and other aspects of the agreement. The winning bidder is chosen on the basis of the smallest present value of toll revenue they will accept. The concession period ends when the toll revenue received by the winning concessionaire reaches the lowest amount that is bid. The concession is then rebid. An LPVR auction moderates the effects of traffic (or revenue) risk to the private partner. If traffic is unexpectedly low, which depresses revenues, the franchise is automatically extended to ensure that investors receive their anticipated return on investment. Conversely, if traffic is unexpectedly high, the franchise period is automatically shortened. LPVR auctions have been used successfully in Chile, and they could help to address competitive concerns when using PPPs in the United States.

V. Summary

PPPs raise competitive neutrality concerns that are relatively new in the United States. Some stem from incumbent public facility operators benefiting from a variety of government-bestowed advantages that may result in an uneven public/private playing field. Because infrastructure often requires massive amounts of investment, the social cost of capital to the public versus the private sector is a particularly prominent issue.

PPPs allow private-sector financing to compete with more traditional project financing forms that, in the United States, rely on the issuance of tax-exempt municipal bonds. Granting tax-exempt status to publicly issued, but not privately issued, debt violates basic principles of competitive neutrality. However, the public sector also benefits from the fact that it need not pay those who bear the risk of public-sector projects—taxpayers—any compensation for providing risk-bearing services. These factors should be taken into account when considering competition issues and competitive neutrality.

Appendix

The standard approach to determining the cost of capital for any firm is the weighted average cost of capital (WACC).[66] The WACC is obtained by weighting the cost of each financing type by its proportion in the capital structure and then summing across all financing types. We consider a firm with a simple capital structure that utilizes only one type of debt and one type of equity capital. For a private firm:

$$\text{WACC} = \frac{E}{V} * Re + \frac{D}{V} * Rd * (1 - Tc)$$

where:

Re = cost of equity capital, which is the expected return paid to equity investors

Rd = cost of debt capital, which is the return paid to debt investors

E = market value of the firm's equity

D = market value of the firm's debt

V = total value of firm's financing from all sources ($V = E + D$)

E/V = percentage of financing from the issuance of equity

D/V = percentage of financing from the issuance of debt

Tc = corporate tax rate. The corporate tax rate is subtracted from the cost of debt capital because the firm is able to expense interest paid on debt.

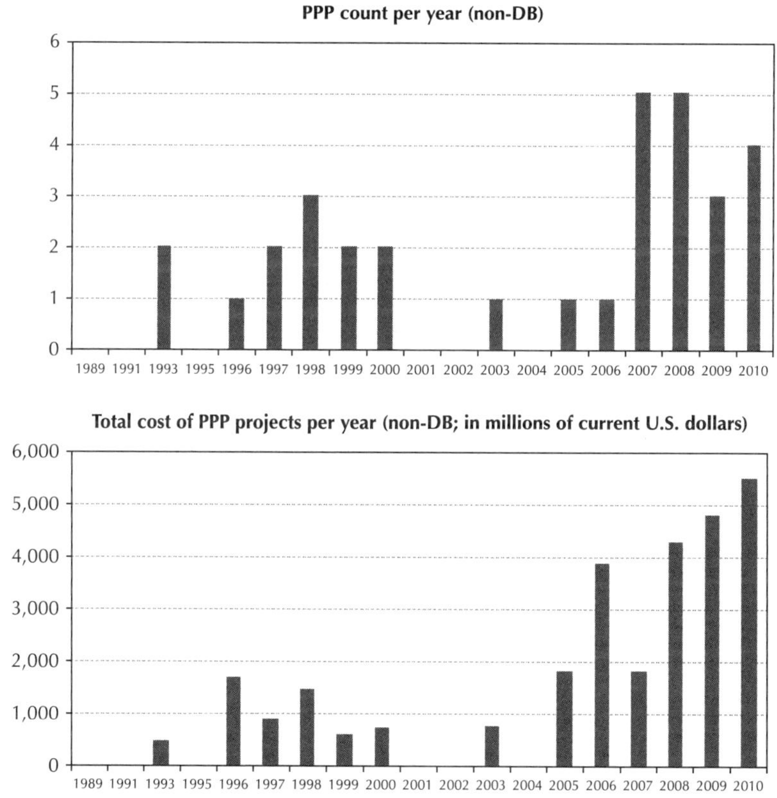

Figure 3.1 Number and total cost of PPP projects in the United States (non-DB only)

SOURCE: *Public Works Financing*, various issues.

NOTE: The majority of non-DB projects are design-build-finance-operate (DBFO) projects.

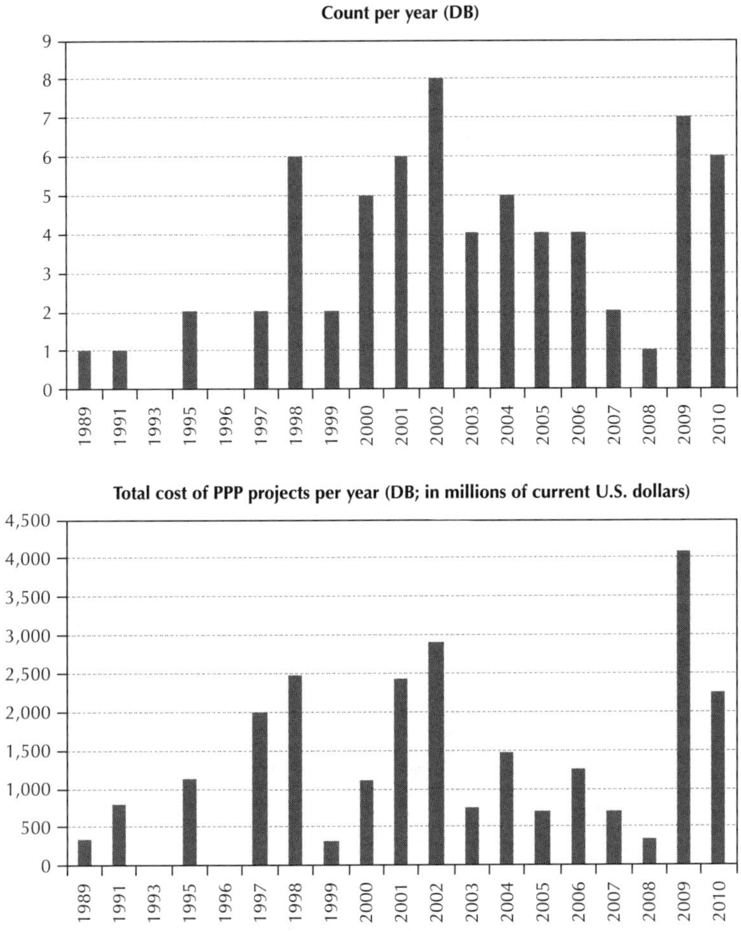

Figure 3.2 Number and total cost of PPP projects in the United States (DB only)

SOURCE: *Public Works Financing,* various issues.

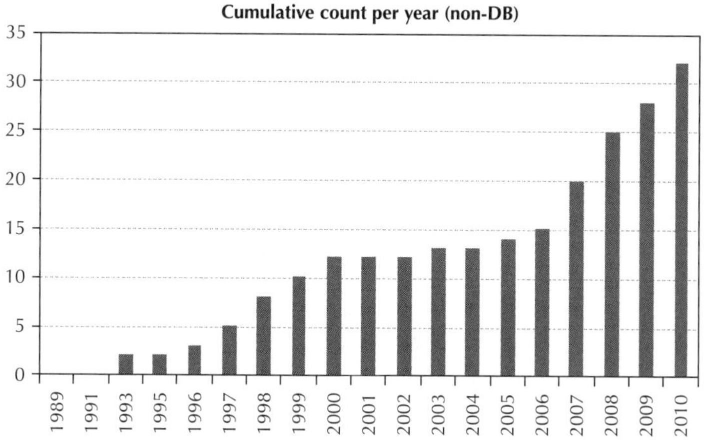

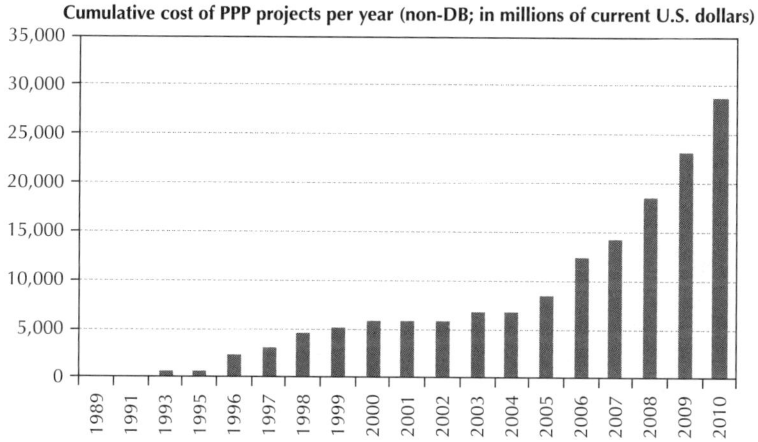

Figure 3.3 Cumulative count and cumulative cost of PPP projects (non-DB only)

SOURCE: *Public Works Financing*, various issues.

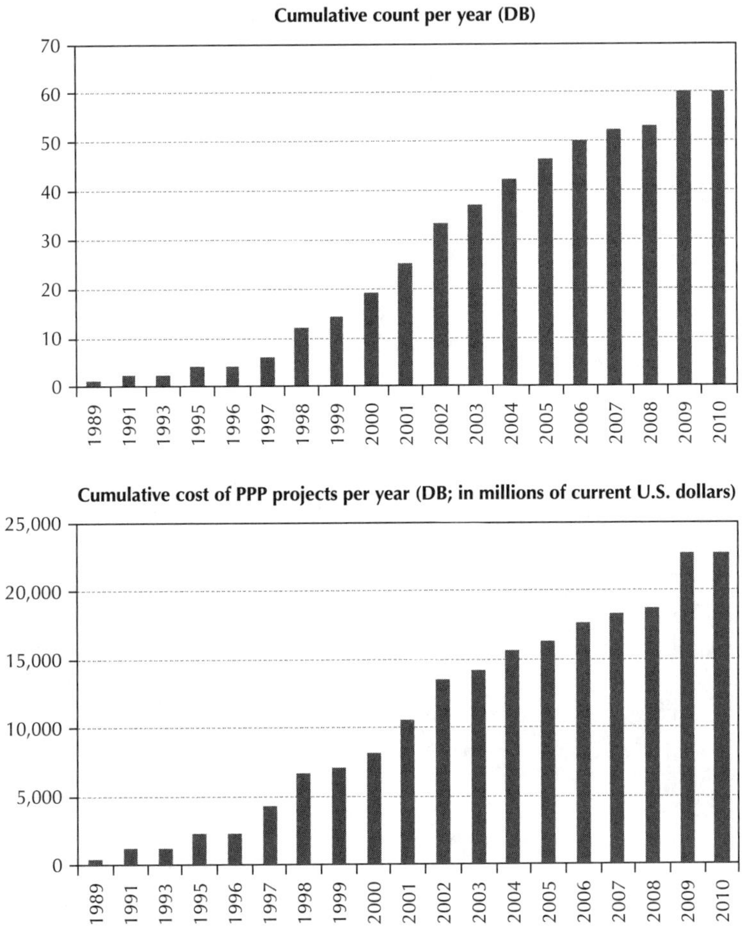

Figure 3.4 Cumulative count and cumulative cost of PPP projects (DB only)

SOURCE: *Public Works Financing*, various issues.

Part II

Is There a Need for a Specific Substantive Legal Framework in Domestic and International Competition Law?

Chapter 4

State-Owned Enterprises versus the State

Lessons from Trade Law

Wentong Zheng

The state plays important roles in affecting conditions of competition in the marketplace. The state is, first and foremost, the regulator of the market and, through exercising its regulatory power, may either promote or lessen competition in the market. The state may also affect competition by directly participating in the market—for example, by producing goods or services through "public enterprises" or "state-owned enterprises" (SOEs).

As this chapter discusses, antitrust law generally applies to conduct by the state as a market participant through SOEs. SOEs, however, may not be purely commercial entities even when engaging in activities of commercial nature. They may coordinate their activities with one another in furtherance of the business interest of their common owner—the state—and may perform policy functions that are not based on the principle of profit maximization.[1] The potential for the state to coordinate SOEs' activities for both commercial and policy purposes raises important questions under antitrust law as to when SOEs should be treated as a single economic entity controlled by the state and when they should be treated as separate economic entities capable of collusion. These questions have important implications for the treatment of SOEs under antitrust law in the areas of horizontal agreements and merger review.

This chapter first discusses the application of antitrust law to SOEs and the special challenges posed by the rise of "state capitalism" to the determination of whether SOEs are separate economic entities. It then points out that international trade law has dealt with similar challenges, albeit in different contexts. It details how international trade law demarcates the boundary between SOEs and the state in two particular areas—antidumping and subsidies—and discusses the lessons that antitrust law could learn from international trade law in this regard.

I. The Application of Antitrust Law to State-Owned Enterprises

Antitrust law in the major jurisdictions of the world generally applies to the commercial activities of the state through SOEs. For example, in the European Union, Articles 101 and 102 of the Treaty on the Functioning of the European Union (TFEU) apply to "public undertakings and undertakings to which member states grant special or exclusive rights,"[2] except when the application of the competition rules "obstructs" the performance of the particular tasks assigned to such undertakings.[3] In China, an "undertaking" that is subject to the Antimonopoly Law is defined as "any natural person, legal person, or organization that engages in the production and distribution of products or the provision of services,"[4] presumably including SOEs. In India, an "enterprise" that is subject to the Competition Act is defined to include a "department of the Government" that is engaged in "any activity relating to the production, storage, supply, distribution, acquisition, or control of articles or goods or the provision of services."[5] In the United States, the applicability of antitrust law to SOEs is complicated. Under the "state action" doctrine first enunciated in *Parker v. Brown*,[6] anticompetitive actions by governments in their capacities as sovereign regulators are exempt from antitrust scrutiny on the theory that the Sherman Act only prohibits restraints of trade by private parties.[7] As far as the commercial activities of the federal government are concerned, whether they are subject to antitrust law depends on many factors. In 2004, in *United States Postal Service v. Flamingo Industries (U.S.A.), Ltd.*, the U.S. Supreme Court held that federal antitrust laws do not apply to the U.S. Postal Service (USPS).[8] The Court based its holding on the fact that the USPS by statute was "an independent establishment of the branch of the Government of the United States."[9] The Court also noted that its holding was consistent with the "public responsibility" of the USPS, which differs from private enterprises in not seeking profits, in its universal service and national security responsibilities, and in its possession of certain government powers.[10] Following the *Flamingo* decision, Congress enacted the Postal Accountability and Enhancement Act (PAEA) that established a new Postal Regulatory Commission as the regulator of USPS's rates for "market-dominant" services.[11] For both competitive products and market-dominant products outside of the statutory letter monopoly, the PAEA explicitly provides that the USPS will be subject to federal antitrust laws.[12]

As for the commercial activities of governments at the state and local levels, there appears to be disagreements among U.S. courts as to whether antitrust law applies to them. In *City of Columbia v. Omni Outdoor Advertising, Inc.*, the U.S. Supreme Court held that "[the state action] immunity does not necessarily obtain where the State acts not in a regulatory capacity but as a commercial participant in a given market,"[13] opening the door to the possibility of creating a "market participant" exception to the state action immunity. Some U.S. courts appear to be willing to create such an exception. In *Genentech, Inc. v. Eli Lilly & Co.*, the Federal Circuit noted in dicta that "the policies underlying *Parker* do not extend to circumstances where the state acts not in a legislative/regulatory capacity but as a commercial participant in a given market."[14] In *A.D. Bedell Wholesale Co. v. Philip Morris Inc.*, the Third Circuit stated that "there is also a market participant exception to actions which might otherwise be entitled to *Parker* immunity."[15] In *Hedgecock v. Blackwell Land Co.*, the Ninth Circuit suggested that "a commercial participant exception to *Parker* might be appropriate in circumstances where an arm of the state enters a market in competition with private actors. . . ."[16] Some other U.S. courts, however, have rejected the "market participant" exception to the state action immunity.[17] One of the reasons why these courts were reluctant to accept a broad market participation exception to the state action immunity is the difficulty in distinguishing the role of the state as a market regulator from the role of the state as a market participant.[18] When the state enters a market in competition with private actors, the state usually adopts accompanying regulatory measures that affect competition between the state actor and private actors. For example, in *Hybud Equipment Corp. v. City of Akron, Ohio*, when a city started operating a solid waste processing plant that converted solid waste to steam, the city required all collectors and haulers to deliver solid waste generated within the city limit to the city plant for disposal.[19]

Despite the lack of clarity as to the applicability of antitrust law to SOEs in the United States, the argument for applying antitrust law to at least the purely commercial activities of the state—to the extent that they are distinguishable from the regulatory activities of the state—appears to be convincing. As Chief Justice Burger argued in his concurrence opinion in *City of Lafayette, La. v. Louisiana Power & Light Co.*, the same Congress that "meant to deal comprehensively and effectively with the evils resulting from contracts, combinations, and conspiracies in restraint of trade" surely would not have intended to allow the government to engage in such conduct without being subject to the Sherman Act.[20]

II. The Rise of "State Capitalism"

Until recently, in many jurisdictions, the applicability of antitrust law to SOEs was a question that did not carry much commercial significance. In the United States, for example, the various entities that are linked to the federal government usually have specialized roles, and the extent of competition between these entities and the private sector is limited.[21] At the state level, SOEs exist in many sectors, including transportation, energy, sports facilities, universities, hospitals, concessions in state-owned parks, buildings, facilities, and distribution of alcoholic beverages, but in most cases the goods or services offered by SOEs are differentiated and provided with a view to achieving a governmental, public service objective.[22] In other words, cases in which the state enters market sectors that are purely commercial in nature had been uncommon.

All of this changed with the rise of what is often referred to as "state capitalism" in emerging markets, particularly China.[23] As is detailed below, successful SOEs exist in almost all industries in state capitalism countries, including petroleum, telecommunications, chemicals, and ports, to name just a few.[24] Thanks to the exponential growth of SOEs in market sectors that are traditionally served by purely commercial entities, the question of whether and how to subject SOEs to antitrust law becomes more consequential. This question is also made realistic by forces of globalization and the extraterritorial reach of antitrust laws.[25] When an SOE is engaged in conduct that has substantial anticompetitive effects in other jurisdictions, antitrust law in other jurisdictions must decide on whether and how to respond to the SOE's conduct.

In a recent special report on state capitalism, *The Economist* provided a sketch of the peculiar development model that blends a dominant role of the state with forces of private markets.[26] According to *The Economist*, state-controlled companies accounted for four of the ten largest global listed companies by revenue as of 2010.[27] SOEs are particularly dominant in certain sectors such as energy, where the 13 biggest oil firms, which together control three-quarters of the world's oil reserves, are all state-backed.[28]

As *The Economist* noted, the idea of having the government play an active role in industrial policy has been around as long as capitalism itself. However, one of the crucial events that led to the prominence of the state capitalism model was the rise of China.[29] Over the past three decades, China has seen its GDP grow at an average of 9.5 percent a year and has overtaken Japan as the world's second largest economy and the United States as the world's largest market for many consumer goods.[30] Chinese SOEs have played a central role in this process. Although the state-owned sector as a whole now accounts only for one-third of China's GDP, individual Chinese SOEs have become more powerful than ever, with the 121 largest SOEs in China increasing their total assets from $360 billion in 2002 to $2.9 trillion in 2010.[31]

Not only have SOEs in China grown in size, but they are being operated under a different model than in the past. Since the late 1970s, the Chinese government has delegated to SOEs the power to make managerial decisions on production volumes, pricing, and wages and has converted SOEs to corporations with Western-style governance structures.[32] China has also undertaken to break up SOE monopolies in key industries.[33] In many of China's industries today, there are multiple, or even numerous, SOEs competing against one another and against private and foreign firms.

III. State-Owned Enterprises as Separate Economic Entities: Challenges of State Capitalism to Antitrust

The existence of many competing SOEs in the same industry poses challenging questions for antitrust law. To be sure, the state is the owner of all SOEs, but that does not necessarily mean that the state will participate in the day-to-day management of the SOEs.[34] The fact that the state is the ultimate owner of all SOEs, however, means that the state may at least in theory coordinate the activities of SOEs.

Whether the state coordinates the activities of SOEs has important implications for antitrust in the areas of horizontal agreements and merger control. In horizontal agreements, if the activities of individual SOEs are controlled and coordinated by the state, then it could be argued that these SOEs constitute a single economic entity despite their separate legal status. Under this "single-entity" theory, units of a single economic entity cannot "conspire" to restrain trade within the meaning of antitrust law.[35] In *Copperweld Corporation v. Independence Tube Corporation*, the U.S. Supreme Court held that "an internal agreement to implement a single, unitary firm's policies does not raise the antitrust dangers that §1 [of the Sherman Act] was designed to police."[36] According to the Court, "the coordinated activity of a parent and its wholly owned subsidiary must be viewed as that of a single enterprise for purposes of §1 of the Sherman Act."[37] Because "a parent and its wholly owned subsidiary have a complete unity of interest,"[38] "the very notion of an 'agreement' in Sherman Act terms between a parent and a wholly owned subsidiary lacks meaning."[39] After *Copperweld*, the single-entity theory has been held to be applicable to forms of affiliation other than the parent–wholly owned subsidiary relationship.[40] So far, courts have not confronted the question of whether SOEs constitute a "single entity" for purposes of Section 1 of the Sherman Act, but an encounter with this question appears to be inevitable given the rising prominence of SOEs from state capitalism countries.

In merger control, the question of whether the state coordinates the activities of SOEs has significant impact on how merger analysis should be conducted when an SOE is a party to the merger. If the state does coordinate the activities of the SOEs, then the merger analysis should focus on not just the notifying SOE but the entire state-owned sector as a whole in the same or other industries on the theory that all SOEs constitute a single economic entity. Furthermore, if the state does coordinate the activities of all SOEs, the turnover of the parties involved in a merger, which is usually the basis for determining whether the notification threshold is triggered, should be expanded to include not just the turnover of the notifying SOEs but the turnover of the entire state-owned sector.[41]

In two jurisdictions, Australia and the European Union, antitrust regulators have recognized the importance of the SOE question for merger analysis. In both jurisdictions, however, antitrust regulators have chosen to dodge this question.

In Australia, the Australian Competition and Consumer Commission (ACCC) evaluated the competitive impact of a proposed acquisition of interests in Rio Tinto by China Aluminum Corporation, or Chinalco.[42] Wholly owned by the government of the People's Republic of China, Chinalco is a mineral resources company and a producer of primary aluminum and alumina.[43] The proposed transaction would form a "strategic alliance" between Chinalco and Rio Tinto and would allow Chinalco to increase its shareholding in the Rio Tinto parent companies and acquire interests in various assets of Rio Tinto.[44] When evaluating the competitive impact of the proposed transaction, the ACCC considered whether the proposed transaction would likely affect iron ore prices by providing Chinalco with the ability and incentive to decrease iron ore prices below competitive levels to the benefit of Chinese steel mills.[45] The ACCC pointed out that Chinalco might have such incentive if Chinalco, the Chinese government, and Chinese steel mills operated as a "single entity."[46] The ACCC determined that it might be worthwhile for Chinalco to try such a strategy because the loss in Chinalco's profits as a shareholder in Rio Tinto caused by the lower iron ore prices would likely be offset by the gain to the Chinese steel mills.[47] The ACCC was ultimately of the view, however, that Rio Tinto would not have the ability to unilaterally influence global iron ore prices to a significant extent.[48] Therefore, the ACCC held that it was not necessary to evaluate whether Chinalco, the Chinese government, and Chinese steel mills constituted a single entity.[49]

In the European Union, Recital 22 of the Preamble to the European Merger Regulation provides that in the evaluation of mergers involving SOEs, account has to be taken of "the undertaking making up an economic unit with an independent power of decision, irrespective of the way in which their capital is held or of the rules of administrative supervision applicable to them."[50] In other words, the antitrust authority will look beyond the nominal shareholding and administrative structures of SOEs and will focus instead on whether SOEs have an "independent power of decision." In several merger cases involving Chinese SOEs so far,[51] however, the European Commission (Commission), like the ACCC, dodged this important inquiry. In *China National Bluestar / Elkem*, for example, China National Bluestar, a Chinese SOE, proposed to acquire Elkem, a Norwegian silicon producer. China National Bluestar is a subsidiary of China National Chemical Corporation (ChemChina), an SOE owned by the Chinese state through the State Assets Supervision and Administration Commission (SASAC).[52] When evaluating the competitive impact of the proposed transaction, the Commission determined that it was relevant to assess whether ChemChina is an independent economic entity or whether it belongs to a wider economic entity, including more enterprises owned by the Chinese state active in the same markets.[53] The parties submitted evidence that ChemChina has independent power of decision from the Chinese state at both the central and local government levels.[54] After going through a lengthy examination of the competitive position of Elkem versus China National Bluestar, ChemChina, and other Chinese SOEs, however, the Commission concluded that "the proposed transaction would not lead to any competition concerns even if ChemChina and other SOEs operating in any of the markets concerned, under the Central and Regional SASACs, were to be regarded as one economic entity."[55] Therefore, according to the Commission, "it is not necessary to conclude definitively on the ultimate control of ChemChina."[56]

IV. State-Owned Enterprises versus the State: Lessons from Trade Law

From the above discussions, it is obvious that despite the importance of the question as to whether SOEs should be treated as separate economic entities that retain independent power of decision from the state, antitrust authorities around the globe so far have not been entirely comfortable with venturing methodologies or guidance on how to answer that question. Below, this chapter discusses how another body of law—international trade law—has delineated the boundary between SOEs and the state and what lessons antitrust law could learn from international trade law in this respect.

Broadly speaking, international trade law is also about competition: it limits the ability of a country to regulate competition between domestic and foreign goods or services. International trade law began dealing with SOEs at a much earlier time than antitrust law, partly because trade between market economies and state-dominant economies occurred at a much earlier time than SOEs from state capitalism countries posed any antitrust concerns.[57] To be sure, international trade law and competition law have different objectives. Unlike competition law, which targets welfare-reducing measures, international trade law focuses on protectionist measures that may or may not be welfare-reducing. In addition, the contexts in which the SOE question arises under international trade law are different from the contexts in which the SOE question arises under competition law. But despite these differences, the way international trade law handles SOEs is still of instructive value to antitrust law. Below, this chapter discusses the handling of SOEs under international trade law in two substantive areas: antidumping and subsidies.

Antidumping. International trade law allows a country to impose antidumping duties on imported merchandise that is "dumped" by foreign firms. To use U.S. antidumping law as an example, "dumping," or "sales at less than fair value," is determined by a comparison of the sales price of an imported product in the importing country with the "normal value" of the imported product. The "normal value" of an imported product is usually the price of the product sold in its home market. When the product is not sold in its home market at all, the normal value of the product will be determined by the price of the product sold in a third country or by the "constructed value" of the product equal to the cost of production of the merchandise plus a reasonable allowance for general, selling, and administrative expenses and profits.[58]

Since the margin of dumping (or the amount by which the export price of a product is exceeded by its normal value) varies based on the firm's pricing structures, the practice under antidumping laws is to assign individual dumping margins to producers and exporters in market-economy countries.[59] However, in cases involving producers and exporters from the so-called "nonmarket economy" (NME) countries, the presumption is that all of the companies in the country are essentially operating units of a single, statewide entity and thus should receive a single antidumping duty rate.[60] In determining whether a foreign country should be designated as an NME, U.S. antidumping law requires the U.S. Department of Commerce (the agency charged with dumping determinations) to take into account six factors aimed at measuring the extent of the government's control of the foreign country's economy. These factors include (1) the extent to which the currency of the foreign country is convertible into the currency of other countries; (2) the extent to which wage rates in the foreign country are determined by free bargaining between labor and management; (3) the extent to which joint ventures or other investments by firms of other foreign countries are permitted in the foreign country; (4) the extent of government ownership or control of the means of production; (5) the extent of government control over the allocation of resources and over the price and output decisions of enterprises; and (6) such other factors as the administering authority considers appropriate.[61]

However, the single-entity presumption in cases involving state-owned exporters from NME countries can be rebutted, and the SOE exporters will receive separate antidumping rates if they can demonstrate that their export activities are sufficiently independent of the government.[62] In evaluating whether an SOE exporter is independent from the government, the Department of Commerce is of the position that ownership "by all the people" as stated on an SOE's business license does not in and of itself require the conclusion of a single, statewide entity.[63] Instead, an SOE can demonstrate its independence by demonstrating an absence of central government control, both in law and in fact, with respect to exports.[64]

When analyzing whether there is de jure absence of control of an SOE by the government, the Department of Commerce examines whether formal laws, regulations, and enactments applicable to the SOE seeking a separate rate indicate the absence of control.[65] In past cases involving SOE exporters from China, for example, the Department of Commerce has found a number of Chinese laws and regulations to be relevant to its analysis of the de jure absence of government control over SOEs' export activities, including the Company Law of the PRC, the Foreign Trade Law of the PRC, the Administrative Regulations of the PRC Governing the Registration of Legal Corporations, the Administrative Regulations of the PRC Governing Enterprise Legal Person Registration, the Law of the PRC on Chinese-Foreign Cooperative Joint Ventures, the Law of the PRC on Industrial Enterprises Owned by the Whole People.[66] Evidence that supports a finding of de jure absence of control includes an absence of restrictive stipulations associated with an individual exporter's business and export licenses; any legislative enactments decentralizing control of companies; or any other formal measures by the government decentralizing control of companies.[67] For example, in *Final Determination of Sales at Less Than Fair Value: Silicon Carbide from the People's Republic of China* (*Silicon Carbide*), one of the laws examined by the Department of Commerce—the Law of the PRC on Industrial Enterprises Owned by the Whole People—states that enterprises have the right to set their own prices. This law, among others, led the Department of Commerce to conclude that there was *de jure* absence of control of the respondent SOE by the government.[68]

However, a demonstration of de jure absence of control is not sufficient to rebut the single-entity presumption. The Department of Commerce recognizes that the implementation of formal laws and regulations on devolution of government control may be uneven. It is the Department of Commerce's policy, therefore, to also conduct a de facto analysis to determine whether the respondent SOEs are, in fact, not subject to government control.[69] In its de facto analysis, the Department of Commerce considers whether the export prices are set by, or subject to the approval of, a governmental authority; whether the respondent has authority to negotiate and sign contracts and other agreements; whether the respondent has autonomy from the government in making decisions regarding the selection of management; and whether the respondent retains the proceeds of its export sales and makes independent decisions regarding the disposition of profits or financing of losses.[70] When conducting its de facto analysis, the Department of Commerce examines and verifies the respondent SOE's correspondence files, bank records, and accounting records relating to investment and other activities.[71]

Subsidies. The question of whether SOEs are subject to the control of the state and therefore are not pure "market participants" also arises under international trade law in the area of subsidies. Generally, under the WTO Agreement on Subsidies and Countervailing Measures (SCM Agreement), a "subsidy" is deemed to exist if there is a "financial contribution" by a government or public body and if a "benefit" is thereby conferred.[72] A "financial contribution" exists if (1) a government or public body makes a direct transfer of funds (e.g., grants, loans, and equity infusion) or potential direct transfers of funds or liabilities (e.g., loan guarantees); (2) a government or public body foregoes or does not collect revenue that is otherwise due (e.g., fiscal incentives such as tax credits); (3) a government or public body provides goods or services other than general infrastructure, or purchases goods; or (4) a government or public body makes payments to a funding mechanism, or entrusts or directs a private body to carry out one or more of the functions illustrated in (1) to (3) above which would normally be vested in the government and the practice, in no real sense, differs from practices normally followed by governments.[73] As for the determination of a "benefit," the SCM Agreement sets out guidelines for the major types of financial contributions. For example, to determine whether a government loan confers a benefit, the criterion is whether there is a difference between the amount that the firm receiving the loan pays on the government loan and the amount the firm would pay on a comparable commercial loan that the firm could actually obtain on the market.[74] To determine whether the provision of goods or services or purchase of goods by a government confers a benefit, the criterion is whether the provision is made for less than adequate remuneration, or the purchase is made for more than adequate remuneration.[75] The adequacy of remuneration, in turn, is determined in relation to prevailing market conditions for the good or service in question in the country of provision or purchase (including price, quality, availability, marketability, transportation, and other conditions of purchase or sale).[76]

In determining the existence of a subsidy, a key issue is the meaning of the term *public body* in the SCM Agreement. According to the SCM Agreement, a subsidy could be conferred by a government, a public body, or a private body that has been "entrusted or directed" by the government to make a financial contribution.[77] But what is the boundary between a government and a *public body*? Are these two terms functionally equivalent, or does the term *public body* cover something that is not covered by the term *government*?

This question is relevant for the subsidy analysis under the SCM Agreement because, in many situations, the state confers a subsidy not through the government itself but through entities affiliated with or controlled by the government. If those entities are classified as public bodies, they will be considered to be capable of conferring subsidies within the meaning of the SCM Agreement. If those entities are classified as private bodies, however, it has to be demonstrated that they are "entrusted or directed" by the government to confer the subsidies in question. In evaluating whether an entity should be considered a public body, the U.S. Department of Commerce (the agency charged with subsidy determinations in the United States) considers five factors to be relevant:

government ownership; the government's presence on the entity's board of directors; the government's control over the entity's activities; the entity's pursuit of governmental policies or interests; and whether the entity is created by statute.[78]

The question of how to determine whether an entity is a public body becomes particularly challenging when the entity involved is an SOE. In *Circular Welded Carbon Quality Steel Pipe from the People's Republic of China*, one of the subsidy programs investigated by the Department of Commerce was the provision of hot-rolled steel (an input for producing the subject merchandise) by the Chinese government through its SOEs for less than adequate remuneration.[79] The Department of Commerce noted that other than the levels of government ownership of certain firms producing hot-rolled steel, the Chinese government failed to provide the information that was necessary for conducting the five-factor analysis to determine whether the firms were public bodies.[80] Therefore, the Department of Commerce applied a rule of majority ownership, under which the Chinese SOEs were treated as public bodies as long as they were majority owned by the government.[81]

In *Light-Walled Rectangular Pipe and Tube from the People's Republic of China*, the Department of Commerce elaborated on why it believed that the information provided by the Chinese parties was insufficient for it to conduct the five-factor analysis.[82] The Chinese parties in that case submitted information that, they argued, proved under the five-factor analysis that one Chinese SOE input supplier, Baosteel, was not a public body.[83] The Department of Commerce noted that because Baosteel was majority owned by the Chinese government, the first of the five factors clearly supported that it was a public body.[84] As for the second factor, the Chinese government argued that there was no evidence indicating that any member of Baosteel's board of directors was a government official. The Department of Commerce, however, cited record evidence suggesting that some members of the board had ties to the government.[85] As for the third factor, the Chinese government argued that there was no evidence of government control over Baosteel's activities because no governmental authority regulated steel producers or set steel prices. The Department of Commerce, however, noted that the Chinese government cited no information specific to the activities of Baosteel to support its claim.[86] As for the fourth factor, the Chinese government argued that Baosteel did not pursue government interests because it had a duty under Chinese law to protect shareholders and maximize profitability. The Department of Commerce rejected this argument, citing statements from Baosteel's annual reports referring to, among others, the implementation of the government's five-year plan and the government's steel industry policy.[87] As for the final factor, the Chinese government argued that Baosteel operated under the same Chinese company law as private enterprises. The Department of Commerce held that this information was not sufficient to determine that Baosteel was not created by statute.[88]

Another type of Chinese SOE that was under subsidy investigation in recent years is China's state-owned commercial banks (SOCBs). In *Coated Free Sheet Paper from the People's Republic of China*, the Department of Commerce investigated whether the Chinese government provided subsidies to the Chinese paper industry through preferential lending by SOCBs.[89] For the subsidies to be countervailable, the entities that were allegedly conferring the subsidies, the SOCBs, must be public bodies. In this context, the Department of Commerce commented on whether China's SOCBs should be treated as public bodies. The Department of Commerce first stated that despite reforms in virtually every sector of the Chinese economy, the Chinese government had been relatively cautious about banking sector reforms and remained very involved in the sector.[90] The Department of Commerce next examined several specific characteristics of China's banking sector relating to the question of whether SOCBs in China allocate credit in accordance with governmental policies. First, the Department of Commerce stated that the government had near complete ownership of the banking sector.[91] Second, the Department of Commerce noted a provision under China's Commercial Banking Law that required banks to "carry out their loan business upon the needs of national economy and the social development and under the guidance of State industrial policies."[92] Third, the Department of Commerce evaluated record evidence regarding China's banking reforms to determine whether there continued to be state influence in the banking sector. In this regard the Department of Commerce pointed out that interest rates remained generally undifferentiated and a risk analysis system was not fully in place for most of the SOCBs.[93] The Department of Commerce concluded, therefore, that China's SOCBs were public bodies and that loans provided by SOCBs constituted a direct financial contribution from the government.[94]

The Department of Commerce's handling of the question of whether SOEs should be treated as public bodies in countervailing duty cases involving Chinese SOEs was challenged before the WTO. The WTO dispute settlement panel hearing the dispute upheld the Department of Commerce's determinations that China's SOE input suppliers and SOCBs were public bodies.[95] On appeal, the Appellate Body of the WTO rejected the Department of

Commerce's handling of the Chinese SOE input suppliers, holding that "evidence of government ownership, in itself, is not evidence of meaningful control of an entity by government and cannot, without more, serve as a basis for establishing that the entity is vested with authority to perform a governmental function."[96] The Appellate Body supported the Department of Commerce's treatment of China's SOCBs as public bodies, holding that the Department of Commerce did consider and discuss evidence indicating that SOCBs in China are controlled by the government and that they effectively exercise certain governmental functions.[97]

From the above discussions of the demarcation of the boundary between SOEs and the state under international trade law, several lessons can be drawn for antitrust law. First, international trade law looks beyond the theoretical ownership of SOEs in determining whether they are separate economic entities. In both the areas of antidumping and subsidies, the ownership of SOEs is only one of many factors to be considered in determining whether SOEs are controlled by the state.[98] This view is consistent with the current EU antitrust practice, under which the focus of the inquiry is whether SOEs retain an "independent power of decision" from the state.[99] Second, the factors examined by international trade law in determining whether SOEs are separate economic entities vary based on the specific context of the matter. In the area of antidumping, for example, international trade law's inquiry is focused on SOEs' autonomy in carrying out activities that are related to their ability to "dump" products, such as their autonomy in pricing, negotiating and signing contracts, selecting management, retaining proceeds of export sales, disposing of profits, and financing losses.[100] In the area of subsidies, international trade law's inquiry is focused on SOEs' obligations to pursue governmental interests and implement governmental policies.[101] The lesson for antitrust law here is that the factors examined under antitrust law in determining whether SOEs are separate economic entities should also vary depending on the context of the inquiry. For example, the main factor in cartel cases should be SOEs' autonomy in management, particularly in pricing, whereas the main factor in merger cases should be SOEs' incentives to coordinate their business activities for purposes of maximizing the gains of the state. Third and finally, international trade law provides an example of conducting facts-intensive inquiries regarding the control of SOEs by the state.[102] Antitrust law has had plenty of experience analyzing whether minority ownership actually results in control,[103] but it is international trade law that has analyzed whether majority ownership (by the state) does *not* result in control.

Chapter 5

What Drives Merger Control?

How Government Sets the Rules and Play

D. Daniel Sokol

Merger control is one of the most important functions of antitrust/competition law. It is the mostly ex ante review to correct for potential anticompetitive behavior through either unilateral or coordinated effects. Mergers tend to be high stakes, and some of the very nature of what might make a merger attractive from a competition perspective, such as efficiencies, might have negative repercussions with regard to noncompetition economic interests such as employment and loss of a national champion or noneconomic political factors such as diversity of choices.

As with antitrust more generally, the number of jurisdictions with a merger control regime have expanded quite rapidly in the past two decades. At present there are in excess of 90 jurisdictions that maintain some level of antitrust review over mergers under their antitrust law. A number of other jurisdictions may lack specific formal merger control powers under antitrust law but may still review mergers under sector-specific regulation, national security regulation, and other non-antitrust review. In the jurisdictions with formal antitrust review, often this review may be concurrent with non-antitrust review.

The state shapes its merger control regime in two fundamental ways. The first is the extent to which noncompetition economic factors may be considered by the antitrust merger system and what remains outside the purview of antitrust (such as sector regulation). The second is the set of assumptions within competition economics that shape both merger control rules and outcomes.

What exactly is and should be the criteria and outcomes for state intervention used in merger control remain open questions around the world.

We begin with the use of an antitrust specific merger control regime. The implementation of merger control may lead to significant tensions domestically. A merger control system based on competition economics may be at odds with policies not based upon competition economics. Issues such as foreign ownership, efficiencies (which may include job losses), and competition economics that may diverge from "industrial policy"[1] of a given country may exacerbate situations in which politics may play a larger role in antitrust either implicitly or explicitly.[2] By politics, this chapter examines issues from the lens of public choice. Politics mean factors that impact merger control are not driven by the latest analysis of neutral competition economics within antitrust decision making. This chapter argues that for purposes of optimal antitrust enforcement in terms of outcome, predictability, and administrability, the setup of antitrust should be designed so as to remove as much of the overt and implicit political choices from antitrust as possible. Instead, these political choices should be made by other parts of government, such as the executive or through legislative fiat. Put differently, antitrust should become as technocratic (based on the latest developments within competition economics) as possible. To do so in any given jurisdictions, it faces certain challenges from both within antitrust and outside competition law.

This chapter identifies three topics related to the extent to which political factors are and should be recognized: within antitrust, outside antitrust law as part of merger control, and how the two analyses interact. This chapter offers an analysis of these themes, along with case studies of each issue to operationalize these issues in real-world settings.

I. The Nature of Political Intervention within Merger Control

The reasons a merger may be blocked by antitrust authorities can have competition economics justifications or some other justifications. In some instances preventing a merger may be based on a particular view of dynamic competition within competition economics, which holds that unless competitors are adequately protected, competition itself will eventually be undermined and consumers will be injured in the long run. In other instances this is based on the view that merger control has substantive objectives beyond competition, such as the protection of employment or preservation of social stability.[3]

The most important factor that impacts how much government intervention there is within merger control is whether to make competition economics / industrial organization the sole factor to determine whether to permit a merger. A regime that makes economic analysis the sole standard of merger control will be a far more permissive merger control system than one that examines noncompetition economics factors because a market-based system will be the default that will shape the permissibility of mergers.[4]

An industrial organization economics-based merger control system removes significant discretion from the merger control system. From a normative standpoint, this is probably for the best because the incorporation of fairness-related concerns in the merger analysis process may lead to results that hurt consumers because "fairness" is highly variable in its meaning. Areeda and Turner described fairness concerns within antitrust concerns as "a vagrant claim applied to any value that one happens to favor."[5] More generally, Kaplow and Shavell suggest:

> [A]dvancing notions of fairness reduce individuals' well-being. By definition, welfare economic analysis is concerned with individuals' well-being, whereas fairness-based analysis (to the extent that it differs from welfare economic analysis) is concerned with adherence to certain stipulated principles that do not depend on individuals' well-being. Thus, promoting notions of fairness may well involve a reduction in individuals' well-being.[6]

Embracing antitrust industrial organization (described herein as competition economics) allows for greater predictability and for outcomes that are less likely to be hijacked by overtly political concerns not based on competition economics.

Several advancements have been made in economics as they relate to merger control that push toward a more technocratic, less overly political antitrust. They include more sophisticated models of unilateral effects,[7] coordinated effects,[8] merger simulation,[9] efficiencies,[10] and upward pricing pressure.[11] When a merger control system focuses on these issues, the implication is that issues such as saving local jobs or protecting smaller competitors for the sake of keeping less efficient competitors in the market play perhaps no role.

Given the nirvana fallacy, this chapter does not suggest that competition economics create a new framework for undertaking merger analysis to incorporate other economic concerns or noneconomic fairness concerns. Rather, the latest developments of competition economics should frame the development of merger control. Overtly political interventions should be moved to those areas of regulation in which alternative frameworks and trade-offs are commonly accepted.

A number of factors account for noneconomic goals in the practice of competition law for merger review. Some of this is due to particular language in the enacting legislation that provides for multiple and sometimes competing goals. These goals may create a path dependency in case law regarding the implementation of merger law. Moreover, even if the statute is silent or has some sort of efficiency justification, the case law may reflect some noneconomic approaches rather than agency thinking based upon competition economics.[12]

There are also situations under both competition law and competition agency analysis in which sophisticated economic theoretical and empirical work and approaches may be ignored or marginalized depending on the particular case. This may be a more implicit political version of merger control in which the agencies strategically pick and choose the economics to adopt based on the outcome they want.[13] In this setting, the state plays a formative role in shaping policy but in a less obvious way than if a sector regulator was to ignore the lack of any negative competitive effects in a decision to block a merger based upon noneconomic factors such as under a "public interest" standard of review.[14]

In some systems, competitor effects still have some salience in merger analysis. Yet, at some level, this focus on competitors rather than on competition is a form of industrial policy because it may favor outcomes inconsistent with either total or consumer welfare. While few merger control systems worldwide assign significance to protecting competitors, some regard protection of competitors as a legitimate concern in their antitrust merger review regarding case outcomes.[15]

The trade-offs between economic and noneconomic goals are not the only set of political trade-offs that the state shapes in its antitrust analysis. Even within a purely competition economics framework, there is a political element to the use of economics. The choice as to the standard used regarding how to assess the effects of a merger is political. The two competing economics-based choices within competition economics are consumer welfare and total welfare. In simple terms, consumer welfare means the effect of the merger on consumers, whereas total welfare is the effect of the merger on both consumers and producers. In many antitrust cases, there is in fact no difference in outcome regardless of the welfare standard.[16] Most mergers that harm consumer welfare will also harm total welfare, such as a merger to monopoly. However, as we discuss below, in some merger cases the welfare standard matters in terms of outcome.

The difference in outcomes can be seen through the example of the use of efficiencies in mergers. Williamson first identified the efficiency trade-off raised by merger-specific efficiencies that may accompany an increase in monopoly power postmerger.[17] There are some instances in which a business practice improves efficiency—that is, reduces costs of production and/or distribution. We set up two basic hypotheticals to illustrate the problem. The easy case is one in which the merger does not enhance market power. As a result, cost savings from the merger will be passed on to some extent to consumers in the form of lower prices. This case is easy because the merger increases both consumer welfare and total welfare. The more difficult case occurs where the improved efficiency accompanies increased market power postmerger that leads to a price increase above the previous level. This situation creates a need to weigh the benefits of improved efficiency against the costs of allocative inefficiency, since on total welfare grounds this merger should be allowed, whereas on consumer welfare grounds it should not.

This situation illustrates the political reason that agencies may choose consumer welfare over total welfare as the basis for an economic analysis of mergers. The political backlash against antitrust policy would be significant under the following circumstances (the hard case): there are job losses and price increases postmerger even though total welfare increases. It is for situations such as these that we suspect that antitrust agencies do not adopt a total welfare standard, even in cases in which economists rather than lawyers head competition authorities due to a fear of lack of funding or of a reduction in the powers of the agency as a result of allowing such mergers.[18]

The decision for a merger regime of its welfare standard also has other impacts regarding the play of merger control. Once an agency decided upon either a total or consumer welfare standard, this creates a certain amount of lock-in regarding the agency's discretion. Certain challenges will be brought or not brought based on the likelihood of success on the merits based upon the merger standard.

In practice, changing enforcement practices for mergers across political regimes is not easy. To a large extent, merger policy is dependent on the particular matters that parties notify to the antitrust authorities. Issues like general economic climate and the strength of the economy will impact the number of merger filings. Other issues such as industry consolidation based on specific industry conditions also impact the opportunities for merger challenges. Finally, judges may be reluctant to change substantive merger law. Together, the political choice that the state makes in its merger standard has a lasting impact on the play of competition policy in a given jurisdiction. Therefore, the choice of economics means less overt political antitrust.

Just as there is an implicit political choice in picking the welfare standard used to analyze mergers, there is a similar implicit political choice as to the aggressiveness of merger enforcement. Yet, on the margins, a shift in administration of an antitrust agency may impact the agency's enforcement posture and how much the state may be willing to support merger enforcement. In this sense, government has the ability, potentially, to decide the temperature of enforcement. That is, government may decide that merger enforcement is too lax or too strong and may shift its enforcement resources as a result of its own preferences for enforcement. This is a political decision, even if done through the lens of competition economics.

Case Study I: United States

Perhaps more than any other antitrust system, the United States' experience with merger control has shown the most dramatic shift in terms of the change from overt political factors to one guided solely by competition economics considerations. The use of merger control in antitrust has been a U.S. export, although the transplant has been different across jurisdictions based on a number of factors. Nevertheless, the long time span of U.S. merger policy and the particular embrace of competition economics illustrate the different tensions of "political" antitrust and how the state shapes antitrust merger enforcement both in terms of explicit and implicit political intervention that has some broader lessons for other merger regimes.

The changes in the United States reflect a similar transition (although in many cases not as far along) in other jurisdictions as to politics in merger control in which technocracy using the latest methods in industrial organization suggest the least political intrusion specific to competition economics into competition policy.[19]

The U.S. experience with regard to the politics of merger control and the potential of shifting political forces on enforcement provides a case study to address how much antitrust agencies can do to change the dynamics of merger enforcement. The U.S. merger regime has been the most studied merger system. Moreover, the U.S. merger regime is the most technocratic in the sense that economists play a significant role in the merger review process within the agencies and with the parties each utilizing economists to make arguments based upon the economic arguments laid out in the merger guidelines.

Given the current state of competition economics, U.S. merger enforcement and case law from the 1950s and 1960s are intellectual embarrassments. The agency priorities and case law reflected the idea that big was bad, that merger efficiencies should play no role in merger analysis, and that the protection of competitors mattered more than efficiencies. Put differently, overt noneconomic political factors mattered within antitrust.[20] This approach in the case law began to change in the late 1970s, although the change specifically in merger case law lagged a bit relative to the abolition of per se rules regarding conduct.[21] Such overt political antitrust considerations (those not based on competition economics) are no longer part of the current antitrust policy discourse within the case law or agency practices as embodied in the merger guidelines. As Judge Ginsburg has noted in the case law development:

> Even in such cases where there is no consensus among economists, there is, nevertheless, virtually universal agreement among antitrust economists and lawyers alike, that the Court should answer questions of antitrust law with reference to economic competition—matters of consumer welfare and economic efficiency—rather than make political judgments about such economically irrelevant matters as the "freedom of traders," or "the desirability of retaining 'local control' over industry and the protection of small businesses."[22]

Changes in priorities became embedded not merely in the case law but also in the agencies with the rise in the importance of economics. In terms of how the incentives impact the role of the state in merger control, discretion in the hands of lawyers will play out differently than that of economists because it will go to questions of how central economic analysis will be in case selection. Froeb and colleagues explain the role of the economist as follows: "Economic methodology is particularly well suited for predicting the causal effects of business practices and for determining the effects of counter-factual scenarios that are used to determine liability and damages."[23] If this analysis is the basis of enforcement decision making, it focuses on effects. In this sense overt political control can be removed from case analysis because it is guided more by empirics. This is not to say that economists are not subject to political motivation. However, economists exercise it less than lawyers because populism was never part of industrial organization's mantra.[24] Lawyers, as part of an investigative team, may be less driven by the empirics of economics. More overt political goals might come into play in their analysis. The greater institutionalization of economics as the central motivation for merger control may have been a causal factor that changed the role of non-antitrust government intervention in merger control and a move away from political antitrust.

Empirical work suggests that overt noncompetition economics-based politics has, for the most part, become a nonissue in U.S. merger enforcement in recent decades. As one economist notes, "Populism was forced to a fringe position."[25] Earlier studies of U.S. merger control that examined the 1980s suggested that there were noneconomic factors at play in merger control.[26] The same work also found that the recommendations of economists carried less weight than those of the lawyers. A greater role for economists merely shifts "political" antitrust from noneconomic politics to politics within economics and the role of the state in merger control. This is implicit politics because both lawyers and economists behave politically, and some are the same in terms of their private incentives.[27]

The quantitative work on the death of overt political antitrust in merger control has been challenged by two sets of critiques that suggest that overt politics still play a role. In these critiques, the state continues to play an overt political role to shape merger enforcement. The first critique is based on a small sample of case studies. One of the harshest critics of "political" enforcement in the United States in recent years has been Robert Pitofsky, who chastised enforcement under the Bush administration as overly lax due to an ideological shift toward strong adherence to Chicago School principles. In a book on Chicago School antitrust, Pitofsky wrote, "The decline of antitrust enforcement against mergers between direct rivals ('horizontal mergers') [under Bush] is the most pronounced and unfortunate effect of the influence of Chicago School economics."[28] Given Pitofsky's hostility to changes after his tenure at the FTC as chairman, what is striking is how close Pitofsky's own enforcement policy was to that of those undertaken by antitrust enforcers under the Bush presidency that preceded and followed his tenure under Clinton.[29] Moreover, Pitofsky's own vision of antitrust articulated in the late 1970s was one in which noneconomic factors should play a role in antitrust enforcement. Yet, as chairman of the FTC, Pitofsky did not allow such nonpolitical factors to play a significant role, and merger control in the late 1990s looked more like the early 1992s or early 2000s than the mid-1970s, or even the mid-1950s, in which government enforcement of merger control was more significant. Pitofsky was constrained significantly because of the technocratic shift within the practice of merger law and changes in case law due to this shift (as embodied under the merger guidelines) that prevented a return to an earlier, more political antitrust.

The other critique suggesting overt political U.S. merger enforcement has come from Carl Shapiro and Jonathan Baker, who offer both quantitative and qualitative critiques of political enforcement. In work that had significant policy traction, Baker and Shapiro undertook a study of mergers under the George W. Bush administration and made the claim that under the Bush administration there was underenforcement of mergers. They claimed that this was particularly true for the Department of Justice than for the Federal Trade Commission.[30]

However, most recent empirical studies that analyze more recent merger enforcement note that across both Republican and Democratic administrations over the past 20 years, merger policy has remained constant—that is, at least since the George H.W. Bush administration.[31] Practitioner survey empirical work also backs up a nonpolitical U.S. antitrust system, even under the George W. Bush administration.[32]

How does one explain the transformation in the United States to significantly reduce overt political considerations (and thus the role of the state) within antitrust merger policy? The U.S. experience is worth noting as an example for other jurisdictions, even those with significantly different institutional designs, largely because the important changes that the United States implemented. This includes the creation of a distinct group within the antitrust agencies of economists, including a chief economist and staff, who are not subordinate to the lawyers.[33] This institutional design allows for a distinct economic voice to influence case selection and analysis to help ensure that there is an economic basis for enforcement decisions.

An additional factor that has changed the approach of the U.S. antitrust agencies to one that is more economics based and technocratic (and thus less overtly political) has been the introduction of economically informed merger guidelines that have been copied in many of the world's jurisdictions. The guidelines have prevented the worst excesses of noneconomically rigorous merger enforcement such as *Von's Grocery*,[34] perhaps the worst merger decision of all time. The importance of the merger guidelines to antitrust analysis of mergers and the use of various economics theories and approaches have been tremendous, and there has been an iterative process of tweaking the guidelines as the economics of the time have advanced. This has been true in the United States with each iteration of the merger guidelines—1968, 1982, 1984, 1992, 1997, and 2010.[35]

Case Study II: Europe

Explicit politics plays a significantly smaller role now than before in European merger analysis. Some of the reasons look very similar to those of the United States, such as developments in case law, the move to a greater "effects-based analysis" that relies more heavily on economics, and the institutionalization of greater economic analysis within DG Competition.[36]

How Europe got to the point of a less active intervention by the state into competition policy is an interesting story. Some have argued that at the Commission level, the 1989 Merger Regulation eschewed industrial policy concerns.[37] However, Europe has become more technocratic in its merger control only more recently.[38]

Historical factors and path dependency explain the greater orientation toward industrial policy of EC merger control. The core of European competition law was to further market integration over other factors such as efficiency. This meant that efficiency (however defined) played a lesser role in the original formulation of European competition law. One might suggest that a reading of *De Havilland / Aerospatiale*, a merger case in 1991 soon after the 1989 merger rules were put into place, about the failing firm defense expressed the tension between industrial policy and competition policy, at least regarding the appropriate use of efficiencies in the failing firm defense context.[39] Put differently, in the early years of the merger regime these overt political factors were more central to European merger policy than is the case today.

Because lawyers played a significant role in merger enforcement, while economists played a minor role, the Commission's decisions to challenge mergers may have lacked a rigorous economic justification. This too has changed due to the institutionalization of greater economic analysis, including the creation of a chief economist and an economics staff not subordinate to lawyers, as well as a series of cases that reversed Commission challenges based upon insufficient economic analysis.[40]

The earlier case law and institutional approaches have impacted on the current structure and nature of merger enforcement in Europe in terms of state intervention. Quantitative research supports that at present, Europe is a stricter enforcer of merger regulation than the United States.[41] Path dependency and earlier nonefficiency legacy may play some role in this orientation toward greater enforcement. One could frame Europe's wariness regarding vertical restraints (including vertical mergers) as an expression of this same sort of legacy.[42] Thus, more aggressive European challenges on mergers that are vertical may be as much political (based on a concern for the competitive process)[43] as economic and a key difference with the United States on competition law and economics.

A second factor that seems to have impacted the development of noneconomic factors in European merger control was what some claimed was an anti-American bias. Empirical work that analyzes this earlier period found that there was protectionism involved in European merger control. DG Competition had a higher probability of intervention against non-European firms when there were European competitors in the same market.[44] In more recent years, empirical work on merger challenges suggests that the protectionist approach seems no longer to be the case at the level of DG Competition.[45]

This rift between Europe and the United States came into play in particular in the late 1990s and early 2000s. A number of high-profile cases before structural changes in the mid-2000s suggest that industrial policy or other political concerns may have been at play that led to particular decisions. These included most notably *Boeing / McDonnell Douglas*,[46] *GE/Honeywell*,[47] and *Oracle/PeopleSoft*.[48] This chapter focuses on *GE/Honeywell* because it illustrates how politics both explicitly and implicitly led to divergent outcomes between Europe and the United States. *Oracle/PeopleSoft*, also discussed, illustrates a situation in which the political dimension may have trumped economics-driven merger analysis to prevent a different enforcement outcome between Europe and the United States.

We begin with a short review of *GE/Honeywell*.[49] The proposed *GE/Honeywell* deal received merger clearance in the United States but was blocked in Europe based on a theory of the bundling of GE's engines with its financial services at a price that was below what its rivals could offer. Third-party complaints drove much of the hostility of the European Commission, but so did a different path dependency based on political considerations on the view of competition in Europe. European competition policy, at the time, was far more likely to be about the preservation of competitors than the United States. Thus, even if there were not some more overt public choice–related explanation for the strategic use of antitrust, the institutional factors also pushed DG Competition to block the deal in Europe and in effect to block the deal globally.[50]

In *Oracle/PeopleSoft*, the Commission approved the merger but did so using the same unilateral effects theory that DOJ had suggested to block the deal. Unlike *Boeing / McDonnell Douglas* and *GE/Honeywell*, the Europeans agreed with the market definition employed by DOJ and yet somehow still cleared the merger after DOJ had lost its merger challenge to the deal before a district court.[51] This is puzzling, since if DG Competition accepted the DOJ market definition, the three-to-two merger most probably should have been challenged by DG Competition.

Politics seems to have played a role in the decision not to challenge the merger in Europe. Because of the very thorough opinion that would have made an appeal incredibly difficult to win, DOJ decided not to appeal the ruling. Had economic analysis been at the forefront of the European decision making, this would have created a potential problem. By challenging a deal that could proceed in the United States, the Commission would only increase transatlantic tensions, just as Commissioner Monti's term was to come to a close and just as efforts on best practices in the ICN for merger control were taking shape. These political factors seem to have been in play in the Commission's decision to clear *Oracle/PeopleSoft*. DOJ's loss in district court provided cover for the Europeans not to challenge the deal aggressively so that Commissioner Monti would not leave a political bomb for his successor Commissioner Kroes and another potential transatlantic rift.[52]

Case Study III: Member State–Level Politics in Mergers—Ireland

Merger control in Europe occurs not merely at the Commission level but at the member state level as well. Given smaller staffs overall and fewer economists than DG Competition, it may be more difficult for member states to be as advanced in their economics. However, institutional design issues also impact the politics of merger control at the member state level. The Irish system illustrates a change in the approach taken at the national level (for the better). Under Ireland's original 1978 merger control regime, the Minister for Industry and Commerce could block or approve mergers and did not have to give a reason for doing so. Under Ireland's Competition Act of 2002, merger control shifted to the Irish Competition Authority. The Competition Act required that a merger be blocked based on a substantial lessening of competition standard.

While there has been some disagreement as to the sophistication of the economics of the Irish merger control regime, the overt political nature of merger control has been removed. In its place is a more implicit set of assumptions over the nature of economic evidence. The ICA has given significant weight to both qualitative and survey evidence and in such cases made arguments that have not always employed the latest econometric tools of analysis.[53] Because qualitative evidence may be more prone to manipulation, there may be some potential political element to its use. Yet, this sort of bias of evidence is more easily corrected than the naked political power play of noneconomic goals over competition economics. Over time, the ICA will improve its economic analysis of merger economics and better integrate it into its merger practice.

Case Study IV: China

China's merger control system is relatively new. China's Anti-Monopoly Law (AML) was adopted by the People's National Congress on August 30, 2007, and went into effect on August 1, 2008. Although China's AML is based in substantial part on the established body of antitrust law in the European Union and the United States, the provisions of the AML reveal interesting ambiguities and uncertainties regarding some basic issues.

Article 27 of the AML lists the factors that may be considered when deciding whether to approve a merger: (1) market share and power, and market concentration; (2) the effect of market concentration on entry and technological innovation; (3) the effects on consumers and other related undertakings; (4) the effect on the development of the national economy; (5) and other factors as determined by the State Council Anti-Monopoly Enforcement Authority. Thus, the fourth and possibly fifth factors allow for MOFCOM to impose conditions that might not be based on traditional competition economics factors. To be sure, China is not the only system in which incorporation of such explicit noneconomic factors is possible but China's merger control is a system in which these factors may be used extensively.

Legal policy of how the merger regime works in practice in China is not clear because few decisions have been made. Some of the emerging scholarship on Chinese merger control examines the existing structure and decided merger cases. Two recent articles reviewed MOFCOM's decided cases to date and conclude that the structure is conceptually for the most part similar to that of the United States and Europe and that decided cases provide evidence that industrial policy considerations do not drive Chinese merger control.[54] These studies have examined fewer than a dozen published decisions. Unfortunately, these decisions represent a small fraction of all mergers, and not all mergers approved with conditions have been published, which has created a selection bias effect to those studies.

In a separate research project, I surveyed nearly all of the Chambers-ranked non-PRC-based law firms about their China-related findings to determine the extent of the political (noneconomic) forces at play in merger control.[55] A few insights from that study show how political Chinese merger control can be. The most important finding has to do with the direct intervention of other parts of government within MOFCOM's merger review process. Other government ministries need to sign off on merger approval. Many months can go by in terms of negotiations with MOFCOM and these other parts of governments (sometimes with the knowledge of the merging parties but not always). These other parts of government can have significant influence in putting certain conditions on the merger approval and may ask questions and force concessions of the merging parties that have nothing to do with competitive effects.

One important finding is the importance of third-party competitor complaints. If there is a Chinese company (particularly an SOE) that competes within the same relevant market or may at some point merely think of entering the market, the merger notification receives significantly more scrutiny. This is the case even if the competitive effects are negligible such that in other merger systems the deal would fall within a presumptive safe harbor because the market shares of the merging parties might be under 25 percent. As a result of these pressures, MOFCOM's decisions at times have been attempts to frame political concerns within the language of economic analysis, even when the economic analysis undertaken is more rudimentary than what one might find in Western Europe or North America.

Case Study V: New Zealand and National Champions

What might create a situation in which there are potential welfare losses at home may be made up for in a merger context with total welfare gains due to greater efficiency regarding the export economy. New Zealand has an efficiency basis in its competition law as well as a goal of protecting the competitive process. In practice, New Zealand looks to a substantial lessening of competition test based on quantitative economic factors to determine if a merger should be approved.[56]

The stage was set when Cavalier Wood Holdings (CWH) acquired a competitor in 2010. CWH applied for and received merger clearance from the New Zealand Commerce Commission. The acquisition left only two players in the New Zealand market: CWH and another wool scourer (and wool wholesaler), New Zealand Wool Services International (WSI). In 2012, CWH applied for merger clearance from the Commerce Commission to acquire WSI. The Commerce Commission approved the merger, which was a merger to monopoly. Third-party respondents contested the merger, which the Commerce Commission approved and which was appealed to the High Court.[57]

The third parties argued that the merger to monopoly lessened competition and made an argument that to approve the merger was to favor an export-oriented industrial policy over consumer interests in New Zealand, which would be harmed by the merger, since even by the Commission's own conclusion, CWH would be able to impose a price increase of between 5 and 10 percent before new entry was likely.[58] If the merger was approved, the implication by the third parties was that competition economics would take a secondary position to trade policy.

In fact, however, there was a competition economics–based reasoning that allowed for the merger to be upheld by the High Court. The Court found that there was a strong efficiencies argument in favor of the merger, given significant overcapacity in the industry and where the possibility of foreign entry would be a credible threat to price increases.[59]

II. Politics in Mergers Outside of Antitrust/Competition Law

The state may intervene in merger policy outside of antitrust by granting concurrent authority for merger approval to both antitrust and sector regulators. When there is overlapping regulation, this means a certain level of compromise so that the more interventionist regulator (usually the sector regulator) has an effective veto on a particular transaction being approved.[60] Because of this possibility of asymmetrical bargaining power, the working relationship between sector and antitrust authorities may become strained. This is particularly so in those countries in which antitrust has become more technocratic and based exclusively on economic analysis and sector regulators who have both an economic and a noneconomic set of goals under a broader "public interest" mission.

A concern of the mixing of economic and noneconomic goals of regulation is that the mixture allows for more ready regulatory capture in the merger setting of the sector regulator. The extensive literature on public choice provides both theoretical and empirical support to the regulatory capture thesis of sector regulators.[61]

Regulatory capture by sector may be more severe than those of antitrust enforcers for two reasons. The first is that sector regulators have more concentrated interest groups, which makes capture more likely. The multiple missions (including noneconomic ones) of sector regulators also creates additional political pressure points for the executive or legislative branches of government to use to leverage noncompetition concerns. This may impact the outcome of particular merger cases.

The second factor that compounds the capture is the pursuit of "public interest" or merely the veneer of public interest. Whereas some notion of efficiency may be (at least in practice) the only factor that determines outcomes in many antitrust systems, sector agencies may need to balance efficiency concerns with the preservation of competitors who may provide consumer choice and diversity.[62] Sometimes these concerns may be valid, but sometimes they may result from rent seeking. The point is not to distinguish between the two but merely to note that sector regulation has divergent interests from antitrust that are not based on some sort of efficiency analysis.

Case Study VI—The United States and Sector Regulation in Financial Regulation

Dodd-Frank has been the most important change to the U.S. financial system in a generation. Certain provisions within Dodd-Frank impact issues of competition within financial services and the role of antitrust. Some provisions within Dodd-Frank explicitly address antitrust. There are provisions in the sections that deal with the seizure of failing firms (using a covered financial company and a bridge financial company) that preserve some form of antitrust merger review during the seizure and sale of assets.

In merger analysis, sector merger requirements—along with all other regulatory requirements—are taken as facts that get plugged into the competition analysis by the Federal Reserve. Given the antitrust savings clause, there seems to be a sector-based exemption from antitrust built in along the *Trinko*[63] and *Credit Suisse*[64] model that allow for sector regulation in lieu of antitrust enforcement. Yet, the Federal Reserve has no previous background in merger control for competition issues to understand the antitrust analysis. There is also the risk of industry capture from special interests,[65] which may have been by design of the interested parties.

In a change from prior law, Dodd-Frank requires the reviewing agency for a merger in the financial system to analyze a merger for how increased concentration might impact systemwide financial stability[66] and "the cost and availability of credit and other financial services to households and businesses in the United States."[67] To prevent concentration, Dodd-Frank imposes market share caps for financial institutions to forbid a merger in which a financial company could hold more than 10 percent of the total liabilities of all financial companies[68] or control more than 10 percent of the total amount of U.S. insured deposits.[69] For example, a nonbank acquisition of $25 billion may lead to a different analysis from DOJ on competition grounds (where there may be no competitive concern) but that would be a concern of the Federal Reserve for issues of systemic risk. Likewise, a deal that may raise antitrust concerns may not impact system risk. Yet, because banking regulators have a different set of economic (and other) assumptions in their review, this may lead to different outcomes than a technocratic antitrust economics analysis.

Case Study VII—Endesa and Spanish Merger Politics

At the level of the creation of national champions (as opposed to European champions), the Commission has been clear. Philip Lowe noted, "National champions are illegal, they're immoral, and they're fat."[70] This is not the case at the national level in Europe. The role of government in merger control as a way to chill merger behavior on the part of foreign firms may have been pushed to the level of member states in Europe. Perhaps the best known of these cases involved the aborted takeover of Endesa, a Spanish company, by E.On, a German company. After receiving competition clearance from the European Commission,[71] the Spanish government used the sector regulator to impose a series of conditions on E.On that crippled its ability to prevail in its bid. Endesa was sold to a consortium that included a Spanish bidder in which E.On was able to acquire some of the non-Spanish assets.[72]

DG Competition brought a case based upon the events that unfolded. The Commission correctly found that the Spanish sectoral measures aimed at blocking the E.On bid violated EC law, and the ECJ found in favor of the Commission.[73] Of course, the damage had already been done, as E.On had to withdraw its bid. The inability of the Spanish Competition authority to challenge the government effectively in advocacy to stop the creation of a national champion has mixed implications. On the one hand, the fact that the CDC found that the merger did not create competition concerns suggests that it was not subject to political capture in spite of significant government pressure. On the other hand, the government was able to use sector regulation to effectively block the merger between E.On and Endesa.

Case Study VIII—British Banking Nationalizations and Bailouts

The most recent financial crisis provides an example of how national-level competition authorities may be less able to stop naked industrial policy mergers that may be anticompetitive because of the influence of sector regulators. In the United Kingdom, if the government wants to nationalize or partially nationalize a company, it does not have to file a merger control notification with the competition authorities. This is distinct from a state-owned enterprise engaged in economic activity, acquiring another business, under which the normal merger rules would apply. During the financial crisis, the British government nationalized Northern Rock and bought 80 percent of Royal Bank of Scotland. This required a fast-tracked act of Parliament but did not involve any antitrust considerations. Moreover, Lloyds Bank was strongly encouraged to acquire Halifax Bank of Scotland (the most exposed UK bank following Lehman Bros). The Office of Fair Trading recommended against the merger on competition grounds, but the Secretary of State for Business created a new public interest ground for circumventing competition concerns. The newly formed bank had to be bailed out anyway, and the UK market has been left with the anticompetitive effects of the merger.[74] In this situation, financial stability concerns trumped competition concerns.

Case Study IX—Export Cartels in Canada

Earlier empirical work on the Canadian merger competition system shows that it has moved toward a technocratic model of enforcement based on factors such as market concentration (based upon HHI) and entry barriers and foreign entry.[75] Yet, a recent case study illustrates that there are still methods outside of competition law that can impact Canadian mergers in the context of foreign acquisitions in which the state can impose industrial policy concerns on merger control. The proposed *BHP Billiton / PotashCorp of Saskatchewan* merger is an example in which foreign ownership law (Investment Canada Act) trumped antitrust concerns.

To set the stage, Investment Canada Act's purpose is to create a mechanism in Canada to align the nature of international investment into the country with Canadian national policy concerns. The Act uses a "net benefit to Canada" test. Issues that emerge in this context include traditional industrial policy concerns such as employment levels of the acquired Canadian firm in Canada and the amount of R&D undertaken postmerger in Canada.

Within the context of Investment Canada Act, BHP Billiton made an unsolicited bid for PotashCorp of Saskatchewan in 2010. The antitrust issue regarding the merger was more interesting than the usual merger analysis. What emerged from BHP is that, postmerger, it would not agree to remain in the international potash export cartel of which PotashCorp was a member. Frederic Jenny details the nature of the international potash market and cartel in his excellent work *Export Cartels in Primary Products: The Potash Case*.[76] In it, he notes the detrimental impact of the potash cartel on developing world markets and the limited ability based on current antitrust tools of developing world consumers to protect themselves against such export cartels.

From the standpoint of the role of antitrust versus other regulation, the Canadian Competition Bureau announced that it would not challenge the deal on competition grounds. After all, the deal did not create competition concerns in Canada given that BHP lacked any potash operations worldwide. However, given the Investment Canada Act review, the Canadian government had a second path to block the merger. It was on Investment Canada Act grounds that it did so. Although membership in the potash export cartel was not explicitly part of the discourse, the Canadian government discussed how the proposed acquisition would result in job losses in Canada.

The complete divorce of industrial policy in the case of potash for the Competition Bureau is an important lesson from this episode. That is, given significant political pressure from the Canadian government, the Competition Bureau kept its analysis limited to competition concerns and moved the nonpolitical merger denial outside the realm of competition law.

* * *

Alternative visions of competition and implementation of political factors explain either explicit or implicit politics and state intervention into merger control. A shift seems to be in place in many jurisdictions but such that these considerations may have been removed from the competition analysis and placed in separate statutory regulatory schemes.

This chapter proposes a merger control system that is competition neutral. In an ideal setting, this means the adoption of a standard of antitrust based exclusively on competition economics (whether total or consumer welfare—the various implicit political trade-offs between these two is a second-order problem relative to the issue of overt political factors in antitrust).[77] Merger control should become completely technocratic in a way that antitrust concerns are the only ones that are taken into account. Any concerns regarding industrial policy, national security, and so on should become a separate screen taken outside of the competition law context. This will allow competition law to remain more technocratic and nonpolitical and to move noncompetition economic considerations to those areas more prone to public choice concerns, such as sector regulation, the legislative process, or executive fiat, that are better equipped than antitrust to deal with political trade-offs. Over time, as the sophistication of an antitrust agency's economic analysis improves, this will lead to more efficient outcomes. Privileging the overt sort of state intervention within merger control through the explicit inclusion of noneconomic concerns in the merger area has the potential to bleed into nonmerger antitrust analysis, which would set back antitrust law and policy in many jurisdictions.

Chapter 6

Antitrust Enforcement and Regulation

Different Standards but Incentive Coherent?

Alberto Heimler

There is a major difference between the approach adopted for economic regulation and that followed in antitrust enforcement. Regulation identifies a specific course of action for firms (i.e., regulation instructs firms on what to do), while in antitrust, firms are informed about what is prohibited—in other words, antitrust tells firms what they cannot do). Antitrust, by not holding firms to a given action, is by definition more market and innovation friendly. Antitrust allows firms to freely choose from a very wide range of possible actions.

Also, the risks associated with antitrust and regulatory decisions differ. In economic regulation there is the risk of capture by the regulator (which may go in either direction, favoring the incumbents or the new entrants) and the associated risk of inefficiency or ineffectiveness. In antitrust, however, the risk is the uncertainty about what is prohibited (except for per se prohibitions) and what is allowed. If such uncertainty is brought to the extreme, firms would not know what is allowed and prohibited, so the law would not be able to influence firms' actions (i.e., if a firm does not know what the law prohibits or allows, it just acts as if the law does not exist), and it would be completely irrelevant.

Contrary to common wisdom, economic regulation is pervasive—for example, price controls of public utility services; concessions for the use of public property, including the radio spectrum; pollution control; information requirements of all sorts; accreditation of suppliers of credence goods; and the introduction of special and exclusive rights. These are only examples of areas where governments intervene, sometimes very intrusively, in our economies. While antitrust enforcement in the last few decades has thoroughly emphasized the positive role incentives play for achieving optimal economic outcomes (making sure that the law is interpreted so as not to block welfare-enhancing firm strategies), such an acknowledgment does not seem to have played a similar role in regulation, trade policies, or even the protection of intellectual property rights.

Sometimes antitrust enforcement adopts the approach of regulation—for example, when a firm is considered to have abused its dominant position by not respecting a regulatory obligation or when a dominant IP holder is obliged to deal at fair, reasonable, and nondiscriminatory (FRAND) terms. By telling firms what to do, antitrust enforcement may become inefficient, abandoning its market orientation. The extent over which the regulatory approach influences antitrust enforcement is an area where the difference among jurisdictions is the largest. Although in recent decades European antitrust enforcement has become closer to that of the United States, in terms using economic analysis to identify a violation and the widespread adoption of an effects-based approach, the infringement of a regulatory obligation (without any further characterization) has a higher probability of being considered an antitrust offense in Europe than in the United States.

The comparison among standards of the approaches being followed cannot be made in the abstract but requires examples from which a general conclusion can be developed. To characterize the regulatory approach, this chapter uses as an example the issue of price regulation in the public utility sector. Furthermore, it addresses the question of FRAND royalties in intellectual property and discusses some applications of trade policy, showing how they may effectively become a protectionist device.

These approaches are compared in terms of their relative efficiencies. In particular, the standard adopted in antitrust, which, at least in principle, is the most incentive coherent, is compared with that followed in other areas of regulation. The huge differences in standards adopted in different systems of law suggest that the many communities that inspire trade liberalization, regulatory reform, the protection of intellectual property rights, and antitrust enforcement could benefit by adopting a more convergent approach, especially because the standards that are being discussed are all centered around competition and therefore do not differ in terms of the general interest being pursued.

I. Price Regulation of Public Utilities

As an example of how regulation may sometimes differ from what the market approach might suggest, I address the issue of price regulation of public utility services, distinguishing the approaches adopted for final prices and access prices.

Gomez-Ibanez[1] provides a convincing theory on the reasons why the prices of monopoly infrastructure services are regulated. He suggests that price regulation is necessary for both producers of these services and consumers. Producers need the regulation to make sure that the regulated prices of public utilities will accommodate the returns on the investment sunk in the infrastructure. Without the regulation, they may risk expropriation ex post by demagogic governments. As for consumers, they need the regulation to make sure that the pricing of final public utility services is not so high as to exploit the market power that public utilities can exercise bilaterally, gaining all the transaction costs associated with switching providers (e.g., changing location if sewage services are too expensive). As a result, prices of regulated infrastructure should not be so low as not to allow normal returns on sunk infrastructure investment and not so high as to exploit the difficulty consumers face in switching (for the type of infrastructure services characterized by some form of demand substitutability).

To avoid the drawbacks of rate-of-return regulation (not enough discipline on the part of the monopolist on the control of its costs), price cap regulation was introduced in the 1980s by UK Treasury economist Stephen Littlechild. Price cap regulation makes sure that the final prices of monopoly public utility services grow with inflation, minus a factor associated with the relative increase in efficiency in the supply of these services with respect to the rest of the economy (CPI-X). The idea of price caps is that the regulated firm maintains the freedom to set individual prices, while a cap is placed on the average increase in the prices of the range of services it provides. As a result, the firm has the incentive to innovate beyond what had been anticipated by the regulator, since any cost savings associated with the innovation translate to higher profits. Price caps are coherent with both the producer and the consumer commitment problems, provided that the initial prices are optimal. Price caps are also incentive coherent because it promotes the introduction of efficiency-enhancing innovations.

What is interesting, however, is that price cap regulation, in leaving the regulated firm free to set individual prices, makes the firm responsible under an antitrust standard for any exclusionary conduct achieved through individual pricing.[2]

The approach with the regulation of access prices has been different. Access problems arise when providers of a competitive service need to purchase essential inputs from the infrastructure service provider and then end up competing with that company. In such circumstances, a competitor must set access prices as low as possible, while still making a profit, and operate only in the competitive segment of the market to compete with the vertically integrated firm. A whole range of access prices have been imposed on the monopoly infrastructure service provider, while the global cap, which has the same properties as the price cap on retail prices, that several economists have suggested[3] was very rarely chosen as the standard to be adopted.

The highest possible nonexclusionary access price is the efficient component access price,[4] where access prices should be equal to the final prices minus the cost the vertically integrated firm has avoided because of the competitor's services. Only competitors that are more efficient than the vertically integrated firm would find it profitable to get involved, and the vertically integrated firm would gain all the profits associated with the monopoly it has. Efficient Component Pricing Rules (ECPR) are incentive compatible because it allows returns on past investments. However, ECPR is difficult to apply if the competitor provides services that are not the same as the incumbent's.[5] In such circumstances the avoided cost has to be calculated by considering the effect of demand substitutability,[6] which is quite complicated and requires a substantial amount of information that is often not available. This is why in practice ECPR has been approximated by a cost plus approach, where the access price was set as equal to the total long-run incremental cost (plus a markup) calculated with respect to the technology adopted by the regulated firm.

Very often, however, regulators have encouraged the entry of competitors in the competitive segment of the market by imposing much lower access prices than those determined by the actual/historical costs of the incumbent. For example, in telecommunications it has been a common practice in many jurisdictions to price access at the total long-run incremental cost calculated at the best-practice technology, believing the regulated firm would be more likely to invest in the best-practice technology. However, this seldom happened. Telecommunications technologies tend to improve over time, and costs usually decrease, so the incumbent may always be in a situation where historical costs are never recovered. As a result, the practice of imposing access prices below cost creates the perverse incentive for the incumbent to try to prevent entry by competitors via illegitimate means (refusal to entry, low-quality access, etc.).[7]

If it is in the public interest to promote entry into telecommunication services, a more efficient public policy would be to subsidize entry directly (e.g., offering tax relief for the new entrant) instead of subsidizing access at the expense of the incumbent.

While price cap regulations on final prices are meant to encourage incumbents to innovate, access price regulations usually only address the competitors' right to access the market. This completely ignores the negative effect such regulations would have on innovation or on the possibility that incumbents might completely refuse access or provide low-quality access to competitors.

II. The Protection of Intellectual Property

According to Harry First, "Intellectual property law is out of control" because "for more than a decade, intellectual property rights holders have constantly pushed at its boundaries, expanding the scope of their rights and thereby increasing the costs for all users of intellectual property products."[8] As the Federal Trade Commission[9] and the National Academy of Science[10] also confirm, the U.S. patent system leads to too many patents because of the looseness of the nonobviousness standard. As a consequence, suggests Carlton, if "obvious ideas are patented, then subsequent innovations that rely on these ideas will be forced to pay for the use of these obvious ideas, and that reduces the incentives to innovate."[11]

Considering that such lack of rigor in the assessment of novelty is not just a simple organizational issue but originates from a combination of high volume of applications and lack of resources of patent offices, Lemley suggests that patent offices should concentrate their resources on the most important patents. Since important patents cannot be recognized ex ante by law, patent applicants should have the option of earning a presumption of validity by paying a fee for a thorough examination of their inventions.[12] Those who are unwilling to go through the expensive process would still receive a patent, but their validity would be subject to full review by the Courts in the event of litigation. In other words, patent applicants would choose by themselves which patent is more important.

This approach is confirmed by the analysis conducted by Acemoglu and Akcigit that concludes that full patent protection is not optimal and that, from the viewpoint of maximizing the growth rate of the economy, it would be more efficient to adopt a more flexible system, one that provides greater protection to technological leaders than to simple followers.[13]

Other economists have proposed much more radical reforms to the whole approach to intellectual property, suggesting that its theoretical foundations are uncertain and unclear. Boldrin and Levine, for example, have strongly criticized the terms of patent protection and conclude, "On the basis of the available evidence, our best estimate of the length of optimal copyright term is about two years and that of patents is about ten years."[14] The huge difference between these estimates and existing terms of patent (20 years) and copyright (75 years after the death of the author) protection shows, at the minimum, how wide the range of options is, especially for copyrights.

As First suggests, "It is innovation, not innovators, which the IP law should protect."[15] First is essentially rephrasing what is probably the most famous statement about the objectives of antitrust enforcement—"It is competition, not competitors, which the Antitrust Act protects"[16]—even though, of course, in the case of IP law, the protected innovator is the successful one, not the weak competitor, as is the case with antitrust enforcement.

While IP law has always protected the innovator under the assumption that by so doing innovation would be promoted, there are some cases where the law was interpreted as aiming at the protection of innovation, not the innovators. For example, in the United States, business methods or research tools patents are granted less and less frequently because that would reduce innovation, not enhance it. As Lemley points out, the stronger rigor in the granting of patents on business methods originates in an organizational innovation within the U.S. Patent Office, where patents on business methods are granted only after a second pair of eyes has reviewed them; this practice would prove to be very costly if done for all patents.[17] This is why Lemley suggests a two-tier system where patent offices would grant two types of patents (distinguished in terms of the degree of validity that they confer), according to how much the applicant was willing to pay.

While the way patents are granted is strictly regulated, there is no regulation on the pricing of intellectual property, and the price of licensing (royalties) is left to the parties' negotiations (and subject to antitrust scrutiny). Sometimes standards-setting organizations arrange the terms by which the standard is to be licensed. One of the most common rules is that patents associated with the standard must be licensed at FRAND terms. These obligations—which the patent holders voluntarily accept—are intended to prevent patent holders from exploiting ex post their advantage in having their patent included in the standard. It also counterbalances the increase in market power associated with the creation of the standard. FRAND terms do not represent a constraint on the general ability of patent holders to ask for royalties. Indeed, the pricing of intellectual property represents a signal for potential innovators to invest resources for making a given patent obsolete. If all royalties, not just those bundled in a standard, were constrained at their FRAND level, such an incentive could disappear, and the rate of innovation would be negatively affected.

III. Trade Policy and Competition

In 1998, the Brookings institution published a study[18] analyzing the relationship between antidumping rules and competition. Using examples from many jurisdictions across the world, the study, which was led by Robert Willig, showed that antidumping measures are very seldom justified under a competition/antitrust standard. Monopoly power is what makes dumping socially harmful. In fact, according to Willig, only "strategic dumping" and "predatory dumping" would indeed be harmful, a very small percentage of all antidumping procedures in the 1990s.[19] The majority of dumping cases, classified as aiming at "market expansion" or caused by "cyclical dumping," prohibited procompetitive behavior, and the underlying cases were mostly motivated by protectionist intent. This did not originate from the different philosophical origins of antitrust and antidumping laws. Indeed, the objective of both sets of laws was to protect the competitive process and protect the consumer from monopoly power. However, over time this common justification was lost. Antitrust law began to emphasize pursuing economic efficiency. Antidumping law continued to concentrate on the protection of domestic producers. This lack of emphasis on competition and efficient outcomes in trade policy is borne out by the fact that the injured jurisdiction could adopt countervailing duties to punish another jurisdiction for providing illegitimate subsidies to a firm. It is difficult to reconcile such a sanction—raising duties on other products—with the damage done by the subsidized firm(s) to domestic industry.

Indeed, the World Trade Organization (WTO) code against subsidies diverges even more deeply from the principles of efficiency. No identification of the relevant market is required in the analysis of anticompetitive subsidies, nor is harm clearly defined. For example, a global monopolist/dominant firm can file a complaint against a subsidized new entrant. In the course of the analysis, an illegal subsidy would be quickly identified, but no assessment would be made as to whether such subsidies were, for example, a reaction to a consolidated strategy of the dominant firm to preempt or foreclose entry. It would only matter that the domestic dominant producer is injured by the subsidy.[20]

A practical application of this approach can be found in a 2011 WTO Appellate Body judgment in the market for commercial aircraft. The United States claimed that Airbus benefited from illegitimate subsidies. In particular, it denounced 300 separate instances of alleged subsidization over a period of almost 40 years by the European Communities and four of its member states—France, Germany, Spain, and the United Kingdom—with respect to large civil aircraft (LCA) developed, produced, and sold by Airbus. The decision of the dispute settlement panel was issued on June 30, 2010. The European Union appealed to the WTO Appellate Body, which issued its report on June 1, 2011, confirming that some of these subsidies were indeed illegitimate.

Hahn and Mehta commented on the Appellate Body report suggesting that the role of competition analysis was not sufficiently robust.[21] For example, when the Appellate Body analyzed the launch subsidies for the construction of large civilian aircraft—while concluding that it was not feasible, given the economic conditions of the time—it did not provide a detailed picture of the other market participants, "considering that Boeing was receiving subsidies over much of the same period."

A more thorough regime such as the European Treaty (where subsidies are prohibited when they negatively affect competition) would have been much more appropriate for the WTO system. In such an agreement, state subsidies would be prohibited if they were anticompetitive and affected international trade.[22] The link with exports would be much more indirect, and competition analysis would play a much larger role in the analysis of harm.

Finally, an example of how well-meaning rules may lead to very inefficient results is the TRIPS provision on the length of a patent protection. The TRIPS agreement requires WTO members to provide protection for a minimum term of 20 years from the filing date of a patent. So the TRIPS provisions will be enforced quickly, the agreement also requires member countries to extend the protection not just to new patents but also to all existing patents. In other words, producers that agreed to supply patented products in jurisdictions with shorter protections would also benefit from extensions. It is quite clear that if the purpose of patent protection is innovation, extending the protection for existing patents to 20 years has no effect on innovation, resulting in a windfall for existing patent holders.[23]

IV. Antitrust Enforcement and Incentive Coherence

This section examines the influence of the regulatory approach on antitrust enforcement, showing that the adoption of a regulatory approach by antitrust enforcers may not always be incentive compatible and may lead to inefficiencies. The relationship between the level of regulated access prices and the finding of an abusive exclusion and the imposition of FRAND license terms as antitrust remedies are analyzed.

A. Access Prices and Antitrust

The opinion of the U.S. Supreme Court in *Verizon v. Trinko*[24] clarifies the extent of antitrust jurisdiction in cases where the sectoral regulator is also in charge. The case was against Verizon, a telecommunications incumbent operator that provided low-quality access to the local loop to competitors at regulated access prices. Because Verizon was obligated to provide access at prices imposed by the U.S. telecom regulator (the Federal Communications Commission [FCC]) to be equal to long-run incremental costs, the Court argued that there was a regulatory infringement, leading the FCC to impose a pecuniary sanction on Verizon. However, according to the Court, there was no antitrust infringement because the regulated access prices were much lower than those that would have prevailed in a regulation-free market (i.e., right below the level where they would be exclusionary). The Court opinion suggests that for an antitrust case to be initiated, the access prices should not be below costs. Then there must be proof that the behavior under scrutiny is exclusionary.

Another important consideration when analyzing the relationship between a regulatory environment and antitrust enforcement is whether the existence of price regulation excludes the possibility of antitrust infringement. The answer is a firm "no." Case law in the United States provides such a clear answer. In the United States, in cases where there is a regulator, the extent of antitrust scrutiny is clearly smaller than in the EU. As the European *Deutsche Telekom* case shows, as long as the regulation is structured so the firm has some autonomy on price formation, then the firm itself is responsible for any possible abuse originating from such an autonomous decision, and the regulation plays no role.[25]

B. FRAND Royalties as an Antitrust Remedy

In a recent paper, Geradin and Rato conclude that FRAND royalties are not an antitrust remedy because "calls for antitrust intervention reflect a preference for a system of pervasive royalty regulation based on a flawed royalty-allocation mechanism that would inevitably hinder innovation."[26] The European General Court in the recent Microsoft judgment[27] does not seem to agree with this statement. The judgment originates from the 2004 European Commission case against the Microsoft Corporation.[28] A key aspect of this case concerned the refusal by Microsoft to provide competitors with information relating to its operating system source code, which, it was alleged, was necessary for the development of competing software products in the group server market.[29] Although the relevant information may have been protected by copyright, the Commission considered it essential for allowing the development of competing applications so they could run smoothly on Windows.

In its defense, Microsoft insisted that its refusal to supply the information was objectively justified by its intellectual property rights because it was entitled to a reward from its investment and because any other result would prejudice its incentives to innovate. The protection of intellectual property was Microsoft's main defense, a point clearly inconsistent with existing case law and a point that was easy for the Court to refute. (By the way, Microsoft had made a similar argument in the United States, and the Court of Appeal wrote that such an argument "borders upon the frivolous" and then went on to conclude that it is "no more correct than the proposition that use of one's personal property, such as a baseball bat, cannot give rise to tort liability."[30])

As to the requirement that competition be eliminated because of Microsoft's refusal to share the information, the Court took the position that the Commission does not need to wait for all competition to be actually eliminated. On the contrary, it is sufficient to show that competition is strongly weakened as a result, as was actually the case, according to the Court, with the group server market where Microsoft was becoming the leading player.

The Microsoft decision on interoperability, besides being in line with the European Court of Justice case law, is also justified economically. In a 2007 paper, Genakos, Kuhn, and Van Reenen elaborate on the economic analysis employed in the EC Microsoft decision.[31] They claim that the economic rationale of the case is the same as that used in 2001 in the United States in *US v. Microsoft*, where the rationale for bundling Internet Explorer in the Windows operating system was to exclude Netscape, a potential base for the development of an alternative operating system, and therefore protect the dominant position of Microsoft in the operating system itself. In the European case, the threat to Microsoft's dominant position was the growth of independent applications for group servers.

This theory of harm is indeed reflected in paragraph 770 of the Commission decision:

> As Microsoft itself acknowledges, software markets are subject to *shifts of paradigms*, of which the evolution from the original centralized computing approach to the modern approach of distributed computing, where processing power is distributed between servers and *fat clients*, constitutes a good example.

> An evolution that would lead the IT industry back to a more server-centric (and *thin client*) approach could in the long term threaten to strip Microsoft's overwhelming dominance on the client PC operating system market of its competitive importance. (Italics added)

Unfortunately, the Court did not pick up this point directly, so the real threat to competition originating from the refusal to share the information on interoperability was not clearly assessed by the Court.

Microsoft claimed it was difficult to comply with the Commission decision because the Commission did not specifically identify the information it had to share with competitors. The Commission only regulated that the information had to allow smooth interoperability and be reasonably priced. Eventually, in 2007, the Commission agreed that a flat fee of €10,000 was a reasonable price. However, the Commission fined Microsoft €899 million because it delayed compliance with its decision for three years.

The Commission's 2007 decision takes a regulatory approach. First, it admits pricing only if "Microsoft's protocol technology must be Microsoft's own creation (and) it must be innovative." Furthermore, according to the Commission, "Remuneration must be in line with a market valuation for comparable technologies." The Commission decision contains a very detailed analysis on what is innovative and what price should be charged, a highly speculative area. Furthermore, the Commission does not explain why it considered €10,000 a reasonable fee instead of, say, €5,000 or €20,000. Also, the Efficient Component Pricing Rule, which economic analysis suggests should represent a free market, not exclusionary, solution, is not even mentioned.

The Commission's decision was appealed, and in 2012, the Court of First Instance delivered its judgment, practically confirming the Commission's decision. Much of the CFI judgment turned on Microsoft's complaint that the Commission had failed to provide it with any guidance as to the sort of terms that would be FRAND-compliant and that it was therefore difficult to know how to comply with its obligations.[32] The Court, however, does not ask whether FRAND royalties are appropriate for enhancing competition in the group server market. In particular, if the issue is the market power that Microsoft can exercise in the Windows operating system, and if the information for smooth interconnection costs only €10,000, who else could challenge Microsoft's market power besides a free operating system like Linux? Imposing reasonable prices reduces the incentives to innovate around the Microsoft "monopoly" and thus reduces competition in the future.

In the United States, there is much more reluctance on the part of competition authorities to set reasonable prices as a remedy. However, in the 2011 merger decision on the creation of a joint venture between Comcast and NBC, the joint venture was ordered to license content to competitors at reasonable terms (with reference to the market price of similar content). Although the FCC and not the Department of Justice[33] determined the prices, it is nonetheless part of an antitrust decision.

The term *reasonable* should not be used in antitrust enforcement; *nonexclusionary* has a much stronger foundation in case law. Otherwise, why aren't *reasonable* prices imposed on all dominant firms?

* * *

Governments play a significant role in promoting competition, and they use a variety of policies for this purpose, including, most prominently, economic regulation, trade policy, and antitrust law enforcement. Some of these policies share the objectives to be achieved (greater competition), whereas others pursue other general interest objectives, although often the instrument they use is not fully in line with the actual achievement of these objectives. As a result, some change is required, either in the legislation itself or in the way it is applied.

While antitrust enforcement in the last few decades has thoroughly emphasized the role of incentives in achieving optimal economic outcomes (making sure that the law is interpreted so as not to block welfare-enhancing firm strategies), such an understanding did not play a similar role in regulation, trade policies, or even the protection of intellectual property rights. This is why competition impact assessment plays such an important role in many jurisdictions.[34]

The problem with regulation is that its standards are not always incentive compatible. For example, in the regulation of access prices, telecom regulators have very often imposed a below-cost price for access in an attempt to encourage new entry. By so doing, however, the incumbent paid the price of the inefficient entry and tried to avoid it (by refusing entry, by providing low-quality entry, etc.). An alternative, more respectful way that both the incumbent and the new entrant could maintain incentives to invest and innovate was to use the tax system, if necessary. In the field of IP protection, the lack of rigor in the enforcement of the novelty standard has led to the granting of many unjustified patents. As a result, some reforms aiming at introducing patents of different legal validity along the lines of the suggestions made by Lemley may be appropriate.

Besides cases of inefficient regulation, there are also instances where the existence of a regulatory standard affects the decision making of antitrust authorities in an inefficient way. For example, while FRAND terms for royalties have been adopted by standard-setting organizations to make sure the market power derived from using the standard is not exploited strategically, they have also been imposed as remedies in antitrust proceedings, especially in Europe. Such an extension—for example, the one adopted by the European Commission in the Microsoft case—implies that the simple use of market power associated with dominance is prohibited in Europe (because the dominant firm's prices have to be reasonable), at least if the market power originates from IP. Furthermore, the Microsoft decision where FRAND royalties have been imposed does not discuss the competition consequences originating from such an imposition. For example, it may be argued that because of artificially low royalties, nobody would have the incentive to innovate around the protected IP. As a result, the dominant company's market power is made more stable and more lasting, contrary to the desired outcome.

The standard to be used for granting access to the intellectual property should have been "nonexclusionary" royalties, not FRAND terms. Nonexclusionary royalties are incentive compatible because they signal to competitors the profitability of investing for overcoming the dominant company's market power.

Finally, sometimes trade policy is not sufficiently pro-competitive either. For example, the WTO antisubsidy code does not require that the negative effects on competition of the subsidy be proved. All that matters is the damage to domestic industry originating from the subsidy abroad. All this may lead to inefficient decisions that do not take into account the purpose of the subsidy by ignoring the full range of strategies adopted in the market, including the strategies of the injured firms.

All this shows us that standards, both in the substance of the legal provisions to be adopted and in the actual enforcement of existing ones, need to be thoroughly analyzed in terms of the incentives they create. The antitrust approach, with its strong emphasis on market incentives and flexibility, is the standard that has mostly benefitted from economic analysis, being based on an evaluation of the effects generated by firms' behaviors. As a result, the antitrust approach (at least when it maintains an efficiency-promoting orientation) can serve as a benchmark for the reforms to be adopted in other areas of economic regulation (price regulation, IP protection, trade policy, etc.).

Chapter 7

International Law and Competition Policy

Paul B. Stephan

States approach the regulation of international commerce with mixed motives. In a static world motivated exclusively by material interests, every state would like its producers to get monopoly rents from their foreign sales and its consumers to benefit from full competition. To the extent an industry has the characteristics of a natural monopoly, due either to positive returns to scale or declining marginal costs, each state would like to host the producer. But in a dynamic world where states can respond to the actions of others, it becomes much more difficult either to predict or prescribe the pattern of international competition regulation that will or should emerge.[1]

The range of possible dynamic responses is great. Only a few narrow international commitments limit what states can do.[2] A pro-competition importing state can go after foreign producers who collude in restricting sales in its import market to raise prices. Alternatively, a state might try to open up foreign export markets for its producers. In either case, it may impose sanctions on foreign firms to further its policy. But what happens if the foreign firms act in coordination with, or under the control of, a foreign state?

As this question indicates, competing competition policies can lead to international conflict. It is the job of public international law to address such sources of tension. Several general international law doctrines apply to competition law conflicts. None, however, has great clarity or definiteness. There remains plenty of room to link arguments for application of these doctrines to claims about optimal international competition policy.

This chapter explores the concepts of territoriality, sovereign immunity, and act of state as used in international law and applied to competition law conflicts. It focuses on U.S. practice, because the United States has been the principal exporter of competition policy and thus has generated the most international conflicts. It argues that current trends in U.S. law bolster these traditional international law doctrines and thus reduce the likelihood of disagreements over competition policy. Whether these developments will bring us closer to an optimal international competition regime is more debatable.

I. Territoriality and National Competition Law

Traditionally, international law stood on two foundations: territoriality and sovereign consent. Both concepts presupposed states as indispensable lawmakers. States function as the ultimate source of authority over particular territory. Endowed with state authority, sovereigns may consent to obligations through agreements with other states. Two hundred years ago, Chief Justice Marshall provided the canonical statement of the doctrine:

> The jurisdiction of the nation within its own territory is necessarily exclusive and absolute. It is susceptible of no limitation not imposed by itself. Any restriction upon it, deriving validity from an external source, would imply a diminution of its sovereignty to the extent of the restriction, and an investment of that sovereignty to the same extent in that power which could impose such restriction.
>
> All exceptions, therefore, to the full and complete power of a nation within its own territories, must be traced up to the consent of the nation itself. They can flow from no other legitimate source.[3]

Accordingly, the traditional conception of international law allocated authority to sovereigns on the basis of territory and then facilitated reallocations of authority that flow from agreements among sovereigns. These agreements could be express, as with treaties, or implied, as with customary international law. The concept of "exclusive and absolute" sovereign authority over its territory itself rested on customary law, although Article 2(1) of the UN Charter ratifies the concept.[4]

Over the last 30 years, advocates and scholars have challenged both of these foundations. Territoriality, they argue, has become obsolete in an increasingly interconnected world.[5] State consent similarly has become less important as coalitions of interested persons take shape across state borders to formulate and implement international norms.[6] These jurists envision a new international law that focuses on human interests without mediation by states or the territory that they occupy or control.[7]

This vision, however, outstrips reality. States remain indispensable to the formation of international law, and the mapping of state authority onto state territory remains central to the international legal system. Recent evidence of the enduring importance of territoriality can be found in the International Court of Justice's decision in *Jurisdictional Immunities of the State*.[8] The Court considered a claim that the traditional immunity enjoyed by one sovereign in another's courts must give way when a state is responsible for war crimes. The prohibition of fundamental norms of international law, the argument went, rests on a higher authority than state consent and thus requires the suspension of the normal privileges that one sovereign accords another.

The Court categorically rejected this argument. It instead ruled that exceptions to immunity always must rest on consent, either express or implied by custom. No such exception exists for even grave breaches of that part of international law that protects individual, rather than state, interests.[9]

Of course, just because the International Court of Justice believes this to be true, it does not make it a fact. International law lacks an authoritative arbiter. But it remains clear that the significance of states and their borders still matters in the international system, changes in the structure of international communication, transportation, and the structure of the world economy notwithstanding.

What does all this mean for competition policy? A wooden application of the principles of territoriality and sovereign consent would seem to lead to an absolute prohibition of any regulation by a state of conduct taking place on another sovereign's territory, absent some agreement to the contrary. Indeed, the United States once embraced this position.[10] The Supreme Court, however, rethought the issue long ago. By the 1920s it approved sanctions imposed on an international price-fixing scheme involving foreign participants because a key meeting of the participants took place in the United States.[11] At the end of World War II, the government argued that international law had evolved to the point where a state could regulate extraterritorial anticompetitive conduct that had a substantial, direct, and intentional effect on the U.S. market.[12] Many other states took serious exception to this position, but the Supreme Court endorsed it in a somewhat careless manner in 1993.[13] At about the same time, the

European Court of Justice did effectively the same thing, holding that the European Economic Community then (now the European Union) could regulate a price-fixing conspiracy among foreign producers that used local agents in its implementation.[14]

All of these cases involved foreign producers who sought to collect monopoly rents from domestic consumers. When the victims of anticompetitive behavior are foreign consumers, different standards have applied. In *Matsushita Electric Industrial Co. v. Zenith Radio Corp.*, the Court gave the back of its hand to the argument that the Sherman Act provided a remedy to a plaintiff who sought compensation for its exclusion from the Japanese domestic market. U.S. antitrust laws, the Court declared, "do not regulate the competitive conditions of other nations' economies."[15] More recently, the Court in *F. Hoffman-La Roche v. Empagran S.A.* ruled that the Sherman Act does not apply to anticompetitive conduct that causes only foreign injury.[16] Exceptionally, the *Hoffman-La Roche* opinion makes much of the customary international law of territoriality, which it invoked to justify its interpretation of the relevant statute. This interpretive tool, the Court argued, "helps the potentially conflicting laws of different nations work together in harmony—a harmony particularly needed in today's highly interdependent commercial world."[17]

The last, cryptic signal from the Court on the question of antitrust extraterritoriality is lodged in a footnote in *Morrison v. National Australia Bank Ltd.*, a recent pronouncements on the presumption against extraterritoriality in U.S. economic regulation.[18] The case is significant both because it involved securities regulation, an area of great importance to international business, and because it repudiated nearly half a century of lower court practice. In distinguishing its earlier antitrust decisions, the Court noted simply that the Sherman Act applied extraterritorially, without explaining why.[19]

Taken together, these cases convey a sense of unease, if not confusion. In other regulatory fields, the Court has seized on territoriality as a means of providing a bright line for managing transnational problems. Congress, the Court seems to believe, may manage international regulatory conflicts as it chooses, but it must take the initiative in doing so. Absent explicit legislative action, the default will be a lack of U.S. supervision of foreign transactions, whatever their effect on U.S. interests.[20] But in the field of antitrust, a different baseline applies. Its dimensions and the reasons for the difference remain murky. Doubtlessly the Justices do not agree among themselves as to these matters.

Looking back at the emerging doctrine, one can detect two competing impulses framed by a structural problem. The structural problem is the cryptic language of the Sherman Act, which forbids collusive actions "in restraint of trade or commerce" but provides no clear guidance as to what this means. Faced with this challenge, the U.S. courts have taken it upon themselves to develop a common law of fair trade that changes with time and fashion.[21] Unlike (perhaps) other regulatory fields, Congress already has taken the initiative in delegating to the courts the responsibility for devising the substantive standards in antitrust.

In developing this common law, the Court has tried to accommodate two competing insights. On the one hand, in a world of international commerce, foreign conspiracies can impose significant harm on U.S. consumers and presumptively should face regulation. On the other hand, judicial assaults on the choices that foreign states make about the organization of their own markets seem quixotic as well as dangerous. The Court plausibly could insist on further direction from Congress before taking on other countries.

A focus not on the location of conduct but rather on the place of harm, to some extent, balances these impulses. If foreign states choose to submit people on their territory to monopoly rents, the case for U.S. courts coming to the rescue of these victims seems especially weak. Thus, territoriality comes back in as a constraint on national regulation, only more loosely than other areas. The "place of harm" standard is necessarily more indefinite, and therefore more debatable, than the "place of sale" rule imposed in *Morrison*.

To be clear, the cases do not explicitly invoke a territorial "place of harm" limit on the Sherman Act. Rather, the courts' behavior and the somewhat confused accounts they give of their conduct seems to fit with such a rule. Thus, one can used territoriality to predict judicial behavior, even if the courts themselves talk about the concept obliquely when they do so at all.[22]

But this modified use of territoriality does not help with one important problem. In many instances, the foreign producers seeking monopoly rents in the United States are arms of a foreign state or otherwise act under state control. Here the economic injury to U.S. consumers results from a direct international conflict based upon opposing state policies. For a court to do nothing would leave the supposed beneficiaries of the Sherman Act without a cause of action. But to allow litigation would put the courts in the position of attacking foreign governments without the clear backing of Congress. If territoriality were the only limit on the Sherman Act, then these suits should proceed. Yet, courts understandably have been queasy about taking on other states directly.

Because territoriality offers no help here, the courts have looked to other doctrines to limit litigation against foreign states and their competition policies.

International law offers two more doctrines of possible relevance—namely, sovereign immunity and the act of state doctrine. Each is relevant, even if only the first reflects a clear obligation imposed by international law.[23]

II. Sovereign Immunity as a Limit on Regulation

Historically international law has blended the concepts of exclusive sovereign control over its territory and of sovereign consent by presupposing that sovereign acts performed on another state's territory rest on the host state's permission and that a promise not to hold the acting state responsible in the host state's courts accompanies this permission. Under traditional doctrines of international law, a state that invades another's territory without consent commits an international wrong, for which retaliation up to and including armed attack was permissible. If the state's presence came with consent, by contrast it would be assumed that the host state's consent embraced a promise not to interfere with the acting state's conduct to any greater degree than the acting state had agreed to at the outset. Out of these implied promises arose a doctrine of sovereign immunity, which instructed domestic courts not to exert their authority against a foreign sovereign without the consent of that sovereign or a command of its own state.[24]

During the twentieth century, this doctrine evolved. After World War II, the United States took the lead in arguing for an exception to a general rule of immunity in cases where a sovereign mimicked a private actor (*acta jure gestionis*), such as by engaging in commercial activity. Congress in 1976 replaced, as to sovereigns but not government officials, the common law of immunity with the Foreign Sovereign Immunities Act (FSIA).[25] This statute constitutes U.S. law, but it does not reflect international practice in all respects, and in a few instances, it may even violate international law.[26]

Under the FSIA, a foreign sovereign, or a legal entity controlled by a foreign sovereign, enjoys immunity from suit only if it satisfies several requirements. First, in the case of a sovereign-owned legal entity, the firm must not be formed under U.S. law.[27] Second, it must be directly owned by a foreign state at the time of the suit.[28] Third, the sovereign or entity must not have consented to the suit.[29] Fourth, the suit must not be based on commercial activity that is either carried on in the United States or has a direct effect in the United States.[30]

The recent OPEC litigation illustrates how these rules apply to a foreign price-fixing cartel aimed at the U.S. market.[31] U.S. subsidiaries of foreign national oil companies (NOCs) enjoy no immunity because they are formed under U.S. law. The NOCs also are subject to suit to the extent that they are responsible for the sale of products in the United States, because this activity fits within the statutory exception for commercial activity. Neither the states that make up OPEC nor the organization itself was a named defendant, even though the organization and its state members made up the heart of the conspiracy.

From a rational plaintiff's perspective, joining OPEC and the member states to the litigation would have been pointless. Both the U.S. subsidiaries and the NOCs were likely to have significant attachable assets in the United States. OPEC has no U.S. presence, and foreign states normally do not own outright attachable assets in foreign states.[32] To the extent that the plaintiffs wanted to make money from the litigation, the available exceptions to foreign sovereign immunity gave them everything they could have wanted.

The U.S. stance on sovereign immunity is not the only one, of course. Some states, including China, still take the position once embraced by the United States that all state acts have a sovereign character and thus enjoy immunity.[33] The International Court of Justice expressly refused to decide whether customary international law still embraces this rule.[34] Even if the old position no longer reflects the international consensus, those states that adhere to it may implement this all-encompassing immunity within their own legal systems.

The practical consequence of broader sovereign immunity outside the United States is limits on enforcement of any judicial awards obtained domestically. A beneficiary of a U.S. judgment would have no ability to reach state-owned assets (including the assets of state-owned companies) located in jurisdictions that embrace the traditional approach. This adds to the already considerable difficulty of enforcing judgments against foreign sovereigns.

At the end of the day, however, sovereign immunity is not a significant constraint on the use of competition law to attack state-organized export cartels. As a general rule, the territoriality principle allows states to impose their own rules on assets invested in, as well as transactions taking place on, that state's territory. This means that retaliation against foreign cartels works only to the extent that the foreign actor has put its people or property at risk in the retaliating state. This fundamental characteristic of the international system is as true for private cartels as those organized by states.[35] But where foreign actors do enter the U.S. market, sovereign immunity does nothing to prevent the full-throated application of U.S. competition rules.

III. The Puzzling Persistence of the Act of State Doctrine

Sovereign immunity is not, however, the end of the story. Other doctrines, emanating from, if not strictly required by, international law also allow courts to manage conflicts between cartel-promoting and consumer-protecting states. In the United States, three overlapping doctrines provide some latitude to courts seeking to avoid confrontations with foreign governments: the act of state doctrine, the foreign sovereign compulsion defense, and the political question doctrine.

The act of state doctrine is, in the United States, one of the more complex and confused bodies of judicially constructed law. It is not a product of international law as such but rather an independent response by some states to problems raised by the territoriality principle. The leading U.S. decision *Banco Nacional de Cuba v. Sabbatino* took great pains to state that neither international law nor the Constitution compels the doctrine.[36] Rather, courts apply the doctrine to avoid judicial interference in decisions best made by the political branches. But unlike the political question doctrine, the matters covered by the doctrine are not inherently incapable of judicial resolution. Thus, the courts accept that Congress can override the doctrine and require them to address particular disputes involving foreign sovereign acts.[37]

Where the act of state doctrine applies, it requires a court to accept the validity of an act of foreign state. Acts by a sovereign of a sovereign nature within its own territory trigger the doctrine. What suffices to override the doctrine, as well as a precise demarcation of its boundaries, remains controversial. But the Supreme Court has passed up at least one opportunity to denounce the doctrine altogether, and the lower courts continue to apply it in a variety of contexts, including antitrust cases.[38]

At first blush, the role of the doctrine in antitrust is puzzling. It is, after all, only a default rule that courts may apply in the absence of any clear instruction from the legislature. Act of state issues typically arise in disputes over property rights, including mining and drilling concessions. Lacking constitutional stature, the doctrine cannot survive a contradictory statutory command. The Sherman Act is just such a command, instructing the courts to address anticompetitive behavior affecting U.S. commerce. One might think that the mandate of Congress would supplant whatever discretionary considerations that motivate the doctrine. And the antitrust laws make no distinction between private and foreign-sovereign acts.

An explanation for the persistence of act of state in this field can be found in a feature noted above: The U.S. courts have understood the antitrust laws as effecting a delegation of common-law powers to the judiciary.[39] The legislative instruction in essence is no instruction, leaving the judiciary vested with the responsibility to grapple with anticompetitive conduct but otherwise without legislative guidance. Congress has neither overridden common-law doctrines, of which act of state is an example, nor expressly endorsed departures from international practice, the territoriality principle in particular. The nature of the statutory delegation thus invites reference to a doctrine that, while not applying of its own force, remains useful as an interpretive template.[40]

By way of comparison, the Supreme Court has found the act of state doctrine and its converse, the revenue rule, irrelevant in two cases involving the scope of criminal fraud. In *W.S. Kirkpatrick & Co. v. Environmental Tectonics Corp., International*, the Court allowed a firm to bring a civil suit against a competitor under the Racketeering Influenced and Corrupt Organizations Act (RICO) for obtaining a government contract through bribery.[41] The Court deemed the relevant question to be whether the payment of a bribe to obtain a governmental favor constituted fraud under federal law, not whether the bribe invalidated the contract under Nigerian law.[42] Accordingly, the act of state doctrine did not apply.

The revenue rule is the logical counterpart of the act of state doctrine. Just as the doctrine requires a court to accept the validity of a sovereign act undertaken with the sovereign's territory, the rule requires a court to give no extraterritorial effect to a sovereign's revenue impost.[43] In *Pasquantino v. United States*, the Court rejected the argument that this common-law rule should illuminate the interpretation of "property" for purposes of wire fraud liability.[44] It accordingly held that an attempt to evade Canadian customs duties constituted criminal fraud because Canada's right to duties is a property interest within the meaning of the statute. The Court asserted that the United States had a legitimate interest in criminalizing fraud carried out on its own territory, even if the prosecution had the collateral effect of strengthening the sanctions for evasion of a foreign revenue law.

Although the concepts of fraud and property both have their roots in the common law, the Court has not understood the criminalization of fraud under federal law as constituting a delegation of general lawmaking power to the judiciary. As a result, common-law doctrines derived from the principle of territoriality do not have the same role to play in illuminating the scope and meaning of the statutes. The Court instead focuses on the purpose of the statute and the reprehensibility of the conduct involved, not on the effect of criminalization on foreign sovereign acts. Antitrust is different precisely because the fact of the delegation of judicial lawmaking power is so clear, while the extent of this power is so undefined.

Even though antitrust in the United States rests on legislation, the courts legitimately may use the act of state doctrine as an interpretive tool. This basic point, however, does not resolve how the doctrine may function in specific cases. In particular, it leaves open the question of what limitations may constrain it. The Supreme Court has identified three possible exceptions, although it has embraced only two.[45] First, an act of positive law can override the doctrine, including rules of international law based on a high degree of codification or consensus.[46] Second, the Court in *Alfred Dunhill of London, Inc. v. Republic of Cuba* held that state entities acting entirely within their civil law competence may do things that do not rise to the level of sovereign acts, and thus fall outside the doctrine.[47] Third, a plurality of the *Dunhill* Court endorsed a commercial exception to the doctrine.[48] In addition, the Court in *W.S. Kirkpatrick & Co.* indicated more generally that the doctrine did not apply when the object of a lawsuit is not to treat a foreign act as a legal nullity but rather to attach adverse consequences to it.[49]

Unless and until international law embraces a norm condemning export cartels, either by treaty or by broad consensus constituting a binding customary norm, the first exception cannot apply. The only body of international law that comes close to creating such a norm is the Uruguay Round Agreements, which regulate trade law and arguably address anticompetitive refusals to export. But both U.S. and EU law expressly bar domestic courts from applying these agreements, instead relegating enforcement exclusively to state-to-state dispute resolution.[50]

The *Dunhill* exceptions, however, have considerably greater purchase. In antitrust cases, courts without exception have rejected the argument that all acts of state-owned entities constitute sovereign acts for purposes of the act of state doctrine. Were the rule otherwise, all activities carried out within the foreign state's territory would enjoy immunity from judicial review, contrary to the clear implication of FSIA's commercial activity exception. The challenge instead is distinguishing sovereign acts from other behavior.[51]

One line of argument focuses on the role of sovereign compulsion. As a formal matter, litigants and courts have treated foreign sovereign compulsion as an analytically distinct issue.[52] As an analytical matter, however, these cases are better seen as applying *Dunhill*. Actions by foreign firms, whether state-owned or not, that comply with a mandatory rule on the territory of the state that issues the mandate are themselves extensions of the state's sovereign authority.

Attacks on those acts are simply assaults on the exercise of sovereign power. The compulsion cases thus distinguish the exercise of civil law rights, to which the doctrine does not apply, from the exercise of sovereign authority.

Another line of cases struggles with *Dunhill's* commercial exception. In the most recent OPEC litigation, the Fifth Circuit ruled that a majority of the Supreme Court had not excluded commercial conduct from the doctrine and therefore refused to consider the issue.[53] The Ninth Circuit reached the same outcome by treating limits on exports of natural resources as inherently noncommercial.[54] Both decisions have the effect of giving conclusive effect to sovereign mandates carried out within the state's territory, even when the mandate involves commercial transactions and results in direct harm to U.S. consumers.

Finally, there remains the general question of whether the act of state doctrine has any relevance to suits that seek compensation for the harm caused by a sovereign act, rather than nullifying the act outright. Read broadly, *W.S. Kirkpatrick & Co.* seems to limit the doctrine only to suits falling into the second category. If so, few if any antitrust suits ever would raise an act of state issue. But the *W.S. Kirkpatrick* opinion is deeply enigmatic, indicating at one point that imposing tort liability for a wrongful detention would constitute the invalidation of the official act of detention.[55] Until the Court revisits the issue, it may be best to treat that case as resting on a narrower ground—namely, the inconsistency between the doctrine and the legislative purpose of regulating the payment of bribes to foreign officials.

As noted above, the Supreme Court has yet to consider whether foreign sovereign compulsion constitutes a valid excuse for conduct that otherwise would be actionable under the antitrust laws.[56] A number of lower courts have applied the defense in instances where the compulsion is transparent and emanates from government policy makers, as opposed to the managers of state-owned enterprises. The prevalence of the defense may indicate that it will endure and ultimately gain the endorsement of the Supreme Court.

Simply as a matter of analytic clarity, however, it does not appear that the foreign sovereign compulsion defense does any useful work.[57] Compulsion requires a credible threat, which as a practical matter involves proposed action or inaction with respect to people or assets on the territory of the threatening sovereign. Anything that should count as foreign sovereign compulsion, accordingly, also would meet the territorial and sovereign-act components of the act of state doctrine as limited by the *Dunhill* majority.

In the recent OPEC lawsuit, the Fifth Circuit invoked an alternative ground for dismissing the complaint, holding that consideration by a court of a claim that maintenance of the OPEC cartel violated the Sherman Act would violate the political question doctrine. In doing this, the Fifth Circuit embraced the position of the Department of Justice in its amicus brief. On its face, however, the holding seems nonsensical.

The political question doctrine, however murky in detail, rests on a bedrock constitutional principle. Due either to an express constitutional assignment of responsibility or the inherent nature of the judicial process, some issues as a constitutional matter may not be resolved by the courts.[58] The doctrine thus delineates an area where courts lack the capacity to adjudicate. But what does an attack on a government-organized cartel have to do with judicial incapacity? Is it plausible that, were Congress to adopt a law that expressly extends the Sherman Act to cartels managed by foreign states, the judiciary would refuse on constitutional grounds to carry out this mandate? If the answer is no, then surely the judiciary has the constitutional capacity to do the same under the currently vague standards of that statute.[59] Accordingly, talk about the doctrine seems more of a distraction than useful in international antitrust litigation, notwithstanding the arguments of the government and the occasional inclination of the lower courts to embrace them.

* * *

In a world where optimal global consumer welfare dominated all other policy objectives, competition authorities probably would not distinguish between private and governmental conspiracies in restraint of trade. But in a world where states pursue other objectives and embrace strategic trade objectives, unilateral pursuit of aggressive proconsumer competition objectives invites trade wars rather than cooperation. In some instances, the risk is worth it, because a risk of sanctions may produce market liberalization. In such conflicts, the court may become useful instruments. But rarely do states regard their judiciary as the best place to locate the decision as to when to go to war.

One can imagine a world where the U.S. judiciary, out of an abundance of caution, fully embraced the territoriality principle and insisted that Congress mandate expressly any imposition of antitrust liability on conduct taking place outside the United States. Instead the courts have taken the riskier course of presumptively allowing lawsuits wherever the harm, rather than the conduct, occurs in the United States. But to ameliorate that risk, the courts, not always with a clear doctrinal basis, have withheld action when anticompetitive acts result directly from a transparent command of a foreign state. In such instances, the willingness of the foreign state to take responsibility for the anticompetitive conduct relocates the dispute to the sphere of state-to-state negotiations. Where negotiations break down, the legislature still may enlist the courts in the battle, but the courts will not start hostilities on their own. This outcome is conservative in the sense that judicial inaction removes pressure that could goad the government to negotiate international agreements that more closely embrace global consumer welfare. But such conservatism is not necessarily a bad thing.

Chapter 8

The Foreign Trade Antitrust Improvements Act

Further Limitations on the Ability of the Antitrust Regime to Promote Consumer Welfare

Joseph P. Bauer

It keeps getting worse and worse. Over the past three and a half decades, the Supreme Court has made countless changes to substantive antitrust doctrine, making successful assertion of an antitrust claim more and more difficult.[1] The procedural obstacles facing a plaintiff even hoping for its day in court to attempt to prove the harms it suffered from a defendant's anticompetitive behavior have also gotten much higher.

About a decade ago, I wrote that these ever-steeper procedural barriers to satisfying the prerequisites for asserting a claim for antitrust relief were an important reflection of judicial hostility to the prosecution of antitrust claims.[2] Subsequently, four years ago, in its much-criticized *Twombly* decision,[3] the Supreme Court imposed new and substantially higher, pleading requirements on victims of alleged antitrust violations. These burdens have made it more difficult to get past the pleading stage and on to pretrial discovery, where the plaintiffs would have access to the evidence demonstrating those violations.

In this chapter, I focus on yet another barrier to the successful assertion of an antitrust claim: the Foreign Trade Antitrust Improvements Act of 1982 (FTAIA).[4] Although there is extensive disagreement about the specifics with respect to what behavior and structure the antitrust laws should seek to prohibit or permit, there is broad, general consensus on the goals of the antitrust laws. They are the enhancement of consumer welfare, the promotion of competition, and compensation of the victims of antitrust violations. Regrettably, the FTAIA has significantly undermined the achievement of these goals.

The obstacles erected by FTAIA are the result both of that initial legislative act and subsequent restrictive judicial interpretation. As described more extensively below, the FTAIA precludes the maintenance of certain claims for behavior occurring in part or in whole outside the United States. The Act continues to make American antitrust laws applicable to *import* trade or commerce. However, under the Act, other anticompetitive behavior is subject to the antitrust laws only if a complicated standard is met: the "foreign" conduct must have a "direct, substantial, and reasonably foreseeable effect" on domestic commerce and that domestic effect must "give rise to" the plaintiff's claim.

The explicitly stated purpose of the Act was to benefit American businesses and in particular the American export trade. The House Report[5] accompanying its passage indicates that the statute had two purposes. In the years leading up to its passage, understandably courts had given different interpretations to the reach of the antitrust laws. Thus, the FTAIA was designed to reduce this uncertainty.[6] But the stated primary purpose of the statute was to address the "apparent perception among businessmen that American antitrust laws are a barrier to joint export activities that promote efficiencies in the export of American goods and services."[7] Withdrawing the application of the antitrust laws to certain export activities presumably would enhance domestic prosperity.

An analysis of the 30 years of judicial treatment of the FTAIA provides a microcosm of the broader theme of this volume: how should the state weigh the promotion of competition with the advancement of a multiplicity of other goals? It is certainly important for any state to maximize commerce and to foster more congenial conditions for its business entities, including in their commercial relations with entities and consumers in other countries. But the state ought to strive to do so, while also continuing to protect the interests of its own consumers, both individual and corporate. Competition (or antitrust) laws are among the most important vehicles for achieving that goal. While accommodating all of these goals sometimes involves a tricky balance, hopefully there is agreement that the promotion of profits in international commerce should not come at the expense of higher prices or fewer choices in the domestic market.

In one sense, the FTAIA sought to achieve this balance—by continuing to include within the reach of the antitrust laws not only import commerce but certain nonimport commerce that has specified domestic effects. However, judicial interpretation of the FTAIA—by giving an increasingly expansive reading to those actions that *cannot* be brought in American courts—has had a most unfortunate, and undoubtedly unintended, effect. These cumulative decisions have contributed to significant reductions in the ability of the antitrust laws to achieve the goals just described.

A major step in that direction was the Supreme Court's *Empagran* decision, in which the Court denied relief to certain plaintiffs complaining of a worldwide price-fixing conspiracy.[8] Subsequently, courts have interpreted the exclusions in the FTAIA even more broadly, thereby undermining the important role for the antitrust laws.

Empagran itself probably had a neutral effect on American businesses and consumers. There, the Supreme Court sought to rein in the use by *non*-American plaintiffs of the Sherman and Clayton Acts to activities that neither took place in the United States nor directly harmed Americans. But, remarkably, more recent case law under FTAIA affirmatively harms American plaintiffs. These decisions deny them relief under the antitrust laws for foreign behavior that raises prices paid by American individuals and business. The result is a reduction in the consumer welfare that the antitrust laws are designed to promote and protect. This can hardly be consistent with the purposes of the FTAIA. This misguided judicial treatment is instructive for persons considering the role of the state in the promotion of competition—since these decisions surely do not advance the interests of the enacting state—in employing the antitrust laws as a vehicle for maximizing national welfare.

I. Extraterritorial Reach of US Antitrust Law

The state of the law with respect to the reach of the American antitrust laws to foreign activities has had a long and twisted history. I start with the seminal case, now over a century old: *American Banana Co. v. United Fruit Co.*[9] The plaintiff and the defendant were both American corporations. The defendant owned numerous banana plantations in Central America and exported bananas to the United States. The plaintiff purchased the interests of someone who had developed a rival plantation in Panama and was building a railway to deliver its bananas to a port for export to the United States.

The plaintiff's lawsuit alleged that a number of acts undertaken by the defendant in Central America—including acquiring real property of and stock interests in competing corporations, entering into price-fixing agreements, and inducing governmental authorities in Panama to seize the plaintiff's plantation[10]—gave rise to claims under the Sherman Act. Notwithstanding the fact that both parties were American—and, although not mentioned in the opinion, that the defendant's acts might have given rise to effects in the United States—the Supreme Court concluded that the Sherman Act did not reach this claim. Speaking for the Court, Justice Holmes proclaimed that "the general and almost universal rule is that the character of an act as lawful or unlawful must be determined wholly by the law of the country where the act is done."[11] A contrary result, the Court declared, "not only would be unjust, but would be an interference with the authority of another sovereign, contrary to the comity of nations."[12] Discerning congressional intent regarding the scope of the Sherman Act, the Court stated that "any statute [is] intended to be confined in its operation and effect to the territorial limits over which the lawmaker has general and legitimate power. . . . It is entirely plain that what the defendant did in Panama or Costa Rica is not within the scope of the statute so far as the present suit is concerned."[13]

Over the following decades, the Supreme Court's interpretation of the Commerce Clause generally gave it an increasingly expansive reach.[14] That same expansion was reflected in decisions on the reach of the antitrust laws to certain intrastate activities.[15] And there were a number of post–*American Banana* decisions by the Supreme Court, expanding the application of American antitrust laws to behavior that occurred in part in the United States but that also involved foreign conduct.[16]

Gradually, courts exercised antitrust jurisdiction over certain forms of purely extraterritorial activities, which had effects on competition in the United States. Before considering the changes wrought by FTAIA, three cases addressing such behavior deserve particular attention. They include two courts of appeals decisions—the Second Circuit's "intent/effects" approach in *Alcoa*[17] and the Ninth Circuit's notably different approach in *Timberlane*[18]—and the Supreme Court's opinion in *Hartford Fire*.[19]

Alcoa is the well-known decision authored by Judge Learned Hand. There, the Second Circuit concluded that the defendant's intentional actions to allow it to retain its decades-long position as the sole domestic manufacturer of aluminum ingot from bauxite ore supported a finding that the defendant was guilty of monopolization, which was in violation of Section 2 of the Sherman Act. *Alcoa* is also a landmark case on the extraterritorial application of the antitrust laws.

In addition to its action against the principal defendant, the government had also named Aluminum Limited, Alcoa's Canadian subsidiary, as a defendant.

One issue was whether the Sherman Act extended to Limited's acts outside the United States, which had effects on competition and the price of aluminum in the United States. Judge Hand distinguished *American Banana* and asserted that it was "settled law" that "any state may impose liabilities, even upon persons not within its allegiance, for conduct outside its borders that has consequences within its borders which the state reprehends."[20] Suggesting a rule that has since been widely adopted by subsequent courts, the court of appeals concluded that the Sherman Act applied to extraterritorial activities if two conditions were satisfied: the activities were intended to have some effect on imports or exports and the "performance [of the agreement] is shown actually to have had some effect upon them."[21] Concluding that here both of these conditions were met, the court declined to decide the applicability of the Sherman Act if only one of them were shown.[22]

In *Timberlane*, the plaintiffs alleged a complicated scheme involving an American bank, a subsidiary of which had an office in Honduras, and several individuals and corporations—some American, some Honduran—to reduce the amount of lumber the plaintiffs could purchase in Honduras and ship to the United States. The bulk of the defendants' activities took place in Honduras, and the principal effect was also felt in that country.[23] The district court, applying a version of *Alcoa*'s "effects" test, had dismissed the action, having concluded that the defendants' conduct did not have the requisite "direct and substantial" effect on U.S. foreign commerce.

The Ninth Circuit rejected that conclusion, holding that a judicial focus solely on the substantiality of the domestic effect of a defendant's extraterritorial conduct, with little or no attention to other considerations, including the degree of comity owed based on the interests of the parties and the countries involved, was "costly" and "risky."[24] Instead, the court suggested a three-step approach,[25] which in turn would require weighing a long list of factors to determine the applicability of the Sherman Act to the challenged conduct.[26] While this far more nuanced approach had the potential virtue of increasing the likelihood of reaching a "correct" result, it was criticized by numerous courts and commentators for the increased burden it placed on courts and parties, as well as the uncertainty of result it presaged.[27]

Hartford Fire involved an alleged conspiracy by American insurance and reinsurance companies and reinsurers based in London to change the terms of commercial general liability insurance policies for risks in the United States. Those non-American insurers did not engage in conduct in the United States, but the effects of their conduct were felt there. The case presented two separate questions: whether the defendants' conduct was immunized by the McCarran-Ferguson Act[28] and "whether certain claims against the London reinsurers should have been dismissed as improper applications of the Sherman Act to foreign conduct."[29]

In a 5 to 4 decision, Justice Souter, writing for the Court,[30] concluded that the district court "undoubtedly had jurisdiction of these Sherman Act claims."[31] The Court noted that it had long ago rejected the limited approach of *American Banana*.[32] Citing to *Alcoa*, Justice Souter stated that "it is well established by now that the Sherman Act applies to foreign conduct that was meant to produce and did in fact produce some substantial effect in the United States."[33]

Justice Scalia dissented from the Court's conclusion that the Sherman Act applied to these defendants.[34] He acknowledged that "it is now well established that the Sherman Act applies extraterritorially."[35] He also agreed that federal courts had "jurisdiction" over these claims, given the fact that the antitrust laws fell within the power of Congress to legislate with respect to commerce with foreign nations. However, for the dissent, "the question . . . is whether and to what extent Congress *has* exercised that undoubted legislative jurisdiction in enacting the Sherman Act."[36] Justice Scalia found the answer in a canon of construction, that "an act of congress ought never to be construed to violate the law of nations if any other possible construction remains."[37] Drawing on principles of customary international law and in particular the comity owed by one country to the interests of other countries, Justice Scalia concluded that the exercise of legislative jurisdiction here was unwarranted.[38]

II. FTAIA Complexity

In addition to these three cases, over the years, numerous other courts have also struggled to create a framework for analyzing the international reach of the antitrust laws. As the legislative history of the FTAIA reflects,[39] prior to its enactment, there was considerable uncertainty regarding that question.[40] The FTAIA was a congressional attempt to state clear rules for identifying the applicability of the antitrust laws to certain foreign activities.

Yet, despite the passage of the FTAIA, the uncertainty persists today, and the controversy about the appropriate scope of the antitrust laws has not ended. The primary difficulty in discerning the scope of these limitations is the "rather convoluted language" of the statute.[41] It provides as follows:

> [The Sherman Act] shall not apply to conduct involving trade or commerce (other than import trade or import commerce) with foreign nations unless—
>
> (1) such conduct has a direct, substantial and reasonably foreseeable effect—
>
> (A) on trade or commerce which is not trade or commerce with foreign nations, or on import trade or import commerce with foreign nations; or
>
> (B) on export trade or export commerce with foreign nations, of a person engaged in such trade or commerce in the United States; and
>
> (2) such effect gives rise to a claim under the provisions of the [Sherman Act], other than this section.[42]

Now, to try to parse this statutory monstrosity, what is the effect of the enactment of the FTAIA on the application of the Sherman Act to extraterritorial behavior?

First, what is clear: the FTAIA seeks to identify situations to which the American antitrust laws are or are not inapplicable. The "other than import trade or import commerce" language, inserted parenthetically in the initial portion of the Act, sets forth the one straightforward exception to the FTAIA. This phrase makes clear that the FTAIA does not apply to, and thus the Sherman Act is fully applicable to, importation activities.[43]

What about other "foreign commerce"?[44] Does the FTAIA limit the application of the Sherman Act to exports from the United States? Does it bar antitrust claims for activities that neither originate in nor terminate in the United States? What different treatment is there for activities involving goods or commodities, as compared to services, financial transactions, and the like? The balance of this chapter seeks to answer these questions and, more importantly, to criticize some of the answers that some courts have given.

III. Current Uncertainty

The Supreme Court has not been particularly helpful in resolving these interpretive questions. *Hartford Fire*[45] was the first post-FTAIA case to address the extraterritorial reach of the antitrust laws. Although that case was decided more than a decade after the enactment of the FTAIA, Justice Souter's opinion there only made passing reference to that statute.[46] Indeed, the Court expressed doubt, without any further explanation, about whether FTAIA even applied to the case.[47] The *Hartford Fire* Court also expressed uncertainty, without feeling a need to resolve the question, "whether the Act's 'direct, substantial, and reasonably foreseeable effect' standard amends existing law or merely codifies it."[48] And on a key issue that divided the majority and the dissent that was authored by Justice Scalia—the extent to which the doctrine of *comity* would counsel an American court to decline to exercise jurisdiction over the foreign defendants—Justice Souter once again found no guidance from the FTAIA.[49]

By contrast, *Empagran* addressed one of the important interpretative issues under the FTAIA: does the Sherman Act continue to apply when the defendant's activity under attack involves "(1) significant foreign anticompetitive conduct with (2) an adverse domestic effect and (3) an independent foreign effect giving rise to the claim?"[50] The Court in *Empagran* began by restating the second "exception" to the FTAIA, in addition to the "import trade or import commerce" exception. The Sherman Act continues to apply where the commerce in question has a "direct, substantial, and reasonably foreseeable effect" on domestic commerce and where that effect gives rise to a Sherman Act claim.[51]

Empagran's restatement of this statutory language does provide a few clear rules. The antitrust laws do not apply to anticompetitive activities where the harm is felt solely outside the United States.[52] Thus, it does not apply either to "export activities" or to "other commercial activities taking place abroad, *unless* those activities adversely affect domestic commerce, imports to the United States, or exporting activities of one engaged in such activities within the United States."[53] But the imprecision of the extent of the second exception—the "unless" clause—still leaves numerous unanswered questions.

Empagran involved an alleged worldwide conspiracy to fix the prices of vitamins. Some of the manufacturers and distributors were American, and some were foreign. Some of the purchasers affected by the price-fixing cartel were American, and some were foreign. But the focus of this appeal was on foreign purchasers who did not purchase any vitamins in the United States.[54] Critically, the Court accepted the lower courts' assumption[55] that the "foreign effect"—that is, the higher prices paid by the foreign plaintiffs—was *independent of* any domestic effect, meaning the higher prices paid by American purchasers.[56]

The Court identified two reasons for finding the Sherman Act inapplicable to the foreign purchasers' claims: history and comity. The FTAIA sought to clarify and limit the extraterritorial scope of the antitrust laws. But it certainly did not seek to expand their reach. The prevailing state of the law in 1982 would have foreclosed the assertion of that kind of antitrust claim.[57]

Considerations of comity were even more important. There is a strong presumption that federal statutes are to be construed to avoid interference with the sovereign interests of other nations.[58] That presumption may be overcome when the foreign activity impacts American consumers and other domestic interests. But in light of the assumption that here the foreign harm was independent of any domestic impact, coupled with recognition of the superior interests of other countries[59] and the extent to which imposition of liability and remedies would be inconsistent with their legal norms, the Sherman Act does not extend to those claims.[60]

All well and good—if there truly was no domestic harm from the defendant's behavior. There must be some "domestic effect" of the antitrust violation to avoid the bar of FTAIA. The United States might view the defendants' behavior as highly problematic, but America has at most only an altruistic interest in having its antitrust statutes apply to all anticompetitive behavior everywhere in the world, while other countries have real interests at stake.

However, in the Supreme Court, the plaintiffs also challenged the assumption that the behavior truly was "independent." Rather, they asserted that even the portion of the price-fixing conspiracy addressed at foreign purchasers did harm American interests. The Court remanded on this point to allow a determination of the relationship between those harms and, if so, whether this would fall within the second exception to FTAIA.

Since *Empagran*, lower courts have considered a variety of interpretative questions under the FTAIA. One is the question that was left for consideration on remand: whether there is the requisite domestic harm if the sellers could not have maintained their international price-fixing arrangement "but for" some adverse domestic effect.

Regrettably, several courts have rejected that assertion. Application of the American antitrust laws is withheld, even where the foreign conduct results in a spillover effect in the United States and when U.S. consumers are harmed by the extraterritorial behavior. The result has been to deny fuller protection to *American consumers* from antitrust violations that take place on a worldwide basis.

The most notable decision to reject the "but for" argument was the D.C. Circuit's opinion on remand in *Empagran*.[61] The plaintiffs contended that in the challenged worldwide price-fixing conspiracy, involving products that were fungible, the defendants were only able to maintain their super-competitive prices outside the United States by inflating prices in the United States as well. Otherwise, domestic purchasers would have been able to act as arbitrageur-exporters, underselling the cartel's elevated foreign prices.[62] Thus, there was a domestic effect.

The court of appeals recognized that the plaintiffs had painted a "plausible scenario under which maintaining super-competitive prices in the United States might well have been a 'but for' cause of the [plaintiffs'] injury."[63] But the court held that this was not enough. The court insisted on a showing of a "direct causal relationship" to the domestic injury—in other words, a showing of "proximate causation." Echoing the Supreme Court's concerns for so-called "prescriptive comity,"[64] the D.C. Circuit insisted that "a more flexible, less direct standard than proximate causation would open the door to just such interference with other nations' prerogative to safeguard their own citizens from anticompetitive activity within their own borders."[65]

Subsequently, a number of other courts have likewise held that a "but for" relationship is insufficient to bring the conduct within the exception to the FTAIA for foreign activities that have a domestic effect. Like the D.C. Circuit in *Empagran*, they have insisted that the FTAIA bars an antitrust claim unless the domestic harm is the "direct" result of the foreign behavior.[66]

This narrow approach to the FTAIA's exception for behavior causing adverse domestic effects is unreasonably constrained and short-sighted. It effectively ignores the very real injury—the spillover effect—that Americans incur from this behavior. It constrains the ability of the United States to deter anticompetitive behavior, and this result is hardly dictated by the language of the Act.

The *Empagran* Court had indeed relied on comity to support its result. But it emphasized that this comity—which is analogous to the balancing of interests undertaken in a conflicts of law analysis—was particularly appropriate when there was no domestic harm from the behavior in question.[67] But here, where the D.C. Circuit accepted the assertion that the defendants' behavior necessarily had a domestic impact, even if one that was arguably only "indirect," the comity analysis differs substantially. Under those circumstances, an American court should be far less reluctant to apply American law to protect American interests.

Another group of decisions is even more problematic. In these cases, although the alleged anticompetitive behavior occurred outside the United States, harm undoubtedly was inflicted on American consumers. Indeed, in several of those cases, at least some portions of the transaction itself occurred in the United States. Nonetheless, in these cases, courts have concluded that FTAIA still bars an antitrust action.

The *Minn-Chem* decision by a three-judge panel of the Seventh Circuit—which was properly overturned by that court in an en banc decision—is the most recent and most prominent illustration of the serious judicial misreadings given to FTAIA.[68] Had that original decision not been set aside, it would have been yet one more instance of the serious erosion of protection against anticompetitive behavior that antitrust laws can and should afford to American consumers.

The plaintiffs complained of a broad price-fixing conspiracy in the potash market. The defendants were non-American companies engaged in mining potash, which is a mineral primarily used as an agricultural fertilizer in Canada, Russia, and Belarus. Together, the defendants accounted for over two-thirds of the world's potash supply.[69] The plaintiffs represented classes of American purchasers of potash who imported potash, both directly and indirectly, into the United States.

The complaint alleged that the defendants had conspired to set the sales prices and output levels of potash in China, Brazil, and India; that those prices served as "benchmarks" for American potash prices; and that this behavior resulted in the higher prices they paid for potash in the United States. Yet, remarkably, the original Seventh Circuit panel held that these claims were barred by the FTAIA. First, it concluded that "it is not enough that the defendants are engaged in the U.S. import market."[70] Rather, it held that FTAIA's "import commerce" provision[71] applies only "*if* the overseas anticompetitive conduct actually 'involves' the U.S. import market."[72] In its view, this in turn required that the specific conduct, here the agreement to fix prices, must "target" U.S. import goods.[73]

Then, in the panel's view, it was not enough that the plaintiffs alleged that the prices they paid were elevated and that this was the known and intended result of the defendants' behavior.[74] Rather, the plaintiffs had to plead facts, showing that the effect on the domestic potash industry was the "direct, substantial, and reasonably foreseeable" result of the foreign anticompetitive activity. The allegations in the complaint about the relationship between the price increases and output restrictions in China, Brazil, and India and the sharply elevated prices the plaintiffs paid in the United States were dismissed as conclusory or inadequate.

In part, the defendant-oriented tilt reflected in that decision is yet another illustration of the serious mischief wrought by *Twombly* and its progeny. The insistence on detailed allegations of fact makes it far more difficult for plaintiffs who have not yet had the benefit of any pretrial discovery to state a claim that will satisfy these elevated standards of Federal Rule 8.[75] However, that decision was also reflective of the substantive shift away from vigorous enforcement of the antitrust laws and toward greater permissiveness of defendants' anticompetitive behavior, described at the outset of this chapter. But the expansion of FTAIA in a situation like the one presented by *Minn-Chem* would have had a particularly invidious result. Nonsensically, the court exempted Canadian, Russian, and Belarus producers from antitrust scrutiny, even when their conduct harmed American importers, American farmers, and American consumers.

In a notable contrast, the en banc panel refused to permit the defendants to invoke FTAIA as a shield from potential antitrust liability. As to some of the charged conduct, the result was straightforward. Some of the allegedly inflated prices were for large quantities of potash shipped directly to the United States. These transactions were part of "import trade" and thus were clearly outside of the FTAIA's coverage.[76] Rejecting any suggestions of "targeting,"[77] the court succinctly concluded that "transactions that are directly between the plaintiff purchasers and the defendant cartel members *are* the import commerce of the United States in this sector."[78]

Closer examination was required of some of the allegations regarding the defendants' global price-fixing conspiracy and the plaintiffs' contention that the elevated prices charged in the United States were the result of the defendants' use of prices set on foreign sales as a benchmark. Since arguably some of those transactions involved potash that was not imported directly into the United States, they were not part of "import trade" or "import commerce." Therefore, it became necessary to consider the requirement for an exception to FTAIA: that the foreign conduct have a "direct, substantial, and reasonably foreseeable effect" on domestic commerce. The latter two requirements were easily met; the trade involved ran into the billions of dollars, the price of potash rose 600 percent, and the defendants certainly could have foreseen that their price strategy would affect the prices paid by American consumers.[79]

But was the effect of this conduct "direct"? Here, the court rejected the more demanding standard suggested by the Ninth Circuit, which required that the domestic effect be the "immediate consequence" of the defendants' illegal conduct.[80] Instead, the Seventh Circuit correctly held that this element only required proof that the prohibited effect on domestic competition was the "proximate result" of the unlawful behavior.[81] And here, since the plaintiffs' complaint plausibly alleged the requisite domestic effect, it was error to dismiss the action.

This decision marks a healthy redirection of FTAIA's exclusion of actions challenging foreign behavior, even when it does not directly involve import commerce. The antitrust laws still apply when that behavior impacts domestic commerce and harms domestic consumers. And despite fears of potential over-application of the Sherman Act, plaintiffs still have to meet the *Alcoa / Hartford Fire* standard for the extraterritorial application of the antitrust laws: "that the conduct of the foreign cartel members was (1) meant to produce and (2) did in fact produce some substantial effect in the United States."[82]

The expansive misinterpretation of the FTAIA's exclusions was properly corrected by the full Seventh Circuit. However, two slightly older decisions involving international air travel by Americans are good examples of the over-broad judicial interpretation of FTAIA. They also illuminate the theme of this book: instances of judicial miscalibration of the proper role that the state should play in protecting competition.

In *McLafferty*,[83] the plaintiff sought to represent a class of Americans who purchased tickets in the United States from several foreign airlines. She alleged that the defendants had engaged in a price-fixing conspiracy to elevate the fares for travel between Europe and Japan, including flights taken by the plaintiff. Yet, the court found that the alleged conspiracy did not have the requisite effect on domestic "commerce" to fall within the exception in the FTAIA. The court stated that its focus was on the "geographic target" of the conspiracy. Then, with little explanation for its conclusion, it asserted that "it is apparent that the conspiracy's target was Europe and Japan and passenger travel between the two."[84] In the court's view, the fact that the claim was by American plaintiffs for purchases made and paid for in the United States was, in the court's view, insufficient to overcome the FTAIA.

It should be obvious that this result seriously diminishes the protection that the antitrust laws are designed to extend to American consumers. Furthermore, this reading of FTAIA was not necessary to accomplish its goals, including whatever comity concerns are suggested by *Empagran*. It should hardly be offensive to foreign countries for the Sherman Act to extend to sales taking place in the United States, even for foreign air travel provided by foreign carriers. The opportunity afforded to the defendants to make sales in the United States and to profit from travel by American consumers should carry with it the obligation to adhere to the rules imposed by U.S. antitrust law.

Even more regrettable is another decision also involving alleged price-fixing by airlines—both American and foreign—flying international routes. Unlike *McLafferty*, where the flights neither originated nor terminated in the United States, in *In re Transpacific Air Transportation Antitrust Litigation*,[85] the plaintiffs complained of overcharges on flights from Asia to the United States.[86] Nonetheless, the court here too held that the claims were barred by FTAIA. It first gave a cramped interpretation to the "import trade" or import commerce" limitation in FTAIA, finding that unlike cargo, international air passengers were not the subject of "importation."[87] Putting aside the fact that the airlines presumably also transported the passengers' luggage,[88] this narrow definition of "import" is inconsistent with the evolving nature of international trade, which is increasingly characterized by the sale of services, intellectual property, or other intangibles across national borders and less by sales of traditional "goods."

The court also dismissed the second "exception" to FTAIA: for foreign conduct having an adverse domestic effect, where "such effect gives rise to the [antitrust] claim."[89] The court conceded that the defendants' overcharges resulted in the requisite effect on American consumers. Yet, it strangely found that the excessive fares those Americans paid to fly to the United States constituted a *foreign injury*—because the flights did not originate in the United States.[90] In doing so, the court rejected the obvious facts that the same planes that flew to the United States were returning to the Asian destinations; that the fares to and from the United States were similar and linked; and, perhaps most important, that the U.S.-based resources of these passengers was diminished by the price-fixing conspiracy.[91]

These instances of limiting protection under the antitrust laws for American consumers—and, ironically, expanding the range of immunity for foreign defendants for their behavior that harms those American consumers[92]—can hardly have been FTAIA's goal. To the contrary, they undermine the goals of the antitrust regime and the interests of the state in protecting its citizens.[93]

Unfortunately, but not surprisingly, these opinions engage merely in an elementary level of statutory interpretation. They leave unexamined the competing values that underlie the possible alternate interpretations. Arguably, the courts are seeking to protect the interests of American companies doing business abroad and of foreign companies that do business in the United States, with the unstated assumption that somehow this will result in a net benefit for the American economy. The judicial unwillingness to allow American consumers harmed by that behavior to sue for antitrust redress may be thought by these courts to be a necessary evil to protect those business entities.

Thankfully, the landscape is not totally bleak. In addition to the recent Seventh Circuit decision in *Minn-Chem*, there are a handful of other decisions that have recognized the broader reach of American antitrust laws, notwithstanding some of the limitations erected by the FTAIA.[94] These courts understand that vigorous application of the American antitrust laws is appropriate to deter and prevent anticompetitive behavior of both foreign and domestic companies, even for conduct undertaken solely outside the United States, to the extent that it results in a reduction in domestic consumer welfare. Regrettably, the majority of courts interpreting and applying FTAIA have been far too concerned about the interests of foreign (and domestic) commercial entities and the perceived interests of foreign countries, while they have been insufficiently attentive to the very real costs of anticompetitive behavior. A reexamination of the goals of the drafters of the FTAIA, as well as a reconsideration of the important role of competition law in promoting consumer welfare, should lead to a sounder balancing of these interests.

* * *

The Foreign Trade Antitrust Improvements Act of 1982 was intended to promote exports from the United States by shielding exporters from antitrust liability for harm to non-American consumers. But under FTAIA, the Sherman Act remains fully applicable to foreign behavior having an adverse effect on domestic commerce and import commerce. The Seventh Circuit's recent *Minn-Chem* decision recognizes the importance of continued application of the antitrust laws to this behavior.

Regrettably, too many other courts have given an unduly expansive reading to the carve-out from the reach of the antitrust to certain foreign behavior. Not only are these decisions inconsistent with the legislative purpose of FTAIA, but they also deny the competitive benefits that the antitrust laws are designed to confer on American consumers.

These cases are part of a larger trend, of the last 35 years, of cutting back on the protections afforded by the antitrust laws. As incorrect as those decisions may be, they may in part be explained by the countervailing concerns of undue burdens imposed on American companies supplying goods and services. But that explanation cannot be extended to conduct undertaken principally by *non-American* suppliers that adversely affect commerce in or to the United States and harming *American* consumers.

Thus, enough already! It is time either for the courts—including the Supreme Court—to correct this misdirection in the interpretation of FTAIA or for Congress to make the necessary statutory revisions to clarify how antitrust laws apply to *all* conduct, domestic and foreign, that harms competition in the United States.

Part III

Jurisdictional Experiences

Chapter 9

Competition Advocacy of the Korean Competition Authority

Dae-Sik Hong

Under the Monopoly Regulation and Fair Trade Act of Korea (MRFTA), the Korea Fair Trade Commission (KFTC) is the principal government agency entrusted with competition law enforcement. Among the KFTC's primary powers is the power to investigate unlawful business practices and issue administrative decisions. Under the MRFTA, unlawful practices include the abuse of dominance, cartels, and anticompetitive mergers, all of which limit competition mechanisms in a free market economy. "Competition Law" refers to the MRFTA provisions that regulate such anticompetitive business practices. When market competition is hindered by private anticompetitive business activity, the KFTC may play a role in protecting competition by enforcing competition law. It is thus a fundamental role for the KFTC to enforce competition law as a solution to market failures that appear in the form of monopolies and oligopolies.

However, market competition is not only deterred by private businesses, but it is also disrupted by public regulatory interventions, regulatory legislation, and other rule-makings. Public regulations differ from private business practices. Even when an existing public regulation may seem to oppose market competition, it is likely that the public regulation was introduced to address a different type of market failure that competition law does not adequately cover. What might be considered anticompetitive when done by private parties may be treated differently by the government when done through public restraints. Public restraints are more difficult for public authorities to understand and to rectify. Accordingly, in many cases it is difficult to legally assign blame to a private business practice that was affected by the central or local government regulations. Thus, as to public restraints and actions of businesses pertaining to such public restraints, there was a clear need for effective facilitation for market competition via means other than enforcement of competition law. The concept that arose in response to this need is "competition advocacy,"[1] which refers to the measures that are applied where an enforcement of competition law is deemed inappropriate. The Korean experience with competition advocacy, given the scope of power granted to the KFTC, provides a unique experiment for a broader set of advocacy powers for competition authorities worldwide.

In the context of its competition advocacy powers, the competition agency is not required to enforce measures pursuant to a specific requirement or to provide for specific remedies. Instead, the competition authority has, in the Korean case, the authority to implement a comprehensive competition policy. In this sense, the agency's act of executing the task of competition advocacy falls under the concept of competition policy implementation that is broader than competition law enforcement. Although the KFTC has broad discretion in deciding the method and substance of the competition advocacy, the agency nevertheless is limited in that the successful implementation of such measures is contingent upon the specific public agency's willingness to cooperate because the KFTC cannot change such regulations on its own. On the one hand, because the KFTC technically has the authority to enforce competition law against anticompetitive practices, if a business practice proves to be anticompetitive, there is a risk of uncertainty because the business can be subject to law enforcement even if its practices had been in accordance with public regulations. Competition law enforcement thereby provides the central and local governments the incentives to cooperate with the KFTC. On the other hand, if competition advocacy is successful, and the anticompetitive public regulation in question is relaxed or eliminated, there is the obvious benefit of creating a competitive market in which the interests and autonomy of businesses are well protected. Thus, successful competition advocacy results in the expansion of the areas where competition law may eventually apply in the future. Hence, competition law enforcement and competition advocacy are not mutually exclusive but rather are mutually reinforcing.[2]

The KFTC's use of competition advocacy has been a domestic development. There was no real exposure to the global community of the role in competition advocacy in other jurisdictions, nor was there any serious academic research done by the local competition community regarding the application of competition advocacy, except for the KFTC's own promotional publications.[3] Given that the application of competition law and competition advocacy both have significant roles in the realm of competition policy, the failure to thoroughly analyze this issue has led to a biased view of competition advocacy in which only the strengths and successes of the system are exposed to the public. There needs to be a more systematic review and critique of the practice of competition advocacy in South Korea to establish an objective view of the system.

Against this background, this chapter provides an overview of the substance and the application of the competition advocacy and presents a more objective view on the competition advocacy system. Section I analyzes the institutional framework from which the competition advocacy stems. Sections II and III provide an overview of the KFTC's activity in the context of the relationship between competition advocacy and competition law enforcement. Section IV objectively evaluates whether the role of competition advocacy is carried out for the rightful purpose within the given institutional framework. The chapter concludes by considering what seems to be the lesson for other jurisdictions and suggests that the KFTC must undertake competition advocacy in a manner appropriate for promoting a pro-competitive environment.

I. Overview of Competition Advocacy in Korea: Institutional Frameworks and Its Constituents

Article 36 of the MRFTA provides that "matters related to competition promotion policies through the consultation and coordination of legislation and administrative measures that restrict competition" are under the KFTC's jurisdiction along with matters related to the enforcement of the competition law. This provision establishes the legal basis for the KFTC's authority with respect to competition advocacy. A plain reading of the text suggests that the KFTC's method of competition advocacy is technically without any legal restriction. However, this provision itself does not ensure the KFTC's participation in legislative regulation, other rule-makings, and their enforcement procedures because there is an information asymmetry. Without knowledge of the proposed regulation, the KFTC cannot act in a timely manner. For the KFTC to act quickly, there needs to be well-organized coordination with other regulatory bodies. Therefore, a prerequisite to an efficient competition advocacy is that the KFTC receive adequate information regarding such regulatory governmental activities in a timely manner.

To promote this cooperation and coordination, Korea's competition law provides a system that allows the KFTC to participate in the public agencies' legislative and regulatory procedures. The competition law mandates that public agencies must provide the KFTC with information regarding the issues that require consultation, a broad range of circumstances where the consultation is mandatory for public agency must be presented, and the KFTC's opinions must be incorporated into legislative and regulatory procedures.

First, Article 63 of the MRFTA imposes obligations on the chief officer of the competent administrative authority to consult or to give prior notice when proposing an administrative legislation or amending enactments that contain anticompetitive regulations. This is called the Prior Statutory Consultation System. According to Article 63, the chief officer of the competent administrative authority has the obligation to consult with the KFTC when planning to enact or amend an anticompetitive statutory law or give approval and other measures involving anticompetitive effect. In addition, although the chief officer of the competent administrative authority has a lesser obligation with regard to the consultation and the service of prior notice to the KFTC when (re)amending other anticompetitive administrative regulations, the KFTC still has the authority to provide opinions requesting modification of such regulations. Although a strict reading of the MRFTA may suggest a differing degree of authority between the KFTC's authority to consult and its authority to voice its opinion, the two authorities are essentially the same in practice, since even when the KFTC has the authority to consult, the role of the KFTC here would still be to voice its opinion to the relevant agency.

Second, legislation in which the KFTC must be consulted includes all official and unofficial administrative legislation drafted by the government or competent administrative agencies[4] as long as the proposed regulation affects factors restricting competition. Consequently, there is a need to define what such factors are and to determine which acts constitute factors that grant the KFTC the authority to step in. While the law provides some examples of actions that qualify as factors that suppress competition, such as restrictions on the setting of prices, conditions on transactions, entry or business activities, and unlawful concerted acts, it does not provide a clear definition of these factors. Nevertheless, the MRFTA does define "practices substantially restricting competition" as "practices that affect or are likely to affect the determination of price, quantity, quality, or other trading terms or conditions by intent of a certain enterprise or an association of enterprises, because of reduced competition in a particular business area" (Article 2(8-2)). We can thus infer the meaning and the scope of "factors restricting competition."

The factors can be categorized into two situations. The first are cases in which, by law or regulation, the government has the express or indirect power to influence such competitive factors as price, quantity, quality, and so on. The second are cases in which the government grants a certain enterprise or an association of enterprises the power to directly or potentially influence those competitive factors.

The KFTC also has arranged an internal standard[5] to increase its efficiency in the consultation process for the proposed regulation. Under this standard, the factors are those that may have a negative effect on a degree of market competition, such as those that reduce or are likely to reduce the number of competitors (including potential competitors). The standard provides the following as categories of competition restricting factors: (a) cases that limit the number or range of suppliers, (b) cases that limit the ability of suppliers to compete, (c) cases that hinder the incentive of suppliers to compete, and (d) cases that limit the choices and information available to consumers.[6]

Third, regardless of whether the KFTC responds to a prior consultation request or provides an opinion in response to prior notice, the KFTC has on its own motion the power to opine on the enactment or amendment of statutory laws and regulations that have anticompetitive elements. Because this kind of opinion only has the legal force of a recommendation and has no binding effect, the competent administrative authority can use it as a reference, and the KFTC cannot require the agency to make modifications to reflect its recommendations. However, statistically, a substantial number of the KFTC's opinions have had an impact on the adoption of the final regulation. For instance, from 1991, the year the KFTC started offering advocacy opinions, to 2003, the KFTC conducted prior consultations 4,396 times with different competent administrative authorities. The KFTC offered 850 opinions, 633 of which were implemented (a 74 percent implementation rate).[7] There has been an upward implementation trend ever since. The KFTC's consultations with the agencies gradually have increased from 483 in 2001 to 1,178 in 2010. In 2010, the KFTC offered 56 correction recommendations, 43 of which were implemented (76.8 percent reflection rate).[8]

Since 1995, the increase in the implementation rate has been more substantial. This may reflect the increase in status of the KFTC within the central government. In terms of institutional structure, prior to 1995, the KFTC was a nonindependent agency within another competent administrative authority. In 1995, it became an independent central administrative authority, and in 1996, the KFTC's chairman was promoted to the level of minister.[9] Also, the chairman, although not a member of the State Council,[10] may attend the Council and take the floor.[11]

In practice, the chairman has participated actively in debates over important anticompetitive policy. Because enactment or amendment of statutory laws is the deliberation matter in the State Council, the chairman can have an impact on the deliberation by giving a different perspective.[12] This institutional arrangement provides a stronger platform to become directly involved in decisions made by other ministries and to participate more actively in decisions about responses to economic crisis conditions.[13]

Because the MRFTA provides the KFTC with comprehensive authority to opine on regulatory and legislative procedures relating to restrictions on competition, in theory, there is no reason for the KFTC to get involved on its own motion. However, even if the competent administrative authority violates its duty to consult or give prior notice to the KFTC, there is no de facto ramification on the effectiveness of the legislation, which follows that any administrative authority that feels pressured by the evaluation of the KFTC may be inclined to avoid the duty. Also, the administrative authority may not recognize that the legislation has some elements of restrictions on competition, so the authority may neglect its duty. Because a legislative bill or draft enforcement ordinance submitted by the government undergoes deliberation at the vice ministry conference or the State Council, it reduces the information asymmetry that the KFTC experiences in situations where the administrative authority does not make a prior consultation request to the KFTC. However, in cases in which measures are not subject to intragovernment deliberation, it is hard for the KFTC to collect relevant information. To remedy this situation, the law authorizes the KFTC, when the competent administrative authority enacts or amends the legislation, to see whether the legislation has the effect of restricting competition via its own motion and, if so, to offer its opinion ex post. But because the authorization only applies to the enactment or amendment of legislation, if the legislation that has some restrictions on competition is already in force or there is no concrete evidence that it adversely affects competition, it is hard for the KFTC to react to these circumstances. In this case, it is necessary for the KFTC to perform competition advocacy.

The MRFTA imposes a duty on the KFTC to establish and implement action plans to promote competition in markets where monopolies or oligopolies have existed for an extended period of time and authorizes the KFTC to offer the heads of the competent administrative authority an opinion on the matters related to the improvement of market structures, including the introduction of competition in the market.[14] The authorization is the foundation for the KFTC's ability to recommend on its own initiative corrective measures for administrative practices that restrict competition.

Since the 1980s, the government has tried to minimize or eliminate, based on a self-limitation approach, the adverse welfare effects of regulations adopted by establishing special committees within the central government and, more specifically, economic development strategy departments. However, due to the problem of neutrality and independence, the role was gradually transferred to the KFTC from April 1997 to March 1998. After the Framework Act on Administrative Regulation (FAAR) went into effect in March 1998, a new committee, the Regulatory Reform Committee, was formed and was granted the power of regulatory impact assessment. The KFTC is ex officio a member of the Regulatory Reform Committee.

The Regulatory Reform Committee not only examines the central government's draft bills or the local governments' draft municipal ordinances/rules that either impose duties on or limit the rights of Korean nationals (and if necessary recommends improvements), but it also studies whether repeal or improvement of these rules is necessary with regard to the legislation already enacted (and, if necessary, recommends improvements). Accordingly, the KFTC's participation in the committee as an ex officio member plays a complementary role to its own competition advocacy task.

The KFTC's competition advocacy through participation in the Regulatory Reform Committee takes the form of internal deliberation. Because of the informal nature of the KFTC's power on the Committee, the KFTC may perform a Competition Impact Assessment as a part of the Regulatory Impact Analysis (RIA).[15] Korea accepted OECD's recommendation to implement an RIA, and the system was enacted into law in 2008. Korea was the first regime in which all administrative departments are statutorily required to create RIA reports about any regulation that will be introduced or strengthened. These reports must undergo strict review of the Committee.[16]

One of the considerations in creating an RIA report is whether to include a discussion of the restrictions on competition.[17] The KFTC receives the RIA report from the chief of the competent administrative authority and performs the Competition Impact Assessment. Because the RIA is designed to undertake a cost-benefit analysis, the inclusion of the Competition Impact Assessment as part of the RIA enables market-oriented assessment and analysis to be performed in the broader context of the RIA.[18] To assist in the RIA process, the KFTC released its *Competition Impact Assessment Manual* in July 2007 that was modeled on the OECD Competition Assessment Toolkit[19] adapted to the Korean context. The manual offers procedures, divisions of labor among authorities, and assessment methodologies of the Competition Impact Assessment.

The KFTC entrusted its regulatory reform responsibilities to its task force of the Competition Restriction Regulation Reform. The task force is responsible for the Competition Impact Assessment. In 2009, the first year of the implementation of the Competition Impact Assessment, the KFTC conducted 330 assessments and proposed alternatives to 35 legislative bills related to restrictions on competition. In 2010, the KFTC conducted 277 assessments and identified problems and proposed alternatives to 36 legislative bills related to restrictions on competition. In addition, the KFTC has presented its Competition Impact Assessment System and its case studies before the Competition Committee of the OECD, and its manual in an English version was made available to other agencies via OECD's Committee Information Service website.[20]

II. Competition Advocacy Complementing Competition Law Enforcement

The area in which competition advocacy was originally needed was where competition law enforcement was not possible because of the public nature of the restraint. In this area, competition advocacy supplements competition law enforcement by attempting to improve the institutional elements that lead to limited competition. The KFTC's competition advocacy activities can be divided into three time periods.

A. Quickening Period of Competition Advocacy: 1991–2000

During this period, the KFTC was not active in competition law enforcement and relied more on competition advocacy to foster competition. The KFTC began its competition advocacy activities in 1991, which was in line with the central government's efforts at deregulation at the time. In 1990, the Korean government established an administrative deregulation committee and two working committees under it.[21] The KFTC was responsible for economic deregulation at the working level.

As noted earlier, the KFTC began to function as an independent central administrative agency in 1995 with policy-making capabilities, along with its chairman being recognized as a minister-level appointee in 1996. Consequently, the status of the KFTC rose rapidly, and it gained more legal power and greater implementation ability to effectively perform competition advocacy. For example, the MRFTA was amended to specify the content of the prior statutory consultation system and to give a legal basis for authority to establish and implement action plans to counter monopolistic or oligopolistic market structures and offer recommendations to the relevant administrative bodies.

Additionally, the KFTC has been an integral part of the public sector reform since the Asian financial crisis at the end of 1997.[22] The reform centered on privatization of public enterprises and management innovation programs. To accomplish this, the KFTC internally formed a privatization task force and used it to provide its opinions in advocating competition for public enterprises. The results were reported via the Public Enterprise Privatization Promotion Committee set up across all governmental organizations.

During this period, the biggest achievement in competition advocacy was the enactment in February 1999 of the Omnibus Cartel Repeal Act. The Act abolished 20 different forms of statutory cartels.[23] For example, statutory cartels that allowed business associations of lawyers, accountants, and seven other professional groups to set fees that required prior approval from supervisory government offices were eliminated. Moreover, improvements were made to the means by which the rate and charge of insurance were set. Prior to the enactment of the aforementioned law, standardized calculation method of the rate and charge of insurance was used and administered by the insurance development institute, which was essentially a conglomerate of different insurance companies.

B. Active Competition Advocacy Connected with Competition Law Enforcement: 2001–2005

During this period, competition law enforcement flourished and the KFTC started to implement competition advocacy in line with enforcement. The revision of the MRFTA in February 1999 granted the KFTC the power to carry out investigation of market structures and publish the results of the analysis. Competition advocacy could be thereby carried out based on empirical studies of individual markets and industries. However, it was not until 2008 that market studies under this authority began on a regular basis.

Using the results of the industry-based research completed since 1999, the KFTC began to push ahead with the Clean Market Project (CMP) annually, in which it selected 3 to 6 fields in which markets were monopolistic or oligopolistic and likely to cause harm to competition. The KFTC would suggest measures to mitigate the anticompetitive effect in these selected industries.[24]

The CMP allowed for systematic changes in a given industry and suggested both behavioral and structural improvements to address anticompetitive practices.[25] The KFTC selected markets that are closely associated with ordinary lives of Korean citizens and prepared overall status analyses and measures. The CMP began with 6 fields, including private education, mobile telecommunications, and medicine/pharmaceuticals. The CMP expanded to 33 fields by 2005.

C. Competition Advocacy Activity Interacting with Competition Law Enforcement: 2006–Present

The KFTC has begun to undertake market studies from 2008.[26] These studies have a different significance from the CMP in the way they focus on the industry-specific market. The studies are based on the Mining and Manufacturing Statistical Survey by the National Statistical Office. Accordingly, the KFTC annually produces a *Market Structure Studies Report* carried out by the Korea Development Institute in association with the KFTC. The market study helps the KFTC analyze the fundamental sources of market distortions and develop measures to counteract these elements. The KFTC also publishes a competition policy report for each main industry analyzed in the market study. The competition policy report publication began with air transport and Internet portal industries in 2008 and expanded to indemnity insurance, movies, petroleum, and pharmaceuticals in 2009. In 2010, the gas and alcoholic beverages industry reports were also published. However, none of these reports have been updated yet.

In 2009, the KFTC embarked upon a project to improve entry regulations.[27] This project is based on the recognition that if Korea is to become a truly advanced market economy, it must urgently overhaul various entry regulations to shift its economy to a more pro-competitive structure. After open forums and informal gatherings for discussion, the KFTC selected 26 tasks in sectors with public monopolies or deep-rooted private monopolies during the first stage, 20 tasks (including easing entry regulations for service sectors and liberalizing monopolistic public sectors to private operators) during the second stage, and 19 tasks (such as in health care, culture, and tourism) during the third stage.

III. Competition Advocacy Fostered by Competition Law Enforcement

Competition law enforcement was weak until the mid-1990s. The defining moment of change was when Korea received bailout funds from the IMF at the end of 1997. Starting with meeting IMF's bailout conditions, government policies began to center on promoting a sound market economy. Consequently, the demand for competition law enforcement increased.[28] Specifically, KFTC enforcement has expanded in cartels, merger control, and unilateral conduct.

Competition law enforcement in Korea targets business activities that are not under or closely related to public regulation. Therefore, competition law assumes a market-based system. But during the period in which government-led growth was the dominant Korean economic policy, regulatory interventions were permitted even in industries that did not present market failures[29] as justification for intervention (such as those industries producing public goods or with a natural monopoly). Consequently, it was difficult for the KFTC to promote competition in such industries and sectors. These difficulties were largely mitigated through the government's efforts to reform existing policies that did not comply with a free market, such as entry restrictions, price controls, and sale restrictions in industries that had a large impact on the economy.[30] As the reforms have lifted restrictions that interfered with autonomous business decisions, businesses were left with a greater room for doing business, and consequently the scope of enforcement also expanded.

But despite no explicit regulation, administrative agencies continued to interfere with autonomous decisions through measures such as administrative guidance, and businesses frequently remained within the traditional anticompetitive boundaries rather than exerting their newly earned freedom.

Regulations such as price controls and sales restrictions in effect promoted or condoned cartels. Through the government's regulatory reform and the KFTC's competition advocacy, these restrictions were either repealed or relaxed. Such actions not only helped businesses operate within a market system but also increased the awareness of the customary restrictions to competition for other noncompetition agency officials. However, agency officials were reluctant to change their customary way of operation, which consisted of implementing policies that determine the number of licenses, size, prices, and quantities of products of an industry; businesses also remained accustomed to doing business through the existing system. To continue to implement conventional anticompetitive policies, officials took unofficial measures—namely, "administrative guidance."[31]

Although administrative guidance works under a legal basis, the specific prerequisites and workings of the system are not necessarily prescribed in the law. Also, administrative guidance has no coercive force and requires voluntary consent for it to take effect, as opposed to administrative measures.[32]

Administrative guidance occurred frequently in fields such as broadcasting, telecommunications, energy, insurance, and finance, where administrative agencies intervened for industrial policy purposes prior to liberalization. In such sectors, government offices used administrative guidance as an unofficial means of intervening and artificially controlling the market once they determined that the market was not operating as they desired. For example, a regulatory agency would determine the maximum limit of a price increase for a certain field or instruct firms how to manage by agreement among themselves. Behind the private anticompetitive agreement, there was administrative guidance from a regulatory government agency. Therefore, determining whether and to what extent competition law would be applied to these kinds of situations was a challenge.

The KFTC has ruled that concerted anticompetitive acts, even if the cause of which was compliance with an administrative guidance, were unlawful in principle and strictly enforced competition law against them, except for acts that complied with a guidance with a clearly lawful basis.[33] The point of the KFTC policy is twofold. First, acts that comply with an administrative guidance that has no clear legal basis are not exempted from sanctions under the MRFTA. Second, even if an act was performed pursuant to an administrative guidance, the administrative guidance does not justify the fact that it was a concerted act, nor does it serve as a standard with which to determine whether it was a concerted act.

With regard to the first point, courts agreed with the KFTC by strictly construing the requirements of Article 58 of the MRFTA. Article 58 exempts from the application "acts of an enterprise or an association of enterprises as committed in accordance with any Act or any of its decrees." By setting a strict limit for the exemption, courts made the exemption applicable only in situations when there was a justifiable reason for limiting competition law enforcement.[34] According to precedents, enterprises that are subject to the Act or its decrees are required to be "regulated by a high level of public regulation if either it would be rational to restrict competition because of the special nature of the industry or the business has been guaranteed a monopolistic position through official approval," while the contents of the Act or its decrees require that "there be recognition of definite exceptions to free competition." Thus, the content of regulations designed to be applied toward justifiable industries, and especially regulations designed to substitute competition that may not be justifiable when applied to certain industries, must be definite and clear, since otherwise it is difficult to satisfy the requirements of this provision. Additionally, even if the business performs an action that satisfies the requirements above, the law requires that it be the minimally necessary action only within the scope allowed by the law. This type of interpretation of precedents seems to have been influenced by the implied exemption principle present in the United States.[35] For example, the Korean Telecommunications Business Act gives the sector regulator the authority to set standards for the terms, procedures, methods, and prices of interconnections of telecommunications facilities through notices,[36] but it cannot be seen as a definite example of an exception to free competition.[37] Thus, even if the sector regulator provided rules regarding burdensome interconnection rates, adhering to these rules would not necessarily mean that their actions would be legally justifiable.[38] Furthermore, the Broadcasting Act gives the broadcasting regulator the authority to accept notification of standard terms of contract from businesses, approve user fees, and mandate the change of terms of contract,[39] but it does not involve a direct, case-by case decision on user fees and thus cannot be seen as a law that recognizes an exception to free competition.[40]

In relation to the second point, the KFTC is not greatly concerned about the influence of administrative guidance when determining whether some behavior amounts to collusion, and it adheres to the view that an act is not justified even when it is recognized as involving the administrative guidance. However, if the administrative guidance is binding de facto and a company is found to be an agent of public behavior, the KFTC only considers these factors for the purposes of decreasing fines. In comparison, courts apply a more relaxed standard. Like the KFTC, the courts consider situations distinct from the administrative guidance that involves separate agreements recognized as collusive as evidence of collusion. However, in case the evidence is confined to mere communication or contact between the businesses and the contents of those communications have been determined to be details related to executing the standards in the administrative guidance, the Korean Supreme Court has held that no collusion existed, overturning the KFTC's decision.[41] Additionally, unlike the KFTC, which rarely finds justification for price-fixing cartels, the Korean Supreme Court has stated that a collusive agreement may be justified in the presence of a special circumstance and found that an instance of a concerted act that followed an administrative guidance based closely on the law was a special circumstance.[42]

Since administrative guidance often is not based on law and lacks enforcement provisions, the actions of administrative agencies based on such guidance are mostly not subject to the prior statutory consultation system regulated by the MRFTA. Still, administrative guidance drives businesses to act in a way that restricts competition and may violate the MRFTA. Neglecting administrative guidance could decrease the influence of competition advocacy. The likely hidden intention behind the KFTC's strict enforcement against concerted acts involving administrative guidance is to force businesses to take more responsibility for these actions as well as bring out the problems and need for reform in the actions of the underlying administrative agency.

In the telecommunications and financial industries, where collusion cases caused controversy over the involvement and validity of the administrative guidance, the KFTC entered into MOUs with the regulatory agencies to facilitate close collaboration to prevent anticompetitive behavior within the jurisdiction covered by the administrative guidance—territory that was not subject to the current system.[43] This is a case in which the territory of competition advocacy has been expanded beyond what has been provided for by the system through competition law enforcement.

IV. Implications and Challenges

The authority given to the KFTC under the MRFTA should not have the nature of narrowly defined regulation but carry the nature of law enforcement. Here, law enforcement implies deferring to self-regulating mechanisms in a market economy, while rectifying anticompetitive behaviors that interfere with those self-regulating mechanisms. That the regulation pursued by the KTFC differs from other types of regulation is also clearly demonstrated by its competition advocacy efforts. Law enforcement is usually implemented by monitoring possible unlawful activities and pursuing remedies targeted at businesses subject to the law. However, competition advocacy is undertaken by persuading other administrative agencies and the general public about the importance and benefits of competition.

The KFTC's competition advocacy has been regarded as a successful example of competition law in the international community of developing countries. Korea developed competition law at a stage before the full development of a free-market economic system. The exogenous shock of the Asian financial crisis in late 1997 resulted in the government's persistent effort to relax regulations, which aided broader competition policy and empowered the KFTC. Subsequently, the KFTC continued to expand its role in promoting competition and achieved significant success for a number of reasons.

First, the KFTC has the institutional means to carry out competition advocacy because it is an independent agency. Furthermore, the MRFTA grants the KFTC a right to prior statutory consultation and a right to submit comments on how to improve competition in situations of monopolistic or oligopolistic market structures. Those rights established the foundation of the KFTC's competition advocacy through participation in legislative procedure and rule-making. Additionally, the Competition Impact Assessment System was rapidly adopted and proved to be successful.

Second, competition advocacy through participation in legislation and rule-making has worked more effectively in Korea, where the executive branch has a right to propose legislation. Unlike in the United States, in Korea, the executive branch may introduce a legislative bill.[44] Thus, a substantial number of Korean statutes have been enacted on the basis of legislative bills introduced by the executive branch. In such cases, until the proposals are confirmed within the government, Prior Statutory Consultation pursuant to the MRFTA and Competition Impact Assessment as a part of the RIA pursuant to the FAAR must be performed. Therefore, the KFTC has a chance to detect and manage, in advance, a given legislative proposal that has anticompetitive effects. In practice, the KFTC's opinions during legislative procedures are highly appreciated. Therefore, in case of conflicts between the KFTC and a department over a piece of proposed legislation, the Prime Minister's Office or Regulatory Reform Committee in charge of mediation recommends the application of the KFTC's opinions. This has had a deterrent effect on other administrative departments, which have themselves relaxed competition-restrictive provisions in the process of proposing legislation.

Third, competition advocacy has expanded its territory as the KFTC has prioritized enforcement of competition law in fields where administrative guidance has considerable influence on businesses. The Prior Statutory Consultation System is intended for new or reinforcing legislation and does not cover official or unofficial activities of the relevant administrative agency that encourages competition-restrictive adaptation according to existing legislations. Especially in cases where the relevant administrative agency encourages businesses to commit competition-restraining acts with unofficial administrative guidance, determining whether the business is liable for such competition-restrictive acts and the legal standards with which to determine such issues can be very vague. The KFTC declared that even though administrative guidance was involved, such a competition-restrictive act violates the MRFTA, and it prioritized the enforcement of competition law. As a result, each industrial regulator could recognize the need for cooperation with the KFTC and improve the general practice of legislation through unofficial means. Accordingly, competition advocacy could expand its territory.

The KFTC's competition advocacy in Korea has received a positive evaluation internationally, as mentioned above. However, the objectives and the scope of the KFTC's competition policy have not been clearly established in practice. Also, because the KFTC has to work on policies besides competition policies, it is hard to make the promotion of competition policy consistent. In contrast, government agents pursuing competition policy are diversified, overlapping the KFTC's task. Thus, the KFTC's competition advocacy has faced a number of challenges.

First, the definition of "competition," which is a premise of the KFTC's competition advocacy, its objectives, and the scope of its competition advocacy powers have not been clearly established. In general, such definition and objectives appear in decisions where the KFTC gives reasons and grounds for violations with respect to enforcing the competition law. However, in the course of enforcing the law, the KFTC considers competition as an ideal model that is close to perfect competition. It acknowledges anticompetitiveness in the market as long as it finds the slightest causal relationship between the functions of competition that seeks static market equilibrium and the negative influences that follow its processes. A business model or strategic act, even though it might fall short of perfect competition, can bring consumer welfare enhancement and the enhancement of economic effectiveness, and be approved as effective competitive means reflecting market characteristics. But there is also the risk of unnecessary negative evaluation for such models and acts, and it has happened when the KFTC was applying provisions regulating the abuse of market dominance for a unilateral act on the part of a business.[45] In the case of cartels, fewer problems arise because courts accept the KFTC's decision on illegality relatively broadly. However, the line in deciding illegal concerted action is vague, which can be worrisome to businesses. The KFTC's recent competition advocacy has focused on providing the market with reform and change against business customs and practices that are considered anticompetitive in some way, and the law enforcement has facilitated such efforts by the KFTC. However, unless competition advocacy in association with the law enforcement reflects the market situations that are experienced in practice, its receptivity and reliability are not sufficiently guaranteed.

Second, the advent of sector specific regulatory institutions means that sector regulators contend with the KFTC for expertise in individual sectors. As a result, the KFTC now faces new challenges to its competition advocacy. For instance, the Korea Communications Commission (KCC) and the Ministry of Science, ICT and Future Planning,[46] which jointly regulate the telecommunications and broadcasting industries, have adopted ex ante regulatory measures to induce competition where competition is not self-initiated by the market. More interestingly, the KCC has also adopted ex post regulatory measures to ensure the effectiveness of its ex ante regulatory measures. The KCC uses these measures to evaluate a business practice on the basis of its restraints on competition or on the harm suffered by users or viewers. As such, these measures compete with competition law enforcement by the KFTC. These measures are emblematic of the KCC's conception of competition: the KCC views the competition process in the telecommunications and broadcasting industries as rather dynamic and interacting with government regulation. In contrast, the KFTC views competition and government regulation as inherently in conflict. Given the prevalence of the KCC's conception of competition and its approach to the relationship between government regulation and competition law enforcement support in the regulated industries, the KFTC's competition advocacy could lose support in regulated fields.

Third, the nature of the KFTC's competition advocacy has changed as the KFTC has come to serve an increasingly important role in recent executive branch policies such as promoting economic growth at all levels of society. This policy of so-called "shared growth" might be an attempt at a "balanced economic development," which is a goal explicitly provided for under Article 1 of the MRFTA. However, commentators have noted that the goal of "balanced economic development" cannot be easily defined in the context of market competition or be easily pursued in practice. Nevertheless, this goal has been actively pursued by the Korean executive branch through the shared growth policy. The most representative measure undertaken by the executive branch of the Korean government to implement the shared growth policy is the "Plan for Shared Growth between Conglomerates and Smaller Businesses," announced in September 2010. In concert, the KFTC set as its most urgent policy goal the improvement of the relationship between conglomerates and smaller businesses. The statutory mechanism through which the KFTC implements this policy goal is the Fair Subcontract Transactions Act (FSTA), which was amended in 2011.[47] The FSTA provides the KFTC with the authority to intervene with respect to unfair subcontracting terms and practices and to promote cooperation between conglomerates and smaller businesses in the interest of fair competition and shared growth. In short, to promote an economic policy with an unclear nexus to market competition, the Korean government has provided the KFTC with unofficial administrative authority as well as official enforcement authority. As a result, the KFTC's competition advocacy could come into conflict with policies pursued by the KFTC.

* * *

Until the KFTC's active involvement in competition advocacy, the Korean government pursued growth-fostering policies as a priority in the economic sphere, while permitting a broad range of regulatory interventions irrespective of any market failure. Against this backdrop, the KFTC, through its competition advocacy, has played a decisive role in promoting a pro-competitive environment by reducing regulatory interventions or at the very least requiring justifications for regulatory interventions.

The success of the KFTC's competition advocacy first manifested itself in industries where regulatory interventions by the Korean government were undertaken to meet industry needs but were not readily justified by market failure. These industries, including petrochemicals, steel, aviation, and automobiles, were mainly developed by government initiatives and as a result were essentially monopolistic or oligopolistic in nature. The success of the KFTC's competition advocacy in these industries was mainly due to two factors. First, it possessed legal/institutional means to participate in regulatory and legislative procedures as a government agency independent from other government agencies charged with implementing economic policies. Second, in the process of implementing regulatory reforms, the Korean government provided the KFTC with an important role and function. In industries such as finance, energy, and telecommunications where regulatory interventions were justified on grounds of market failure, the KFTC engaged in competition law enforcement as a matter of principle even where business activities were influenced by unofficial regulatory interventions such as administrative guidance. In these sectors, the KFTC expanded the reach of competition advocacy to regulatory interventions undertaken through unofficial means.

In developing and emerging countries, the market and its internal competition mechanisms are not yet in place. In these countries, the government plays a greater role as the creator or supporter of market competition rather than the enforcer of it. In the process, the government of a developing or emerging country tends to promote policies aimed at protecting or supporting competitors rather than promoting competition itself. Thus, in a developing or emerging country, even the adoption of the competition regime of an advanced country, including competition law and a competition agency, is unlikely to lead to the mutually complementary interaction between competition advocacy and competition law enforcement as long as the competition agency does not possess the legal means to play a leading role in market competition in its relationship with economic agencies charged with industrial policies. In that sense, Korea, which provides for the independence of the KFTC and its right to participate in the regulatory and legislative procedures, serves as a positive example for countries experiencing difficulties in promoting economic development.

For all foreign jurisdictions, the lesson to be gained from the KFTC's experience with competition advocacy concerns the importance of establishing a proper relationship between the competition agency and other government agencies charged with economic policies. Even if the KFTC further develops the statutory basis for regulatory interventions through competition advocacy, the legacy of sector-specific industrial policies remains. More specifically, agencies charged with the regulation of particular industries view monopolies/oligopolies created by their regulation as justified and seek to protect competitors within their regulatory purview. Because of the KFTC's competition advocacy, there have been fewer instances of new or heightened regulatory activities based on new legislation or regulations, so regulatory agencies have not been able to maximize their power. Consequently, sector-specific regulatory agencies in need of new regulatory powers have at times avoided collaboration with the KFTC by relying on legislation introduced by members of the Korean National Assembly because the KFTC does not have any institutional means of participating in the legislation process initiated by the members of the National Assembly. Such lack of collaboration on the part of sector-specific regulatory agencies arises at least in part from their less than complete trust in the KFTC. This problem cannot be resolved simply by the introduction of an institutional measure. Hence, it is ultimately in the KFTC's interest to differentiate itself from other regulatory agencies by clarifying the meaning of market competition in the context of its competition policies and by undertaking competition advocacy in a manner appropriate for promoting a pro-competitive environment.

Chapter 10

Competition and the State in China

Thomas K. Cheng

In China, the role of the state in markets is complicated. In capitalist economies, private ownership is more common, but in China, state-owned enterprises (SOEs) prevail. SOEs are not only found in sectors in which state presence has generally been accepted in other countries, such as utilities and natural monopoly industries, but they are also active in industries that are generally left to the private sector elsewhere, such as retail, restaurants, and tourism. SOEs are owned by all levels of government, from the central government to provincial and local governments. Given the prevalence of SOEs in the Chinese economy, it is imperative that the Chinese authorities make a concerted effort to ensure a level playing field between public and private enterprises and that competition law be enforced consistently. Enforcement of competition law against Chinese SOEs is not without controversy.

Until the recent investigation by the National Development and Reform Commission (NDRC), one of the Anti-Monopoly Law (AML) enforcers, into the major SOEs in the telecom sector, it was not at all clear that the AML applied to SOEs.[1] The ambiguous language of Article 7 of the AML can be interpreted as exempting SOEs from the AML. Even if the AML were established to apply in full to the SOEs, it is still very difficult for one part of the Chinese state to take enforcement action against another part of the state. This difficulty is compounded by the fact that China lacks an impartial third-party arbiter in disputes between different parts of the administrative state—an independent judiciary—to adjudicate such enforcement actions. Furthermore, a full application of the AML to the SOEs would still fall short of ensuring a level playing field between public and private firms. The AML does not regulate public subsidies or preferential access to credit offered by the state to SOEs, which tilts the playing field in favor of these enterprises.

The odds are further stacked against private enterprises in China due to a phenomenon known as "abuse of administrative monopoly." While the term is unique to China, the phenomenon is by no means unique to it, although it may be more common in China than elsewhere.[2] This refers to governments using administrative means to disrupt the competitive process by offering protection to or favoring certain market participants, often SOEs owned by that government body. Examples include application of discriminatory inspection standards, registration requirements, compulsory purchase of goods from designated sellers, or the most egregious of all, outright blockade of nonlocal goods. Abuse of administrative monopoly is widely acknowledged by Chinese scholars as the most serious competition problem in China.[3] Chapter 5 of the AML is devoted entirely to it. Enforcement efforts thus far, however, have been scant.

Despite the best intentions in enforcing the AML against anticompetitive conduct by SOEs and abuse of administrative monopoly, the relationship between the state and the markets will not be satisfactorily resolved until some deeper systemic issues are addressed. An appropriate calibration of the role of SOEs in the economy will not be attained until the Chinese state has determined a suitable role for itself in the economy. Are SOEs only to be deployed when there is market failure or when the provision of public goods is at issue? Or are SOEs to serve as an extension of the state to control the economy and the country? Moreover, SOEs and abuse of administrative monopoly are closely related to central-local relationships. It is a widely noted fact that provincial and local governments groom provincial and local champions because of regional rivalry among the provinces and the inadequacy of central government funding for local governments. Local governments thus rely on local SOEs for revenue to make up for the shortfall. To maximize the revenue that could be gained from their SOEs, local governments pursue abuse of administrative monopoly to protect their market share. This incentive to protect local enterprises will not be fully eradicated until fiscal reforms are introduced to address the local government revenue shortfall. In short, the role of the state in competition is not purely a competition law issue in China. As is to be expected given the pervasive presence of the state in Chinese society, the issue has broader political economy implications and cannot be satisfactorily resolved until these broader issues are addressed.

I. Competition Law and State-Owned Enterprises in China

One of the most prominent features of competition and the state in China is the prevalence of SOEs in the economy. When assessing the extent of state intervention in the economy, it is important to bear in mind that China began its journey from a different starting point from most Western capitalist economies. In the latter, the presumption is private ownership of property and productive resources. State ownership only steps in when justified by circumstances, such as market failure, natural monopoly, provision of public goods, performance of universal service obligations, and so forth. In stark contrast, the modern, post-reform Chinese economy began when state ownership was omnipresent. In 1978, when economic reform began, SOEs controlled 99.8 percent of the national economy.[4] What has followed since then has been a gradual reduction of state presence in the economy and reform and restructuring of SOEs. Despite more than 30 years of reform, however, SOEs have still maintained a strong presence in many sectors.

A. An Overview of State-Owned Enterprises in the Chinese Economy

When China began its "Open Door" policy in the late 1970s, it was very much a centrally planned economy with close to no private ownership of productive resources. SOEs dominated practically every sector of the economy. SOE reforms were conducted in conjunction with the liberalization of the price system, both of which proceeded in a gradualist manner. The first step in the reform process was a transition to the contract responsibility system, introduced in 1987, under which SOEs were obliged to submit a certain predetermined amount of their profit to the state.[5] The rest of the profit was to be kept by the SOEs. This system was put in place to provide incentives to SOEs to become more productive and focus more on profit and was quite successful.[6] Meanwhile, managers of SOEs were given greater autonomy to decide what, how much, and how to produce.

In the 1990s, the government accelerated the pace of reform. It actively pursued a policy that has come to be known as "grasping the large and letting go of the small."[7] Under this policy, the government focused on turning around large SOEs. Small SOEs were either merged with one another, merged into larger SOEs, or allowed to go bust. As a result, the number of

SOEs dropped, and so did their relevance in the economy. SOEs' share in industrial output fell from 78 percent in 1978 to 33 percent in 1996. Over the same period, SOE profit fell from accounting for 14 percent of GDP to almost zero by 1996. Between 1998 and 2010, SOEs' share in the total number of industrial enterprises fell from 39.2 percent to 4.5 percent, its share in total industrial assets from 68.8 percent to 42.4 percent, and its share in national employment from 60.5 percent to 19.4 percent.[8] Their share in China's exports dropped from 57 percent in 1997 to 15 percent in 2010.[9] These statistics show that although the absolute number of SOEs has declined, they have become larger and more capital intensive.

Over time, the government's SOE policy has taken on a sectoral focus. This approach has been described as a "backward and forward" approach by Chinese scholars.[10] It has moved forward in the sense that SOEs have exited certain industries, while private enterprises are encouraged to enter these industries and compete. These industries included electronics, chemicals and textiles.[11] Through several rounds of restructuring, the government dissolved the ministries that oversaw these industries and replaced them with industrial associations.[12] Between 2005 and 2009, SOEs retreated from 20 manufacturing industries that were characterized as generally competitive. It has moved backward in the sense that it has identified a number of strategic sectors over which the state would maintain tight control to the exclusion of private firms. These sectors would be dominated by enterprises directly owned by the state.

In 1999, the Fourth Plenary of the 15th Chinese Communist Party Central Committee identified four areas that SOEs must control: national security, natural monopoly, vital public services and pillar industries, and key high-tech industries. In 2006, the State-Owned Assets Supervision and Administration Commission (SASAC) issued the "Guidelines for Adjusting State Capital Structure and Deepening SOEs' Restructuring," which further defined natural monopoly as important infrastructure and natural resources. In 2006, a former director of the SASAC identified seven strategic sectors over which the state would maintain absolute control. These included defense, electric generation and distribution, petroleum and petrochemicals, telecom, coal, civil aviation, and waterway transport.[13] In these sectors, a number of SOEs compete with one another while being protected from new entry. Some of the firms in these sectors are groomed to be national champions, which are given privileged positions in the domestic market to allow them to grow to a sufficient size to be competitive internationally. Examples include the three dominant state-owned oil companies.

The government also designated as pillar industries machinery, automobiles, IT, construction, steel, base metals, and chemicals, where the state would maintain somewhat strong influence.[14] In these sectors, private participants could face a range of entry barriers or other constraints on operation and expansion. Basically, the Chinese government's current SOE policy consists of (1) dominate and expand in key industries affecting national security and the "commanding heights" of the national economy, (2) compete on equal footing with nonstate enterprises in competitive industries, (3) compete mainly among SOEs in natural monopoly industries such as telecom and electricity, and (4) serve as the main instrument of industrial policy: develop pillar industries such as steel and automobiles and create national champions to compete internationally.

In addition to policy changes, legal and institutional reforms were put in place in the 2000s to strengthen the governance of the SOEs. SASAC was formed in 2003 to serve as the controlling shareholder and the government's representative in managing SOEs. SASAC is a ministry under the State Council. It is an institution that represents the state, exercises the state's ownership rights and equity rights, and takes the obligations and responsibilities of the state. Somewhat confusing for the governance of SOEs, SASAC is both a regulator and a controlling shareholder of SOEs. It sends representatives to the SOEs' boards to the extent that there is one[15] and supervises the appointment of key personnel in SOEs in conjunction with other government ministries and the Communist Party. It has been described as the largest shareholder of the world. SOEs under SASAC control account for a significant share of the Chinese state sector. These SOEs accounted for 88.1 percent of the revenue, 84.1 percent of the profits, and 86.4 percent of the net assets of the nonfinancial SOEs nationwide. Legally, the Law of State-Owned Assets of Enterprises, which was ratified in October 2008 and came into effect in May 2009, formally recognizes SASAC as an investor—a shareholder of the SOEs with the ordinary rights and duties of a shareholder. However, in reality, the powers given to the SASAC under this law are greater than those of a shareholder under the PRC Company Law.

With these reform measures, SOEs in China have continued to grow in size. Fifty-five of the Fortune Global 500 Companies in 2011 were Chinese SOEs. Of the top 500 Chinese companies, 316 were SOEs. Their shares of revenues, profits, and assets among the top 500 firms were 83 percent, 82 percent, and 90 percent, respectively. The top ten industrial SOEs accounted for 82.8 percent of total industrial SOE production and 81.4 percent of the total net profits. Despite the government's effort to merge SOEs and reduce their number, there were still 20,510 SOEs in the industrial sector and about 10,000 nonfinancial SOEs in the service sector in 2010. The industrial SOEs are mainly found in energy, raw materials, and equipment manufacturing, while the service SOEs tend to operate in construction, telecom, aviation, shipping, retail, restaurants, tourism, and real estate.

Consistent with the government's sectoral focus for SOEs, SOEs have only a small share of production in retail and restaurants; an over 20 percent share in construction, real estate, and wholesale; and between an 80 percent and 90 percent share in telecom and aviation. SOEs also dominate banking and the insurance sector. However, despite the deemphasis on wholesale trade, retail, and restaurants, SOEs operating in these sectors still took up 17.8 percent of all SOEs.[16] Not all SOEs are owned by the central government. Provincial and local governments also operate many SOEs. In 2006, there were about 21,000 centrally owned SOEs and about 95,000 SOEs owned by provincial and local governments. In 2010, SOEs owned by the central government accounted for 54.9 percent of the total assets of all SOEs nationwide. Furthermore, the non-financial SOEs owned by the central government accounted for 63.3 percent of the revenue, 67.5 percent of the profits, and 62.4 percent of the net assets of all SOEs nationwide.

In short, after decades of reform, state presence in the Chinese economy has shrunk. The state is involved in fewer sectors than it was when reform began, although one wonders what economic purpose state presence in retail, restaurants, and tourism serves. Given the sectoral focus of the government's SOE policy, SOE presence is strongest in select sectors that have been deemed to be particularly important to national economic development. In light of the importance of these strategic sectors, it is fair to say that SOEs still play a prominent role in the Chinese economy. As Professor Huang Yong, a leading competition law scholar in China, observed, "After the adoption of the reform and opening-up to the outside world policy, SOEs still act as the foundation of the development of the entire Chinese economy and the industrial sectors in which they are playing a role are more and more concentrated."[17] In light of the prevalence of SOEs in the Chinese economy, their treatment under the AML will have important implications for the development of competition law in China. Exempting them from the AML would mean that a significant portion of the economy is carved out of competition law enforcement. For quite some time, that seemed to be a distinct possibility. This is evident from reported instances of mergers between SOEs that were not reported to MOFCOM.

B. Article 7 of the Anti-Monopoly Law

There was much controversy regarding the application of the AML to SOEs during the drafting of the law. Ministries responsible for supervising various SOEs lobbied for exemptions from the AML.[18] SOEs clearly qualify as undertakings under Article 12 of the AML and prima facie should be fully subject to it. The ambiguity comes from Article 7, which specifically addresses the role of SOEs in the economy and their treatment under the AML. In the end, drafters of the law opted for open-ended language in that Article that seems to leave the question at the discretion of the enforcement authority.[19] Article 7 states:

> In industries that are vital to the national economy and those implicating national security, which are controlled by state-owned enterprises and in industries in which there are legal monopolies, the state shall protect the lawful business activities of those enterprises, supervise and control their conduct and prices for the products and services pursuant to law, protect the interests of consumers and promote technological progress.
>
> The undertakings in the industries specified in the preceding paragraph shall conduct their business according to law, act in good faith, observe strict self-discipline, subject themselves to the supervision from the public and shall not impair the interests of the consumer by exploitation of their controlling or exclusive and monopoly positions.[20]

Some scholars have argued that the first paragraph of the Article on its face seems to imply an exemption of SOEs in strategic sectors from the AML. Professor Eleanor Fox has concluded from the language of Article 7 that "the dominant SOEs are in strategic sectors and the strategic sectors are all but exempted from the prohibitions of the AML"[21] and that "the state—and not the antimonopoly agencies—has jurisdiction to control, or not, the anticompetitive behavior of the most powerful state monopolies."[22] Meanwhile, others have argued that Article 7 enacts no such exemption and that the AML should apply fully to SOEs. Mehra and Meng suggest that "[t]he dominant view is that [the AML] should apply to all restrictive or monopolistic practices, without discrimination among subjects for their differences in ownership, legal form, or industry."[23] Some scholars have argued for a more nuanced position, proposing that "Clause 1 and Clause 2 of Article 7 can and should be read to allow for a workable relationship between regulation and competition law in the fully regulated industries and among state-sponsored dominant firms and for regulation and competition law to coexist to their mutual benefit."[24] Specifically, these authors argue that AML cannot apply to the pricing behavior of a dominant firm as regulated by a relevant regulatory agency but may apply to other types of abuse of dominance.[25]

This author is of the view that Article 7 does not exempt SOEs from the AML. Paragraph 1 speaks only of the state protecting the SOEs; it does not indicate that the state will shield SOEs from the reach of the AML. Immediately following that sentence, Paragraph 1 goes on to state that the state shall supervise SOEs' conduct and prices pursuant to law in the interest of consumers. Unless the reference to "law" excludes the AML, and there is no reason why it should, this clause can be interpreted as suggesting that the state shall supervise SOE conduct according to the AML. Similarly, in Paragraph 2, it is said that undertakings in those industries shall conduct their business according to the law. The paragraph ends with a mention of consumer interest against SOE exploitation of their monopoly position. The reference to abuse of dominance is unmistakable.

Thankfully, this issue can be said to have been definitively resolved by the recent NDRC investigation of China Telecom and China Unicom, both of which are state-owned dominant firms in the telecom sector. In fact, they are two of the only three major telecom operators in China after the recent restructuring of the industry. In November 2011, the NDRC announced that it had launched an investigation of China Telecom and China Unicom over their alleged anticompetitive practices in the broadband market.[26] The practices consisted of discriminatory charges of Internet service providers for interconnecting with the two companies' networks and failure to fully integrate their networks.[27] Apparently, what motivated the investigation was the constant complaint by Chinese Internet users of the slow broadband connection speed offered by the two companies, which was apparently considerably slower than the connection speed commonly found in developed countries.[28] This investigation, which is still ongoing at the time of writing, positively affirms that the AML applies to SOEs no matter how big or how important they are. China Telecom and China Unicom are two of the largest SOEs in China, and the telecom sector is one of the sectors identified as strategic by the SASAC.

The fact that the NDRC took such a high-profile route to announce its investigation—with a press conference on national TV threatening to fine the two operators should violations be proven—emphatically settles the debate about the applicability of the AML to SOEs in favor of full applicability. A further noteworthy feature of the investigation is that the alleged abuses of the two telecom operators—discriminatory interconnection charges and integration of their networks—are presumably issues that are well within the scope of the telecom regulatory regime and could have been settled as regulatory issues. The fact that the NDRC proceeded to pursue them in a competition law investigation, no doubt after consultation with the telecom regulator, the Ministry of Industry and Information Technology, in the State Council, can be interpreted as a sign that competition law enforcement does not defer to sectoral regulation with respect to these dominant SOEs. The investigation was an unequivocally positive development in competition law enforcement in China.

C. Possible Anticompetitive Conduct by SOEs

Having established that the AML applies to SOEs, it is important to examine what types of anticompetitive conduct are particularly common among SOEs in general and what types of such conduct have been perpetrated by Chinese SOEs. This will indicate to the AML enforcers what type of conduct to look out for. Given that many Chinese SOEs have protected market positions in their sectors, abuse of dominance should be a high priority for competitive law enforcement against SOEs. The types of anticompetitive conduct that SOEs in China have reportedly engaged in or that are especially common include predatory pricing, raising rivals' costs, excessive pricing, tying, price discrimination, refusal to interconnect, and cross-subsidization. Moreover, Chinese SOEs have been known to have consummated a number of potentially anticompetitive mergers without submitting the transactions to merger review by the relevant enforcement authority, the Ministry of Commerce (MOFCOM).

Professors Sappington and Sidak have convincingly illustrated that with a reduced focus on profits, SOEs may have greater incentives than profit-maximizing firms to pursue activities that disadvantage competitors.[29] Because of their dual interest in both revenue and profits, SOEs are less concerned about the impact of higher costs on their profits. They are hence less concerned about the costs of predation and more prone to pursue predatory pricing. SOEs may be interested in expanding their scale of operation and thus maximizing their revenue for a variety of reasons. An SOE's profit can be capped by government regulation. Therefore, SOEs may be constrained in their pursuit of profit maximization. Moreover, SOEs may have been instructed by the government to increase local employment or increase the provision of product or service to low-income families.[30] An SOE manager's personal prestige may also be enhanced by the company's scale of operation. The desire to increase revenue and output may thus give SOEs the incentive to harm their competitors by depressing their output. Coupled with a reduced concern about costs, which is often the result of the soft budget constraint to which SOEs are subject, SOEs have both the incentive and the ability to pursue predatory pricing strategies against their rivals. Particularly worrying for SOE rivals is that SOEs may have the incentive to pursue predatory pricing even if their ultimate objective is not to recoup the loss by driving rivals out.[31] Recoupment of losses need not concern SOE managers because, unlike managers of private, profit-maximizing firms, SOE managers are not accountable to their shareholders for losses.[32] Also, because of their desire to increase their output and therefore revenue, SOEs have great incentives to pursue strategies to raise their rivals' costs.[33] Raising rivals' costs may force rivals to raise their prices and thus reduce their output, which will divert more sales to SOEs.

Although this author is not aware of any incidents of Chinese SOEs pursuing predatory pricing or raising rivals' costs, Chinese SOEs are well positioned to do so. Managers of Chinese SOEs are usually left with greater discretion. And it has been pointed out that manager-led SOEs have significant incentives for scale expansion, which in turn creates a conducive environment for predatory pricing.[34] Firms subject to a soft budget constraint are also better positioned to pursue predatory pricing, since there is less pressure to recoup costs. The Chinese state collected no dividends from SOEs until 2007. And even then, it only does so from wholly owned subsidiaries at below-market rate. Budgetary pressure on Chinese SOEs can be said to be low. Sappington and Sidak further argue that an SOE that values both revenue and profit typically will have stronger incentives than a profit-maximizing firm to overinvest in capital to secure an abnormally low marginal cost to relax a binding prohibition on pricing below cost.[35] As noted earlier, Chinese SOEs have tended to be capital intensive. And there are suggestions that their use of capital is inefficient, which could be signs of overinvestment. It is possible that Chinese SOEs may have achieved an abnormally low marginal cost through their capital overinvestment that will allow them considerable room to pursue predatory pricing. Predatory pricing is prohibited by Article 17(2) of the AML.

A host of anticompetitive conduct has already been observed among Chinese SOEs. State-run utility companies have been known to have required customers to purchase a particular product from a designated manufacturer to obtain service from the utility company. For example, water companies force customers to purchase designated water supply equipment.[36] Gas companies require residents to purchase gas stoves from them before installing natural gas pipelines in residential areas.[37] Electricity companies have also compelled customers to purchase electric meters from them before supplying service.[38]

Such conduct would be treated as tying, which is expressly prohibited by Article 17(5) of the AML.

There have been reported instances of excessive pricing by the national railroad and a Beijing cable TV operator.[39] China Unicom has also been subject to excessive interconnection charges.[40] Article 17(1) of the AML prohibits undertakings from selling their goods or services at unfairly high prices. While there are valid objections to enforcement against excessive pricing in a competitive, unregulated market, where firms are given monopoly rights but not subject to effective rate regulation, there are good reasons for the competition enforcement authority to step in to pursue excessive pricing.

Cross-subsidization is reportedly common among Chinese state-run utility companies. China Telecom used revenue from its protected fixed-line business to cross-subsidize its operation in the competitive radio paging business.[41] Cross-subsidization can result in significant distortions in the market and allow the SOE to gain an unfair advantage over rivals in competitive markets. The AML currently contains no enumerated prohibition of anticompetitive cross-subsidization. However, given the likely prevalence and harmful effects of anticompetitive cross-subsidization, the AML enforcers may consider deeming it illegal under Article 17 of the AML. To clamp down on anticompetitive conduct by Chinese SOEs, the AML enforcers will need to be watchful for the aforementioned conduct.

In addition to anticompetitive conduct, potentially anticompetitive mergers have been consummated by Chinese SOEs without a formal merger review by MOFCOM. In 2009, Shanghai Airlines merged with China Eastern Airlines in an effort to cut costs and improve profitability. MOFCOM did not undertake a formal review of the transaction under the AML.[42] Without a proper review of the merger, it is hard to conclude with confidence whether the merger would have presented competition issues. Evidence, however, suggests that it probably would have. It has been noted that the merged entity would hold a 50 percent market share of air transportation out of Shanghai, one of the largest aviation markets in China.[43] This would at least raise some prima facie unilateral effects concerns. Aside from unilateral effects, the merger was also likely to have created coordinated effects. There was evidence that the Chinese airlines had been colluding in the domestic aviation market prior to the merger. They had formed so-called "price alliances" to stabilize prices, which were believed to have raised prices by 10 to 20 percent.[44] In particular, Chinese economists have concluded that there was price collusion on the immensely competitive Shanghai-Beijing route by the major airlines, which resulted in the elimination of discounts, which had been very common in the market.[45] The elimination of one rival may further stabilize the cartel and render continual collusion more likely.

Another example of potentially anticompetitive mergers that were consummated without passing through proper merger review was the restructuring of the telecom sector in 2008–2009. Prior to the restructuring, there had been six telecom operators in China. The market, especially in mobile telephony, however, had been quite lopsided, with China Mobile accounting for 69 percent of the market.[46] In an effort to spur competition, the Ministry of Industry of Information Technology ordered the restructuring of the industry, which saw China Mobile merge with the smaller, fixed-line operator China Tietong, China Telecom acquire China Unicom's CDMA network, and China Unicom's remaining assets merge with China Netcom.[47] After the restructuring, three main telecom operators have emerged in China: China Telecom, China Mobile, and China Unicom. Again, none of these mergers was submitted to MOFCOM. Given the high degree of concentration in the telecom sector in China at the time of these mergers, it is highly likely that these mergers at least would have warranted close scrutiny by MOFCOM. The cavalier attitude toward merger notification by SOEs partly reflects the turf battle between the Chinese sectoral regulators and the AML enforcers and partly recalls the centrally planned economy days of the country a few decades ago, when enterprises could be merged and restructured through administrative edict without regard to the economic effects of the transactions. For competition law enforcement against SOEs to be given full effect in China, mergers between SOEs that meet MOFCOM's notification thresholds must be reported to and reviewed by MOFCOM for potential anticompetitive effects. Industry restructuring in China must be undertaken with full regard to its impact on competition.

II. Abuse of Administrative Monopoly in China

Another type of state intervention in competition that is related to the SOEs is what is known in China as "abuse of administrative monopoly." Abuse of administrative monopoly refers to administrative measures or conduct adopted by government agencies to distort competition or to erect barriers to market entry. It has been said that in light of the pervasiveness of regulation and government intervention in the economy, abuse of administrative monopoly poses a much more serious threat to free competition in China than does monopolization by private enterprises.[48] The phenomenon of abuse of administrative monopoly is related to SOEs because the government bodies to which SOEs are affiliated are concerned about the profitability of the enterprises. One way for the government bodies to boost the profitability of their enterprises is to erect artificial barriers to competition from rivals by way of administrative measures.[49] The government bodies have the incentive to create a favorable environment for their affiliated enterprises.

Despite the prevalence of abuse of administrative monopoly and its negative impact on the continual development of the Chinese economy, Chinese scholars are split on whether abuse of administrative monopoly should be dealt with in the AML. Professor Wang Xiaoye, one of the leading competition law scholars in China, asserts that that the AML should reflect the Chinese economic reality, which features abuse of administrative monopoly as the most pernicious distortion of competition.[50] This dictates that abuse of administrative monopoly must be included within the ambit of the AML. A contrary view is held by Professor Shi Jichun of Renmin University, who argues that abuse of administrative monopoly is ultimately a political problem that can be dealt with only through political reforms and not competition law enforcement.[51] This division of opinions was reflected during the drafting process of the AML, during which the chapter proscribing abuse of administrative monopoly was taken out and then reinstated.[52] In fact, the treatment of abuse of administrative monopoly was highly controversial and resulted in delay of the overall legislation. The provisions that were eventually adopted were detailed in their proscription but lacking in penalty.

Abuse of administrative monopoly is common in China. Examples have included discriminatory license fees, discriminatory inspection and technical standards, compulsory purchase of locally produced goods, and even outright road blockade. For instance, in 1996, the Shanghai municipal government issued regulations prohibiting taxi companies from buying cars with engines smaller than 1.6 liters in capacity, which effectively blocked the import of the popular Shali taxi model produced in Tianjin, the main competitor of locally produced taxi cars. In 1996, the Beijing municipal government ordered that cars with engines over 1 liter in capacity could only be used every other day but exempted vehicles produced by Beijing Jeep Corp from the order.[53] In 1999, Hubei Province, which produces Citroen cars, imposed an RMB 70,000 fee on the purchase of Shanghai-produced Santana cars. This measure was a reaction to the Shanghai municipal government's discriminatory licensing policy, which imposed an RMB 20,000 license fee for Santana cars and an RMB

80,000 fee for other cars. In 2001, the Guangzhou government stopped issuing licenses to cars with 1-liter or smaller engines, effectively preventing smaller cars produced in Sichuan Province and Tianjin from competing with the larger Accord cars produced locally.[54] In the same year, the Shanghai municipal government banned cars over a certain weight from using major roads, which effectively excluded larger cars produced in Sichuan from the local market.[55] These incidents all aptly illustrate how local governments use administrative measures to protect local companies from outside competition.

Egregious examples of abuse of administrative monopoly abound. Some local governments compel government subunits, businesses, and consumers to purchase local goods. A good example is Shuchen County in Anhui Province, whose protective measures have been widely reported, including by the official national TV network CCTV. The county government adopted the *Shuchen County Commercial Reorganization, Management and Examination Proposal*, which set out market share targets for local products, such as wine and cement. In addition, the government set up a special unit to protect local businesses and used a wide range of administrative measures to ensure that market share targets were reached. These measures included requiring government employees to purchase local products (in 2000, county teachers were paid three bottles of local wine in lieu of RMB 60 as part of their salary); requiring consumers to use local products (civilians who wanted to build a house were required to use locally produced cement or their construction permit applications would not be processed); requiring government units to purchase local products (under the *Regulations on Government Purchase of Alcohol*, county government units must use local wine for official functions); and requiring manufacturers to purchase locally produced inputs (under a number of county regulations on cement use in construction projects, construction material manufacturers must purchase locally produced cement). Furthermore, some local governments have set up checkpoints at regional borders to obstruct entry of goods from other regions. Examples include the governments of the City of Liangping and Nanchuan County in Sichuan Province, which set up roadblocks on highways to prevent entry of fertilizers from outside their respective regions in 2002.[56]

To combat these abuses of administrative power, the Chinese government has adopted a number of laws and regulations. These have included Article 6 of the Temporary Stipulation of the State Council on the Promotion and Protection of Socialist Competition in 1980, the Circular Concerning the Prohibition of Blockages in Purchasing and Marketing Industrial Products in 1982, the Circular Concerning Breaking Down Inter-Regional Market Blockages and

Further Invigorating Commodity Circulation in 1990, Article 7 of the Anti-Unfair Competition Law in 1993, and the Regulations on Prohibiting Local Blockade in Market Economic Activities in 2001. However, these were all deemed to be inadequate due to deficient penalties or ineffective enforcement, which eventually led to the adoption of Chapter 5 of the AML.

Chapter 5 of the AML contains six Articles. Article 32 prohibits government bodies from compelling purchases of goods or services from designated undertakings. Article 33 proscribes administrative measures that impede the free movement of goods, including discriminatory charges, discriminatory technical or inspection standards, discriminatory licensing procedures, and roadblocks. Article 34 ensures equal treatment of nonlocal firms in public procurement exercises. Article 35 bans discrimination against nonlocal investments. Article 36 prevents government bodies from compelling undertakings to engage in anticompetitive conduct otherwise proscribed by the AML. And Article 37 instructs government bodies not to issue regulations that eliminate or restrict competition.

Despite its comprehensive nature, the AML has not addressed what has plagued enforcement against the abuse of administrative monopoly thus far: the lack of effective penalties. As suggested earlier, the previous laws and regulations failed to stamp out abuse of administrative monopoly largely because of ineffective enforcement and deficient penalties. The AML suffers from the same inadequacy, because Article 51 provides only for admonition by the superior authority for an offending government body and disciplinary measures for the responsible individuals. The superior authority is unlikely to have the incentive to be vigilant against the abuse of administrative monopoly, since any measure or conduct that benefits a lower-level government body may indirectly benefit the superior authority. Scholars have suggested that there should be civil liability for government agencies in violation of the abuse of administrative monopoly provisions.[57]

Harsher penalties, however, are unlikely to resolve the lack of effective enforcement of these provisions. The fact remains that the AML expects one part of the Chinese bureaucracy to bring enforcement actions against another part of the bureaucracy, an event that is highly unlikely to happen under the current Chinese political system. An enforcement mechanism that utilizes a third-party adjudication system, as is done in most other jurisdictions, such as the United States and the European Union, would sidestep this problem. This option, however, is unavailable in China because the judiciary lacks independence and is very much under the control of the executive. It is highly unlikely that the judiciary would rule against the executive branch of the same level of government in an abuse of administrative monopoly case. Absent an impartial enforcement agency and adjudicator, the abuse of administrative monopoly provisions of the AML are likely to remain sporadically enforced and unlikely to provide an effective antidote to the widespread abuse of administrative monopoly in China.

* * *

Despite the heavy focus on AML enforcement against SOE anticompetitive behavior and abuse of administrative monopoly, a fundamental solution to the problem of the role of the state in the Chinese economy requires addressing some systemic issues. Professor Shi Jichun made a valid observation when he opined that abuse of administrative monopoly is ultimately more than a legal problem. Together with SOE anticompetitive conduct, the causes of abuse of administrative monopoly have systemic roots, and these competition problems can only be solved if the underlying systemic causes are addressed. The first of these causes is the government's conception of its role in the economy. Ultimately, SOE anticompetitive conduct and abuse of administrative monopoly are manifestations of the Chinese government's extensive intervention in the economy. Only a retrenched role of the state in the economy will minimize SOE presence and take away the incentives for local governments to harm competition through administrative measures. Should the government be unwilling to retreat from the economy, the competition law enforcement authorities will need to be particularly vigilant against SOEs in light of their greater incentives and ability to pursue certain types of anticompetitive conduct. Given the support from the government enjoyed by the SOEs, private enterprises will surely need the protection of the competition law enforcement authorities to ensure a level playing field. SOEs are also intimately linked to China's industrial policy. SOEs have been the main vehicle through which China has pursued its industrial policy, especially its national champion policy. A level playing field between public and private firms will never be attained unless China slows down in its relentless drive for national champions.

To look even deeper, the current Chinese political system is conducive to regional rivalries and gives provincial and local governments the incentives to groom local enterprises as local champions and to offer them protection through administrative measures. The Chinese economy is highly decentralized, and the provinces are often given the leeway to develop local champions. This, together with the fact that Chinese officials are evaluated on their performance by the GDP growth of the area for which they are responsible, gives these officials incentives to protect local enterprises. Furthermore, under the current fiscal system, tax revenues and expenditure responsibilities are not matched evenly, often leaving local governments with a substantial revenue shortfall. As such, local governments often have to rely on local enterprises to make up for this shortfall. This fiscal reliance on local enterprises gives local governments further incentives to protect these enterprises through administrative means. Until these systemic issues are addressed and the fiscal distribution system reformed, the incentives to groom and protect local champions will persist and AML enforcement will remain a palliative, but not a cure, for SOE anticompetitive conduct and abuse of administrative monopoly.

Chapter 11

State Aids in European Union Competition Law

Leigh Hancher and Francesco Salerno

The financial crisis of 2008 provided a sharp reminder that the European Union (EU) is the only international economic organization or quasi-federal arrangement or union that subjects its members to rigorous control over their ability to disburse subsidies to attract—or retain—industry.[1] Thus, a key paradox facing the European institutions responsible for state aid control under the European Treaties is that they have rather limited financial resources at their disposal to stimulate change and transition. Member states hold the purse strings, but the European Commission, entrusted with the exclusive task of assessing the compatibility of national state aid or subsidy measures, can wield substantial power in deciding how that money should be spent. At the same time, from its forgotten status as the Cinderella of competition policy, in the past decade European state aid policy and law has evolved into a major pillar of Europe's industrial, financial, and economic policy to realize the goals of the "Europe 2020 strategy for growth" and indeed as a key tool for the EU's aim to ensure a transition to a smart, inclusive, low-carbon economy by 2050.

The focus of this chapter is on the actions of member states as opposed to firms and, more specifically, on how state aid rules shape member states' intervention in the economy. In so doing, the chapter broadly follows a two-part structure that mirrors the structure of state aid control under EU law. If a measure is "aid," it requires Commission approval before it can be put into effect. If aid is disbursed without Commission approval, the beneficiary must repay the amount received, with compound interest. Subsequent approval will not remedy this illegality.[2] As a result, before deciding on a policy measure, a member state must first examine whether the measure falls within the scope of the EU state aid rules. If the answer is in the affirmative, the member state will have to canvass the measure so it can obtain approval at the Commission level. The chapter tracks this decision-making process and first discusses recent case law on the concept of aid. Next, the chapter reviews the most important substantive features of the approval process,[3] including the recent "modernization" effort the Commission launched in May 2012.[4]

In our concluding remarks we argue that, given its increasing penchant for using state aid as a tool of industrial policy, the Commission is, albeit indirectly, providing incentives for member states to devise measures that fall outside the state aid regime altogether.

I. The Notion of State Aid: Form versus Effects

Although to a non-European reader, *all* the measures the state-shareholder has undertaken in Europe in the present financial crisis may seem like a form of state subsidy, the first step in EU state aid law is to determine whether a state measure is state aid. This task is not as easy as it might seem.

The concept of an aid is not defined in the Lisbon Treaty (nor was it defined in the now expired European Coal and Steel Community Treaty, which had also prohibited state aid to those sectors of the economy). Article 107 TFEU refers to aid in any form whatsoever that distorts competition.[5] As with its interpretation of other treaty articles, the Court has focused on the purpose of this provision. In Case C-83/98P *Ladbroke*, the Court of Justice of the EU (CJEU) ruled that the concept of aid was an objective one.[6] The CJEU has also explained that it is *the effect*, and not the form, of the aid that is crucial. As the Court of First Instance (now General Court—GC) recalled in its ruling in Case T-613/97 *Ufex*:

> The aim of Article 92(1) EEC [now Article 107(1) TFEU] is to prevent trade between member states from being affected by advantages granted by public authorities which in various forms, distort or threaten to distort competition by favouring certain undertakings or certain products. The concept of aid thus encompasses not only positive benefits, such as subsidies, but also interventions which, in various forms, mitigate the charges which are normally included in the budget of an undertaking and which, without therefore being subsidies in the strict sense of the word, are of the same character and have the same effect.

Although it may seem that it is the effects of a measure that carry the day and that, as a result, a wide range of measures can be covered by the definition, we shall see below that form can play a crucial role in state aid analysis. This is especially important in that the more refined economic approach to the assessment of state aid, discussed in Section II, is only related to the assessment of the aid measure in question and not to its initial classification as state aid as such. This first section covers the steps in the state aid analysis that are used to determine if a state measure can be considered "state aid," with the groundbreaking *EdF* case as an example, and discusses the role of the *EdF* case in state aid analysis and how it can impact the way in which the Commission and member states interact in this area.

A. Three Steps in the State Aid Analysis

Can the measure fall outside the scope of state aid because it is not intended to confer an advantage on a beneficiary / group of beneficiaries but rather aims at fostering a given policy (e.g., environmental policy,[7] industrial policy, regional policy, etc.)? The answer to this question is no. According to a very well-established body of precedents, the concept of state aid is not dependent on the objectives underlying a given measure.[8]

Is the form of the measure relevant?

An often repeated formula is as follows:

> The concept of aid embraces all measures which, in various forms, mitigate the charges which are normally borne out by the budget of an undertaking and which, without therefore being subsidies in the strict meaning of the word, are similar in character and have the same effect.[9]
>
> It is thus clear that the second level of state aid analysis focuses on the effects of a given measure rather than its form. This is precisely the reason why Article 107 TFEU was drafted in a very general way, i.e., that Article makes reference to aid in "*any form whatsoever*."[10]

How should the effects of a measure be analyzed to determine if it is state aid? In Case C-280/00 *Altmark*,[11] Advocate General Leger drew a distinction between measures adopted by the state in the exercise of its prerogatives and those adopted in its capacity as a provider of, or alternatively a purchaser of, goods and services in the market. This distinction carries momentous consequences because the type of effects analysis depends on it.

Indeed, an *actus iure imperii* triggers what could be defined as a "simplified effect analysis." In this category of cases, there appears to be little interest in the underlying economics of the transaction or the "cost" of the measure to the state.[12]

Quite to the contrary, when the state acts through the adoption of an *actus iure gestionis*, there will be room for a "sophisticated effect analysis"—the so-called Market Economy Investor Principle analysis (MEIP).[13] In this second category of cases, greater emphasis appears to be placed on the net financial burden borne by the state or the net financial advantage conferred on the beneficiary of the measure. Thus, it is true that state aid law is an effects-oriented doctrine, but such effects can be determined depends on the form of the measure under scrutiny. This is why form plays a crucial role in this regard.[14]

In joined cases C-72 and C-73/91 *Sloman Neptun*,[15] the GC had already referred to "the object and general structure" of a measure to determine if it was state aid, thus signaling an important shift toward a more empirically rooted state aid analysis.[16] This trend continued in the *Ryanair* case.[17] But in the *EdF* case this approach was put to a key test because the state used fiscal power and legislation—that is, the archetypical prerogative power of *acta iure imperii*. We now turn to the *EdF* case.

B. The EdF Case

The measure at issue in the *EdF* case concerned the use of fiscal powers to exempt a transaction (the requalification of the network assets) from taxation, thereby using the resulting tax advantage to increase EdF's balance sheet. The Commission relied on its well-established practice and concluded that the use of fiscal powers was a typical *actus iure imperii*, deserving nothing more than a simplified effects analysis. Not surprisingly, the Commission then found that EdF enjoyed a preferential tax treatment and, consequently, a selective advantage triggering a finding of state aid.[18]

On appeal,[19] the starting point of the GC's reasoning was to preserve the long-standing case law regarding the need to differentiate between *acta iure imperii* and *acta iure gestionis*. Nevertheless, what the GC tried to explain is that when carrying out this step of the analysis, it was not sufficient for the Commission to look exclusively at the form of the measure at issue. In other words, the GC thought it was not possible to automatically conclude that the measure at issue constitutes an *actus iure imperii* on the sole basis of its form—that is, of its being a tax measure. On the facts of the case, the GC was not prepared to allow the Commission to confine itself to a simplified effects analysis.

At paragraphs 229–233, the GC advocated a contextual analysis that looks at a number of factors, including the objective of the tax measure.[20] The GC by no means implied that a different type of effects analysis would have led to a different conclusion—in other words, to a finding of nonaid. Quite to the contrary, it seemed to hint that the tax measure could have constituted state aid even applying a sophisticated effects analysis.[21] In this light, it was clear that the GC's main focus lay in the methodology to be followed when analyzing the form of a given measure. This process pertained to the third level of state aid analysis that has been illustrated above. The examination of the form of the measure defined the type of effects analysis to be applied.

C. The CJEU Judgment

On June 5, 2012, the *EdF* saga came to an end when the CJEU decided not to follow the AG's opinion and to uphold the GC's judgment. Three main areas needed to be addressed. First, the CJEU rejected the Commission's first ground of appeal according to which the GC had distorted the clear sense of the evidence before it. The CJEU noted that even if such a distortion of the facts existed, the "*modus operandi chosen by the member state is irrelevant for the purposes of assessing whether that test [MEIP test] applies*."[22] In other words, a superficial look at the form of the measure was not sufficient to dismiss the applicability of the MEIP test. Echoing the General Court's language, the CJEU called upon the Commission to carry out a "global assessment" that takes into account the nature and subject matter of the measure at issue, as well as its context, the rules applicable to it, and, more interestingly, its objective. This global assessment played a crucial role when analyzing the form of a given measure and determines what type of effect analysis has to be carried out. This consideration leads to the second area of focus.

Next, the CJEU upheld the General Court's idea that the examination of the objectives is inherent to this level of state aid analysis. In other words, the European Court of Justice confirms that while objectives do not play any role at the stage of the jurisdictional analysis, they are crucial when carrying out the above-mentioned global assessment.

Finally, the third area of focus concerns the substantial shift in the center of gravity of state aid analysis. The CJEU turned state aid analysis into an evidentiary matter.[23] In particular, the judgment lay down clear rules as to the parties bearing the burden of proof and identifies the type of evidence to be analyzed.[24] As a result, the judicial debate on the possible lack of advantage—in consequence of the application of the MEIP test—had been moved to a different level; in other words, it became a question of evidence. This reverberates on both the member states and the Commission.

On the one hand, the member states have now clear indications as to the type of evidentiary material that will have to be produced. Such evidence must—in accordance with established case law—predate the decision to make the investment in question, as it is not enough to rely on ex post economic evaluations in regard to its profitability.[25] On the other, the Commission bears a duty to ask the member states to provide all the information necessary to determine whether the conditions of applicability of the MEIP test are met. In conclusion, the European Court of Justice's stance is largely coherent with the judgment at first instance and reinforces the General Court's call for a deeper state aid analysis, where the Commission cannot confine itself to looking exclusively at the form of a measure.

The recent increase of state involvement in the economy—notably through the acquisition of shares in listed companies—demands state aid law to hone its analytical tools. It is imperative to grasp fully what the state is actually doing in the market and to distinguish between *acta iure imperii* and *acta iure gestionis*. This analysis has to be imbued with more realism. The fact that the state intervenes through the adoption of tax measures by no means implies automatically that it is adopting an *actus iure imperii*, justifying only a simplified effect analysis. In this regard, the analysis of the objective pursued by the state is inherent to this type of investigation. In addition, the adoption of the approach presented in this section would not open the floodgates to hundreds of measures, allowing them to escape state aid scrutiny. The result of the application of a sophisticated effects analysis may in fact be the opposite. The state engages in economic activities for a variety of reasons—for example, to pursue objectives of general interest—something that no normal shareholder or investor would do. However, only a stricter focus on the third level of state aid analysis—that is, a closer scrutiny of the form of a given measure—can allow the Commission to understand more precisely what is actually happening in the market and to apply the correct type of effect analysis. The CJEU's judgment reckons this need for more realism in state aid analysis and confirms the spirit of the GC's approach. Thus, the *EdF* saga brings about a significant development in the case law, obliging the Commission to look at the increasing involvement of the member states in the economy in a more empirically rooted way.

II. The Compatibility Assessment: The Different Roles of the State and the State Aid Analysis

The European state aid regime has been put to its most severe test during the recent financial crisis. Despite initial protectionist instincts in some member states, the Commission was able on the basis of this unique regime to coordinate national action to limit negative spillover effects, such as untenable subsidy races and distortions of competition that would have fragmented the internal market.[26] This recent experience again reminds us that the treaty state aid provisions essentially aim at reducing, if not eliminating, distortions of production and location decisions across member states; this regime relates to competition between member states, not just competition between undertakings. The Commission's compatibility assessment should be focussed on distinguishing "good aid" from "bad aid" in respect to its impact on competition among member states.

In this light, treaty state aid rules may share more chromosomes with the internal market rules and the rules on free movement than with its competition or antitrust rules, such as Articles 101 and 102 TFEU. Nevertheless, irrespective of its genetic makeup, the reach of the treaty state aid regime into national economies remains extensive, especially as long as the courts continue to give a generous interpretation to the final condition: the effect on trade test. At least prior to the financial crisis, the Commission's decisions on swimming pools, zebras, and ski lifts were far better known, and more widely criticized, than its decisions on major bank restructuring packages.[27]

If the focus of the state aid regime differs from antitrust, then it also follows that economic analysis of the impact of national support measures should be of a different order and purpose when it is concerned with the actions of member states as opposed to firms. The assessment of financial support to firms should therefore not only be based solely on its effect on competition in markets or its potential to boost market power but on other factors involving its eventual impact on trade and also its potentially positive effects, including social and political objectives.[28] As we shall argue, the Commission's views on the role of state aid control policy, and the new State Aid Modernisation (SAM) initiative for achieving the Europe 2020 Strategy objectives by supporting smart, sustainable, and inclusive initiatives of general common interest, confirm this approach.

To date, the Commission has preferred to take these types of policy objectives into account exclusively within its compatibility assessment. In doing so, the Commission draws heavily on soft law instruments when carrying out such compatibility assessment, including communications, guidelines, and frameworks. Indeed, the Commission continues to prefer to use guidelines in certain fields, such as the environment or broadband, even though the Enabling Regulation on the application of Articles 92 and 93 (now 107 and 108 TFEU, respectively) of the treaty establishing the European Community to certain categories of horizontal state aid provides it with a formal legal basis to adopt binding rules, which national courts could enforce, in this area.[29]

The current architecture of compatibility assessment is based on a "three-tiered" system: block exemption, standard assessment, and detailed assessment.

1. Following the 2005 reforms, the SAAP,[30] the Block Exemption Regulation of 2008 allows for automatic exemption of a variety of aids across a number of sectors.[31]
2. Measures that do not satisfy the Block Exemption conditions must be notified and will be assessed under the relevant guidelines. In certain cases the compatibility assessment can be carried out on a "standardized basis"—that is, just by applying the guidelines.[32]
3. For larger amounts of aid, the measure will have to be subject to a detailed assessment.

With respect to the last tier, the Commission must examine whether the aid measure is aimed at a well-defined objective of common interest and must be designed to address market failure or other, equity-related objectives. The next step is to identify whether the aid measure is the appropriate policy instrument. Does it provide an appropriate incentive effect that modifies the behavior of the recipient firm to do something that it would not otherwise have done without government intervention? The third and final step is to evaluate the proportionality of the aid measure. This involves considering both the positive and negative effects of the proposed aid measure—the so-called "balancing test," also known as "the refined economic approach." All state aid that falls outside the scope of block exemption regulations and guidelines is subject to a detailed assessment and balancing test, irrespective of the amount of aid or the size of the beneficiaries. Aid falling within the scope of the relevant "soft law" guidelines, discussed in this section, will only be subject to a detailed assessment, based on the refined economic approach, in cases involving large amounts of aid.[33]

With this premise in mind, we can now turn first to a discussion of the recent modernization efforts—the SAAP and the SAM—and then (1) provide an analysis on the interactions between the state industrial policy and state aid policy through the case of broadband, and (2) discuss the interface between the state as provider of Services of General Economic Interest (SGEI) and state aid.

A. The Europe 2020 Strategy and State Aid Modernization

In June 2011, the Commission produced a report on "State Aid Contribution to Europe 2020 Strategy" in its Spring State Aid Scoreboard.[34] This report provides an interesting overview of state aid in areas of particular relevance to the Europe 2020 Strategy for smart, sustainable, and inclusive growth.[35]

The report reviews state aid trends in a number of areas, including research and development, and innovation; environmental protection; regional development; broadband; small and medium-sized enterprises; and employment training—all of which are key action points in the Europe 2020 Strategy. This report raises some interesting questions about the role of state aid policy in the Commission's overall strategy to ensure smart growth, which is developing an economy based on knowledge and innovation; sustainable growth, which is promoting a more resource efficient, greener, and more competitive economy; and inclusive growth, which is fostering a high-employment economy delivering economic, territorial, and social cohesion. The Europe 2020 Strategy outlines various priorities for which state aid instruments can be used in a policy mix to contribute to a number of "flagship initiatives."

The analysis reveals that by far the largest number of national support measures or schemes fall under the scope of block exemption regulations and can be disbursed without prior Commission authorization, and it confirms that in all these areas the Commission only very rarely opposes a measure.

The measures that fall outside a block exemption regulation and require the so-called detailed assessment are approximately 5 to 9 percent of all the measures notified. The remainder are approved under the standard assessment provided for in the relevant sectoral guidelines. Regional aid, which can be block exempted under certain conditions, continues to account for the highest share of total aid to Europe's industry and services.[36] As the report comments, this type of aid is meant to address the "cohesion disequilibrium" rather than market failures only.

Large disparities between the member states in the volume of aid granted demonstrate different policy approaches, however, and the report confirms that it is not the purpose of the state aid rules, or indeed the Commission's policy goal of ensuring "less and better targeted aid," to arrive at a level playing field in terms of public support for any of these six areas across the member states.

The detailed review of the level of aid in these six areas analyzed in the 2011 Spring Scoreboard appears to indicate that the Commission would even welcome more rather than less aid to secure the fulfilment of the "flagship initiatives" embraced in the Europe 2020 Strategy. In any event, the report confirms the importance of state aid control as an important tool in achieving wider European industrial policy goals because measures canvassed to match the requirements of the block exemption regulation can almost automatically be implemented.

Indeed, even in areas where the refined economic approach has been taken seriously, or at least applied with some conviction, very large sums of money are still being approved. Even if as required by the SAAP, state aid is better targeted, it is difficult to conclude that this has led to a reduction in the volume of state aid disbursed. For example, in 2010 alone, the Commission approved under its 2009 guidelines for state aid to broadband the use of over €1.8 billion public funds for broadband development. Total aid for broadband and "next-generation infrastructure" (NGA) has been estimated at €9 billion. The Europe 2020 Strategy sets ambitious targets for broadband development (discussed below), estimated to require some €330 billion in investment. The 2011 State Aid Scoreboard indicates that of the 75 decisions adopted in relation to broadband support between 2004 and 2010, the Commission adopted 65 compatible decisions, 6 "no aid" decisions, and 1 negative decision. As discussed below, in April 2011, the Commission announced a review of the 2009 guidelines,[37] and this initial consultation has now led to a revised set of draft guidelines designed to meet the challenges of achieving the Europe 2020 Strategy and the Commission's Digital Agenda for Europe.[38]

In May 2012, the Commission launched a further initiative to reform the application of the state aid regime—the State Aid Modernisation program (SAM). According to the Commissioner responsible for competition, "The most important objective of the overhaul of the state aid regime is to help Europe's governments spend more wisely in these difficult times to prepare the ground for the recovery, keep the right priorities in times of fiscal consolidation, and, of course, mitigate the social effects of the crisis."[39]

The proposed reform is based on three pillars. The first and most important pillar of the reform process rests on the need to encourage more focused and better-quality aid. Apart from targeting market failures, "good aid" is aid that:

- has a real incentive effect and therefore fosters growth;
- is designed in a way that avoids waste of public money and thus minimizes the cost to the taxpayer;
- has no better market alternative; and
- strengthens the internal market by keeping the sectors open and competitive and avoiding imbalances among member states.

Put differently, "good aid" is "aid that promotes research and development; makes access to finance easier for SMEs; gives the right incentives for the development of the digital economy; protects the environment; and attracts investment toward the weaker regions of Europe," while "bad aid" "crowds out private investment; keeps inefficient and nonviable companies on indefinite life support; and generally wastes taxpayer's money."[40]

The second pillar of the reform package is simplification. The present system of guidelines and notices on different types of aid has grown in complexity and now includes some 40 different texts. The reforms should lead to a leaner and clearer regime, on the promise that the Commission will be able to make faster decisions.

The third pillar reflects a shift of focus in control from a case-to-case to a more structured policy approach. This will also allow the Commission to set out its own priorities, start more investigations ex officio, and look more systematically into those sectors that practice indicates could raise competition concerns.

In its Communication[41] launching the SAM, the Commission confirms an important shift in its policy objectives:

> State aid control can also help member states to strengthen budgetary discipline and improve the quality of public finances—resulting in a better use of taxpayers' money. It is particularly important in order to achieve smart fiscal consolidation, reconciling the role of targeted public spending in generating growth with the need to bring budgets under control. There is therefore also a need to embed State aid control and more general competition concerns in the EU Semester procedure.[42]

Last but not least, the SAM envisages an important role for national authorities, including national regulatory authorities, and the new draft broadband guidelines reflect this move toward enhanced policy coordination at the national level. If the Commission succeeds in realizing this objective, it may make further inroads into national preferences for economic intervention and industrial policy—an objective that it failed to achieve with the earlier reforms introduced by the SAAP of 2005.[43]

B. Correcting Market Failures: Broadband

State aid to broadband provides an excellent test for the implementation of the principles set out in the new SAM plans (together with the new package on services of general economic interest [SGEI], adopted in December 2011, discussed below). Broadband can be considered as a mixed good mingling private, public, and merit goods, including SGEI. Consequently there is no one-size-fits-all approach to pricing or business models—allowing some considerable scope for Commission policy to shape state intervention. Even though the electronic communications sector is fully liberalized in Europe and subject to detailed sectoral regulation,[44] the Commission has accepted that market-driven private investment alone would not be sufficient to realize its ambitions for broadband connectivity and that the use of additional public funds may be a necessity. Further, in the context of the financial and economic crisis, broadband infrastructural investment is considered to be effective in bringing about both short-term recovery and longer-term competitive advantages.

In several early broadband cases, the Commission held that the financial support would amount to an aid to both the proposed operator and to end users, even though the former had been selected by negotiated tender procedures. It ruled that the measures still amounted to aid, albeit that they were eventually exempted, subject to conditions, under Article 107(3)(c) TFEU. Tenders of this variety have been referred to as a form of "competition for subsidy," which may result in the member state paying the lowest level of subsidy, but do not necessarily rule out the existence of a subsidy as such.[45]

The guidelines of 2009[46] lay down the conditions under which public funding should be granted to broadband development in line with the EU state aid rules and codify the Commission's extensive decision-making practice (developed since 2003) concerning basic broadband networks, extrapolate their fundamental tenets, and apply them to the new area of very high-speed, fiber optic–based Next Generation Access (NGA) networks.[47] In other words, by bringing national measures within the compatibility assessment, the Commission can pursue its wider policy goals.

The guidelines distinguish among "white," "gray," and "black" areas, depending on whether there are already adequate private infrastructures in place. Public funding to roll out a broadband network in (mostly rural) white areas where no adequate infrastructure exists is generally regarded as unproblematic. Conversely, investment in (densely populated) areas where already competing broadband infrastructures exist (black) is prohibited, while a state aid project for gray areas requires a more in-depth analysis. A similar logic is applied in cases of aid to NGA networks, distinguishing between "white NGA," "gray NGA," and "black NGA" areas.[48]

Where the Commission authorizes state aid, a number of compatibility conditions must be fulfilled (as detailed in paragraph 51 of the guidelines). Public authorities must carry out a detailed mapping of the target areas, and the use of open tender mechanisms to grant the aid remains crucial. Effective open wholesale access to the subsidized network must be guaranteed to allow alternative operators to compete and avoid recreation of telecoms monopolies. Moreover, the measures have to be technology neutral, and price benchmarking and claw-back mechanisms need to be put in place to avoid overcompensation. Because the risk of distorting competition could be higher (since basic broadband infrastructures may be already in place in the targeted areas), additional compatibility conditions must be met for aid to NGA networks. The white/black/gray area distinction is adapted to the situation of NGA networks by requiring member states to take into account not only existing NGA infrastructures but also concrete investment plans by telecom operators to deploy such networks in the near future.[49]

In April 2011, the Commission published a detailed questionnaire to invite comments on the proposed revision of the 2009 guidelines, scheduled for late 2012. This early revision date reflects the view that at the time of adoption of the 2009 guidelines, there was relatively limited experience on dealing with NGA networks. In June 2012, the Commission came forward with new draft guidelines,[50] building on the principles set out in the new SAM plans, and the new package on services of general economic interest (SGEI), adopted in December 2011 (see below). The new guidelines aim to shift the focus of public investment to passive infrastructure elements of the networks (ducts, manholes, dark fiber)[51] to further strengthen competition and to impose stricter access conditions for wholesale providers to allow the use of the subsidized infrastructure and further foster competition at the retail level. In particular, a publicly funded network set up within the context of a public service or SGEI must be available to all interested operators, and the provision of an infrastructure in an area where private investment is already available cannot be considered as an SGEI. An SGEI mission should only cover the deployment of a broadband network providing universal connectivity and the provision of related wholesale access services, but it should not include retail communication services (see paragraphs 20 to 23 of the draft). As explained below, member states normally enjoy wide discretion in defining the types of services or activities to be designated as SGEIs, but the draft guidelines would considerably encroach on the scope of that discretion.[52]

In this respect the Commission proposes to clarify the role of national telecoms regulators (NRAs) in designing and monitoring effective, pro-competitive state aid measures and to ensure their alignment with the principles adopted in the NGA Recommendation of 2010 on wholesale access to NGAs.[53] For example, NRAs should be consulted on the prices and related terms and conditions for wholesale access. This is a significant policy shift, since normally national regulators are not involved in the process of granting or monitoring state aid at the national level. So far it has met with mixed reactions from the regulators themselves, given that in most jurisdictions, NRAs lack the legal competence to take on the types of tasks envisaged for them in the draft guidelines.[54]

C. Caring for the Elderly and the Sick: The State as Provider of SGEI and State Aid

As Mario Monti concluded in May 2010, "The place of public services within the single market has been a persistent irritant in the European public debate."[55] Following the entry into force of the Lisbon Treaty, SGEIs—also referred to as public service obligations—featured more prominently in the European primary law framework. First, a specific protocol on SGEIs, Protocol 26, was annexed to the treaties to emphasize their importance. Second, the Lisbon Treaty gave legal force to Article 36 of the Charter of Fundamental Rights of the EU on access to SGEIs by citizens.[56]

When granting compensation for the provision of these types of services, the state is again wearing a specific hat, and support for SGEIs is normally assessed under state aid rules by reference to Article 106(2) TFEU, which states that undertakings entrusted with the operation of services of general economic interest are subject to the rules contained in the treaty, in particular to the rules on competition, insofar as the application of such rules do not obstruct, in law or in fact, the performance of the tasks assigned. This wording has to be read in conjunction with the so-called *Altmark* case law.[57] In *Altmark*, the European Court of Justice analyzed compensation paid by a member state to an undertaking entrusted with a SGEI. The ruling clarified under which conditions this compensation falls outside Article 107(1) TFEU—that is, it is not state aid at all.

In particular, under the *Altmark* case law, there are four cumulative criteria: the recipient undertaking must actually have public service obligations to discharge, and the obligations must be clearly defined; the parameters on the basis of which the compensation is calculated must be established in advance in an objective and transparent manner; the compensation cannot exceed what is necessary to cover all or part of the costs incurred in the discharge of the public service obligations, taking into account the relevant receipts and a reasonable profit; and where the undertaking that is to discharge public service obligations, in a specific case, is not chosen pursuant to a public procurement procedure that would allow for the selection of the tenderer capable of providing those services at the least cost to the community, the level of compensation needed must be determined on the basis of an analysis of the costs that a typical undertaking, well run and adequately provided with the relevant means, would have incurred.[58]

If the measure does not respect the *Altmark* criteria, then it is considered state aid and must be notified to and subsequently authorized by the Commission. Given that the *Altmark* criteria are extremely strict, more often than not a member state will find itself under an obligation to notify SGEI compensation measures and to obtain Commission approval. In December 2011,[59] the Commission adopted a package of measures intended to clarify further and streamline its approach to the compatibility assessment of SGEI under the state aid rules.[60] At the same time, the Commission also issued the so-called "Quality Framework for Services of General Interest in Europe,"[61] where it argues in favor of more convergence between state aid and the EU public procurement rules to facilitate their application for member states. In particular, at paragraph 19 of the Framework on compatibility of state aid granted as compensation for SGEIs,[62] it seems to suggest that compliance with the relevant procurement rules—usually a competitive tender—is a necessary condition for a state measure to be deemed compatible with the state aid rules. The aim here is to secure "value for money" by ensuring that the lowest tender wins. This is a very strict interpretation of the *Altmark* ruling and has attracted criticism.[63] Furthermore, it is not entirely clear that by having more recourse to public procurement procedures, the Commission might obtain "less and better-targeted state aid" because public procurement can also be used to foster policy goals, which may not always deliver lower public costs. Indeed, a contracting authority may choose to award a contract either on the basis of the lowest price or "the most economically advantageous tender." The latter criterion allows for the consideration of a wider range of factors than price alone, including social and environmental goals, as the Commission itself recognizes at paragraph 67 of the Framework.

According to the rules contained in the 2011 Package, if a given measure grants an amount exceeding a given threshold, it will have to be notified and assessed by the Commission in accordance with the principles set out in the Package. In essence, compensation for an SGEI must not exceed what is necessary to cover the net cost of discharging the public service obligations,[64] including a reasonable profit.[65] However, the Communication acknowledges that:

> In the absence of specific Union rules defining the scope for the existence of an SGEI, member states have a wide margin of discretion in defining a given service as an SGEI and in granting compensation to the service provider. The Commission's competence in this respect is limited to checking whether the member state has made a manifest error when defining the service as an SGEI and to assessing any state aid involved in the compensation.[66]

An example drawn from a sector where there are no such Union harmonization rules may be useful to illustrate these principles. If a member state decides to provide top-quality health care by means of high-level or "gold-plated" hospital services, the Commission will not be entitled to second guess such a choice, as its scrutiny must be limited primarily to an analysis of costs with a view to identifying possible instances of overcompensation.[67] Overcompensation is a cause of concern because the recipient could use this revenue to cross-subsidize activities that are subject to full competition—a particular concern in the broadcasting sector, for example.[68]

The wide discretion left to member states to designate particular activities as SGEIs,[69] of course, raises a number of questions regarding the scope and level of scrutiny that the Commission, and eventually the European courts, must respect, while carrying out a compatibility review of SGEIs and their financing. Two cases illustrate this point. In *Endesa and Endesa Generación v. Commission*,[70] Spain had granted financial compensation in return for the obligation to use indigenous coal to generate electricity. The Commission had—with some hesitation—approved the measure, and its decision was subsequently challenged by a number of utilities. In the decision on whether to suspend the Commission decision, the GC, in its Order of February 2011, recalled that member states have a "wide discretion" to define what they regard as SGEIs and that the definition of such services by a member state can be questioned by the Commission only in the event of manifest error. In this regard, the member states have to (1) demonstrate the presence of an act of the public authority entrusting the operators in question with an SGEI mission and the universal and compulsory nature of that mission and (2) indicate the reasons why it considers that the service in question, because of its specific nature, deserves to be characterized as an SGEI.[71]

In this light, the Commission's review is necessarily limited to ascertaining whether first, the system is founded on economic and factual premises that are *manifestly* erroneous and second, whether the system, including its financing, is *manifestly* inappropriate for achieving the objectives pursued.[72] In other words, the Commission cannot usually replace the member state's assessment of what the latter regards as an SGEI, and how much money to throw at it, although as we have seen above, it intends to narrow that assessment under its draft broadband guidelines. Yet, the *Endesa* case, decided before the new SGEI package was adopted, suggests that if a member state claims a situation of security of energy supply—as Spain did in the case at issue—the Commission may only check if this claim is manifestly erroneous. If not, the Commission has no leeway to hear arguments questioning the level of a security of supply risk, or the cost of responding to it, and has to accept the member state's resolve to adopt SGEI measures, even if the risk is minor or even remote. This in turn limits the General Court's ensuing review, which will be confined to ascertaining whether the Commission's assessment is sufficiently plausible to support the necessity for the system in question.[73]

In *Enel*,[74] the Court of Justice has provided a possible counterbalance to the wide discretion of member states in defining SGEIs. This is because while member states are free to designate an SGEI, once they do so, they must respect the principle of proportionality, especially if the sector is subject to harmonizing legislation.[75] In *Enel*, the CJEU examined Italian legislation mandating electricity-generating companies holding essential installations to make available specified volumes of energy at a price not determined by the producer but imposed by the regulator. Even though the Court in the end concluded that the Italian legislation was proportionate, it nonetheless subjected it to a rigorous test. Applied in the context of a state aid analysis, this rationale would mean that, through stricter conditions on how compensation is to be calculated, the Commission may be able to steer the way SGEIs are organized at the national level toward greater efficiency and transparency.

Indeed, in a very recent case,[76] the Commission opened an in-depth investigation to establish whether the compensation received by Société Nationale Corse-Méditerranée (SNCM) and Compagnie Maritime de Navigation (CMN) for operating the sea routes between Corsica and Marseille are in line with EU state aid rules. In particular, the Commission indicated that it had doubts about the need for and proportionality of the SGEI and also about the compensation mechanism. SNCM and CMN operate the route between Corsica and Marseille for the period 2007–2013 under a public service agreement concluded with the Corsican regional authorities. The public service obligation encompasses both the basic service (permanent passenger and freight service) and the additional service (passenger service provided for traffic peaks during holiday periods and the summer season). The French authorities are being asked to demonstrate that there is a real public service need and whether the additional service cannot be ensured by market forces alone.[77]

* * *

After more than 50 years of European law, the concept of "state aid" remains open ended. This enables the European Courts to play a key role. Their recent approach in the *EdF* case shows that, through jurisprudence, the concept of state aid can be aligned with economic and political developments affecting the role of the state intervention in the economy. A clearer analysis of the type of "hat" the state is wearing—as a market investor—as the corrector of market failures or as the guarantor of public services—may well be required in the future before turning to the effects of the measure under scrutiny. This may appear an excessively formalistic approach and one that might lead to substantial gaps in the Commission's powers to fight distortions of competition, but it must also be recalled that the European Courts have rejected Commission attempts to stretch the concept of aid to cover "measures having equivalent effect" to state subsidies.[78]

At the same time, and especially in the current financial crisis, the European Commission is inclined to use the state aid rules as a tool to shape member states' industrial and fiscal policies and encroach on national preferences and to impose stricter fiscal control. The interplay between the legal openness of the concept of state aid and the Commission's more interventionist policy stance may give rise to member states having a greater incentive to design measures that fall outside the scope of the state aid provisions to escape the Commission's ever more intrusive appraisal of their compatibility. However, this approach is far from failsafe.[79] As an alternative, member states may be forced to try to comply with the soft law rules—such as the broadband guidelines discussed above—under which the Commission predetermines the contours of its compatibility assessment according to its own, changing policy agenda. In both scenarios, the potential impact of state aid control remains a powerful force in shaping member states' policies toward supporting and steering their economies.

Chapter 12

Australian Experience with Competition Law

The State as a Market Actor

Deborah Healey

The application of competition law and policy to government in Australia is comprehensive. The role of government in Australian markets was historically very significant, but there was early acceptance of the implications of this expanded government role, resulting in the early imposition of general legal liability on "the Crown" (government). Application of statutes to the Crown and its entities was, however, a different story. A rule of construction, the doctrine of Crown immunity (also known as "shield of the Crown") protected many government activities from the application of laws, including the competition law. Microeconomic reforms of the 1980s and 1990s resulted in large-scale restructuring of government entities in the name of efficiency and productivity. Following an important holistic review of Australian competition law and policy in the mid-1990s, competition law prohibitions were applied generally to all government business activities. Simultaneous reforms curtailed other government impacts on markets.

This chapter outlines the history of the role of government and competition law in Australia, the impact of law and policy reform, and the current state of play in the interface between state and competition. It looks primarily at the role of government as market actor in the sense of a business market participant and how it is subject to competition law. Some government conduct that has the capacity to impact the market is still immune from competition law, and until recently the law on Crown (government) immunity also significantly advantaged those dealing with immune government bodies.[1] The chapter also touches on competition policy initiatives aimed at the market impact of government in its roles as lawmaker and regulator. The results of competition policy reform in Australia are impressive, but the reforms were essential to revitalize markets, benefiting both the economy and consumers. Reform initiatives continue. Given the substantial capacity of government bodies to affect markets, the chapter also considers briefly whether aspects of the competition law reforms relating to government have gone far enough. This chapter has broader implications for other countries with centralized structures in which state and competition interface.

I. Law and Government in Australia

A. Historical Role of Government in Australia

Despite the continuing role of the sovereign and the influence of England on the legal system, the role of responsible government in Australia does not simply replicate the English system. While "a dominant Anglo-centric view was an inevitable product of the course of Australia's colonization,"[2] there were significant differences in the way government developed and the roles it adopted here. Australia developed a centralized government power structure at state level that bypassed local authorities, fostering a relationship of the citizen to the state that was quite different from that in England. This centralized power structure and other unique circumstances fostered an attitude in the citizens whereby they "looked to the central federal and state governments for the satisfaction of needs."[3] Isolation of the country and its small number of citizens from Europe and the other Australian colonies, primitive conditions, patterns of settlement in coastal pockets, and imperatives of development all resulted in government involvement in activities that in Britain would have been the function of local government, private enterprise, or private and charitable organizations. Government had significant roles in areas such as public utilities, infrastructure, capital formation, and the labor market that did not exist in England.[4] For the 40 years prior to Federation, public capital formation progressively exceeded private, and after Federation, state governments required federal government support to promote progress.[5] The nature of the expanded role of government in Australia meant that governments at both federal and state levels became major players in areas such as communications, roads, ports, electricity and gas supply, and banking.

Traditionally, all activities of government, even those in the market, were undertaken in Australia in two forms: by government departments (which were not separate legal entities) discharging executive functions under ministerial direction and directly responsible to a minister or by statutory authorities. Government departments had advantages over private competitors such as the ability to obtain land and resources, access to statute to assist their actions, government guarantees on borrowings, access to consolidated revenue to fund losses, and taxation advantages.[6] However, they also had some disadvantages: government departments operated under inflexible employment arrangements, were directed by political agendas that included rigid pricing and cross-subsidization, and were hamstrung by a multiplicity of nonbusiness objectives.[7] Statutory authorities were separate legal bodies under the control of government-appointed independent boards. Statutory authorities rather than departments were used where goods or services were provided in markets or where independence from direct political control was desirable.[8] While the market presence of government and government-controlled bodies was extremely well established, shortcomings in business operations such as poor pricing practices and poor productivity had a negative impact on the economy.[9]

B. Public Sector Reform

A more robust and broader market approach was taken in the country in the 1980s when economic progress appeared to falter.[10] As Australian Competition and Consumer Commission (ACCC) chairman Rod Sims describes, "There was a questioning of whether Australia was benefiting from the continuation of centralized wage fixing, tariff protection, government ownership of trading enterprises such as QANTAS and the Commonwealth Bank as well as rigid regulation and government ownership in the transport and public utility sectors."[11]

In response to the economic downturn of the 1980s, the Australian government floated the Australian currency, cut tariffs, eliminated import quotas, and deregulated the financial system. Australia in essence transformed from a closed domestic economy to an open economy capable of supplying global markets. Microeconomic reforms aimed at improving government administrative and economic efficiency were undertaken. The government introduced competition in some regulated industries. The reforms to government enterprises were sweeping; they "modified and removed day-to-day government controls, revised corporate and financial structures, and established new planning and accountability mechanisms."[12] Changes to government operations included privatization of some government businesses, corporatization (as a statutory corporation with all shares owned by government) of others, and commercialization,[13] where a separate business unit within government was operated on a commercial basis. Public enterprise reform was part of an increased focus on competition, which included the *Hilmer Review*, discussed below. Given the important role that government and its entities played in the market at that time, the extent to which competition law should apply to government was also a significant question.

C. Government Immunity in Australia: The General Picture

Government in Australia was known as "the Crown" for historical reasons and because of the common law origins of the legal system. In England, at common law the Crown could not be sued under the rationale that it was inappropriate for the king to be subject to his own courts. This protection from lawsuit extended beyond the king in his personal capacity and also protected the king's government, also known as "the Crown." While there were some exceptions to the rule, they did not consistently apply.[14] In the Australian Federation, each government, both federal and state, is a separate legal person, falling within the category of legal entity known as a body politic.[15] Each of these bodies politic was known as "the Crown." In addition to governments, statutory corporations in Australia are sometimes called "the Crown."[16]

The position of Crown legal liability in Australia was originally the same as in England, but whether it was because of the prominent role of government in the Australian economy or for some other reason, most Australian states had legislated to make the Crown generally legally liable far earlier than was the case in England.[17] The application of statute law to the Crown was, however, a different situation altogether. The general position with respect to the application of legislation to the Crown is that there is a principle of statutory construction known as "Crown immunity" that has been described as "by far the most important surviving immunity" of the Crown.[18]

In short, the Crown is not bound by statute except by express words or by necessary implication,[19] and in this respect, legislative intent prevails.[20] The presumption of immunity extends to the Crown in its commonwealth, state, and territory capacities. Where a nongovernment party is in a transaction with the Crown that has the benefit of this immunity, an additional question arises about the extent to which relief can be obtained against the nongovernment party. The effect of the doctrine of Crown immunity and the complex federal system, meant that many government businesses were not subject to competition law prior to the Hilmer reforms, to which we now turn.

II. Competition Law in Australia

Australia was an early adopter of competition law (in 1906), although it did not have an effective law until the enactment of the Trade Practices Act 1974 (the "Act"),[21] which was modeled on U.S. and EU statutes operative at that time. However, the Act was subject to significant limitations on coverage, mainly for constitutional reasons. The constitutional powers of the Australian Parliament to make laws with respect to specific matters including corporations[22] and interstate or overseas trade or commerce[23] provided the main Constitutional basis for the Act.[24] Bodies that are not trading, financial or foreign corporations under Section 51(xx) or bodies that are not engaged in constitutional trade or commerce under Section 51(i) of the Constitution of Australia are not within the constitutional power of the commonwealth to regulate in this context. Other factors affecting coverage were first, the commonwealth could not legislate to bind government bodies of states or territories and second, the state and territory governments were free to enact laws within their own jurisdictions expressly exempting specified conduct or certain bodies from the application of the Act.[25] The states and territories often made laws and regulations favoring their own industries and undertakings, and the commonwealth could not control this. Finally, the common law doctrine of Crown immunity, discussed above, meant that many government bodies, both federal and state, were immune from the Act. In 1977, the commonwealth Parliament recognized that it was inappropriate for government bodies carrying on business to have immunity from the Act and rectified the situation to the extent that it had power to do so. The Act was amended so that it applied to commonwealth Crown bodies carrying on business.[26] The commonwealth was, however, powerless to make similar amendments in respect of the Crown bodies of the states or territories.

A. The Hilmer Review

The process of economic reform in the 1980s identified the need for competition policy reform because some aspects of the competition policy framework were "impeding performance across the economy and constraining the scope to create national markets for infrastructure and other services."[27] A major review of Australian competition law and policy was undertaken by an expert committee in 1992. The Hilmer Review was undertaken with the agreement of the commonwealth, all states, and the territories.[28] It took a national approach to competition policy, and it emphasized two important facts: Australia was one economy, and competition policy embraces a range of laws and policies, not just the actual competition law itself. The report emanating from the Hilmer Review, the *Hilmer Report*, recommended a large number of significant reforms.[29] The *Hilmer Report* concluded that an effective competition policy for Australia should address six main concerns:

- Anticompetitive conduct of firms;
- Unjustified regulatory restrictions on competition;
- Inappropriate structures of public monopolies;
- Denial of access to certain facilities that are essential for effective competition;
- Monopoly pricing; and
- Competitive neutrality when government businesses compete with private firms.[30]

The recommendations of the *Hilmer Report* were adopted by agreement,[31] and the process became known as National Competition Policy (NCP). The legislative package comprised the Commonwealth Competition Policy Reform Act 1995 and associated state and territory application legislation. These amended the Act to incorporate Hilmer recommendations and applied the changes at state and territory level to those bodies that the federal government was constitutionally incapable of covering. The prohibitions of the Act on anticompetitive conduct were contained in Part IV of the Act. A new Part XIA was inserted into the Act that created mirror provisions in a Competition Code. Under NCP, each of the states and territories agreed to enact and maintain this Competition Code as uniform legislation to create a uniform competition statute for the country, and this was done by application legislation in each state and territory.[32] All of the governments also signed three agreements: the Competition Principles Agreement, which set out the principles for implementing other NCP reforms, such as prices oversight, structural reform of public monopolies, review and reform of restrictive regulation, competitive neutrality, third-party access to infrastructure services and application of these principles to local government; the Conduct Code Agreement, which also required state and territory governments to notify the ACCC if they enacted laws exempting bodies or conduct under Section 51 of the Act; and the Agreement to Implement the National Competition Policy and Related Reforms, which contained other commitments and provided for three tranches of payments to the states and territories on a per capita basis, subject to satisfactory compliance with NCP commitments. The National Competition Council (NCC) was established to support the implementation of NCP. It could recommend that the treasurer reduce the expected payment for noncompliance.

The next section considers individual NCP reforms that significantly impacted government and markets.

III. Application of Competition Law to Government

A foundational principle of the *Hilmer Report* was that, as a matter of policy, competition law should apply to all entities carrying on business. Hilmer approached the issue of exemptions or immunity on the basis that they should be of limited nature and implemented only after a transparent process.[33] This meant that the competition law should apply to state and territory government business enterprises in the same way that it already applied to commonwealth government business enterprises.[34] In practice, a number of categories of conduct were exempt.[35] The Act was amended to apply to state and territory government bodies to the extent that they carry on business. In practical terms, this means that status as a body entitled to crown immunity does not now exempt a business entity from the application of the competition law.

The wording of the provisions that apply the Act to Crown bodies is generally similar, but there are some distinctions. Section 2A, adopted in 1977 prior to the *Hilmer Report*, states that, subject to the provision itself, Section 44AC, Section 44E, and Section 95AD,[36] the Act binds the Crown in right of the commonwealth insofar as it carries on business, either directly or by an authority of the commonwealth. "Authority of the commonwealth" has two categories: a body corporate established for the purposes of the commonwealth by a law of the commonwealth or a territory, and an incorporated company in which the commonwealth (or another commonwealth body corporate) has a controlling interest.[37] In each case, Section 2A applies as if the commonwealth or the authority is a corporation.[38] The Crown in right of the commonwealth is not liable to be prosecuted for an offense under the Act, but an authority of the commonwealth may be.[39] Curiously, Section 2A contains an express exemption: Part IV does not apply to the business carried on by the commonwealth in developing and disposing of interests in land in the Australian Capital Territory (ACT).

Section 2B applies to the state and territory Crown and applies only to Part IV (anticompetitive conduct prohibitions), Part XIB (anticompetitive conduct in relation to telecommunications), and their related provisions.[40] It provides that the Act binds the Crown in right of each of the states and territories as far as the Crown carries on business, either directly or indirectly or by an authority of a state or territory. "Authority" has a similar definition but only in relation to a state or territory.[41] Similarly to Section 2A, the Crown in right of a state or territory is not liable to a pecuniary penalty or able to be prosecuted for an offense, and this protection does not extend to an authority of a state or territory.[42] The two provisions thus differ in respect of the scope of the Act that applies to the Crown when carrying business and also because the commonwealth Crown is bound as if it were a corporation.[43]

A brief word on local government is appropriate here. Local government consists of incorporated bodies under legislation in all states except New South Wales and Queensland. This means that Crown immunity is unlikely to apply in most states. In any event, Section 2BA(1) provides that Part IV applies only to the extent that a local government body is carrying on business, either directly or by an incorporated company in which it has a controlling interest.

The provisions raise two key questions that must be answered in determining the application of the Act to a government body. First, can the body be categorized as "the Crown" (in other words, does it represent the government)? If the body does not represent the Crown, the Act applies to trading or financial corporations, or bodies engaged in interstate or overseas trade or commerce. Legal "persons" outside these categories are caught under the Competition Act of the relevant state or territory.

Second, if the body does represent the Crown, is it "carrying on business"? If it is not, it is still entitled to immunity. In considering whether a body entitled to Crown immunity is carrying on business, it should be noted that the Act provides specific exceptions in Section 2C, discussed below. The next two sections consider these two important questions in more detail.

A. Does the Body Represent the "Crown"? (Or, Which Bodies Are "the Government"?)

Many bodies in Australia are linked to government. Some are government departments carrying out government functions. Some have been corporatized. Some are corporatized but are still wholly owned by government. Some are partially government owned. Various laws govern their status and operation, depending on the nature of their functions, the way they are intended to be managed, and the degree of autonomy that they have over day-to-day matters. Some government bodies, statutory authorities, and corporations legally or beneficially owned by government may still be manifestations of the Crown (i.e., represent the Crown). Some are not. Importantly, as Seddon noted, "The exact status of a government body is not merely an academic or pragmatic question because substantive rights may turn on what kind of entity it is."[44]

To determine whether a body is part of the Crown, or government (and thus whether it is entitled to Crown immunity), the courts have traditionally relied upon two tests—the incorporation test and the control test—to determine governmental purpose. The incorporation test asks whether the body has been incorporated and the way in which this has been done. The fact that the government has decided to create a separate body to perform a particular activity, for example, is an indication that it is not meant to be the Crown. To determine whether an incorporated body is the Crown, it is necessary to review the legislation establishing the body to ascertain the intention of the legislators. In many cases statutes setting up a body expressly state whether or not it represents the Crown and has immunity. If the legislation setting up the body is silent on the issue of whether it is part of the Crown, it is likely that it is not. The courts generally require clear wording indicating that the body forms part of the Crown for this to be the case. If a body is set up under the general Corporations Act, for example, it is unlikely that the body represents the Crown.[45]

The position of government-owned corporations under the laws of the commonwealth, the states, and the territories establishing them differs. Seddon[46] canvassed these laws and concluded there is no unanimity. The Commonwealth Authorities and Companies Act 1997, for example, binds the Crown in right of the commonwealth but is silent on whether commonwealth authorities or companies represent the crown.[47] By way of contrast, the State Owned Corporations Act (NSW) 1989 binds the Crown but expressly provides that state-owned corporations do not represent the Crown. There is no law dealing with the issue in Western Australia. The Public Corporations Act 1993 of South Australia provides that a public corporation (statutory corporation) and any subsidiaries are instrumentalities of the Crown. Some judgments have suggested that the starting point should be that corporatized bodies do not have immunity, but not all decisions confirm this.[48]

Where there is no legislative specification, the issue is determined by considering the functions of the body and the degree of control exercised over those functions by government. Under this control test, a government body is entitled to Crown immunity if a Minister of the Crown controls and directs its activities. Control in this context refers to the right to control, rather than the actual exercise of control. If a body has independent discretions, it is less likely to be entitled to immunity.

The important case of *Bropho v. Western Australia*[49] decided by the High Court, the final court of review in Australia, emphasized the importance of the overall context of the statute, its disclosed purpose and policy in determining the issue of Crown immunity.[50] This approach was a substantial change in emphasis from preceding decisions applying the test. Prior to this, courts had applied a test of "necessary implication" very strictly, so it was quite difficult to satisfy, and the Crown was usually not bound by a statute.[51] The *Bropho* case abandoned the strict application of necessary implication, giving predominance to statutory construction.[52] In doing so, the *Bropho* case expressly recognized that historical considerations supporting the presumption that legislation would not have been intended to bind the Crown were largely irrelevant in Australia with its different government market role.[53]

The *NT Power* case is a good example of the application of the *Bropho* approach, although it is important to mention that there was substantial diversity in judicial opinion among the lower-level courts.[54] The issues were ultimately determined by the High Court. There were a number of interesting aspects of the case in the context of the changing nature of government bodies and their anticompetitive behavior. The Crown immunity issue related to a subsidiary of the main respondent, Power and Water Authority (PAWA), which itself was clearly entitled to immunity. PAWA owned shares in the subsidiary trading corporation, Gasgo. Gasgo allegedly engaged in misuse of market power in breach of s46 of the Act, and it argued that it was entitled to Crown immunity because it represented the Crown. Gasgo was a trading corporation at general law, with standard commercial articles, and its directors had the usual functions of directors. This made it harder, the High Court said, to identify any legislative intention that it should have Crown immunity. Nothing suggested that its directors were under a duty to obey directions from PAWA or the government, so there was no indication of Crown control or intention to control. The purchasers of its gas were not Crown bodies but ordinary commercial corporations. The High Court found that the fact that its purchasers were not Crown emanations, particularly undermined its attempt to characterize itself as part of the Northern Territory government. Neither the giving of guarantees by the government on its behalf nor an agreement for it to exercise certain rights in consultation with NTEC was sufficient to suggest that Gasgo should have immunity.[55]

Where corporatized bodies are subject to ministerial directions to their boards, it is likely they are entitled to Crown immunity. In some cases, shareholding ministers have reserve powers, or the power to issue ministerial directions.[56] It may be that some bodies are entitled to Crown immunity in respect of some activities and not others—for example, where legislation allows for ministerial directions in respect to only certain conduct.

B. Government as Business: Is the Government Body Carrying on Business?

Once the body is characterized as the Crown, the next question is whether its activities can be considered to be carrying on business to determine whether the Act applies. At the outset, however, it is important to note what is *not* considered carrying on business. Section 2C of the Act lists a number of activities that do not constitute carrying on business by a body that is entitled to Crown immunity:

- Imposing or collecting taxes, levies, or fees for licenses;
- Granting, refusing to grant, or suspending licenses, whether or not they are subject to conductions;
- Transactions involving only persons acting for the Crown, the same right (i.e., both for the commonwealth Crown and none of whom is an authority for that Crown);
- Where one of the entities is a noncommercial authority of the commonwealth, a state, or a territory. A body is "noncommercial" if it is constituted only by one person and is neither a trading nor a financial corporation;
- Where only noncommercial authorities of the same commonwealth, state, or territory Crown are involved; and
- The compulsory acquisition of primary products by a government body under laws unless it is exercising or has not exercised a discretion that it does not have to acquire the products.

These listed exceptions to Sections 2A and 2B are not exhaustive.[57] The High Court in the *NT Power* case[58] characterized a "license" for the purposes of Section 2C as one necessary to prevent an illegality or wrong against the Crown. In other words, engaging in certain conduct, such as selling liquor or drugs without a license, would be contrary to an enactment.

Many cases have considered the meaning of "conducting business" for the purposes of the Act. It does not, for example, require a profit motive.[59] Whether the activities undertaken are in the nature of government activities or would usually be undertaken by business is important. The nature of the statute setting up the relevant government body is also important. The High Court emphasized in the *NT Power* case that the Act should be given a broad application rather than a narrow one. If activities are carried on in a regular manner with repetition and system, they are likely to involve carrying on business.[60]

Procuring goods or services for use by a government body is, however, unlikely to be carrying on business. This conclusion arises from the influential *McMillan* case,[61] where the sale of the printing business unit of a government department was found not to involve carrying on business because the government was not in the business of selling assets, although it was in the business of selling the publications printed by the business. The case has been followed on a number of occasions, and it is now generally accepted that the commonwealth is not bound by the Act in respect of tendering or procuring. This is a very important competition law immunity when one considers that procurement is a major commercial activity of government and, depending on the circumstances, one in which it has the capacity to exercise a substantial degree of market power as an acquirer.[62]

Activities that have been determined not to be carrying on business for the purposes of Section 2C and the similar state provisions include inviting tenders to sell off part of an existing business (the *McMillan* case);[63] running immigration detention centers for profit;[64] managing a national park;[65] running the Trade Practices Commission;[66] and operating a public hospital providing services to public patients through a contractor.[67]

The *NT Power* case[68] mentioned earlier considered a number of significant issues of principle in relation to government business: what happens when a body not previously exposed to competition and traditionally performing a public service is faced with a competitive "threat"; what happens when a government body entitled to crown immunity is "carrying on business"; the extent to which the Act applies to a refusal to enter a new business area or to assist others to do so; and what happens when the subsidiary of an immune body is entitled to crown immunity. Some of these already have been discussed, but for contextual reasons, a full discussion of other aspects of the case is warranted at this point.

In the case, Power and Water Authority (PAWA) was a government body set up under a special law and subject to directions of the minister. It generated electricity and purchased electricity from others, transported electricity from generation sites to distribution points and distributed the electricity to customers. It had issued NT Power Generation Pty Ltd (NT Power) a license to generate electricity. NT Power wanted to sell power it generated to customers but could not do so without access to the electricity transmission and distribution infrastructure owned by PAWA. It sought access to this infrastructure, but PAWA refused to grant it. It was accepted by the parties that PAWA was entitled to Crown immunity because it was set up under special legislation and was subject to ministerial direction, but one of the issues before the High Court was whether it was carrying on business when it refused the use of infrastructure. If it was carrying on business, it would have been subject to the Act (by Section 2B) and potentially liable for contravention. The fact was that it had never allowed anyone to have access before (and presumably no one had ever asked prior to restructuring of the industry). At the time of the request PAWA was setting up an access regime for its infrastructure under the relatively new Access provisions of Part IIIA of the Act, but this had not been finalized. PAWA refused access for reasons that included wanting all access seekers to be dealt with under its standard Part IIIA regime once it was finalized.

PAWA argued strenuously that it was not carrying on business when it refused the request. The High Court found that, on the contrary, PAWA was in fact carrying on business and using the infrastructure as a significant part of that business. The High Court found that relevant considerations included that it had an express duty under its legislation to act in a commercial manner and that it described its transmission and distribution facilities as "business products" in its documentation. The High Court characterized the actual refusal as conduct that advanced PAWA's business and found that it had taken the decision not to supply because of the negative impact that this would have in the short term on its business of selling electricity. The fact that it had not supplied the access before was not the point. Ultimately the High Court found that PAWA had breached Section 46 of the Act, Misuse of Market Power, in refusing to allow NT Power to use the infrastructure.[69]

While the amendments prior to the *Hilmer Report* for the commonwealth Crown and after it for the state and territory Crown assume it is appropriate to apply the Act to the business activities of government, the traditional legal concept of carrying on business fails to encapsulate the substantial business activities of government in the context of procurement and particularly the demonstrable advantage that government may have in procurement and contracting situations. This is a major gap in the way the current legislation deals with the activities of government (to be discussed later).

Of course, governments will not always be in a position of market power in their procurement activities, as the situation in *ACCC v. Baxter Healthcare*[70] indicates, but there are a range of situations that might foreseeably fall within the prohibitions of Part IV of the Act that could apply to governments.

C. Dealing with Immune Government: Derivative Crown Immunity

"Derivative Crown immunity" is the name given to immunity that applies in some circumstances to nongovernment bodies engaged in dealings with an immune Crown body. Where there is conduct in breach of the Act and one of the parties is entitled to Crown immunity, the other party may also be entitled to immunity on the basis that making orders against it would have the effect of indirectly applying the Act to the Crown and prejudicing its interests. This approach was applied in a number of cases and in effect has allowed parties dealing with immune government bodies to escape liability for breaches of the Act in the past.[71]

The issue has recently been raised in two important High Court cases. The first, the *NT Power* case that was discussed previously, involved arguments by Gasgo that had unsuccessfully claimed Crown immunity and also argued for derivative Crown immunity. Gasgo, the subsidiary of PAWA was a party to a contract with the Mereenie Gas Producers (Mereenie) that gave Gasgo pre-emptive rights over gas supplies. Neither Gasgo nor Mereenie was entitled to Crown immunity. NT Power required gas to generate electricity and sought an undertaking from Gasgo that it would not insist on its preemptive rights. Gasgo refused to give the undertaking, and NT Power claimed that this was a breach of Section 46, Misuse of Market Power, of the Act. Gasgo argued that it was entitled to derivative Crown immunity because the Northern Territory government would suffer financial prejudice if immunity was not extended to Gasgo. This was on the basis that if Gasgo did not exercise its preemptive right, PAWA would have to seek additional supplies of gas in a competitive market. The High Court rejected this argument on the basis that financial prejudice was insufficient to ground derivative Crown immunity. To ground derivative Crown immunity, the High Court said, it was necessary to show that the application of the Act in the circumstances would adversely affect a legal prerogative, or a statutory, proprietary, contractual, or other legal or equitable right or interest of the government.[72]

A more recent High Court case has further clarified and narrowed the scope of derivative Crown immunity. Baxter Healthcare Pty Ltd (Baxter) responded to requests for tender from a number of State and Territory Purchasing Authorities (SPAs) that were entitled to Crown immunity because they were not carrying on business.[73] Baxter was found by the lower courts to have breached the provisions of the Act on misuse of market power (Section 46) and exclusive dealing (Section 47) by supplying bundled products, despite this being envisaged in the request for tender documentation.[74] The lower courts found (reluctantly) on the basis of previous law[75] that derivative Crown immunity extended to commercial negotiations between an immune Crown body and a commercial body in breach of the Act. The High Court overruled these decisions and declined to follow the *Bradken* case on the basis that the existing approach to Crown immunity based on *Bradken* was too broad after the later *Bropho* decision.[76] In addition, because the doctrine was a principle of statutory construction, changes to the Act since the *Bradken* case were relevant. The High Court found that it was not Parliament's intention to excuse trading corporations that were doing business with government from the consequences of their breach of the Act. The overall purpose of the Act is to promote competition and fair trading,[77] and this would not be achieved if derivative Crown immunity could be claimed in circumstances such as the present.

A number of features of the case are perplexing. The fact that Baxter's bundling of its offers in the tender process was encouraged by the SPAs is problematic in the context of the result, although it was really the pricing strategy of the bundled alternatives that gave rise to the competition problems, not the mere fact that products were bundled. The concept of a private company misusing its market power against government is somewhat counterintuitive, although when one considers the issue more carefully, it is apparent governments may not always have market power when dealing with private business, particularly where, as here, the other party is a monopolist in relation to one of the required products.

IV. Other Competition Policy Initiatives

This section briefly outlines competition policy initiatives that restrict government legislative and regulatory market impact. The NCP initiatives were agreed to formally by the states in return for large payments based on estimated productivity gains resulting from compliance with the written national reform agenda.[78]

A. Government as a Lawmaker

Each of the states and territories agreed to maintain the standard Part IV Restrictive Trade Practices provisions in the individual Competition Acts to create a single, ongoing law.

B. Limits on Exceptions by Statute or Regulation

Conduct specifically authorized by commonwealth,[79] state, or territory statute or regulation[80] was not traditionally subject to the Act. The power to except conduct was broad and was used particularly in relation to the conduct of "professional associations, agricultural marketing bodies, and some state- and territory-owned businesses."[81] On the recommendation of the *Hilmer Report*, Section 51 of the Act was substantially narrowed to prevent these exceptions except in limited well-justified circumstances with a sunset clause. Excepting laws must now state specifically the conduct to be authorized and refer to the Act.

C. Review of Laws Restricting Competition

The *Hilmer Report* recommended the review by governments at commonwealth, state, and territory levels of all laws to identify and amend those that unnecessarily restricted competition and to review all new legislation to prevent laws that hinder competition without examination under a transparent process.[82] Importantly, the test reversed the usual onus of proof: legislation should not restrict competition unless it can be demonstrated that the benefits to the community as a whole outweigh the costs and the objectives of the legislation can only be achieved by restricting competition. Approximately 1,800 laws were reviewed under this test during NCP, in areas such as water, primary industries, communications, consumer protection, insurance and superannuation, health, the professions, planning and construction, retailing, social regulation, and transport.[83] Many important reforms were implemented.[84] The states have agreed to continue this legislative review.[85]

D. Government as a Regulator: Structural Reform of Public Monopolies

The *Hilmer Report* endorsed structural reform of public monopolies to facilitate competition. Existing reform programs for electricity, gas, and water—sectors previously dominated by public monopolies—continued under NCP.[86]

E. Government as a Facilities Owner: Third-Party Access

The government introduced a third-party access regime as Part IIIA of the Act to facilitate access to significant "essential" infrastructure facilities, both government and privately owned, on recommendation of the *Hilmer Report*.[87] The policy objective was to enhance consumer welfare by ensuring that facilities exhibiting natural monopoly characteristics that could not be economically duplicated did not become "bottlenecks." This would facilitate competition in upstream and downstream markets to maximize efficiency in the supply of goods or services to consumers, while at the same time not acting as a disincentive to further investment.[88]

Part IIIA provides a detailed framework for the grant of access to a "service by means of a facility" based on analysis of specified factors, including that the facility is uneconomical to duplicate.[89] The access regime is made up of a complex web of declaration, negotiation, and arbitration; dispute resolution; certification of state and territory regimes; access undertakings; and industry codes that are too detailed to set out in full here.[90] The National Competition Council, the ACCC, and the Australian Competition Tribunal are involved in these processes at the national level.[91] The Part IIIA general access scheme is supplemented by other federal and state access regimes. Access regimes are in place under the generic law or special regulations in sectors.

F. Government as a Price Setter: Monopoly Price Oversight

The *Hilmer Report* also recommended establishment of independent price oversight for monopolistic government business enterprises in each jurisdiction to set, administer, or oversee prices for enterprises that remained monopoly service providers. The ACCC was given responsibility for setting and overseeing businesses not under state or territory control. Part VIIA of the Act, implemented in 2004, applies in markets that are uncompetitive, and the minister may require the ACCC to hold an inquiry into prices. The minister may also direct the ACCC to monitor prices in a specified industry and has done so in respect to gas prices.

G. Government and the Level Playing Field: Competitive Neutrality

Competitive neutrality is recognition that where significant government business activities are in competition with the private sector, market distortions and inefficient resource allocation can occur. Government businesses should not have a competitive advantage or disadvantage simply by virtue of their ownership or control. Advantage accruing to the bodies, such the lack of a requirement to recover costs or to price efficiently, the nonaccountability of managers for their business performance, and the conferral of monopoly rights on businesses (sheltering them from competitive pressures and discipline), can occur. Potential disadvantages of government ownership such as community service obligations, greater accountability obligations, reduced managerial autonomy, and requirements to comply with government policies on wages, employment, and industrial relations were identified well prior to the *Hilmer Report*, and governments had pursued a variety of reforms such as corporatization,[92] commercialization, privatization, and competitive tendering and contracting to address them.[93] The *Hilmer Report* recommended the adoption of mechanisms to ensure competitive neutrality, and commonwealth, state, and territory governments agreed.

* * *

In 2005 the Productivity Commission reviewed the impact of NCP reforms,[94] noting that as part of NCP, A$834 million was paid to the states and territories between 1998 and 2003. It concluded that NCP had delivered substantial benefits, contributing to a productivity surge that underpinned 13 years of continuous economic growth and associated increases in household incomes and that these and other benefits had greatly outweighed its costs. The annual benefit to the Australian economy was estimated at 2.5 percent of GDP or A$20 billion. Lower prices made possible by cheaper infrastructure inputs for businesses and longer-term stimulus to employment had benefited consumers.[95] Business innovation, customer responsiveness, and choice had been stimulated.[96]

Following the Productivity Commission Review of NCP, COAG in 2006 undertook a new reform agenda,[97] the National Reform Agenda (NRA). Poor recent productivity figures have focused attention on areas for development such as infrastructure.[98] The government established Infrastructure Australia in 2008 to advise governments, investors, and owners on planning and development, develop a strategic blueprint for major infrastructure, and review infrastructure finance.[99] As part of the NRA, infrastructure reform is supported by agreements and financial incentives for states,[100] monitored by the COAG Reform Council. The NRA focuses on competition, regulation, and human capital, and the competition reform stream reviews productivity and economic efficiency in transport, energy, infrastructure regulation, and planning and climate change.[101] Concerns about the burden of government regulation[102] underpin a regulatory review stream promoting best practice regulation to reduce the regulatory burden on business.[103] As part of this, the National Partnership Agreement to Deliver a Seamless National Economy[104] aims to replace piecemeal state and territory laws with uniform national regulation.[105]

Commentators have noted the significant gap in competition law coverage of government procurement that still remains. Seddon, for example, described the Hilmer reforms in respect of government as "limited" because they presume that governments should be bound by the competition law only insofar as they carry on business[106] and give an unfair advantage to public commercial bodies.

Review of the actual wording in the *Hilmer Report* on this issue is instructive: it recommends the removal of the shield of the Crown doctrine "insofar as the Crown in question carries on a business *or engages in a commercial activity in competition (actual or potential) with other businesses*" (italics added).[107] These words indicate that the intention of the recommendation was broader than merely "carrying on business" and extended to "commercial activity," arguably a much broader concept. Presumably the government is engaged in commercial activity in competition, actual or potential, with other acquirers when it is involved in procurement. In amending the Act in relation to state and territory Crown immunity, it is possible that too much emphasis was placed by the drafters on the wording of existing Section 2A, already making the Act applicable to the commonwealth Crown and not enough on the intention of the *Hilmer Report*, which appears to go further than the provisions that eventuated. Additional support for revisiting this issue comes from the Productivity Commission, which stated in relation to Crown immunity and the issue of procurement in its 2005 review of NCP that "lack of clarity in current arrangements may be frustrating the intent of NCP reforms" and that an inclusion in relation to procurement could have merit.[108] Given the size of government procurement activities, it is clear that it has significant impact on markets in this respect.

The Australian NCP reforms provide a model for a holistic consideration of the role of government in the market. The reforms produced significant identified benefits for the whole community. Continuing focus on competition through the existing processes and an additional focus on incentives will ensure continuing productivity in Australian markets.[109]

At the time of finalizing this chapter, a new Australian government had announced the first comprehensive review of competition law and policy in 20 years. The review, described as a "root and branch review," will examine both the current laws and the broader competition framework to "increase productivity and efficiency in markets, drive benefits to ease cost of living pressures, and raise living standards of all Australians."[110]

Chapter 13

Merger Analysis and Public Transport Service Contracts

Philippe Gagnepain, Marc Ivaldi, and Chantal Latgé-Roucolle

The assessment of unilateral effects of a merger in the urban transport industry raises specific questions, mainly because the mechanisms of competition in this sector are closely intertwined in the regulatory rules that structure its industrial organization. When an operator submits an offer for the management of a network, thereby competing with rivals in the market, it can only do that by taking into account the provisions and criteria of the contract that defines the regulatory environment.

One of the main features of this sector is that it clearly calls for competition for the market. Because of economies of scale that characterize the activity of urban transport, it is usually inefficient to have more than one transport operator in a given urban area. This fundamental technological characteristic drives its industrial organization: the management of transport services in this given territory is entrusted to an operator after a call for tenders to a range of potential operators. This competition for the market de facto combines with regulation, since the management contract by which the authority grants a service to an operator defines the legal framework that, in turn, specifies the rules that will be applied to assess the performance of the concessionaire.

As Marina Androulakakis stated, "When awarding public contracts, contracting authorities must ensure open and effective competition between economic operators."[1] Their aim is to ensure that the relevant public purchasing contracts are open to competition for suppliers across the internal market. To safeguard genuine competition among tenderers, the European law expressly states that contracting authorities must treat economic operators equally and nondiscriminatorily and that they must act in a transparent manner. (See Directives 2004/17/EC and 2004/18/EC.[2]) By applying these principles, public authorities can obtain products and services of the highest available quality at the best price under keener competition. The procurement procedures put in place must ensure the fair treatment of any economic operator who wishes to take part in a public tender. Tenderers must be in a position of equality both when they formulate their tenders and when those tenders are being assessed by the adjudicating authority.

To do so, at least two conditions must be satisfied. First, the process must be transparent to prevent favoritism or arbitrariness by contracting authorities. To ensure transparency, the authorities must set all the conditions and detailed rules of the award procedure in a clear, precise, and unequivocal manner in the notice or contract documents. Usually it is required that the information be publicly available. Second, any tenders must satisfy all the conditions that are fixed by the authorities to allow for an objective comparison among tenders—that is, for an equal treatment of bidders. Because authorities have freely chosen the tender specifications, they are committed to strictly observe their terms and conditions.

Now, assuming that these level playing fields are satisfied to ensure the working of the competition for the market, the application of competition law to public contracts raises critical issues because it cannot be independent of the rules enacted by the contracts themselves. Consider the case of France. There, we observe—for the sake of simplicity—two types of regulatory schemes or public contracts in the public transport industry: fixed-price and cost-plus contracts. In the case of a cost-plus contract, the organizing authority (the principal or the regulator) reimburses all costs ex post, so the operator has no incentive to improve productivity. In the case of a fixed-price contract, the authority is providing a subsidy ex ante regardless of changes in income received and costs incurred by the operator. This type of contract provides strong incentives to be efficient. Contracts, regardless of their type, are defined by a level of subsidy (which can be nil) paid by the authority to the operator as a compensation for its mission of managing the network under the conditions specified in the contract. Hence, the effectiveness of competition for the market is rooted in the regulation contained in the contract rules.

The theory of optimal regulation provides a theoretical framework to explain the economic rationale of these contracts.[3] It shows that it is optimal for a regulator to offer a menu of contracts to engage operators in a self-selection process by which they are forced to choose the contract that corresponds to their level of efficiency or inefficiencies. This mechanism prevails because the regulator is in a situation of asymmetric information, since it has incomplete information on the efficiency of the operator and on the actions that the operator takes to solve inefficiencies in operation or management.

Regarding contracts performed in France, we therefore would expect that the highly efficient networks are managed under fixed-price contracts, while the less efficient networks are covered by cost-plus contracts. Indeed, in theory, one should avoid that an inefficient firm chooses a too incentivized contract because it increases the risk of bankruptcy for the inefficient firm. As such, the authority must exclude the inefficient firm, since it is mandatory to provide a public service to consumers.[4] However, one must balance this overview to avoid caricature. Thus, when it is optimal for the regulator to offer a cost-plus contract when the network is less efficient, it means that the network has high costs and therefore the wages of bus drivers are higher. In other words, the regulator has perhaps not as her sole objective the maximization of urban transport end users' welfare, but she may wish to take into account other interest groups.[5]

Intuitively, in the case of a merger between operators, the industrial organization of urban transport sector is fraught with consequences due to the regulatory nature of the industry.[6] For a network managed under a cost-plus contract, the merger might not have direct effect, since in this case, all costs are reimbursed. However, should we consider that the impacts of the concentration should be assessed only for fixed-price contracts that have strong impacts in terms of efficiency? Is this sufficient and correct? Moreover, as the authorities often impose a price cap on average prices applied in the networks, the concentration should not have any effect on prices paid by consumers/users. However, the merger might affect the situation of consumers/taxpayers because it might have an impact on network efficiency. It is therefore necessary both to assess the effectiveness of networks and link it with the level of subsidies, which is in the spirit of optimal regulation theory.

How could we assess the impact of mergers when the competition is organized by means of public contracts? To our knowledge, no guidelines are available to answer this question. In the perspective to remedy this lack of precise rules of investigation, this chapter presents a framework for economic analysis of the urban transport industry. Specifically it proposes an analytical model that simultaneously analyzes the choice and the effectiveness of management contracts. In other words, it seeks to explain what the bases for the choice of management types are and how these management types affect the economic performance of urban transport networks. Furthermore, this chapter proposes tools to better understand how consumers' welfare depends on the operating conditions of contracts on which it would be desirable to build a better analysis of the impacts of the proposed merger or possible remedies to apply thereto. It is also necessary that the theoretical framework can explain the choice of network management mode and the impact of this mode on economic efficiency. In other words, we must test the relevance of the theoretical framework for the analysis of urban transport management contracts. For this, after the specification of a cost model and a model of choice of contract, based on economic theory of regulation, we estimate the economic efficiency using data related to management contracts of urban transport systems in France.

Yet, as is often the case—unfortunately—competition authorities favor a formal approach focusing on the number of firms responding (or likely to respond) to the tender, with the idea that only preliminary conditions to tenders (hence the number of candidates) are important to ensure a competitive situation. We do not discuss in this chapter the question of the impact of the number of applicants for tendering of transport authorities. That is to say, we do not seek to measure how the number of operators that meet a call to take charge of a concession of urban transport affects the conditions of performing the contract. Due to the low number of changes in types of contracts, and even fewer changes of operators on the same network, it would be difficult to obtain a robust measure of the impact of the number of players. We believe that this issue should be discussed in future research. However, this chapter points out the structural elements that explain the operation of service outsourcing and that should be considered in assessing the impacts of concentrations. Above all, this chapter shows that the reference to a pure auction model cannot capture the different dimensions of contracts for concession.

The results of econometric estimations validate the theoretical framework developed and highlight the fundamental role of operators' productivity efforts, which are imperfectly observable by the authority. This means that information asymmetries play a central role in management contracts. These results lead to a first conclusion: the choice of the operator is not decisive per se because consumers' welfare depends on the operation and implementation of the contract. We can therefore make the conjecture that the authority will use the contract period to gain information on the operator. This might have two consequences: a regular renegotiation of the terms of the contract, including the amount of subsidies that the authority may even be encouraged to increase ex ante, to give incentives to the operator to ever higher levels of effort, and an incentive to renew the contract with the same operator at the end of the normal duration of the contract (usually a five-year period, often considered too short by authorities and operators). This conjecture is based on the idea that renegotiation is actually cheaper—directly and indirectly—for the authority and for the incumbent than changing the type of contract and/or the operator with a new tender.

The main contribution of the proposed model is to include the possibility of network effects through productivity improvements. More precisely, we assume that the efficiency gains achieved by a group in the networks it operates under fixed-price contracts (which are more incentive powered for efficiency) benefit each network. Network effects are statistically significant and are relatively high. They represent an average of 17 or 22 percent of the level of costs that would have been observed in a network under cost-plus contracts or under fixed-price contracts, respectively, in the absence of network effects. Note that these network effects—that come from the incentive nature of management contracts—are not, strictly speaking, barriers to entry, since one does not see how a change in regulations may affect them, except depriving the authorities the choice of the operator, which would be unacceptable. One consequence of these effects is that the more the number of groups that operate networks increases, the less the gains in efficiency are obtained. Thus, we can expect a limited number of operators fighting in tenders in urban transportation industry.

The next section presents our structural model. Empirical results are shown in Section II.

I. A Structural Model of the Industry

We present now the different ingredients of the model, which entails discussing the variables at stake, the various equations that describe the contractual relationships between the local regulators and the operator, and the likelihood associated with the econometrical model.

A. The Actors and Their Contractual Relationships

The industry includes a quantity O of operators $o = 1, \ldots, O$. They provide a service in the total set of networks in France, denoted P, whose number is $\text{card}(P) = R$. A network is indexed by the scalar $r = 1, \ldots, R$.

Each urban network is regulated by a local authority, the regulator, that selects the regulatory framework, defines objectives, and sets the constraints imposed on pricing and investment policies. The authority selects the operator that is responsible for the implementation of the provisions of the management contract that is based on these regulations, objectives, and constraints. Note that the operator brings its management teams and skills but must use the facilities and manpower already present in the network.

Two types of management contracts are generally used: the fixed-price contracts (FP) and management contracts or cost-plus contracts (CP).[7] In the first case, the operator receives the revenue from the commercial revenue and a subsidy, paid at the beginning of the year or prearranged, and in all cases independent of the level of network activity during the period. If revenues do not cover the costs, the operator must bear the deficit of the network; otherwise, it makes a profit. Thus, under this type of contract, the operator is given a strong incentive to produce efforts. In the case of a CP contract, however, the authority receives the commercial revenue and covers all costs of the network, which does not provide any incentive to reduce costs. The authority offers such a contract for at least two reasons: it can be selected by the operator if the network is relatively inefficient,[8] and it allows the operator to provide higher remunerations to, for example, workers (such as bus drivers) who play a crucial role in the functioning of a network.

Thus, each contract implies a transfer between the authority and the operator of the network r. Denote by τ the type of contract that takes value FP or CP. The transfer t is then defined as

$$t_r = \begin{cases} B_r & \text{if} \quad \tau = \text{FP} \\ C_r - I_r & \text{if} \quad \tau = \text{CP} \end{cases}, \tag{1}$$

where B is the fixed compensation received by the operator in the case of an FP contract, whereas in the case of a CP contract, the compensation received is equal to the real deficit faced by the network—that is, to the difference between the cost C and commercial revenues I.[9]

Each operator o operates a set of networks P_o, whose number is card(P_o) = R_o. Let P_o^f (P_o^c, respectively) denote the set of networks that the operator o operates under an FP contract (CP, respectively), which includes card(P_o^f) = R_o^f (card(P_o^c) = R_o^c, respectively) networks. In other terms, $P_o = P_o^f \cup P_o^c$.

B. The Program of the Operator

1. Operating Costs and Cost of Effort The operating cost of the network r operated by firm o is

$$C_r = \theta_r - e_r - \delta_o \sum_{r' \neq r, r' \in P_o^f} e_{r'}, \tag{2}$$

where θ_r is the intrinsic level of inefficiency for network *r*, where e_r is the effort exerted by the operator of network *r* in order to reduce its inefficiency, and where the parameter δ_o is nonnegative.

The effort allows accounting for the effects of moral hazard—that is, the impact of the operator actions that are unobservable to the regulator. Note that the efforts of managers of other networks (distinct from the network *r* run by the operator *o*) under FP contracts can bring efficiency gains, independently from the fact that the contract *r* is of type FP or CP. We call this effect the "network effect of contracts"; it measures for an operator the impact on any of his networks of the incentives to reduce costs in its other networks regulated under an FP contract. Note also that the authority does not observe the level of inefficiency of the network nor the productivity efforts of the operator in the network *r*.

Finally, the cost of effort is given by the expression:

$$\psi(e_r) = \exp\left(\frac{e_r}{\alpha_r}\right) - 1, \tag{3}$$

where the parameter α_r is positive.

2. Optimal Effort Level The operator maximizes the profit of the network *r* given by

$$U_r = t_r + I_r - C_r - \psi(e_r), \tag{4}$$

where I_r are the commercial revenues. If the contract is of type CP, the transfer allows covering the costs, $t_r = C_r - I_r$ and $U_r = -\psi(e_r)$. It is convenient in this case to normalize the profit to zero, which implies that the effort level under a CP contract is normalized to zero as well. If the contract is of FP type, the first-order condition entails that $\psi'(e_r) = 1$ and then $e_r = \alpha_r \ln \alpha_r$. Note that the effort function makes sense (the effort must be positive or nil) only if α is greater than one.

In a nutshell, the cost function associated to the optimal decisions of operator *o* for network *r* is

$$\tilde{C}_{r\tau} = \begin{cases} \theta_r - \alpha_r \ln\alpha_r - \delta_o\alpha_r\left[\left(R_o^f - 1\right)\ln\alpha_r\right] & \text{if} \quad \tau = \text{FP} \\ \theta_r - \delta_o\alpha_r R_o^f \ln\alpha_r & \text{if} \quad \tau = \text{CP} \end{cases}, \tag{5}$$

C. The Program of the Authority

The authority maximizes the following social welfare function:

$$W_r = S_r - I_r - (1 + \lambda)t_r + \mu_r U_r, \tag{6}$$

where S is the consumer surplus for network r and λ is the cost of public funds, since the transfer is costly for society. Note that the operator has a weight μ in the objective function of the regulator. We need $\mu_r < 1 + \lambda_r$ so that our problem makes sense from an economic point of view. We assume that the consumer surplus is constant given that demand elasticity is quite low in the short term. At the optimum, the welfare is

$$\tilde{W}_{r\tau} = \begin{cases} S_r - I_r - (1+\lambda)B_r + \mu_r U_r & \text{if} \quad \tau = \text{FP} \\ S_r - I_r - (1+\lambda)(C_r - I_r) & \text{if} \quad \tau = \text{CP} \end{cases}, \tag{7}$$

D. Statistical Hypotheses and Likelihood

We assume that the inefficiency θ_r is normally distributed with mean $\bar{\theta}_r$ and variance $\sigma\theta$. Conditionally to the type of contract, the likelihood associated to the observed cost C_r for network r is

$$L(C_r|\tau) = \frac{1}{\sigma_\theta}\phi\left(\frac{C_r - \bar{\tilde{C}}_{r\tau}}{\sigma_\theta}\right), \tag{8}$$

where ϕ is the normal density and where

$$\bar{\tilde{C}}_{r\tau} = \begin{cases} \theta_r - \alpha_r \ln\alpha_r - \delta_o\alpha_r\left[\left(R_o^f - 1\right)\ln\alpha\right] & \text{if} \quad \tau = \text{FP} \\ \theta_r - \delta_o\alpha_r R_o^f \ln\alpha_r & \text{if} \quad \tau = \text{CP} \end{cases}, \tag{9}$$

Assume moreover that the welfare function is stochastic, since the econometrician imperfectly observes welfare. The welfare index W_r is then

$$W_{r\tau} = \tilde{W}_{r\tau} + \varepsilon_{r\tau}, \tag{10}$$

where ε_r is an error term that follows a Gumbel distribution. Hence, the probability to choose a type of contract τ (FP or CP) instead of the other type τ' (CP or FP, respectively) is given by

$$L(\tau) = \frac{\exp\left(\tilde{W}_{r\tau}\right)}{\exp\left(\tilde{W}_{r\tau}\right) + \exp\left(\tilde{W}_{r\tau'}\right)}. \tag{11}$$

The likelihood associated to the sample of R networks is written as

$$\ln L(C,\tau) = \sum_r L(C_r|\tau)L(\tau). \tag{12}$$

E. Specifications

The network heterogeneity can be captured through a set of exogenous factors. We assume that the parameters θ_r, α_r, μ_r, and δ_o are linear functions of explanatory variables—that is,

$$\theta_r = \gamma_0 + \sum_i \gamma_i x^1_{i,r},\ \alpha_r = \eta_0 + \sum_i \eta_i x^2_{i,r},\ \mu_r = \zeta_0 + \sum_i \zeta_i x^3_{i,r},\ \delta_o = \psi_0 + \sum_i \psi_i x^4_{i,o}, \tag{13}$$

where x^1, x^2, x^3, and x^4 are vectors of exogenous variables.

The specification of the probability of selecting a contract type, as defined by equation (11), requires knowing what would have been the characteristics of the alternative that has not been chosen, since we observe only the characteristics of the selected alternative. Thus, if a contract type CP is chosen, we need to know the amount of the fixed compensation B that would have prevailed if the choice of type of contract had focused on an FP regime. The simplest solution is to use a regression to recover the missing information. We propose to use the sample of observed compensations given under FP contracts, to regress them on the characteristics of the networks, and finally use the estimated values to infer what would have been the level of compensation if an FP type of contract had been chosen.

II. Empirical Analysis

We have a sample of 1,702 observations corresponding to 424 contracts signed in 195 French urban networks over the period 1995–2008. Such a database was created in the early 1980s from the results of an annual survey conducted by the Centre d'Etude et de Recherche du Transport Urbain (CERTU, Lyon) with the support of the Groupement des Autorités Responsables du Transport (GART, Paris), a nationwide trade organization that gathers most of the local authorities in charge of a urban transport network.

The estimation results are reported in the Statistical Annex. The overall fit is very satisfactory because the coefficient of determination of the cost equation is 87 percent, although we note that the fit is not as good for CP contracts as for FP contracts. Table 13.1 shows that the parameters are highly significant. We believe that if we had more variables characterizing the networks, we could further improve the quality of the fit. Two elements suggest that estimates lead to a coherent economic model (Table 13.2). On the one hand, the values of α are all greater than one, and on the other hand, the values of μ are mostly below 1.6, while we choose $\lambda = 0.6$.

Three main results are noteworthy. First, the effort is a variable that plays a significant role that validates our moral hazard model. Second, the network effect of contracts is significant. The operating activity in the other FP networks managed by the same group affect the efficiency of each network, whether it is furnished under an FP or a CP regime. Third, the authority does not only maximize consumer surplus but a linear combination of consumer surplus and operator's profit. In other words, the competition analysis cannot escape the incentive forces that prevail in the regulatory arrangements between the local authority and the operator. Finally, the inefficiency of networks increases over time, all else being equal. However, the growth in costs is less important since 2002. The annual growth rate of the trend is 38 percent in 1996–2002 and 14 percent only over the period 2003–2008.

Finally, some simple algebra sheds light on the respective role of the effort and the network effect in our model: According to our results (Table 13.3), a reduction of costs down to a level of 100 requires in the case of an FP contract an effort of 25 and a network effect of 36. Otherwise the cost would be 161. In the case of a PC contract, in the absence of network effect, costs would increase by 42 percent.

III. Summary

The mechanisms of competition in the urban transport industry are closely intertwined in regulatory rules that structure its industrial organization. This organization, strongly conditioned by the intrinsic characteristics of the sector, in particular with the presence of economies of scale, must combine competition for the market through the organization of tenders for public services delegation and regulation by establishing a legal framework that allows evaluating the performance of the concessionaire.

The presence of asymmetric information related to operators' efforts to improve their performance drives contracts analysis through the theoretical framework of optimal regulation. In this context, questions concerning the consequences of a particular concentration can be captured thanks to the measurement of the effectiveness of networks in relation to the incentive scheme management agreements and therefore the level of compensation.

Laffont and Tirole show that the theoretical properties of any incentive contract for the management of network that would be obtained with an auction mechanism are very similar to the properties of optimal contract that regulates monopolies.[10] The auction mechanism allows revealing information in the same way as a menu of optimal contracts, and vice versa. Consequently, the auction mechanisms for management contracts should be evaluated based on the incentive system they support.

In this perspective, we proposed an analysis that simultaneously considers the choice of the type of contract and its impact on the conditions of network management. We have shown that the observed data on French urban transport networks validate the structural model that we have defined on this industry. The different criteria assessing the statistical validity of the model are satisfied, thus confirming the relevance of the estimated model. This approach allows us to measure the relationship between level of efficiency and level of subsidies. The detection of significant network effects in the sector into consideration confirms the potential efficiencies that a merger could help achieve.

To conclude, the model developed here affirms that the analysis of competition in urban transport industry cannot be reduced to a pure auction mechanism. Instead, the regulatory framework must be taken into consideration. On the one hand, the regulatory framework impacts the level of costs and therefore, ultimately, the level of subsidies, through the incentive mechanisms it wishes to implement. Everything else being constant, lower costs will result in lower compensations. On the other hand, the regulation itself creates network effects between operators within the same group through incentive schemes. This might be allowed only by the presence of a limited number of operators on the market. Finally, the incentive scheme worn by the regulatory framework reflects the regulator's objectives, which may differ from the sole welfare of urban transport services users. In other words, the level of subsidies is not uniquely the result of the conditions of bidding implementation (such as number of participants, for example), but it also results from the operating conditions of management contracts.[11]

Appendix

Many specification tests were implemented before obtaining the model presented in this note. The specification process has highlighted the need to add more heterogeneity for the identification of the parameters. This is why the parameters in the cost and welfare functions are expressed as linear combinations of exogenous variables. The model finally selected is the one that better fits the data—that is, the one for which the statistical criteria for quality are the highest. The values of the estimated parameters also have to satisfy the constraints related to the structure of the model.

Table 13.2 shows that the two structural constraints of the model are satisfied: α is greater than 1, and μ is on average lower than $1 + \lambda$, which is equal to 1.6. Moreover, the R^2 related to cost estimations is 0.8763. Students' statistics are, with the exception of four annual dummies and a parameter of μ, greater than 2 in absolute value.

The estimated theoretical costs are expressed as

$$\bar{\tilde{C}}_{r\tau} = \begin{cases} \theta_r - \alpha_r \ln\alpha_r - \delta_o\alpha_r\left[\left(R_o^f - 1\right)\ln\alpha\right] & \text{if } \tau = \text{FP} \\ \theta_r - \delta_o\alpha_r R_o^f \ln\alpha_r & \text{if } \tau = \text{CP'} \end{cases}$$

Table 13.1 Estimation results

Parameter	*Variable*	*Estimate*	*Std. error*	*Est. / S.E.*
A	Constant	2.6803	0.0734	36.4970
	Number of cities in the network / 10	0.1524	0.0511	2.9850
Θ	Population / 10^5	15.1716	0.3889	39.0110
	Dummy 1996	–2.5805	0.6632	–3.8910
	Dummy 1997	–2.4564	0.6158	–3.9890
	Dummy 1998	–1.7228	0.6105	–2.8220
	Dummy 1999	–1.1414	0.6906	–1.6530
	Dummy 2000	–0.2780	0.7206	–0.3860
	Dummy 2001	0.2726	0.8209	0.3320
	Dummy 2002	1.5438	0.9202	1.6780
	Dummy 2003	7.8844	1.6843	4.6810
	Dummy 2004	4.5833	0.8525	5.3770
	Dummy 2005	4.6549	0.8381	5.5540
	Dummy 2006	4.7768	0.8313	5.7460
	Dummy 2007	5.3830	0.8530	6.3110
	Dummy 2008	5.3537	0.8654	6.1860
Δ	Dummy operator *C*	0.0916	0.0187	4.9100
	Dummy operator *A*	0.0369	0.0066	5.6150
	Dummy operator *D*	0.0471	0.0079	5.9610
	Dummy operator *B*	0.0384	0.0066	5.8550
	Dummy operator NA	0.0545	0.0095	5.7080
μ	Constant	8.5197	2.0260	4.2050
	Population / 10^5	5.1301	2.6963	1.9030
	Annual trend / 100	-97.9458	30.8293	-3.1770
Σ	Variance	6.8377	0.2933	23.3160

SOURCE: Annual survey conducted by the Centre d'Etude et de Recherche du Transport Urbain (CERTU, Lyon) with the support of the Groupement des Autorités Responsables du Transport (GART, Paris).

Table 13.2 Statistics on estimated parameters

	N	*Mean*	*Std. dev.*	*Min*	*Max*
α	1702	2.855	0.205	2.696	4.433
θ	1702	18.893	18.482	–1.063	113.794
δ	1702	0.045	0.016	0.000	0.092
μ	1506	1.252	0.541	0.012	1.600
Observed costs	1702	11.615	19.445	0.058	143.047
Observed costs under fixed-price contracts	1506	11.614	20.136	0.058	143.047
Observed costs under cost-plus contracts	196	11.623	13.000	0.096	76.021
Estimated costs	1702	12.154	17.868	–8.273	104.008
Estimated costs under fixed-price contracts	1506	11.558	17.923	–8.273	104.008
Estimated costs under cost-plus contracts	196	16.730	16.792	–5.412	98.913
Inefficiency under fixed-price contracts	1506	18.704	18.681	–1.063	113.794
Inefficiency under cost-plus contracts	196	20.344	16.852	–0.608	105.566
Effort under fixed-price contracts	1506	2.991	0.410	2.673	6.601
Network effect under fixed-price contracts	1506	4.155	1.415	0.000	11.378
Network effect under cost-plus contracts	196	3.614	1.864	0.000	10.323

SOURCE: Annual survey conducted by the Centre d'Etude et de Recherche du Transport Urbain (CERTU, Lyon) with the support of the Groupement des Autorités Responsables du Transport (GART, Paris).
NOTE: Values are expressed in 10e6 €.

The network inefficiency, θ, depends on the network population and on annual fixed effects. The parameter α, which influences the optimal level of effort of fixed-price contracts, depends on a constant and on the number of cities within the network. Finally, the parameter δ weighs the network effects and depends on operators' specific fixed effects.

The Authority, responsible for the service, maximizes the social welfare. The welfare function is expressed as

$$\tilde{W}_{r\tau} = \begin{cases} S_r - I_r - (1+\lambda)B_r + \mu_r U_r & \text{if } \tau = \text{FP} \\ S_r - I_r - (1+\lambda)(C_r - I_r) & \text{if } \tau = \text{CP'} \end{cases}$$

where S_r is the surplus of consumers/customers/users of the network *r*. I_r is business income. B_r is the subsidy paid to networks managed under fixed-price contracts. C_r denotes the expenses for networks managed under cost-plus contracts. U_r is the profit generated by the operators of networks managed under fixed-price contracts. Finally, λ denotes the cost of public funds set at 0.6. The parameter μ depends on a constant, on the network population, and on an annual trend. Remember that μ has to be lower than $1 + \lambda$. The values of the estimated parameter and the corresponding Student's test statistics are presented in Table 13.1.

The estimated parameters allow assessing the various components of cost and welfare functions that are defined in the structural model (Table 13.2). The level of network inefficiency on average reaches 18 million for fixed-price contracts and 20 million for cost-plus contracts. The level of inefficiency, however, is highly variable from one network to another; the standard deviations of these variables are high compared to their related means. The level of effort for fixed-price contracts is on average €2.99 million. The network effects are on average €4.1 million and €3.6 million for fixed-price and cost-plus contracts, respectively.

With the above-defined structural model, the expenses, which are the observed costs, can be split into three components: the network inefficiency, the effort in productivity, and the network effects that allow reducing this inefficiency. Table 13.3 summarizes this decomposition, distinguishing between fixed-price and cost-plus networks.

Regarding fixed-price contracts, for a level of expenses of 100, the level of effort in productivity is 25.75, and the network effects account for 35.77. These two effects altogether lead to a reduction in the level of network inefficiency from 161 down to 100, which corresponds to a 38 percent decrease. Regarding cost-plus contracts, given that the level of effort is zero by definition, for a level

Table 13.3 Observed and estimated expenses

	Fixed-price contracts			
	Level of inefficiency	*Effort*	*Network effect*	*Measurement error*
Observed expenses				
11.614	18.704	2.991	4.155	0.055
100.000	161.051	25.755	35.773	0.477
62.092	100.000	15.992	22.212	0.296
Estimated expenses				
11.558	18.704	2.991	4.155	
100.000	161.823	25.878	35.945	
61.796	100.000	15.992	22.212	
	Cost-plus contracts			
	Level of inefficiency	*Effort*	*Network effect*	*Measurement error*
Observed expenses				
11.623	20.344	0.000	3.614	–5.107
100.000	175.027	0.000	31.091	–43.936
57.134	100.000	0.000	17.764	–25.102
Estimated expenses				
16.730	20.344	0.000	3.614	
100.000	121.601	0.000	21.601	
82.236	100.000	0.000	17.764	

NOTE: Values are expressed in 10e6 €.

Table 13.4 Simulated postmerger efficiency gains under fixed-price contracts

Network and operator	*Forecasted expenses before merger*	*Forecasted expenses after merger*	*Gains in costs from the merger (%)*
1	1.958	1.958	0.000
2	3.688	3.688	0.000
3	7.888	7.888	0.000
4	18.227	14.869	18.425
5	4.644	0.711	84.682
6	9.859	3.189	67.652
7	4.398	4.398	0.000
8	9.052	9.052	0.000
9	22.493	18.246	18.883
10	37.139	37.139	0.000
11	13.843	13.843	0.000
12	26.192	26.192	0.000
13	2.174	2.174	0.000

SOURCE: Annual survey conducted by the Centre d'Etude et de Recherche du Transport Urbain (CERTU, Lyon) with the support of the Groupement des Autorités Responsables du Transport (GART, Paris).

Table 13.5 Simulated postmerger efficiency gains under cost-plus contracts

Network and operator	*Forecasted expenses before merger*	*Forecasted expenses after merger*	*Efficiency gains (%)*
1	2.676	2.676	0.000
2	15.778	15.778	0.000
3	16.467	12.767	22.469
4	15.841	12.370	21.913
5	44.222	44.222	0.000
6	4.192	4.192	0.000
7	1.599	0.818	48.866
8	27.923	24.185	13.388
9	28.723	28.723	0.000
10	7.089	1.740	75.456
11	3.064	3.064	0.000

SOURCE: Annual survey conducted by the Centre d'Etude et de Recherche du Transport Urbain (CERTU, Lyon) with the support of the Groupement des Autorités Responsables du Transport (GART, Paris).

in expenses up to 100, the network effects are 31 and lead to a reduction in the level of inefficiency from 175 down to 100, which corresponds to a 42 percent decrease.

Tables 13.4 and 13.5 show the simulation results of the gains in cost due to the concentration for each network according to its fixed-price or cost-plus contract type.

Notes

Introduction

1. We use the terms *government* and *state* interchangeably. *See, e.g.,* the recent best practices roundtables at the OECD directly addressing the application of competition law to government activities: OECD, Regulated Conduct Defence, DAF/COMP(2011)3; OECD, Competition, State aids and Subsidies, DAF/COMP/GF(2010)5; OECD, State-Owned Enterprises and the Principle of Competitive Neutrality, DAF/COMP(2009)37; *see also* the work of the International Competition Network (ICN) Working Group on Competition Advocacy, *available at* http://www.internationalcompetitionnetwork.org/working-groups/current/advocacy.aspx.

2. *Competition Authorities: Independence and Advocacy, in* The Global Limits of Competition Law 171 (Ioannis Lianos & D. Daniel Sokol eds., 2012).

3. *See* OECD, Factbook, 2011–2012 (general government expenditures as a percentage of GDP), *available at* http://www.oecd-ilibrary.org/sites/factbook-2011-en.

4. Giuseppe Nicoletti & Stefano Scarpetta, *Regulation, Productivity and Growth: OECD Evidence*, 18 Econ. Pol'y, 9 (2003).

5. Alberto Alesina et al., *Regulation and Investment*, 3 J. Eur. Econ. Ass'n 791 (2005).

6. Helge Berger & Stephan Danninger, *The Employment Effects of Labor and Product Market Deregulation and Their Implications for Structural Reform* (54 IMF Staff Papers 591, 2007).

7. Giuseppe Nicoletti & Stefano Scarpetta, *Regulation, Productivity and Growth: OECD Evidence*, 18 Econ. Pol'y, 9 (2003).

8. Sébastien Miroudot et al., *Measuring the Cost of International Trade in Services* (MPRA Paper No. 27655, 2010); James E. Anderson & Eric van Wincoop, *Trade Costs*, 42 J. Econ. Lit. 691 (2004).

9. On average, public procurement accounts for 25 percent of the OECD countries' GDP. OECD Competition Committee, Competition and Procurement 8 (2011).

10. Li-Wen Lin & Curtis J. Milhaupt, *We Are the (National) Champions: Understanding the Mechanisms of State Capitalism in China*, 65 Stan. L. Rev. 697 (2013).

11. On the historical development of the theory of "government failure," *see* Steven G. Medema, The Hesitant Hand 77–159 (2009); on corruption and government, *see* Susan Rose-Ackerman, Corruption and Government—Causes, Consequences and Reform (1999).

12. For a historical perspective, *see* Robert Millward, Private and Public Enterprise in Europe—Energy, Telecommunications and Transport, 1830–1990 (2005).

13. Wolf Sauter & Harm Schepel, State and Market in European Union Law (2009).

14. For analysis, *see* Eleanor Fox & Daniel Crane, Global Issues in Antitrust and Competition Law 353–418 (2010).

15. Panel Report, Mexico-Measures Affecting Telecommunications Services, WT/DS204/R (April 2, 2004) (adopted June 1, 2004).

16. The Understanding of Commitments in Financial Services, §§ B1 and B10.

17. Appellate Body, Canada—Measures Relating to Exports of Wheat and Treatment of Imported Grain WT/DS276/AB/R (August 13, 2004). On the basis of Article XVII GATS, although in Canada Wheat neither the panel nor the Appellate Body found such a violation.

18. *See* http://www.internationalcompetitionnetwork.org/working-groups/current/advocacy.aspx.

19. *See* ICN Advocacy and Competition Policy Report 2002, *available at* www.internationalcompetitionnetwork.org/uploads/library/doc358.pdf.

20. Antonio Capobianco & Hans Christiansen, *Competitive Neutrality and State-Owned Enterprises: Challenges and Policy Options* (OECD Corporate Governance, Working Paper No. 1, 2011), *available at* http://dx.doi.org/10.1787/5kg9xfgjdhg6-en.

21. For the view that state-owned enterprises should be subject to a more stringent competition law regime than private undertakings, *see* David E. M. Sappington & Gregory Sidak, *Competition Law for State-Owned Enterprises*, 71 Antitrust L.J. 479 (2003).

Chapter 1

I am grateful to D. Daniel Sokol for his helpful comments. I am also grateful to the law librarians at Emory Law School.

1. *See* Section I.C.

2. D. Daniel Sokol, *Competition Policy and Comparative Corporate Governance of State-Owned Enterprises*, 2009 BYU L. Rev. 1713, 1718, 1773.

3. Peter F. Drucker, The Age of Discontinuity 229 (1969).

4. Germà Bel, *Retrospectives: The Coining of "Privatization" and Germany's National Socialist Party*, J. Econ. Persp., Summer 2006, at 187, 188–91.

5. Jeremy Bentham, Principles of Penal Law, pt. II, bk.V, ch. III, *in* 1 The Works of Jeremy Bentham 496 (William Tait 1838–43); Jeremy Bentham, Panopticon; or, The Inspection-House, postscript, pt. II, § II, at 125 (1787).

6. William L. Megginson & Jeffry M. Netter, *From State to Market: A Survey of Empirical Studies on Privatization*, 39 J. Econ. Lit. 321, 322–23 (2001).

7. J. A. Kay & D. J. Thompson, *Privatisation: A Policy in Search of a Rationale*, 96 Econ. J. 18 (1986).

8. David E. M. Sappington & Joseph E. Stiglitz, *Privatization, Information and Incentives*, 6 J. Pol'y Anal. & Mgmt. 567 (1987).

9. This is conceptually similar to the equivalence (in simple models) between strict liability and negligence in tort law. *See* Steven Shavell, Foundations of Economic Analysis of Law 178–93 (2004).

10. Sappington & Stiglitz, *supra* note 8. This idea had already been anticipated in 1979 by Martin Loeb and Wesley Magat, though not in the context of privatization. Martin Loeb & Wesley A. Magat, *A Decentralized Method for Utility Regulation*, 22 J.L. & Econ. 399 (1979).

11. John Vickers & George Yarrow, *Economic Perspectives on Privatization*, J. Econ. Persp., Spring 1991, at 111, 114–16.

12. Jean-Jacques Laffont & Jean Tirole, *Privatization and Incentives*, 7 J.L. Econ. & Org. 84, 87–88 (special issue Jan. 1991).

13. *See* Andrei Shleifer, *State versus Private Ownership*, J. Econ. Persp., Fall 1998, at 133, 136.

14. *See* Paul R. Verkuil, *The Publicization of Airport Security*, 27 Cardozo L. Rev. 2243 (2006).

15. Sanford Grossman & Oliver Hart, *The Costs and Benefits of Ownership: A Theory of Vertical and Lateral Integration*, 94 J. Pol. Econ. 691 (1986); Oliver Hart & John Moore, *Property Rights and the Nature of the Firm*, 98 J. Pol. Econ. 1119 (1990).

16. Klaus M. Schmidt, *The Costs and Benefits of Privatization: An Incomplete Contracts Approach*, 12 J.L. Econ. & Org. 1, 2–3 (1996); *see also* Carl Shapiro & Robert D. Willig, *Economic Rationales for the Scope of Privatization, in* The Political Economy of Public Sector Reform and Privatization 55, 66–69 (Ezra N. Suleiman & John Waterbury eds., 1990); Laffont & Tirole, *supra* note 12, at 85, 88–89.

17. Laffont & Tirole, *supra* note 12, at 85.

18. *Id.*

19. Schmidt, *supra* note 16.

20. Oliver Hart et al., *The Proper Scope of Government: Theory and an Application to Prisons*, 112 Q.J. Econ. 1127 (1997).

21. Oliver Hart, *Incomplete Contracts and Public Ownership: Remarks and an Application to Public-Private Partnerships*, 113 Econ. J. C69 (2003). PPPs and the "to bundle or not to bundle" aspect have been the focus of much of the recent literature. *See, e.g.*, John Bennett & Elisabetta Iossa, *Building and Managing Facilities for Public Services*, 90 J. Pub. Econ. 2143 (2006); Eric Maskin & Jean Tirole, *Public-Private Partnerships and Government Spending Limits*, 26 Int'l J. Ind. Org. 412 (2008).

22. Patrick W. Schmitz, *Partial Privatization and Incomplete Contracts: The Proper Scope of Government Reconsidered*, 57 FinanzArchiv 394 (2000).

23. Timothy Besley & Maitreesh Ghatak, *Government versus Private Ownership of Public Goods*, 116 Q.J. Econ. 1343 (2001).

24. Schmidt, *supra* note 16, at 11, assumes that the government maximizes the sum of everything except the manager's own utility, which makes it *almost* benevolent. Laffont & Tirole, *supra* note 12, assume a completely social-welfare-maximizing government.

25. Hart, Shleifer, and Vishny assume that the government doesn't care about the manager's utility and that the contract price is a cost to the government. Hart et al., *supra* note 20. Besley and Ghatak likewise assume that the government's valuation of a project includes neither the provider's valuation nor its costs. Besley & Ghatak, *supra* note 23, at 1347; *see also* Schmitz, *supra* note 22, at 400.

26. Shapiro & Willig, *supra* note 16.

27. Andrei Shleifer & Robert W. Vishny, *Politicians and Firms*, 109 Q.J. Econ. 995, 997 (1994).

28. *Id.* at 1015.

29. Hart et al., *supra* note 20, at 1144–47 (distinguishing between "corruption" and "patronage"); Edward L. Glaeser, *Public Ownership in the American City*, *in* City Taxes, City Spending: Essays in Honor of Dick Netzer 130, 138–47 (Amy Ellen Schwartz ed., 2004).

30. Shleifer & Vishny, *supra* note 27, at 1022.

31. Saul Estrin et al., *The Effects of Privatization and Ownership in Transition Economies*, 47 J. Econ. Lit. 699, 708, 710 (2009).

32. Josef C. Brada, *Privatization is Transition—Or Is It?*, J. Econ. Persp., Spring 1996, at 67, 81; Gordon H. Hanson, *Antitrust in Post-Privatization Latin America: An Analysis of the Mexican Airlines Industry*, 34 Q. Rev. Econ. & Fin. 199, 204 (special issue Summer 1994).

33. I discuss the pitfalls of selection bias in, *e.g.*, Alexander Volokh, *Privatization and the Law and Economics of Political Advocacy*, 60 Stan. L. Rev. 1197, 1245–47 (2008); Alexander Volokh, *Privatization, Free Riding and Industry-Expanding Lobbying*, 30 Int'l Rev. L. & Econ. 62, 68 (2010); Alexander Volokh, *Choosing Interpretive Methods: A Positive Theory of Judges and Everyone Else*, 83 NYU L. Rev. 769, 803–29 (2008); Alexander Volokh, *Do Faith-Based Prisons Work?*, 63 Ala. L. Rev. 43 (2011).

34. Estrin et al., *supra* note 31, at 702.

35. *Id.* at 719.

36. Megginson & Netter, *supra* note 6, at 356.

37. *Id.* at 378.

38. *Id.* at 381.

39. Rafael La Porta et al., *Government Ownership of Banks*, 57 J. Finance 265 (2002).

40. Svetlana Andrianova et al., *Government Ownership of Banks, Institutions and Economic Growth*, 79 Economica 449 (2012).

41. Volokh, *Privatization and the Law and Economics of Political Advocacy*, *supra* note 33.

42. *Developments in the Law—The Law of Prisons*, 115 Harv. L. Rev. 1838, 1880 (2002) (my student note).

43. Jon D. Michaels, *Beyond Accountability: The Constitutional, Democratic and Strategic Problems with Privatizing War*, 82 Wash. U. L. Q. 1001, 1090 (2004).

44. For a nuanced take on this, *see* Carol M. Rose, *Privatization—The Road to Democracy?*, 50 St. Louis Univ. L.J. 691 (2006).

45. Padma Desai, *Russian Retrospectives on Reforms from Yeltsin to Putin*, J. Econ. Persp., Winter 2005, at 87, 97; Kay & Thompson, *supra* note 7, at 19; Samuel Brittan, *Privatisation: A Comment on Kay and Thompson*, 96 Econ. J. 33, 36 (1986); Vickers & Yarrow, *supra* note 11, at 120–21.

46. Megginson & Netter, *supra* note 6, at 324, 372–76.

47. For the "restructure before privatization" prescription, *see* Jean Tirole, *Privatization in Eastern Europe: Incentives and the Economics of Transition*, NBER Macroeconomics Annual 1991, at 221, 238–40 (Olivier Jean Blanchard & Stanley Fischer eds., 1991). Russian reformers haven't followed that suggested order. *See* Paul L. Joskow et al., *Competition Policy in Russia during and after Privatization*, Brookings Papers on Economic Activity: Microeconomics 301, 305 (1994); Desai, *supra* note 45, at 91; *see also* Vickers & Yarrow, *supra* note 11, at 128–29.

48. Desai, *supra* note 45, at 94–95; Maxim Boycko et al., *Privatizing Russia*, 2 Brookings Papers on Economic Activity 139, 147–48 (1993).

49. *See* Estrin et al., *supra* note 31, at 702, 707.

50. Desai, *supra* note 45, at 97.

51. *Id.* at 88, 96–97.

52. Bernard Black et al., *Russian Privatization and Corporate Governance: What Went Wrong?*, 52 Stan. L. Rev. 1731 (2000).

53. Estrin et al., *supra* note 31, at 713.

54. Sokol, *supra* note 2.

55. Edward L. Glaeser & Andrei Shleifer, *Not-for-Profit Entrepreneurs*, 81 J. Pub. Econ. 99 (2001).

56. Besley & Ghatak, *supra* note 25.

57. Hart et al., *supra* note 20, at 1144; *see also* Shleifer, *supra* note 13, at 139; Vickers & Yarrow, *supra* note 11, at 116.

58. *See* W. Kip Viscusi et al., Economics of Regulation and Antitrust 401–26 (4th ed. 2005), for a discussion of the theory of natural monopoly.

59. William D. Eggers, Competitive Neutrality: Ensuring a Level Playing Field in Managed Competitions (Reason Pub. Pol'y Inst., How-To Guide 18, Mar. 1998); Richard W. Harding, Private Prisons and Public Accountability 158–65 (1997).

60. *See, e.g.*, Harold Demsetz, *Why Regulate Utilities?*, 11 J.L. & Econ. 55 (1968); Viscusi et al., *supra* note 58, at 465–501.

61. *See* Harding, *supra* note 59, at 158–65.

62. Mark A. Zupan, *The Efficacy of Franchise Bidding Schemes in the Case of Cable Television: Some Systematic Evidence*, 32 J.L. & Econ. 401 (1989).

63. U.S. Dep't of Justice, Bur. of Just. Stats., Prisoners in 2010, at 31 appx. tbl. 20 (rev. Feb. 9, 2012).

64. Alexander Volokh, *Prison Accountability and Performance Measures*, 63 Emory L.J. ___ (forthcoming 2014).

65. *Id.* at ___.

66. *See, e.g.*, Dolovich, *supra* note 42, at 500–06.

67. Volokh, *supra* note 64, at ___.

68. Volokh, *supra* note 41, at 1221–31.

69. *Id.* at 1253.

70. One of these is Richard Schmalensee, The Control of Natural Monopolies (1979).

71. *See* Viscusi et al., *supra* note 58, at 429–64.

72. For a specific critique in the British context, *see* Kay & Thompson, *supra* note 7.

73. *See* text accompanying notes 47–48 *supra*.

74. Kay & Thompson, *supra* note 7, at 27; Estrin et al., *supra* note 31, at 706; Vickers & Yarrow, *supra* note 11, at 120.

75. Mexicana went bankrupt in 2010.

76. *See, e.g.*, Damien Geradin, *Price Discrimination in the Postal Sector and Competition Law*, *in* Reinventing the Postal Sector in an Electronic Age 230 (Michael A. Crew & Paul R. Kleindorfer eds., 2011).

77. Robert M. Feinberg & Mieke Meurs, *Privatization and Antitrust in Eastern Europe: The Importance of Entry*, 39 Antitrust Bull. 797, 806 (1994).

78. *See, e.g.*, Douglas H. Ginsburg & Joshua D. Wright, *Antitrust Sanctions*, Competition Pol'y Int'l, Autumn 2010, at 3.

79. Mark S. LeClair, *Exigency and Innovation in Collusion*, 8 J. Competition L. & Econ. 399 (2012).

80. Frank H. Easterbrook, *The Limits of Antitrust*, 63 Tex. L. Rev. 1, 2–3 (1984).

81. *See* A. E. Rodriguez & Ashok Menon, The Limits of Competition Policy: The Shortcomings of Antitrust in Developing and Reforming Countries (2010).

82. *Id.*

83. *See* Vickers & Yarrow, *supra* note 11, at 116.

84. Sam Peltzman, *Pricing in Public and Private Enterprises: Electric Utilities in the United States*, 14 J.L. & Econ. 109 (1971).

85. James F. Ponsoldt, *Balancing Federalism and Free Markets: Toward Renewed Antitrust Policing, Privatization, or a "State Supervision" Screen for Municipal Market Participant Conduct*, 48 SMU L. Rev. 1783, 1787 (1995).

86. 317 U.S. 341, 350–51 (1943).

87. Lafayette v. La. Power & Light Co., 435 U.S. 389, 410 (1978) (opinion of Brennan, J.).

88. 471 U.S. 34, 42 (1985).

89. *Id.* at 45 & n.9.

90. *See* text accompanying note 84 *supra*.

91. *See also* Fed. Trade Comm'n, Office of Policy Planning, Report of the State Action Task Force 25–36 (Sept. 2003).

92. Bates v. State Bar of Ariz., 433 U.S. 350, 362 (1977); Lafayette v. La. Power & Light Co, 435 U.S. 389, 410 (1978) (plurality opinion).

93. Report of the State Action Task Force, *supra* note 91, at 36–37.

94. *Hallie*, 471 U.S. at 46.

95. Report of the State Action Task Force, *supra* note 91, at 37.

96. *Id.* at 50–57.

97. Brooke Group Ltd. v. Brown & Williamson Tobacco Corp., 509 U.S. 209 (1993).

98. Sokol, *supra* note 2, at 1809–11.

99. 511 U.S. 383, 392 (1994).

100. 550 U.S. 330, 342–43 (2007).

101. *Id.* at 358 (Alito, J., dissenting) (citing *Carbone*, 511 U.S. at 387).

102. *Id.* at 359.

103. *See* Hughes v. Alexandria Scrap Corp., 426 U.S. 794, 809 (1976); Dep't of Rev. of Ky. v. Davis, 553 U.S. 328, 339 (2008).

104. Steven Semeraro, *The Antitrust-Telecom Connection*, 40 San Diego L. Rev. 555, 556 (2003).

105. College Savings Bank v. Fla. Prepaid Postsecondary Educ. Expense Bd., 527 U.S. 666, 684–86 (1999).

106. *See, e.g.*, 28 U.S.C. § 2680(a); 1 Civ. Actions Against State & Loc. Gov't § 2:7, :11; Minneci v. Pollard, 132 S. Ct. 617 (2012).

107. Richardson v. McKnight, 521 U.S. 399 (1997).

108. Alexander Volokh, *Privatization and the Elusive Employee-Contractor Distinction*, 46 UC Davis L. Rev. 133, 142, 147–52 (2012).

109. J. W. Verret, *Treasury Inc.: How the Bailout Reshapes Corporate Theory and Practice*, 27 Yale J. on Reg. 283, 318 & n.171 (2010).

110. Brada, *supra* note 32, at 79–81, 84.

111. Caroline M. Hoxby, *School Choice and School Productivity: Could School Choice Be a Tide That Lifts All Boats?*, *in* The Economics of School Choice 287 (Caroline M. Hoxby ed., 2003).

112. Eggers, *supra* note 59; Harding, *supra* note 59, at 158–65.

113. Boycko et al., *supra* note 48, at 144.

114. *Id.* at 145.

115. *See, e.g.*, Todd Zywicki, *The Auto Bailout and the Rule of Law*, 7 Nat'l Affairs 66, 76–80 (Spring 2011).

Chapter 2

1. *See* Milton Friedman, Capitalism and Freedom, ch. 2 (1962).

2. Stephen G. Medema, The Hesitant Hand: Taming Self-Interest in the History of Economic Ideas, chs. 4–6 (2009).

3. D. Daniel Sokol, *Anticompetitive Government Regulation*, *in* The Global Limits of Competition Law 83 (Ioannis Lianos & Daniel Sokol ed., 2012); D. Daniel Sokol, *Limiting Anti-Competitive Government Interventions That Benefit Special Interests*, 17 Geo. Mason L. Rev. 119 (2009).

4. Herbert Hovenkamp, Federal Antitrust Policy (4th ed., 2011), 747; Einer Elhauge, *The Scope of Antitrust Process*, 104 Harv. L. Rev. 667 (1991).

5. Chicago authors may support this statement in view of their conception of the relations between political and economic freedom. *See* Milton Friedman, 10 (1962) ("It is therefore clearly possible to have economic arrangements that are fundamentally capitalist [preserving economic freedom] and political arrangements that are not free").

6. *See, e.g.*, Case T-321/05 AstraZeneca AB and AstraZeneca plc v. European Commission [2010] ECR II-2085; Case C-457/10 P AstraZeneca AB and AstraZeneca plc v. Commission [December 6, 2012, not yet published] (abuse of procedures relating to supplementary protection certificates for medicinal products) and the vexatious (sham) litigation theory in EU and U.S. competition law.

7. *See, e.g.*, the criticisms to public choice by political scientists advancing a more pluralistic research agenda: Donald Green & Ian Shapiro, Pathologies of Rational Choice Theory: A Critique of Applications in Political Science (1994).

8. Max Weber, Economy and Society 1041 (1978) defines "patrimonial state" as one where "practically everything depends explicitly upon personal considerations: upon the attitude toward the concrete applicant and his concrete request and upon purely personal connections, favors, promises, and privileges." These distinctions are, of course, ideal types, since in reality some of the characteristics of each form of state may coexist for a certain time.

9. Daniel A. Crane, *Technocracy and Antitrust*, 86 Tex. L. Rev. 1159 (2008).

10. Defining neoliberalism or the concept of the neoliberal state may be challenging in view of the various perspectives adopted by the literature. *See generally* David Harvey, A Brief History of Neoliberalism (2005) 71–81. Some authors have defined neoliberalism as "the ongoing contest between the imperatives of market economies and nonmarket values grounded in the requirements of democratic legitimacy," neoliberalism advancing "the market side of this contest"; David Singh Grewal & Jedediah Purdy, *Introduction: Law and Neo-Liberalism* (Yale Law Sch. Pub. Law Research Paper No. 313, 2013), 1–2. It follows that in a neoliberal state there might be tensions between democratic demands "that go beyond or contradict market logic" and market imperatives. According to the tenants of neoliberalism, these tensions should be resolved, while making an effort to preserve "market relations from particular kinds of politicization" and to expand markets in areas from which they were previously excluded. *Id.* at 2.

11. Michel Foucault, The Birth of Biopolitics—Lectures at the Collège de France 1978–1979, 39 (2010).

12. *Id.* at 15.

13. *Id.* at 32.

14. *Id.* at 115.

15. Robert Hoppe, *Rethinking the Science-Policy Nexus: from Knowledge Utilization and Science Technology Studies to Types of Boundary Arrangements*, 3 Poiesis & Praxis 199 (2005).

16. Max Weber, Economy and Society 975 (1978).

17. *See, e.g.*, the establishment of the Conseil d'Etat in France in 1799 inaugurating the distinction between public and private law in some continental European legal traditions, an influential model to this day. The aim was to exclude from the scope of ordinary general courts the administrative functions of the state, thus providing more discretion to government bureaucracies. By focusing on the control of legality only and providing government discretion in complex economic and technical matters, administrative courts ensured that bureaucracy was acting according to the limits set to its rational-legal authority.

18. Robert Merton, *The Unanticipated Consequences of Purposive Social Action*, 1 Am. Soc. Rev. 894 (1936); Robert Merton, *Bureaucratic Structure and Personality*, *in* Social Theory and Social Structure 249–60 (Robert Merton ed., 1968).

19. Michel Crozier, The Bureaucratic Phenomenon 186–87 (1964).

20. *Id.* at 195.

21. Harold D. Lasswell, A Pre-View of the Policy Sciences (1971).

22. Dennis C. Mueller, Public Choice III 359 (2003).

23. Jessica Leight, *Public Choice: A Critical Reassessment*, in Government and Markets—Towards a New Theory of Regulation 213–55 (Edward J. Balleisen & David A. Moss eds., 2010).

24. Mark W. Crain & Robert Tollison, *The Executive Branch in the Interest-Group Theory of Government*, 8 J. Legal Stud. 165 (1979); William Landes & Richard Posner, *The Independent Judiciary in an Interest-Group Perspective*, 18 J.L. & Econ. 875 (1975); Thomas W. Merrill, *Capture Theory and the Courts: 1967–1983*, 72 Chi.-Kent L. Rev. 1039 (1997).

25. William Niskanen Jr., Bureaucracy and Representative Government (1971); Jean-Jacques Laffont & Jean Tirole, *The Politics of Government Decision-Making: A Theory of Regulatory Capture*, 106 Q.J. Econ. 1089 (1991).

26. *See, e.g.*, the studies listed by Dennis C. Mueller, Public Choice III 373–79.

27. *Id.* at 384; Donald Wittman, *The End of Special Interests Theory and the Beginning of a More Positive View of Democratic Politics*, *in* Government and Markets—Towards a New Theory of Regulation 193–212 (Edward J. Balleisen & David A. Moss eds., 2010).

28. Leight, *supra* note 23; Green & Shapiro, *supra* note 7; Einer R. Elhauge, *Does Interest Group Theory Justify More Intrusive Judicial Review?*, 101 Yale L.J. 31 (1991).

29. Richard D. Auster & Morris Silver, The State as a Firm (1979).

30. Wittman, *supra* note 27, at 207.

31. Walter Eucken, The Foundations of Economics—History and Theory in the Analysis of Economic Reality (London, 1950); Hanz Rieter & Matthias Schmolz, *The Ideas of German Ordoliberalism 1938–1945: Pointing the Way to a New Economic Order*, 1 Euro. J. Hist. Econ. Thought 87 (1993).

32. Foucault, *supra* note 11, at 116.

33. *Id.* at 119–21.

34. Viktor J. Vamberg, *The Freiburg School: Walter Eucken and Ordoliberalism* 7 (Freiburg Discussion Papers on Constitutional Economics, April 2011).

35. Fred S. McChesney & William F. Shughart II, The Causes and Consequences of Antitrust: The Public Choice Perspective (1995).

36. Hoppe, *supra* note 15, at 208–10.

37. Sheila Jasanoff, The Fifth Branch (1990).

38. Inbal Faibish & Michal Gal, *Six Principles for Limiting Government-Facilitated Restrictions on Competition*, 44 Common Mkt. L. Rev. 69 (2007).

39. Marion Fourcade, Economists and Societies: Discipline and Profession in the United States, Britain and France, 1890s to 1990s (2009).

40. *See, e.g.*, in the United States, Credit Suisse Securities v. Billing, 551 U.S. 264 (2007) (noting there is a serious risk that antitrust courts with different nonexpert judges and different nonexpert juries will produce inconsistent results and mistakes). Of course, this is not the only source of antitrust immunity of regulation. One could add the dual federalism nature of the U.S. Constitution for the antitrust immunity offered to state regulation.

41. *See, e.g.*, Case 13/77, SA GB-Inno BM v. Association des détaillants en tabac (ATAB) [1977] ECR 2115, ¶ 29; C-260/89, Elliniki Radiophonia Tileorasi AE & Panellinia Omospondia Syllogon Prossopikou v. Dimotiki Etairia Pliroforissis et al. [1991] ECR I-2925, ¶ 27; Case 229/83, Association des Centres distributeurs Edouard Leclerc v. SARL "Au blé vert" [1985] ECR 1, ¶ 9.

42. Case C-67/96, Albany International BV v. Stichting Bedrijfspensioenfonds Textielindustrie [1999] ECR I-5751; Case C-309/99, J. C. J. Wouters et al. v. Algemene Raad can de Nederlandse Orde van Advocaten [2002] ECR I-1577.

43. Case C-289/04P, Showa Denko KK v. Commission [2006] ECR I-5859, ¶ 55; Joined Cases T-259–264 and 271/02, Raiffeisen Zentralbank Österreich AG and Others v. Commission [2006] ECR II-5169, ¶ 255.

44. Case C-198/01, Consorzio Industrie Fiammiferi [2003] ECR I-8055, ¶¶ 54–55.

45. On the various interpretative choices offered by the Treaty of Lisbon, *see* Ioannis Lianos, *Competition Law in the European Union after the Treaty of Lisbon*, *in* The European Union after the Treaty of Lisbon 252–84 (Diamond Ashiagbor et al. eds., 2012).

46. *See*, more recently, Case C-280/08 P, Deutsche Telekom AG v. European Commission [2010] ECR I-9555. For a commentary, *see* Javier Tapia & Despoina Mantzari, *The Regulation/Competition Interaction*, *in* Handbook on European Competition Law, Vol. I (Damien Geradin & Ioannis Lianos eds., 2013).

47. *See*, more recently, the adoption of the Services of General Economic Interest Package by the European Commission in April 2012 regarding the conciliation between the competition law provisions of the treaty and the provision of services of general interest, *available at* http://ec.europa.eu/competition/state_aid/legislation/sgei.html.

48. *See* Article 106 TFEU, subjecting public undertakings and undertakings with special or exclusive rights to the application of the general competition law provisions of the treaty "insofar as the application of such rules does not obstruct the performance, in law or in fact, of the particular tasks assigned to them (services of general economic interest)." Nonmarket services (compulsory education, social protection, etc.) and sovereign tasks (such as security, justice) are also excluded from the scope of competition law, following the case law of the European courts. Article 14 of the Treaty on the Functioning of the European Union acknowledges the place occupied by services of general economic interest among the shared values of the EU, thus balancing the constitutional dimension of the competition law provisions. Article 36 of the Charter of Fundamental Rights, now binding, confirms the importance of Article 14 TFEU and acknowledges the need for EU citizens to have access to services of general economic interest.

49. Kenneth Kernaghan, *The Post-Bureaucratic Organization and Public Service Values*, 66 Int'l Rev. Admin. Sci. 91 (2000)

50. HM Government, Open Public Services (July 2011) (white paper), *available at* http://www.openpublicservices.cabinetoffice.gov.uk/.

51. *Id.* at 39–49.

52. OECD, Competition Assessment Toolkit, Vol. 1, 8–9 (2011).

53. *Id.* at 63.

54. *See, e.g.*, European Commission, Better Regulation: A Guide to Competition Screening (2005), *available at* http://ec.europa.eu/competition/publications/archive.html; OFT 876, Completing Competition Assessments in Impact Assessments (August 2007), *available at* http://www.oft.gov.uk/shared_oft/reports/comp_policy/oft876.pdf.

55. European Commission, Impact Assessment Guidelines (Jan. 15, 2009), *available at* http://ec.europa.eu/governance/impact/commission_guidelines/commission_guidelines_en.htm.

56. OECD, *supra* note 52, at 37–38.

57. For a recent discussion, *see* OFT, Article 101(3)—A Discussion of Narrow versus Broad Definition of Benefits (2010) (noting that regarding the difference between cost benefit analysis techniques employed in RIA, competition authorities do not take a positive view toward aggregation of the costs and benefits across relevant markets). Yet, competition screening, if taken seriously, should lead to the aggregation of costs and benefits across markets in the last step of the analysis.

58. The competition assessment may be performed by the competition authority (*e.g.*, UK, Mexico, Korea, Hungary, Greece) or by an independent external authority (*e.g.*, the National Competition Council in Australia).

59. For example, the procedure provided in Article 63 of the Korean MRFTA, according to which other government bodies intending to legislate or amend the laws under their jurisdiction should ask the KFTC for review of any possible anticompetitiveness of the laws concerned, the KFTC conducting prior-consultation with them. OECD, *Korea*, ¶ 63, *available at* http://www.oecd.org/korea/39554122.pdf.

60. *See, e.g.*, OFT 876, Completing Competition Assessments in Impact Assessments, *supra* note 54.

61. *Id.* at ¶¶ 1.2, 1.3.

62. *See* Frederic Jenny, *Competition Authorities: Independence and Advocacy*, *in* The Global Limits of Competition Law 158–76 (Ioannis Lianos & D. Daniel Sokol eds., 2012).

63. Part I of the NHS and Community Care Act 1990; Julian Le Grand, *Quasi-Markets and Social Policy*, 101 Econ. J. 1256 (1991).

64. This may be understood in view of the information asymmetry between providers and users of health care services: Kenneth J. Arrow, *Uncertainty and the Welfare Economics of Medical Care*, 53 Am. Econ. Rev. 941 (1963).

65. Zack Cooper, The Very English Experience with Competition: Lessons from Britain's National Health Service, OECD, DAF/COMP(2012)9, 313–31.

66. The possibility of private actors to provide NHS services is guaranteed by the provisions conferring the power to regulate procurement, patient choice, and competition under Section 75 of the Health and Social Care Act and the licensing requirement in Section 81. Qualified providers should be registered with the CQC and licensed by Monitor, where required, or meet equivalent assurance requirements. They should also, among other requirements, accept NHS prices and meet the terms and conditions of the NHS Standard Contract, which includes an obligation to have regard to the NHS Constitution, relevant guidance, and law.

67. Cooper, *supra* note 65 at 317.

68. Martin Gaynor, Reform, Competition and Policy in Hospital Markets, OECD, DAF/COMP(2012)9, 333–58. Office of Health Economics, Competition in the NHS (January 2012).

69. *Id.* at 321, noting that a growing body of empirical research suggests that for-profit and non-profit hospitals behave similarly if allowed to retain surpluses.

70. OFT1242, Competition in Mixed Markets: Ensuring Competitive Neutrality (July 2010), *available at* http://www.oft.gov.uk/shared_oft/economic_research/oft1242.pdf. A narrowly defined requirement of competitive neutrality would aim to ensure that state-owned and private businesses compete on a level playing field.

71. Case C-41/90 Höfner v. Macrotron [1991] ECR I-1979.

72. For an analysis of the different positions, *see* Okeoghene Odudu, *Are State-Owned Health-Care Providers' Undertakings Subject to Competition Law?*, 5 Eur. Common L. Rev. 231 (2011).

73. Case C-205/03 P, Fenin v. Commission [2006] ECR I-6295.

74. Odudu, *supra* note 72, at 236.

75. *See* the profit structure deal signed with the transfer of the Hichinbrooke's public hospital management to Circle, a private firm co-owned by doctors (*available at* http://www.bbc.co.uk/news/

uk-england-cambridgeshire-16812998), according to which, if Circle succeeds in reversing the debt-hit hospital's fortunes, then it will receive a predefined part of the yearly surplus.

76. OECD, Secretariat, Competition in Hospital Services—The Policy Dimension, DAF/COMP(2012)9, 23–67, in particular at 28.

77. Section 61(1) of the Health and Social Care Act 2012.

78. Section 62(3) of the Health and Social Care Act 2012.

79. Sections 62(4) and 66 of the Health and Social Care Act 2012.

80. Routine elective services are paid for at a uniform national tariff for each procedure (subject to local flexibilities), so there is little scope for some forms of price-related anticompetitive activity (price fixing by providers). However, for other services, the price paid may be determined by negotiation or a competitive tender, in which case there might be scope for price fixing.

81. Cooperation and Competition Panel, Conduct Guidelines (October 2010); Cooperation and Competition Panel, Merger Guidelines (October 2010).

82. As a result of these modifications, the PRCC will not apply the same as general competition law. On the definition of anticompetitive behavior in this context, *see* Section 10 of The National Health Service (Procurement, Patient Choice, and Competition) Regulations 2013. In addition to (i) the PRCC and (ii) the concurrent powers to enforce general competition law, the Monitor may also tackle anticompetitive behavior through (iii) the enforcement of license conditions (relating to choice and competition or Condition C2).

83. To some extent, the UK model constitutes a step in a continuum moving from the nonapplication of competition law, to the application of competition law–inspired principles, to the enforcement of general competition law by a sector-specific regulator (in conjunction with the competition authority), and to the application of general competition law by the regular institutional mechanism (albeit with some guidance on the way this will be applied). The last model is that followed in the United States: statements of the USDOJ and the FTC on antitrust enforcement policy in health care, *available at* http://www.justice.gov/atr/public/guidelines/0000.htm.

84. Department of Health, Response to Opinions of David Lock and the Opinion of Ligia Osepsiu, published by 38 degrees, on the application of the NHS (Procurement, Patient Choice and Competition) Regulations 2013, ¶ 25. *See also*, on the competition framework to be applied by Monitor and on the need to preserve "patient choice," Sections 9 and 10 in Monitor, Substantive Guidance on the Procurement, Patient Choice, and Competition Regulations (May 20, 2013). This takes into account different objectives than those usually taken by the OFT and more generalist competition authorities. Monitor may also have different priorities from the OFT, in view of its wide-ranging role as economic and competition regulator. *See* Section 3, Monitor, Enforcement Guidance on the Procurement, Patient Choice and Competition Regulations 2013 (May 20, 2013).

85. For an account of a comparative institutional analysis using transaction costs economics, *see* Oliver Williamson, *Public and Private Bureaucracies: A Transaction Cost Economics Perspective*, 15 J.L. Econ. & Org. 306 (1999). For a framework focusing on "participation," *see* Neil Komesar, Imperfect Alternatives: Choosing Institutions in Law, Economics and Public Policy (1994).

86. Williamson, *supra* note 85, at 318.

Chapter 3

1. *See* the appendix for a discussion of the standard measurement of a firm's cost of capital.

2. *See, e.g.*, Jean-Jacques Laffont & David Martimort, The Theory of Incentives: The Principal-Agent Model (2002); David E. M. Sappington, *Incentives in Principal-Agent Relationships*, 5 J. Econ. Persp. 45 (1991).

3. R. Richard Geddes & Benjamin L. Wagner, *Why Do States Adopt Laws Enabling Public-Private Partnerships?*, 78 J. Urb. Econ. 30 (2013).

4. J. W. Fischer, *From Interstates to an Uncharted Future: A Short History of the Modern Federal-Aid Highway Program*, *in* 21st Century Highways: Innovative Solutions to America's Transportation Needs (W. Cox et al. eds., 2005).

5. David Schrank et al., *Urban Mobility Report 2010* (2010).

6. *See* Jack Wells, Chief Economist, U.S. Department of Transportation, Presentation to the National Surface Transportation Policy and Revenue Study Commission: The Role of Transportation in the U.S. Economy (June 26, 2006).

7. American Society of Civil Engineers, *Bridges*, in 2013 Report Card for America's Infrastructure (2013), *available at* http://www.infrastructurereportcard.org/a/#p/bridges/overview.

8. *See, e.g.*, Allen Consulting Group, Performance of PPPs and Traditional Procurement in Australia (2007); David Czerwinski & R. Richard Geddes, Policy Issues in U.S. Transportation Public-Private Partnerships: Lessons from Australia (Mineta Transportation Institute Report 2010).

9. *See* Aidan R. Vining & Anthony E. Boardman, *Public-Private Partnerships in Canada: Theory and Evidence*, 51 Can. Pub. Admin. 9 (2008).

10. *See* Federal Highway Administration, Public-Private Partnerships for Highway Infrastructure: Capitalizing on International Experience (2009).

11. *See* Daniel Albalate et al., *Privatization and Regulatory Reform of Toll Motorways in Europe*, 22 Governance 295 (2009).

12. *See, e.g.*, Werner Troesken & Rick Geddes, *Municipalizing American Waterworks, 1897–1915*, 19 J.L. Econ. & Org. 373 (2003) (discussing private investment in the water sector); Douglass North, Institutions, Institutional Change and Economic Performance (1981) (discussing the importance of legal institutions in attracting private investment).

13. Dan Klein & G. J. Fielding, *Private Toll Roads: Learning from the Nineteenth Century*, 46 Transp. Q. 321 (1992)

14. The concession term was 99 years in the case of the Chicago Skyway lease and 75 years in the case of the Indiana Toll Road lease.

15. Jose A. Gomez-Ibanez, Regulating Infrastructure: Monopoly, Contracts and Discretion 109–56 (2003).

16. The noncompete clause contained in the concession contract for the SR-91 freeway in southern California created substantial controversy. The noncompete clause blocked improvements along the congested corridor and was only lifted when the Orange County Transportation Authority purchased the express lanes from their private owners in January 2003.

17. *See* Parker v. Brown, 317 U.S. 341 (1943).

18. Goldfarb v. Virginia State Bar, 421 U.S. 773, 791 (1975).

19. California Retail Liquour Dealers Ass'n v. Midcal Aluminum, 445 U.S. 97, 105.

20. City of Columbia v. Omni Outdoor Advertising, 499 U.S. 365, 372–73 (quoting Hallie v. Eau Claire, 471 U.S. 34, 42 (1985)).

21. We were unable to locate any cases that address the standard necessary to meet this test.

22. Partnerships Victoria 2001.

23. *Id.* at 6.

24. *See, e.g.*, Queensland Competition Authority, Competitive Neutrality, *available at* http://www.qca.org.au/competitive-n/ (accessed December 23, 2013).

25. *See*, however, R. Richard Geddes, Competing with the Government (2004) for examples of such competition in the United States. The World Bank defines SOEs as "government-owned or government-controlled economic entities that generate the bulk of their revenues from selling goods and services." *See* World Bank, Bureaucrats in Business: The Economics and Politics of Government Ownership (1995).

26. *See* D. Daniel Sokol, *Competition Policy and Comparative Corporate Governance of State-Owned Enterprises*, 2009 BYU L. Rev. 1713 (2009), discussing the limitations of antitrust law in addressing anticompetitive behavior by SOEs, in particular with regard to predatory pricing.

27. *Id.*

28. OECD, State Owned Enterprises and the Principle of Competitive Neutrality (2009).

29. Partnerships Victoria, *supra* note 22, at 7 ("Competitive neutrality adjustments remove any net competitive advantages that accrue to a government business by virtue of its public ownership. This allows a fair and equitable assessment between a PSC and bidders").

30. Mathias Dewatripont & Gérard Roland, *Soft Budget Constraints, Transition and Financial Systems*, 156 J. Inst. & Theoretical Econ. 245 (2000).

31. OECD (2009), *supra* note 28.

32. *See, e.g.*, John Kay, *The Structure of Strategy*, 4 Bus. Strat. Rev. 17 (1993).

33. U.S. policy has attempted to address this issue through the use of private activity bonds, or PABs. PABs are bonds issued by or on behalf of local or state government for the purpose of financing the project of a private user. They effectively allow a PPP to benefit from the same tax exemption granted to municipalities.

34. James M. Poterba, *Tax Reform and the Market for Tax-Exempt Debt*, 19 Reg'l Sci. & Urb. Econ. 537 (1989).

35. The risk to taxpayers is higher in general-obligation bonds. We are unaware of any studies that provide estimates of the reduction in interest rates on municipal debt caused by tax policy relative to implicit taxpayer guarantees.

36. Kay, *supra* note 32, at 63, notes that willingness to lend to the government depends on the fact that it is backed by an implicit promise to tax, stating, "We would lend money to the government even if we thought it would burn the money or fire it off into space."

37. For example, Lucas and Phaup (2010, 34) state, "When the government finances risky investments by selling safe Treasury securities, investment risk is shifted onto current and future taxpayers and other federal stakeholders, who effectively become equity holders in a leveraged investment." D. Lucas & M. Phaup, *The Cost of Risk to the Government and Its Implications for Federal Budgeting, in* Measuring and Managing Federal Financial Risk (D. Lucas ed., 2010). Similarly, R. A. Brealey et al., *Investment Appraisal in the Public Sector*, 13 Oxford Rev. Econ. Pol'y 12, 22 (1997), state, "Taxpayers bear the residual risk of government investment, particularly that of making good on obligations to debt holders, in much the same way as the shareholders of a private-sector firm." Taxpayers may be thought of as residual claimants only rarely because property rights to public-sector residual claims are poorly defined in that they lack the basic components of rights such as exclusivity and transferability. Although they may not be adequately reflected on public-sector balance sheets, taxpayers nevertheless bear substantial risk, as the taxpayer liability resulting from the 2008 financial crisis suggests.

38. Dale W. Jorgenson, William Vickrey, Tjalling C. Koopmans, & Paul A. Samuelson, *Principles of Efficiency: Discussion*, 63 Am. Econ. Rev. 54, No. 3, Papers and Proceedings of the Seventy-sixth Annual Meeting of the American Economic Association (May 1964), 86–96.

39. Kenneth J. Arrow & Robert C. Lind, *Uncertainty and the Evaluation of Public Investment Decisions*, 60 Am. Econ. Rev. 364 (1970).

40. Anthony C. Fisher, An Introduction to Applied Macroeconomics 722 (1973).

41. We refer to the residual claimants as taxpayers because taxes are the channel through which aggregate risk bearing takes place in the Arrow-Lind model.

42. *See, e.g.*, Ziemowit Bednarek & Marian Moszoro, The Arrow-Lind Theorem Revisited in Turmoil Times (2011) (working paper).

43. J. Kay, Foundations of Corporate Success (1993); Paul A. Grout & Margaret Stevens, *The Assessment: Financing and Managing Public Services*, 19 Oxford Rev. Econ. Pol'y 215 (2003).

44. Coleman Bazelon & Kent Smetters, *Discounting Inside the Washington D.C. Beltway*, 13 J. Econ. Persp. 213, 216 (1999), state, "In sum, there is little evidence supporting the argument that government should price risks at less than the private market. Indeed, the distorting costs of taxation and the positive long-run correlation between stocks and wages suggest that the government should possibly overprice risks relative to the private market."

45. Kenneth A. Small, *Private Provision of Highways: Economic Issues*, 30 Transport Rev. 11 (2010).

46. Although there has been no comprehensive analysis, Brealey et al., *supra* note 37, consider how some aspects of the different legal arrangements surrounding public- versus private-sector investment are likely to affect the cost of capital.

47. For example, before the 1790s, the State of New York assessed eligible males a minimum of three days of roadwork per year under penalty of fines.

48. *See, e.g.*, Dennis J. Enright, *The Public Versus Private Toll Road Choice in the United States*, NW Financial Group, LLC (June 2007).

49. Harold Demsetz & Kenneth Lehn, *The Structure of Corporate Ownership: Causes and Consequences*, 93 J. Pol. Econ. 1155 (1985), for example, consider several measures of ownership concentration, such as the fraction of total outstanding equity held by the largest four shareholders and a Herfindahl-type measure.

50. Stanford J. Grossman & Oliver D. Hart, *The Costs and Benefits of Ownership: A Theory of Vertical Integration*, 94 J. Pol. Econ. 691 (1986); Oliver Hart & John Moore, *Property Rights and the Nature of the Firm*, 98 J. Pol. Econ. 1119 (1990); Oliver Hart, Firms, Contracts and Financial Structure (1995).

51. Michael C. Jensen & William H. Meckling, *Theory of the Firm: Managerial Behavior, Agency Costs and Ownership Structure*, 3 J. Fin. Econ. 305 (1976).

52. Adolf A. Berle Jr. & Gardiner C. Means, The Modern Corporation and Private Property 3–4 (Transaction Publishers 1991) (1932).

53. Demsetz & Lehn, *supra* note 49, at 1156, in discussing the costs and benefits to firm owners from increased dispersion of ownership, state, "The most obvious disadvantage is the greater incentive for shirking by owners that results."

54. S. Kole & K. Lehn, *Deregulation and the Adaptation of Governance Structure: The Case of U.S. Airline Industry*, 52 J. Fin. Econ. 79 (1999).

55. Brealey et al., *supra* note 37.

56. We recognize that this finding is probabilistic because there are many other factors that are likely to affect both public- and private-sector firm governance and agency costs, such as budget limits and administrative rules for state-owned enterprises. *See* Geddes (1994) for a comparison of methods in public and private firms to control agency costs. Poor governance stemming from the lack of residual claims has been stressed by other authors. *See, e.g.*, Morten Bennedsen, *Political Ownership*, 76 J. Pub. Econ. 559 (2000).

57. Christian Leuz, Karl V. Lins, & Francis E. Warnock, *Do Foreigners Invest Less in Poorly Governed Firms?*, 23 Rev. Fin. Stud. 3245–85 (2010). Demsetz and Lehn recognized the reduced value of the firm created by shareholder shirking of monitoring duties and stated, "The cost of this shirking, presumably the poorer performance of the firm, is shared by all owners in proportion to the number of shares of stock they own." Stated differently, there is profit potential associated with exercising greater control over the firm: "Control potential is the wealth gain achievable through more effective monitoring of managerial performance by a firm's owners."

58. Michael C. Jensen, *Takeovers: Their Causes and Consequences*, 2 J. Econ. Persp. 21 (1988).

59. Private-sector residual claims may also be linked to key decision agents, such as sole proprietors or partners. *See, e.g.*, Eugene F. Fama & Michael C. Jensen, *Separation of Ownership and Control*, 26 J.L. & Econ. 301 (1983).

60. This has been noted by other commentators. *See* OECD *supra* note 28, at 10, which states, "Concerning substantive challenges, competition law enforcers may have to deal with the fact that obtaining relevant information from SOEs could be very difficult due to lack of transparency regarding costs and insufficient standard accounting procedures."

61. *See* Leuz et al., *supra* note 57.

62. We are unaware of any attempts to measure empirically the magnitude of the effect of non-transferability on the relative cost of SOE capital.

63. Edwin Chadwick, *Results of Different Principles of Legislation and Administration in Europe; of Competition for the Field, as Compared with Competition within the Field, for Service*, J. Royal Stat. Soc'y 381 (1859).

64. Harold Demsetz, *Why Regulate Utilities?*, 11 J.L. & Econ. 55–65 (1968).

65. *See, e.g.*, Eduardo Engel, Ronald Fischer, & Alexander Galetovic, *Privatizing Highways in the United States*, 29 Rev. Indus. Org. 27–53 (2006).

66. *See, e.g.*, Richard A. Brealey & Stewart C. Meyers, Principles of Corporate Finance (2008).

Chapter 4

1. *See* D. Daniel Sokol, *Competition Policy and Comparative Corporate Governance of State-Owned Enterprises*, 2009 BYU L. Rev. 1713, 1727–28 (2009) (noting that SOEs are not "necessarily profit-maximizers" and that some of their "functions are based on nonfinancial goals"); *see also* David E. M. Sappington & J. Gregory Sidak, *Competition Law for State-Owned Enterprises*, 71 Antitrust L.J. 479, 479 (2003).

2. *See* Treaty on the Functioning of the European Union art. 106(1) [hereinafter TFEU].

3. *Id.* art. 106(2).

4. *See* The Antimonopoly Law of the People's Republic of China art. 12.

5. *See* The Competition Act of India art. 2(h).

6. 317 U.S. 341 (1943).

7. *See* Parker, 317 U.S. at 352 ("Here the state command . . . is not rendered unlawful by the Sherman Act, since, in view of the latter's words and history, it must be taken to be a prohibition of individual not state action").

8. 540 U.S. 736 (2004).

9. *Id.* at 746.

10. *Id.* at 747.

11. 39 U.S.C. § 3642(b).

12. 39 U.S.C. § 409(e)(1).

13. 499 U.S. 365, 374–75 (1991).

14. 998 F.2d 931, 948 (Fed. Cir. 1993).

15. 263 F.3d 239, 265 n.55 (3d Cir. 2001).

16. No. 93-16604, 1995 WL 161649, at 2 (9th Cir. Apr. 7, 1995) (unpublished opinion).

17. *See, e.g.*, Paragould Cablevision, Inc. v. City of Paragould, 930 F.2d 1310 (8th Cir. 1991); McCallum v. City of Athens, 976 F.2d 649 (11th Cir. 1992).

18. *See* Federal Trade Commission Office of Policy Planning, Report of the State Action Task Force, at 48–49.

19. 742 F.2d 949, 951–52 (1984).

20. 435 U.S. 389, 419 (1978).

21. *See* OECD, Roundtable on the Application of Antitrust Law to State-Owned Enterprises: Discussion on Corporate Governance and the Principle of Competitive Neutrality for State-Owned Enterprises, Oct. 20, 2009, ¶ 2.

22. *Id.* ¶ 18.

23. See *State Capitalism: The Visible Hand*, Economist, Jan. 21, 2012, *available at* http://www.economist.com/node/21542931.

24. *Id.* at 2.

25. For example, U.S. antitrust law has long embraced the notion that anticompetitive conduct may violate U.S. antitrust law regardless of where such conduct occurs or the nationality of the party concerned. The European Union also views agreements or practices between companies in terms of the "effects" that the agreements or practices have within the EU, regardless of the location of the party involved. For an overview of the extraterritorial reach of U.S. and EU antitrust laws, *see* Ivo Van Bael & Jean-François Bellis, Competition Law of the European Community 152–58 (2005).

26. *See supra* note 23.

27. *Id.* at 2.

28. *Id.*

29. *Id.* at 3.

30. *Id.* at 1.

31. *Id.* at 4.

32. *See* Wentong Zheng, *Transplanting Antitrust in China: Economic Transition, Market Structure and State Control*, 32 U. Penn. J. Int'l L. 643, 662–64 (2010).

33. China has broken up the state monopoly in telecommunications and has reshuffled the state owned assets among several SOE telecommunication firms in several rounds of industry restructuring. *See id.* at 701–02 n.251. China has also broken up the state monopoly in the electricity sector into five electricity generation firms and two electricity grids firms. *See id.* at 703 n.254.

34. Indeed, one of the basic principles enunciated by the Organisation for Economic Co-operation and Development (OECD) for SOE governance is that the state, acting as the owner of SOEs, should allow SOEs full operational autonomy and should not be involved in the day-to-day management of SOEs. *See* OECD, OECD Guidelines on the Corporate Governance of State-Owned Enterprises, Part II.A.

35. For example, Section 1 of the Sherman Act prohibits "every contract, combination in the form of a trust or otherwise, or, conspiracy, in restraint of trade." Sherman Antitrust Act, July 2, 1890, 15 U.S.C. §1.

36. 467 U.S. 752, 769 (1984).

37. *Id.* at 771.

38. *Id.*

39. *Id.*

40. *See, e.g.*, Pink Supply Corp. v. Hiebert, Inc., 788 F.2d 1313 (8th Cir. 1986) (holding that sales agents are not capable of conspiring with manufacturers); Oksanen v. Page Mem. Hospital, 945 F.2d 696 (4th Cir. 1991) (holding that board of trustees and medical staff of a hospital comprised a single entity during the peer review process and thus could not conspire with each other for purposes of Section 1 restraint of trade claim under the Sherman Act).

41. *See* Angela Huyue Zhang, *The Single Entity Theory: An Antitrust Time-Bomb for Chinese State-Owned Enterprises?* 8 J. Comp. L. & Econ. 805, 810 (2012).

42. *See* ACCC, Public Competition Assessment, Chinalco (Aluminum Corporation of China)—Proposed Acquisition of Interests in Rio Tinto plc and Rio Tinto Ltd., Mar. 25, 2009, *available at* http://www.accc.gov.au/content/index.phtml/itemId/866064/fromItemId/751043.

43. *Id.* ¶ 12.

44. *Id.* ¶ 15.

45. *Id.* ¶ 36.
46. *Id.* ¶ 37.
47. *Id.* ¶ 40.
48. *Id.* ¶ 41.
49. *Id.* ¶ 42.
50. *See* Recital 22, Preamble to the Council Regulation (EC) No. 139/2004 of Jan. 20, 2004, on the control of concentrations between undertakings.
51. *See* Case COMP/M.6082, China National Bluestar / Elkem, Commission decision of March 31, 2011; Case COM/M.6151, Petrochina/Ineos, Commission decision of May 13, 2011; Case COMP/M.6113, DSM/Sinochem/JV, Commission decision of May 19, 2011; Case COM/M.6141, China National Agrochemical / Makhteshim Agan, Commission decision of Oct. 3, 2011. For detailed discussions of the Commission's analysis in these cases, *see* Zhang, *supra* note 41.
52. *See* Case COMP/M.6082, China National Bluestar / Elkem, Commission decision of Mar. 31, 2011, ¶¶ 2–4.
53. *Id.* ¶ 7.
54. *Id.* ¶¶ 18–32.
55. *Id.* ¶ 34. For the Commission's competitive assessment, see *id.* ¶¶ 36–134.
56. *Id.* ¶ 34.
57. The original 23 contracting parties of the General Agreement on Tariffs and Trade ("GATT") in 1947 included both Western countries, such as the United States, the United Kingdom and Australia and state-dominant economies such as Cuba, Czechoslovakia and India. *See* Barry J. Eichengreen, Europe's Post-War Recovery 133 Tab. 5.1 (1995).
58. *See* Wentong Zheng, *Reforming Trade Remedies*, 34 Mich. J. Int'l L. 151, 159–60 (2012).
59. *See* U.S. Import Administration Antidumping Manual, Ch. 10, at 3, *available at* http://ia.ita.doc.gov/admanual/index.html [hereinafter Antidumping Manual].
60. *Id.*
61. 19 U.S.C. §1677(18).
62. Antidumping Manual, *supra* note 59, Ch. 10, at 4.
63. *See* Final Determination of Sales at Less Than Fair Value: Silicon Carbide from the People's Republic of China, 59 Fed. Reg. 22585, 22587 (Dep't of Comm. May 2, 1994) [hereinafter Silicon Carbide].
64. *See* Final Determination of Sales at Less Than Fair Value: Sparklers from the People's Republic of China, 56 Fed. Reg. 20588, 20589 (Dep't of Comm. May 6, 1991) [hereinafter Sparklers].
65. Antidumping Manual, *supra* note 59, Ch. 10, at 4.
66. *Id.*
67. Sparklers, *supra* note 64, at 20,589.
68. Silicon Carbide, *supra* note 63, at 22,587.
69. *Id.*
70. *Id.*
71. In Silicon Carbide, for example, the Department of Commerce concluded that the respondent SOE demonstrated de facto absence of control based on examinations of those records. *See id.*
72. SCM Agreement art. 1.1.
73. *Id.* art.1.1(a)(1).
74. *Id.* art. 14(b).
75. *Id.* art. 14(d).
76. *Id.*
77. *Id.* art. 1.1(a)(1).
78. Issues and Decision Memorandum for the Final Determination in the Countervailing Duty Investigation of Dynamic Random Access Memory Semiconductors from the Republic of Korea (June 16, 2003), at 16.
79. Issues and Decision Memorandum for the Final Determination in the Countervailing Duty Investigation of Circular Welded Carbon Quality Steel Pipe from the People's Republic of China (May 29, 2008), at 9.
80. *Id.* at 62–63.
81. *Id.* at 63.

82. *See* Issues and Decision Memorandum for the Final Determination in the Countervailing Duty Investigation of Light-Walled Rectangular Pipe and Tube from the People's Republic of China (June 13, 2008).

83. *Id.* at 26–30.

84. *Id.* at 29.

85. *Id.*

86. *Id.* at 30.

87. *Id.*

88. *Id.*

89. *See* Issues and Decision Memorandum for the Final Determination in the Countervailing Duty Investigation of Coated Free Sheet Paper from the People's Republic of China (Oct. 17, 2007).

90. *Id.* at 56.

91. *Id.* at 58.

92. *Id.*

93. *Id.* at 59.

94. *Id.* at 61.

95. *See* Report of the Panel, United States—Definitive Anti-Dumping and Countervailing Duties on Certain Products from China, WT/DS379/R, Oct. 22, 2010, at 58–64.

96. *See* Report of the Appellate Body, United States—Definitive Anti-Dumping and Countervailing Duties on Certain Products from China, WT/DS379/AB/R, Mar. 11, 2011, ¶ 346.

97. *Id.* ¶ 355.

98. *See supra* notes 64, 79 and accompanying text.

99. *See supra* note 50 and accompanying text.

100. *See supra* note 71 and accompanying text.

101. *See supra* note 79 and accompanying text.

102. For example, in an antidumping proceeding, the U.S. Department of Commerce examined a respondent SOE's correspondence files, bank records, and accounting records to determine whether the SOE should be treated as a separate entity from the Chinese state. *See supra* note 68 and accompanying text.

103. *See generally* OECD, Antitrust Issues Involving Minority Shareholding and Interlocking Directorates, DAF/COMP/WP3/WD(2008)(26), Feb. 19, 2008.

Chapter 5

1. Industrial policy has a number of different meanings. *See* Lawrence J. White, Antitrust Policy and Industrial Policy: A View from the U.S. (Jan. 14, 2008), NYU Law and Economics Research Paper No. 08-05, for both narrow and broad definitions.

2. There is a rich literature on public choice and antitrust. *See* Fred S. McChesney et al., *Competition Policy in Public Choice Perspective*, *in* Handbook of International Antitrust Economics (Roger D. Blair & D. Daniel Sokol eds., forthcoming) for an overview.

3. ICN, Advocacy and Competition Policy Report (ICN Conference, Italy, 2002), *available at* http://www.internationalcompetitionnetwork.org/uploads/library/doc358.pdf, 32.

4. Stephen Calkins, The Merger Guidelines and the Herfindahl Index, 71 Cal. L. Rev. 402 (1983).

5. 4 Phillip Areeda & Donald F. Turner, Antitrust Law 21 (1980).

6. Louis Kaplow & Steven Shavell, *Fairness Versus Welfare*, 114 Harv. L. Rev. 961, 971 (2001).

7. Jonathan B. Baker & David Reitman, *Research Topics in Unilateral Effects Analysis*, *in* Research Handbook on the Economics of Antitrust Law (Einer Elhauge ed., 2011).

8. William Kovacic et al., *Coordinated Effects in Merger Review: Quantifying the Payoffs from Collusion*, *in* International Antitrust Law & Policy: Fordham Corporate Law 2006 (Barry Hawk ed., 2006).

9. Roy J. Epstein & Daniel L. Rubinfeld, *Merger Simulation: A Simplified Approach with New Applications*, 69 Antitrust L.J. 883 (2001); Gregory J. Werden & Luke M. Froeb, *Simulation as an Alternative to Structural Merger Policy in Differentiated Product Industries*, *in* The Economics of the Antitrust Process (Malcolm B. Coate & Andrew N. Kleit eds., 1996).

10. William J. Kolasky & Andrew R. Dick, *The Merger Guidelines and the Integration of Efficiencies into Antitrust Review of Horizontal Mergers*, 71 Antitrust L.J. 207 (2003); Johan N. M. Lagerlof & Paul Heidhues, *On Desirability of an Efficiency Defense in Merger Control*, 23 Int'l J. Indus. Org. 803 (2005).

11. Joseph Farrell & Carl Shapiro, *Antitrust Evaluation of Horizontal Mergers: An Economic Alternative to Market Definition,* 10 BE J. Theoretical Econ. Policies & Perspectives 10 art. 9 (2010), *available at* http://faculty.haas.berkeley.edu/shapiro/alternative.pdf.

12. For example, in the United States, cases such as Brown Shoe Co. v. United States, 370 U.S. 294 (1962) and United States v. Philadelphia National Bank, 374 U.S. 321 (1963) remain good case law, and the agencies still cite such cases when they want to block a merger because the case law is favorable to such an outcome even though the economic understanding of those cases is retrograde by today's standards.

13. William Shughart II, The Government's War on Mergers: The Fatal Conceit of Antitrust Policy, Cato Policy Analysis No. 323 (Oct. 22, 1998); William F. Shughart II, Monopoly and the Problem of the Economists, in Economic Inputs, Legal Outputs: The Role of Economists in Modern Antitrust 149–62 (Fred S. McChesney ed., 1998).

14. Howard A. Shelanski, *Justice Breyer, Professor Kahn, and Antitrust Enforcement in Regulated Industries,* 100 Cal. L. Rev. 487 (2012).

15. *See, e.g.*, South African Competition Act 89 of 1998, as amended by Competition Second Amendment Act 39 of 2000, Chapter 1, § 2; Canadian Competition Act § 1.1 (R.S.C., 1985, c. C-34); Walmart Stores Inc. / Massmart Holdings Ltd. (73/LM/Nov10) (providing an application in the merger setting).

16. Roger D. Blair & D. Daniel Sokol, *The Rule of Reason and the Goals of Antitrust: An Economic Approach*, 78 Antitrust L.J. 471 (2012); Ken Heyer, *Welfare Standards and Merger Analysis Revisited*, 8 Competition Pol'y Int'l 143 (2012).

17. The antitrust problem addressed by Oliver Williamson provides a good illustration of the required balancing. *See* Oliver E. Williamson, *Economies as an Antitrust Defense: The Welfare Trade-Offs*, 58 Am. Econ. Rev. 18 (1968).

18. *See generally* Svetlana Avdasheva et al., *Collective Dominance and Its Abuse Under the Competition Law of the Russian Federation*, 35 World Competition 249, 269 (2012); Malcolm B. Coate & Shawn W. Ulrick, *Transparency at the Federal Trade Commission: The Horizontal Merger Review Process: 1996–2003*, 73 Antitrust L.J. 531, 543 (2006); Timothy J. Muris & Bilal K. Sayyed, *The Long Shadow of Standard Oil: Policy Petroleum, and Politics at the Federal Trade Commission*, 85 S. Cal. L. Rev. 843, 848 (2012).

19. *See* Mats Bergman et al., *Comparing Merger Policies in European Union and the United States*, 36 Rev. Ind. Org. 305 (2010); Ulrich Schwalbe & Daniel Zimmer, *Law and Economics in European Merger Control* (OUP 2009); Tomaso Duso et al., An Empirical Assessment of the 2004 EU Merger Policy Reform (2010) (WZP discussion paper), *available at* http://papers.ssrn.com/sol3/papers.cfm?abstract_id=1721412.

20. *See, e.g.*, Robert Pitofsky, *The Political Content of Antitrust*, 127 U. Pa. L. Rev. 1051 (1979).

21. Hillary Greene, *Guideline Institutionalization: The Role of Merger Guidelines in Antitrust Discourse*, 48 Wm. & Mary L. Rev. 771 (2006).

22. Leah Brannon & Douglas H. Ginsburg, *Antitrust Decisions of the Supreme Court: 1967 to 2007*, 3 Competition Pol'y Int'l 1, 22 (2007).

23. Luke M. Froeb et al., *The Economics of Organizing Economists*, 76 Antitrust L.J. 569, 573 (2009).

24. Daniel Crane, *Technocracy and Antitrust*, 86 Texas L. Rev. 1159, 1211–20 (2008).

25. Malcolm B. Coate, Bush, Clinton, Bush: Twenty Years of Merger Enforcement at the Federal Trade Commission 24 (Sept. 2009) (working paper).

26. Malcolm B. Coate, *A Test of Political Control of the Bureaucracy: The Case of Mergers*, 14 Econ. & Pol. 1 (2002).

27. *See* McChesney et al., *supra* note 2.

28. Robert Pitofsky, How the Chicago School Overshot the Mark: The Effect of Conservative Economic Analysis on U.S. Antitrust 233 (2008).

29. Ilene Knable Gotts & James F. Rill, *Reflections on Bush Administration M&A Antitrust Enforcement and Beyond*, 5 Competition Pol'y Int'l 91 (2009).

30. Jonathan B. Baker & Carl Shapiro, *Reinvigorating Horizontal Merger Enforcement, in* How the Chicago School Overshot the Mark: the Effect of Conservative Economic Analysis on U.S. Antitrust 109, 109–10 (Robert Pitofsky ed., 2008).

31. Malcolm B. Coate, Bush, Clinton, Bush: Twenty Years of Merger Enforcement at the Federal Trade Commission 24 (Sept. 2009) (unpublished manuscript), *available at* http://papers.ssrn.com/sol3/papers.cfm?abstract_id=1314924. ("Little evidence can be found to suggest that the enforcement

regime changed [across Bush, Clinton, and Bush administrations] in response to either political control or the specific wording of the Merger Guidelines."); Daniel A. Crane, *Has the Obama Justice Department Reinvigorated Antitrust Enforcement?*, 65 Stan. L. Rev. Online 13 (2012).

32. D. Daniel Sokol, *Antitrust, Institutions, and Merger Control*, 17 Geo. Mason L. Rev. 1055 (2010).

33. Luke M. Froeb et al., *The Economics of Organizing Economists*, 76 Antitrust L.J. 569 (2009).

34. United States v. Von's Grocery Co., 384 U.S. 270 (1966).

35. D. Daniel Sokol, *Antitrust, Institutions, and Merger Control*, 17 Geo. Mason L. Rev. 1055 (2010).

36. Ulrich Schwalbe & Daniel Zimmer, Law and Economics in European Merger Control (OUP 2009); Tomaso Duso et al., An Empirical Assessment of the 2004 EU Merger Policy Reform (2010) (WZP discussion paper), *available at* http://papers.ssrn.com/sol3/papers.cfm?abstract_id=1721412.

37. Damien Geradin & Ianis Girgenson, Industrial Policy and European Merger Control—A Reassessment (working paper 2011).

38. *See* Mats Bergman et al., *Comparing Merger Policies in European Union and the United States*, 36 Rev. Ind. Org. 305 (2010).

39. Aerospatiale-Alenia / de Havilland (91/619/EEC), 1991 O.J. (L 334) 42.

40. Francesco Russo et al., European Commission Decisions on Competition: Economic Perspectives on Landmark Antitrust and Merger Cases (2010).

41. Mats A. Bergman et al., Atlantic Divide or Gulf Stream Convergence: Merger Policies in the European Union and the United States (Apr. 13, 2010). *Available at* http://ssrn.com/abstract=975102.

42. James C. Cooper et al., *Vertical Antitrust Policy as a Problem of Inference*, 23 Int'l J. Indus. Org. 639 (2005).

43. Eleanor M. Fox, *Mergers in Global Markets: GE/Honeywell and the Future of Merger Control*, 23 U. Pa. J. Int'l Econ. L. 457 (2002).

44. Nihat Aktas et al., *European M&A Regulation Is Protectionist*, 117 Econ. J. 1096 (2007); Tomaso Duso et al., *The Political Economy of European Merger Control: Evidence Using Stock Market Data*, 50 J.L. & Econ. 455 (2007); Serdar Dinc & Isil Erel, Economic Nationalism in Mergers & Acquisitions (2011) (working paper). On the use of financial stock market return event studies for competition policy, *see* Tomaso Duso et al., *Is the Event Study Methodology Useful for Merger Analysis? A Comparison of Stock Market and Accounting Data*, 30 Int'l Rev. L. & Econ. 186 (2010).

45. Nihat Aktas et al., Market Reactions to European Merger Regulation: A Reexamination of the Protectionism Hypothesis, (2011) (working paper).

46. Commission Decision Case IV/M.877, Boeing / McDonnell Douglas, 1997 O.J. (L 335).

47. Commission Decision Case COMP/M.2220, General Electric / Honeywell, 2001, 2004 O.J. (L 48) 1, prohibition aff'd, Case T-210/10, Court of First Instance, Dec. 14, 2005 (EU).

48. Commission Decision Case COMP/M.3216, Oracle/PeopleSoft, 2004, 2005 O.J. (L 218).

49. *See generally* Eleanor M. Fox, GE Honeywell: *The U.S. Merger that Europe Stopped—A Story of the Politics of Convergence*, *in* Antitrust Stories (Daniel A. Crane & Eleanor M. Fox eds., 2007).

50. Daniel J. Gifford & Robert T. Kudrle, *European Union Competition Law and Policy: How Much Latitude for Convergence with the United States?*, 48 Antitrust Bull. 727 (2003).

51. The EU even incorporated evidence from the U.S. trial. Press Release, European Comm'n, Commission Clears Oracle's Takeover Bid for PeopleSoft (Oct. 26, 2004), *available at* http://europa.eu.int.

52. Christian Duvernoy & Sven Völcker, Oracle in Brussels, M&A Lawyer (Sept. 2005). ("One theory is that after GE/Honeywell, the Commission was making a political decision and hiding that fact: 'Let's look different and independent, but let's also come out with the same result.'")

53. Patrick Massey, *Taking Politics Out of Mergers: A Review of Irish Experience*, 6 J. Competition L. & Econ. 853 (2010).

54. Ping Lin & Jingjing Zhao, *Merger Control Policy under China's Anti-Monopoly Law*, 41 Rev. Ind. Org. 109 (2012); Pingpin Shan et al., *China's Anti-Monopoly Law: What Is the Welfare Standard?*, 41 Rev. Ind. Org. 31 (2012).

55. D. Daniel Sokol, Merger Control under China's Anti-Monopoly Law (2013) (working paper).

56. Air New Zealand v. Commerce Commission (No. 6) (2004) 11 TCLR 347 (HC), at 42.

57. In New Zealand competition law cases, the High Court judge sits with a lay expert as part of his court, usually an economist.

58. Godfrey Hirst NZ Limited, Judgment of Court CIV 2011-485-1257 at ¶ 5.

59. *Id.* at ¶ 327.

60. Int'l Competition Network, Antitrust Enforcement in Regulated Sectors Working Group, Subgroup 1: Limits and Constraints Facing Antitrust Authorities Intervening in Regulated Sectors (2004).

61. *See generally* Dennis Mueller, Public Choice III (2003).

62. Howard A. Shelanski, *Antitrust Law as Mass Media Regulation: Can Merger Standards Protect the Public Interest?*, 94 Cal. L. Rev. 371, 394 (2006).

63. Verizon Comm., Inc. v. Law Offices of Curtis V. Trinko, LLP, 540 U.S. 398 (2004).

64. Credit Suisse Securities LLC v. Billing, 551 U.S. 264, 284 (2007).

65. George J. Stigler, *The Theory of Economic Regulation*, 2 Bell J. Econ. & Mgmt. Sci. 3 (1971).

66. Dodd-Frank, §§ 604, 622(e).

67. *Id.* § 622(e)(1)(A).

68. *Id.* § 622(b)-(c).

69. *Id.* § 623(c).

70. Philip Lowe, Speech to the Enforcing Competition Law Conference, London: What Is Wrong with National Champions? (June 23, 2006).

71. Under the two-thirds rule, a merger has an EU-wide dimension for merger control if two-thirds of the turnover of each of the merging parties is in the same member state.

72. Damien Gerard, *Protectionist Threats against Cross-Border Mergers: Unexplored Avenues to Strengthen the Effectiveness of Article 21 ECMR*, 45 Common Mkt. L. Rev. (2008).

73. Case C-196/07 Commission v. Spain, judgment of Mar. 6, 2008.

74. Andreas Stephan, *Did Lloyds/HBOS Mark the Failure of an Enduring Economics Based System of Merger Regulation?*, 62 N. Ireland Legal Q. 539 (2011).

75. R. S. Khemani & D. M. Shapiro, *An Empirical Analysis of Canadian Merger Policy*, 41 J. Indus. Econ. 161 (1993).

76. Frederic Jenny, *Export Cartels in Primary Products: The Potash Case in Perspective*, *in* Trade, Competition and the Pricing Commodities (Frederic Jenny & Simon Evenett eds., 2012).

77. Although elsewhere I have argued for a total welfare standard, here my broader point is that the sole standard for antitrust should be the political choice between an antitrust-specific welfare standard, not between antitrust economics and other non-antitrust economics considerations.

Chapter 6

1. Jose A. Gomez-Ibanez, Regulating Infrastructure: Monopoly, Contracts and Discretion (2003).

2. The point will be addressed in Section IV.

3. Jean-Jacques Laffont & Jean Tirole, Competition in Telecommunications § 4.5.3(2000).

4. The efficient component pricing rule was introduced in the literature by Robert Willig, *The Theory of Network Access Pricing*, *in* Issues in Public Utility Regulation (H. M. Trebbing ed., 1979). It was further developed by William J. Baumol & Robert D. Willig, *Fixed Costs, Sunk Costs, Entry Barriers, and the Sustainability of Monopoly*, 96 Q.J. Econ. 405 (1981); William J. Baumol & J. Gregory Sidak, Toward Competition in Local Telephony (1994). ECPR preserves the profits of the integrated supplier and maintains the right incentives to invest/innovate.

5. Nicholas Economides & Lawrence J. White, *Access and Interconnection Pricing: How Efficient Is the "Efficient Component Pricing Rule"?*, 40 Antitrust Bull. 557 (1995).

6. *See id.*

7. *See* Section IV.

8. Harry First, *Controlling the Intellectual Property Grab: Protect Innovation, Not Innovators*, 38 Rutgers L.J. 365, 365 (2007).

9. Fed. Trade Comm'n, to Promote Innovation: The Proper Balance of Competition and Patent Law and Policy (2003).

10. Nat'l Research Council, A Patent System for the 21st Century (Stephen A. Merrill et al. eds., 2004).

11. Dennis W. Carlton, *Does Antitrust Need to Be Modernized?*, 21 J. Econ. Persp. 155 (2007). These criticisms are now revamped by the 2012 Apple-Samsung Court decision in California. As *The Economist* suggests in its comments on the Court decisions, "To award a monopoly right to finger gestures and rounded rectangles is to stretch the definition of novel and nonobvious to breaking points." *Apple v. Samsung. iPhone, uCopy, iSue*, Economist, Sept. 1, 2012.

12. Mark A. Lemley, *Can the Patent Office Be Fixed?*, *in* Rules for Growth (Robert Litan ed., 2011).

13. Daron Acemoglu & Ufuk Akcigit, State-Dependent Intellectual Property Rights Policy Nat'l Bureau of Econ. Res., Working Paper No. 12775, Dec. 2006).

14. Michele Boldrin & David Levine, Growth and Intellectual Property (NBER Working Paper Series No. 12769, 2006).

15. First, *supra* note 8, at 367.

16. Brunswick Corp. v. Pueblo Bowl-O-Mat, Inc., 429 U.S. 477, 488 (1977) (quoting Brown Shoe Co. v. United States, 370 U.S. 294, 320 (1962)).

17. Lemley, *supra* note 12.

18. Robert Z. Lawrence, Brookings Trade Forum (1998).

19. Robert D. Willig, *Economic Effects of Antidumping Policy*, *in* Brookings Trade Forum (Robert Z. Lawrence ed., 1998).

20. Such a thorough analysis should be required for so-called actionable subsidies that, according to the WTO rules, can be prohibited when the complaining country shows that the subsidy has an adverse effect on its interests. Actionable subsidies can be prohibited when they seriously injure the importing country's domestic industry, rival exporters in a third country trying to compete with a subsidized exporter, or exporters trying to compete with subsidized domestic firms.

21. Michael Hahn & Kirtikumar Mehta, *It's a Bird, It's a Plane: Some Remarks on the Airbus Appellate Body Report* (EC and Certain Member States—Large Civil Aircraft, WT/DS316/AB/R), 12 World Trade Rev. 139 (2013).

22. In the interpretation of the rules, economic analysis should play a much more prominent role than in the EU.

23. Carsten Fink & Keith E. Maskus, Intellectual Property and Development: Lessons from Recent Economic Research (2004).

24. Verizon Communications Inc. v. Law Offices of Curtis V. Trinko 124 S. Ct. 872 (2004), *rev'g* 305, F.3d 89 (2d Cir. 2002).

25. In the Court of First Instance (CFI), judgment on the validity of the Commission decision that found that Deutsche Telekom had abused its dominant position by making it impossible for competitors to enter in the competitive segment of the market, the CFI claimed that there is an abuse "if the difference between the retail prices charged by a dominant undertaking and the wholesale prices it charges its competitors for comparable services is negative, or insufficient to cover the product-specific costs to the dominant operator of providing its own retail services on the downstream market." The fact that Deutsche Telekom was subject to a price cap regulation would have made a difference only insofar as the regulation would have imposed on Deutsche Telekom the contested behavior. Alberto Heimler, *Is Margin Squeeze an Antitrust or a Regulatory Violation?*, 6 J. Competition L. & Econ. 879 (2011).

26. Damien Geradin & Miguel Rato, FRAND Commitments and EC Competition Law, (2010), *available at* http://ssrn.com/abstract=1527407.

27. *See* Case T-167/08.

28. European Commission Case No. COMP/37.792 Microsoft of 24.3.2004. *See* Robert D. Anderson & Alberto Heimler, *What Has Competition Done for Europe? An Inter-Disciplinary Answer*, 4 Aussenwirtschaft (2007).

29. Another aspect of the case that involves the bundling of Microsoft's Media Player software with its operating system is not discussed in the paper.

30. *See* First, *supra* note 8.

31. Christos Genakos et al., The European Commission vs. Microsoft: Competition Policy in High-Tech Industries (2007) (LSE working paper).

32. *See also* on this Ravi Mehta, Imprecise Legal Concepts Are No Excuse, Competition Law View from Blackstone Chambers, *available at* http://competitionbulletin.com/.

33. *See* the Justice Department press release, *available at* http://www.justice.gov/atr/public/press_releases/2011/266149.htm.

34. *See* Chapter 2.

Chapter 7

1. *See generally* Paul B. Stephan, *Global Governance, Antitrust, and the Limits of International Cooperation*, 38 Cornell Int'l L.J. 173 (2005); Edward Iacobucci, *The Interdependence of Trade and Competition Policies*, 21 World Competition L. & Econ. Rev. 5 (1997).

2. In theory the Uruguay Round Agreements allow one state to challenge another's competition policy as inconsistent with the General Agreement on Tariffs and Trade or the Agreement on Technical Barriers to Trade. A few cases have arisen, including one under the General Agreement on Trade in Services (which applies only when a government agrees to open up a particular industry to discipline under that Agreement) and a rather idiosyncratic attack on a little used U.S. antidumping statute. For proposals to bring export cartels under WTO regulation, *see* Marek Martyniszyn, *Export Cartels: Is It Legal to Target Your Neighbor? Analysis in Light of Recent Case Law*, 15 J. Int'l Econ. L. 181 (2012); Florian Becker, *The Case of Export Cartel Exemptions: Between Competition and Protectionism*, 3 J. Competition L. & Econ. 97 (2007); D. Daniel Sokol, *What Do We Really Know About Export Cartels and What Is the Appropriate Solution?*, 4 J. Competition L. & Econ. 967 (2008); Andrew T. Guzman, *International Antitrust and the WTO—The Lessons from Intellectual Property*, 43 Va. J. Int'l L. 933 (2003); Eleanor M. Fox, *International Antitrust and the Doha Round*, 43 Va. J. Int'l L. 911 (2003); H. C. Claus-Dieter Ehlermann & Lothar Ehring, *WTO Dispute and Competition Law: Views from the Perspective of the Appellate Body's Experience*, 26 Ford. Int'l L.J. 1505 (2002); Ernst-Ulrich Petersmann, *International Competition Rules for Governments and for Private Business: A "Trade Law Approach" for Linking Trade and Competition Rules in the WTO*, 72 Chi.-Kent L. Rev. 545 (1996). After originally embracing increased linkage between trade and competition law in the Doha Round, the WTO members subsequently rejected the idea. *See* DOHA Work Program—Decision Adopted by the General Council on August 1, 2004, WT/L/579, ¶ 1(g), *available at* http://www.wto.org/english/tratop_e/dda_e/ddadraft_31jul04_e.pdf.

3. Schooner Exchange v. M'Faddon, 11 U.S. (7 Cranch) 116, 136 (1812).

4. Jurisdictional Immunities of the State (Germany v. Italy: Greece Intervening), [2012] I.C.J. 143 ¶ 57.

5. *See, e.g.*, Marko Milanovic, Extraterritorial Application of Human Rights Treaties—Law, Principles, and Policy (2011); Kal Raustila, Does the Constitution Follow the Flag? (2009).

6. *See* Paul B. Stephan, *Privatizing International Law*, 97 Va. L. Rev. 1573 (2011).

7. Louis B. Sohn, *The New International Law: Protection of the Rights of Individuals Rather Than States*, 32 Am. U. L. Rev. 1 (1982).

8. *See supra* note 4.

9. The one dissent in the case did advance a theory of international law that marginalized state consent in favor of ethical values. Jurisdictional Immunities of the State (Germany v. Italy: Greece Intervening), *supra* note 4 (Cançado Trindade, J., dissenting). The most noteworthy thing about that dissent, however, is that no other member of the Court joined it.

10. American Banana Co. v. United Fruit Co., 213 U.S. 347 (1909).

11. United States v. Sisal Sales Corp., 274 U.S. 268 (1927).

12. United States v. Aluminum Co. of America, 148 F.2d 416 (2d Cir. 1945). Because the Supreme Court lacked a quorum to consider this case, the court of appeals decision accepting the government's contention remained the final word for nearly half a century.

13. Hartford Fire Insurance Co. v. California, 509 U.S. 764 (1993). The Court expressly disavowed relying on the 1982 Foreign Trade Antitrust Improvements Act, which at least by negative inference might have supported the outcome. 509 U.S. at 796 n.23, 798. Evidence of the hostility of other states includes both clawback regimes that allowed defendants in U.S. courts to sue for restitution of the punitive component of antitrust damages and blocking statutes that forbade cooperation with civil or criminal cases brought in the United States. For a review of this legislation, *see* Gary B. Born & Peter B. Rutledge, International Civil Litigation in United States Courts 680–83, 972–77 (5th ed. 2011).

14. In re Wood Pulp Cartel: A Ahlström Osakeytiö v. EC Commission (Joined Cases 89, 104, 116, 117, & 125–129/85), [1988] E.C.R. 5193. *See also* Gencor Ltd. v. Comm'n (Case T-102/96), [1999] E.C.R. II-753, ¶ 90.

15. 475 U.S. 574, 582 (1986). In a footnote, the Court clarified that "the Sherman Act does reach conduct outside our borders, but only when the conduct has an effect on American commerce." *Id.* at 582 n.6. It then cited Continental Ore Co. v. Union Carbide & Carbon Corp., 370 U.S. 690 (1962), a case where foreign and domestic producers colluded in a price-fixing cartel directed at the U.S. market. Nowhere in the opinion did the Court refer to the 1982 Foreign Trade Antitrust Improvements Act, which seemed to mandate an exclusion from Sherman Act coverage for foreign economic injuries. In a leading case decided not long after *Matsushita*, a court of appeals ignored this language altogether when considering a challenge to a state policy of limiting the carriage of bulk imported cargo to national

carriers. O.N.E. Shipping Ltd. v. Flota Mercante Grancolombiana, S.A., 830 F.2d 449 (2d Cir. 1987). It instead based its decision on the act of state doctrine, discussed below.

16. 542 U.S. 155 (2004). The Court did recognize an exception to this rule in cases where a price-fixing conspiracy targeted at the U.S. market "gives rise to" a foreign injury. The reach of this exception depends on what standard one employs for causation. At least so far, the courts have understood the standard to be demanding. On remand, the lower court ruled that foreign consumers did not have a claim under the Sherman Act when the price-fixing conspiracy as to the U.S. market merely facilitated their injury. Empagran S.A. v. F. Hoffmann-La Roche, Ltd., 417 F.2d 1267 (D.C. Cir. 2005), *cert. denied*, 546 U.S. 1092 (2006).

17. 542 U.S. at 164–65.

18. 561 U.S. 247 (2010). The repudiated cases include IIT, Int'l Inv. Trust v. Cornfeld, 619 F.2d 909 (2d Cir. 1980); Bersch v. Drexel Firestone, Inc., 519 F.2d 974 (2d Cir. 1975); IIT v. Vencap, Ltd., 519 F.2d 1001 (2d Cir. 1975); Leasco Data Processing Equip. Corp. v. Maxwell, 468 F.2d 1326 (2d Cir. 1972); Schoenbaum v. Firstbrook, 405 F.2d 200 (2d Cir.), *reheard en banc*, 405 F.2d 215 (2d Cir. 1968).

19. *Id.* at 258 note 11 (citing Continental Ore, *supra* note 15). The footnote then explains that some earlier cases involved "conspiracies to restrain trade in the United States," but did not indicate that this was an essential element of a Sherman Act violation. *Id.* In particular, the Court made no mention of the 1982 amendments to the antitrust statutes as perhaps providing an independent basis for extraterritorial application.

20. In addition to Morrison v. National Australia Bank, Ltd., the leading cases are Kiobel v. Royal Dutch Petroleum Co., 133 S. Ct. 1659 (2013), and Equal Employment Opportunity Comm'n v. Arabian American Oil Co (Aramco), 499 U.S. 244 (1991). Congress responded to Aramco by adopting Section 109 of the Civil Rights Act of 1991, Pub. L. 102-166, 105 Stat. 1071 (1991), which imposes limited nondiscrimination obligations on U.S. employers operating overseas. It reacted to Morrison through Section 929P(b) of the Dodd-Frank Wall Street Reform and Consumer Protection Act, Pub. L. No. 111-203, 124 Stat. 1376 (2010), which attempts to restore the SEC's jurisdiction over some foreign sales of securities but does not apply to private suits. It has not yet reacted to Kiobel. *See* Paul B. Stephan, *The Political Economy of Extraterritoriality*, 1 Pol. & Gov. 92 (2013).

21. National Society of Professional Engineers v. United States, 435 U.S. 679, 688 (1977); Northern Securities Co. v. United States, 193 U.S. 197, 361–62 (1904) (Brewer, J., concurring). For examples of shifts in doctrine in the face of changed perceptions of optimal market structure, *see, e.g.*, Leegin Creative Leather Products, Inc. v. PSKS, Inc., 551 U.S. 877 (2007).

22. The Court also can avoid international conflicts by treating foreign state–managed conduct as not harmful and thus outside the scope of regulation altogether. In *Matsushita*, the Court ruled that U.S. law did not apply to a scheme, allegedly managed by the Japanese government, to capture market share in the United States through low prices absent credible evidence that the scheme, once successful, would create a durable barrier to entry. This ruling made unnecessary an inquiry into the availability of a foreign sovereign compulsion defense, the question on which the Court originally had granted certiorari. I discuss this defense and its relationship to the act of state doctrine below. European case law is less clear on this point and might allow government regulation of underpricing even in the absence of clear evidence of a stable barrier to entry. One complicating factor, however, is that many of the cases implicate the separate doctrine under European law disallowing improper government subsidies (state aids). For a review of the cases, *see* D. Daniel Sokol, *Competition Policy and Comparative Corporate Governance of State-Owned Enterprises*, 2009 BYU L. Rev. 1713, 1788–92.

23. *See also* Marek Martyniszyn, Avoidance Techniques: State Related Defences in International Antitrust Cases (UCD Working Papers in Law, Criminology & Socio-Legal Studies Research Paper No. 46/2011, 2012) (reviewing U.S., British, and EC use of sovereign immunity; act of state doctrine; political question doctrine; and foreign state compulsion in antitrust cases).

24. Schooner Exchange v. M'Faddon, 11 U.S. (7 Cranch) 116 (1812).

25. 28 U.S.C. §§ 1602–11; Samantar v. Yousuf, 560 U.S. 305 (2010).

26. In particular, the refusal of the United States to recognize state immunity in certain cases involving torture seems inconsistent with the International Court of Justice's understanding of the present state of customary international law.

27. 28 U.S.C. §§ 1603(b)(3).

28. Dole Food Co. v. Patrickson, 538 U.S. 468 (2003).

29. 1605(a)(1). Consent can be implied by failure to object to jurisdiction at the first opportunity.

30. 28 U.S.C. § 1605(a)(2). I ignore for present purposes other statutory exceptions to state immunity, which do not seem relevant to antitrust issues.

31. Spectrum Stores, Inc. v. Citgo Petroleum Corp., 632 F.3d 938 (5th Cir. 2011).

32. Earlier litigation established that OPEC cannot be subjected to service of process in the United States. Prewitt Enterprises, Inc. v. OPEC, 353 F.3d 916 (11th Cir. 2003). Under FSIA, immunity from attachment is broader than immunity from litigation. 28 U.S.C. §§ 1609–11.

33. *See* Simon N.M. Young, *Immunity in Hong Kong for Kleptocrats and Human Rights Violators*, 41 Hong Kong L.J. 421 (2011).

34. *See* Jurisdictional Immunities of the State (Germany v. Italy: Greece Intervening), *supra* note 4, at ¶ 59.

35. *See* Joel I. Klein, The Internationalization of Antitrust: Bilateral and Multilateral Responses. Presented at The European University Institute Conference on Competition, June 13, 1997, *available at* http://www.justice.gov/atr/public/speeches/1580.htm.

36. 376 U.S. 398, 427–28 (1964).

37. Immediately after the Supreme Court decided Sabbatino, Congress overruled the case as to expropriations of the property of foreign investors. 22 U.S.C. s 2370(e)(2). The Supreme Court has not found an opportunity to consider a case where that statute applied, but the lower courts have accepted the congressional mandate.

38. W. S. Kirkpatrick & Co., Inc. v. Environmental Tectonics Corp., International, 493 U.S. 400 (1990). For lower federal court resort to the doctrine in antitrust cases, *see* Spectrum Stores, Inc. v. Citgo Petroleum Corp., 632 F.3d 938 (5th Cir. 2011); O.N.E. Shipping Ltd. v. Flota Mercante Grancolombiana, S.A., 830 F.2d 449 (2d Cir. 1987); Clayco Petroleum Corp. v. Occidental Petroleum Corp., 712 F.2d 404 (9th Cir. 1983); IAM v. OPEC, 649 F.2d 1354 (9th Cir. 1980); Hunt v. Mobil Oil Corp., 550 F.2d 68 (2d Cir. 1977).

39. *See supra* note 21.

40. The U.S. government accepts that the doctrine applies in antitrust cases, "if the facts and circumstances indicate that: (1) the specific conduct complained of is a public act of the sovereign, (2) the act was taken within the territorial jurisdiction of the sovereign, and (3) the matter is governmental, rather than commercial." U.S. Department of Justice & Federal Trade Commission, Antitrust Enforcement Guidelines for International Operations, Antitrust Enforcement Guidelines for International Operations, Antitrust Enforcement Guidelines for International Operations § 3.33 (1995) [hereinafter Antitrust Enforcement Guidelines].

41. 493 U.S. 400 (1990).

42. RICO does not independently criminalize conduct but rather enhances penalties and provides for civil treble damages suits for specific crimes, if carried out in an organized fashion within the meaning of the statute. The predicate offenses in W. S. Kirkpatrick were mail and wire fraud under 18 U.S.C. §§ 1341, 1343. Environmental Tectonics Corp. v. W. S. Kirkpatrick & Co., 659 F. Supp. 1381, 1391 (D.N.J. 1987).

43. The United States recognized the revenue rule in The Antelope, 23 U.S. (10 Wheat.) 66, 123 (1825).

44. 544 U.S. 349 (2005).

45. The existence of a fourth exception, where the Executive Branch seeks to override the doctrine without relying on a statute or treaty, is not clear. In First National City Bank v. Banco Nacional de Cuba, 406 U.S. 759 (1972), a three-justice plurality asserted that the Executive Branch had this discretion. Five members of that Court rejected the claim. In W. S. Kirkpatrick & Co., Inc. v. Environmental Tectonics Corp., International, 493 U.S. 400 (1990), the Court suggested that factors such as the views of the Executive might justify constriction of the doctrine but in no event could justify expansion of its scope.

46. 376 U.S. at 428. At least one lower court has expanded this point by treating all so-called *jus cogens* norms of international law as overriding the doctrine. Sarei v. Rio Tinto PLC, 671 F.3d 736, 757 (9th Cir. 2011), *vacated and remanded*, 133 S. Ct. 1995 (2013), *reversed on other grounds*, 722 F.3d 1109 (9th Cir. 2013). For criticism of such a use of the *jus cogens* concept, *see* Paul B. Stephan, The Political Economy of Jus Cogens, 44 Vand. J. Transnat'l L. 1073 (2011). In essence, this supposed exception rests on confusion about the doctrine's role as an interstitial rule, rather than as an independent source of legal authority.

47. Alfred Dunhill of London, Inc. v. Republic of Cuba, 425 U.S. 682, 693 (1976). The government does not seem to recognize *Dunhill's* distinction between a civil law act and a commercial act. Antitrust Enforcement Guidelines, *supra* note 40.

48. *Id.* at 695–96 (plurality opinion).

49. 493 U.S. at 405–06.

50. Portuguese Republic v. Council (Case C-149/96), [1999] E.C.R. I-8395; Uruguay Round Agreements Act. At least two lower court cases have intimated that a violation of the Uruguay Round Agreements might negate a sovereign compulsion defense to an antitrust claim. Resco Products, Inc. v. Bosai Mineral Group Co., Ltd., 2010-1 Trade Cas. ¶ 77.061 (W.D. Pa. 2011); Animal Science Products, Inc. v. China National Metals & Minerals Import & Export Corp., 702 F. Supp. 320 (E.N.J. 2010), *rev'd on other grounds*, 654 F.3d 462 (3d Cir. 2011). Neither case explored whether such an approach would be consistent with the statutory command not to incorporate the Uruguay Round Agreements into domestic law.

51. *See* Continental Ore Co. v. Union Carbide & Carbon Corp., 370 U.S. 690, 707–08 (1962) (involvement of government agent in anticompetitive conspiracy does not insulate other participants from antitrust liability); Williams v. Curtiss-Wright Corporation, 694 F.2d 300, 304 (3d Cir. 1982) (allegation that defendant induced foreign governments not to deal with plaintiff does not trigger act of state doctrine); Mannington Mills, Inc. v. Congoleum Corp., 595 F.2d 1287, 1293–94 (3d Cir. 1979) (allegation that defendant induced the grant of foreign patents for anticompetitive reasons does not trigger act of state doctrine); Industrial Investment Development Corp. v. Mitsui & Co., Ltd., 594 F.2d 48, 53 (5th Cir. 1979) (allegation that defendant induced government agency to withhold license does not trigger act of state doctrine); Sage International, Ltd. v. Cadillac Gage Co., 534 F. Supp. 896 (E.D. Mich. 1981) (allegation that defendant induced foreign governments not to buy plaintiff's product does not trigger act of state doctrine).

52. In re Japanese Electronic Products Antitrust Litigation, 723 F.3d 238, 315 (3d Cir. 1983), *rev'd on other grounds*, 475 U.S. 574 (1986); In re Vitamin C Litigation, 810 F. Supp. 2d 522 (E.D.N.Y. 2011); Animal Science Products, Inc. v. China National Metals & Minerals Import & Export Corp., 702 F. Supp. 320 (E.N.J. 2010), *rev'd on other grounds*, 654 F.3d 462 (3d Cir. 2011). *See* Marek Martyniszyn, *supra* note 23.

53. 632 F.3d at 955 n.16.

54. MOL, Inc. v. People's Republic of Bangladesh, 736 F.2d 1326 (9th Cir. 1984). *MOL* involved the commercial exception to FSIA, not the act of state doctrine, and probably no longer is good law as to that statute. *See* Republic of Argentina v. Weltover, Inc., 504 U.S. 607 (1992). But the broad scope of the statutory exception need not be read into the common-law act of state doctrine.

55. 493 U.S. at 405–06 (distinguishing Underhill v. Hernandez, 168 U.S. 250 (1897). *See* Paul B. Stephan, International Law in the Supreme Court, 1990 Sup. Ct. Rev. 133, 149–50.

56. The Justice Department's Antitrust Guidelines also recognized this defense. Antitrust Enforcement Guidelines, *supra* note 40, at § 3.32.

57. In several recent cases, district courts have addressed the defense, one holding that it did not apply and the other that it might apply to some but not all of the defendants' conduct. In each instance, the court just as easily could have held that the government acts in question did or did not come within *Dunhill's* civil law exception to the act of state doctrine. In re Vitamin C Litigation, 810 F. Supp. 2d 522 (E.D.N.Y. 2011); Animal Science Products, Inc. v. China National Metals & Minerals Import & Export Corp., 702 F. Supp. 320 (E.N.J. 2010), *rev'd on other grounds*, 654 F.3d 462 (3d Cir. 2011).

58. For the Court's most recent pronouncements, *see* Zivotofsky v. Clinton, 132 S. Ct. 1421 (2012).

59. The *Spectrum* court recognized that Congress had considered legislation that would have applied criminal and civil sanctions to the OPEC cartel. The court did not see the prospect of such legislation as undermining an argument based on constitutional capacity of the judiciary, however, because the envisioned statute would not authorize private civil litigation. 632 F.3d at 653–54 n.15. Why a claim would become justiciable if the government were to bring it if it were not as long as a private person asserted it was not explained (and does not seem to have a valid explanation).

Chapter 8

I wish to thank Erin Orndorff, Notre Dame Law class of 2013, for her assistance with this chapter. An expanded version of this chapter is available in the *Maine Law Review* (65) 1, 2012.

1. Among the "highlights" of this litany of cases is Leegin Creative Leather Prods., Inc. v. PSKS, Inc., 551 U.S. 877 (2007) (overruling Dr. Miles Med. Co. v. John D. Park & Sons Co., 220 U.S. 373

(1911) and holding that vertical price restraints are unlawful only under a rule of reason analysis and are not subject to a standard of per se unreasonableness); Illinois Tool Works Inc. v. Independent Ink, Inc., 547 U.S. 28 (2006) (overruling portions of several prior cases and rejecting the previously approved presumption regarding a tying arrangement that a patent confers the requisite power on the seller of the tying product); Northwest Wholesale Stationers, Inc. v. Pacific Stationery & Printing Co., 472 U.S. 284 (1985) (holding that only certain concerted refusals to deal are subject to a standard of per se unreasonableness and that most such restraints will be tested under the rule of reason); Continental T.V., Inc. v. GTE Sylvania, 433 U.S. 36 (1977) (overruling Arnold, Schwinn & Co. v. United States, 388 U.S. 365 (1967) and holding that vertical nonprice restraints are unlawful only under a rule of reason analysis and are not subject to a standard of per se unreasonableness).

2. Joseph P. Bauer, *The Stealth Assault on Antitrust Enforcement: Raising the Barriers for Antitrust Injury and Standing*, 62 U. Pitt. L. Rev. 437 (2001).

3. Bell Atl. Corp. v. Twombly, 550 U.S. 544 (2007).

4. 96 Stat. 1246 (codified at 15 U.S.C. § 6a).

5. H.R. Rep. No. 97-686 (1982).

6. *Id.* at 2.

7. *Id.*

8. F. Hoffman-LaRoche, Ltd. v. Empagran S.A., 542 U.S. 155 (2004).

9. 213 U.S. 347 (1909).

10. This particular claim also asserted cooperation in that seizure by Costa Rican government authorities.

11. *Id.* at 356.

12. *Id.*

13. *Id.* at 357. Because the complaint alleged that the plaintiff's harm was the result of the acts of the governments of Panama and Costa Rica but done pursuant to the defendant's intervention, the plaintiff's claims also implicated the "act of state" doctrine.

14. *See, e.g.*, Wickard v. Filburn, 317 U.S. 111 (1942) (upholding authority of Congress to regulate production of wheat a farmer uses for his own needs, because those intrastate activities had an effect on interstate commerce).

15. *See, e.g.*, Summit Health, Ltd. v. Pinhas, 500 U.S. 322, 328 n.7 (1991); McLain v. Real Estate Bd. of New Orleans, Inc., 444 U.S. 232 (1980); Goldfarb v. Va. State Bar, 421 U.S. 773 (1975).

16. *See, e.g.*, United States v. Sisal Sales Corp., 274 U.S. 268 (1927) (applying Sherman Act to alleged conspiracy carried out in part in the United States but implemented through actions of Mexican officials, which affected prices of rope fiber in the United States); Thomsen v. Cayser, 243 U.S. 66 (1917) (applying Sherman Act to claims against agents of foreign shipping lines, based on agreements made in London to charge discriminatory rates on freight shipped between the United States and the foreign country); United States v. Pac. & Arctic Ry., 228 U.S. 87 (1913) (applying Sherman Act to conspiracy to set rates on shipments between the United States and Canada, which was effectuated in part by control of wharves located in the United States).

17. United States v. Aluminum Co. of Am., 148 F.2d 416 (2d Cir. 1945).

18. Timberlane Lumber Co. v. Bank of Am., 549 F.2d 597 (9th Cir. 1976).

19. Hartford Fire Ins. Co. v. Cal., 509 U.S. 764 (1993).

20. *Id.* at 443.

21. *Id.* at 444. The court relied in part for its conclusion on the Supreme Court decisions cited *supra* note 16.

22. *Id.* at 443–44.

23. Some of the activities included resort to Honduran courts and involvement by Honduran government officials. The court of appeals rejected the argument that the plaintiffs' claims were foreclosed by the "act of state" doctrine. *Timberlane*, 549 F.2d, at 605–08.

24. *Id.* at 612.

25. *Id.* at 613.

26. *Id.* at 614.

27. *See, e.g.*, Laker Airways Ltd. v. Sabena, Belgian World Airlines, 731 F.2d 909, 948–49 (D.C. Cir. 1984) (concluding that *Timberlane* factors "are not useful in resolving the controversy"); Nat'l Bank of Canada v. Interbank Card Ass'n, 666 F.2d 6, 8 (2d Cir. 1981) (rejecting the *Timberlane* test); Lionel Kestenbaum, *Antitrust's Extraterritorial Jurisdiction: A Progress Report on the Balancing of Interests Test*, 18 Stan. J.

Int'l L. 311 (1982). *But see Hartford Fire*, 509 U.S. at 817–19 (Souter, J. dissenting) (citing with approval to *Timberlane* and its multi-factor approach).

28. 59 Stat. 33 (codified at 15 U.S.C. § 1013). The McCarran-Ferguson Act provides immunity from the antitrust laws for "the business of insurance." However, that exemption is lost if the defendants' behavior constitutes a "boycott," *id.* § 1013(b). The Court concluded that the Act did not foreclose scrutiny of this conduct, since at least some of the plaintiffs' allegations complained of "boycotts."

29. *Hartford Fire*, 509 U.S. at 794–95.

30. Justice Souter was joined in this part of the opinion by Chief Justice Rehnquist and Justices White, Blackmun, and Stevens.

31. *Id.* at 795.

32. *Id.* at 795–96. In addition to several earlier cases in which the Supreme Court had distinguished *American Banana*, more recent case law had also indicated that that decision was of limited precedential value. *See* Matsushita Elec. Indus. Co. v. Zenith Radio Corp., 475 U.S. 574, 582 n.6 (1986).

33. *Id.* at 796. The Court asserted that the plaintiffs' allegations satisfied this standard. "Such is the conduct alleged here: that the London reinsurers engaged in unlawful conspiracies to affect the market for insurance in the United States and that their conduct in fact produced substantial effect." *Id. See* Carrier Corp. v. Outokumpu Oyj, 673 F.3d 430, 438–40 (6th Cir. 2012) (concluding that court has jurisdiction under Sherman Act for claims involving foreign conduct that has domestic effects; relying on *Hartford Fire* and *Alcoa*).

34. He was joined in this dissent by Justices O'Connor, Kennedy, and Thomas.

35. 509 U.S. at 814 (Scalia, J., dissenting).

36. *Id.* (emphasis in original).

37. *Id.* at 814–15 (quoting from Murray v. Schooner Charming Betsy, 2 Cranch 64 (1804)).

38. "I think it unimaginable that an assertion of legislative jurisdiction by the United States would be considered reasonable." *Id.* at 819.

39. *See supra* notes 5–7 and accompanying text.

40. *See* Timberlane Lumber Co. v. Bank of Am., 549 F.2d 597, 610 (9th Cir. 1976).

41. Turicentro, S.A. v. Am. Airlines Inc., 303 F.3d 293, 300 (3d Cir. 2002) (also describing statute as "inelegantly phrased").

42. 15 U.S.C. § 6a.

43. *See, e.g.*, Carrier Corp. v. Outokumpu Oyj, 673 F.3d 430, 438 n.3 (6th Cir. 2012) (noting that FTAIA clearly permits antitrust actions for claim challenging foreign price-fixing conspiracy on goods exported to the United States); In re Cathode Ray Tube (CRT) Antitrust Litig., 738 F. Supp. 2d 1011, 1022–23 (N.D. Cal. 2010) (upholding jurisdiction over claims for products sold or distributed in the United States, either directly or through subsidiaries or affiliated companies).

44. The second, and more convoluted, exception applies where the commerce in question has a "direct, substantial, and reasonably foreseeable effect" on domestic commerce and where that effect gives rise to a Sherman Act claim.

45. Hartford Fire Ins. Co. v. Cal., 509 U.S. 764 (1993).

46. Justice Scalia's dissent did not even take note of FTAIA or its implications for the case.

47. "It is unclear how [FTAIA] might apply to the conduct alleged here. . . . Assuming that FTAIA's standard affects this litigation, . . . the conduct alleged plainly meets its requirements." 509 U.S. at 796 n.23. Why? How? The Court was silent.

48. *Id. Compare* U.S. v. LSL Biotechs., 379 F.3d 672, 679 (9th Cir. 2004) (concluding that FTAIA's requirement of "direct" effect in the United States cut back on the *Alcoa* test for reach of Sherman Act), *with id.*, 379 F.3d at 684 ("I believe that the new statute merely codifies existing antitrust law in the use of the word 'direct.'") (Aldisert, J., dissenting); Kruman v. Christie's Int'l, PLC, 284 F.3d 384, 389–90, 399–401 (2d Cir. 2002) (FTAIA "does not alter" preexisting standards for extraterritorial reach of antitrust laws), *cert. dismissed*, 539 U.S. 978 (2003).

49. "When it enacted the FTAIA, . . . Congress expressed no view on the question whether a court with Sherman Act jurisdiction should ever decline to exercise such jurisdiction on grounds of international comity. . . . We need not decide that question here, however, [because] international comity would not counsel against exercising jurisdiction in the circumstances alleged here." *Id.* at 798.

50. *Empagran*, 542 U.S. at 159.

51. *Id.*

52. "[T]he Sherman Act does not prevent [American exporters] from entering into business arrangements (say, joint selling arrangements), however anticompetitive, as long as those arrangements adversely affect only foreign markets." *Id.* at 161. This conclusion is consistent with the primary purpose given for the enactment of FTAIA—the removal of "barrier[s] to join export activities."

53. *Id.* (emphasis in original). The "other commercial activities" would encompass transactions solely within, between, or among foreign countries.

54. The court of appeals had concluded that these purchases, as part of a global price-fixing conspiracy, were within the "exception" to the FTAIA. 315 F.3d 338 (D.C. Cir. 2003).

55. 542 U.S. at 160.

56. "[W]e base our decision upon the following: The price-fixing conduct significantly and adversely affects both customers outside the United States and customers within the United States, but the adverse foreign effect is independent of any adverse domestic effect." *Id.* at 164.

57. "[W]e have found no significant indication that at the time Congress wrote this statute courts would have thought the Sherman Act applicable in these circumstances." *Id.* at 169.

58. *Id.* at 164. This approach echoes the canon of construction invoked by Justice Scalia in dissent in *Hartford Fire.*

59. The strength of those interests and the American sensitivity to those interests were demonstrated in part by appearances as amici curiae by the Federal Republic of Germany and the government of Canada and by the U.S. Department of Justice and Federal Trade Commission, all arguing for inapplicability of the American antitrust laws.

60. *Id.* at 165 (finding that justification for "interference with a foreign nation's ability independently to regulate its own commercial affairs" was "insubstantial").

61. Empagran S.A. v. Hoffmann-LaRoche, Ltd., 417 F.3d 1267 (D.C. Cir. 2005).

62. *Id.* at 1270.

63. *Id.*

64. 542 U.S. at 164–69.

65. 417 F.3d at 1271.

66. *See, e.g.*, In re Dynamic Random Access Memory (DRAM) Antitrust Litig., 546 F.3d 981, 985–90 (9th Cir. 2008); In re Monosodium Glutamate Antitrust Litig., 477 F.3d 535, 537–40 (8th Cir. 2007); Emerson Elec. Co. v. Le Carbone Lorraine, S.A., 500 F. Supp. 2d 437, 442–47 (D.N.J. 2007).

67. "Our courts have long held that application of our antitrust laws to foreign anticompetitive conduct is nonetheless reasonable and hence consistent with principles of prescriptive comity, insofar as they reflect a legislative effort to redress *domestic* antitrust injury that foreign anticompetitive conduct has caused." *Empagran*, 509 U.S. at 165 (emphasis in original).

68. Minn-Chem, Inc. v. Agrium Inc., 657 F.3d 650 (7th Cir. 2011), *set aside after rehearing en banc*, 683 F.3d.845 (7th Cir. 2012).

69. *See* Chapter 5.

70. 657 F.3d at 661.

71. Recall that this "exception" to FTAIA—more accurately, a provision dictating that the FTAIA never reaches "import commerce"—permits the assertion of an antitrust claim.

72. *Id.* (emphasis in original).

73. *Id.*

74. As the court noted, "From 2003 to 2008, potash prices in the United States increased by a staggering amount—roughly 600%." *Id.* at 654.

75. Fed. R. Civ. P. 8(a)(2).

76. As the court explained, "The applicability of U.S. law to transactions in which a good or service is being sent directly into the United States, with no intermediate stops, is both fully predictable to foreign entities and necessary for the protection of U.S. consumers." 683 F.3d at 854.

77. Regrettably, other cases have also insisted on proof that the defendants' conduct "targeted" the United States or U.S. imports. *See, e.g.*, McLafferty v. Deutsche Lufthansa A.G., 2009 WL 3365881 (E.D. Pa. Oct. 16, 2009) (discussed *infra* notes 83–84 and accompanying text). However, as the Seventh Circuit correctly concluded, the proper reading of FTAIA only requires that the defendants' conduct have the requisite "effect" on either U.S. domestic commerce or U.S. import commerce—irrespective of the defendants' intent. Thus, the test is "objective," looking at the actual effect, rather than adding some "subjective" requirement.

78. *Id.* at 683 F.3d at 855 (emphasis in original).

79. *Id.* at 856.

80. United States v. LSL Biotechnologies, 379 F.3d 672, 680 (9th Cir. 2004).

81. "The word 'direct' addresses the classic concern about remoteness. . . . [T]he FTAIA exclude[s] from the Sherman Act foreign activities that are too remote from the ultimate effects on U.S. domestic or import commerce." *Id.* at 683 F.3d at 857.

82. *Id.* at 858. Here, the court concluded that "[t]he inference from [the plaintiffs'] allegations is not just plausible but compelling, that the cartel meant to and did in fact keep prices artificially high in the United States." *Id.* at 858–59.

83. McLafferty v. Deutsche Lufthansa A.G., 2009 WL 3365881 (E.D. Pa. Oct. 16, 2009).

84. *Id.* at *4.

85. 2011 WL 1753738 (N.D. Cal. May 9, 2011).

86. The class of plaintiffs was all passengers purchasing overpriced tickets on these flights. While these passengers were not all Americans, undoubtedly a large fraction were.

87. On this basis, the court distinguished In re Air Cargo Shipping Serv. Antitrust Litig., 2008 WL 5958061 (E.D.N.Y. Sept. 26, 2008).

88. Today, of course, that carriage would probably be subject to various limitations, surcharges, penalties and so forth.

89. FTAIA, 15 U.S.C. § 6a.

90. 2011 WL 1753738, at *5–8.

91. *Id.*

92. *See also* Animal Science Prods., Inc. v. China Nat'l Metals & Minerals Imp. & Exp. Corp., 702 F. Supp. 2d 320, 369 (D.N.J. 2010) (holding that "import" provision in FTAIA applied only if the defendants were the physical importers of the goods).

93. The case law under the FTAIA also reflects a significantly reduced solicitude under the American antitrust laws for injury to *non*-Americans, even if that harm is the result of anticompetitive behavior taking place in the United States. A leading example is Turicentro, S.A. v. American Airlines, 303 F.3d 293 (3d Cir. 2002). The plaintiffs were travel agents located in Central America. They alleged that the defendants—American air carriers and a U.S. airline trade association—had conspired to reduce the commissions paid to them for air travel both in the United States and between the United States and Latin America. The court of appeals concluded that these claims were barred by the FTAIA because they did not have the requisite "effect" on U.S. commerce. "United States antitrust laws only apply when a price-fixing conspiracy affects the domestic economy." *Id.* at 305.

Although some might argue that this result is "unfortunate," it presents the obverse situation from the *McLafferty* and *Transpacific Air Transp.* decisions. As a matter of policy, *Empagran* can be read for the sound proposition that the American antitrust laws are not designed to protect the world from all types of anticompetitive behavior. Thus, these non-American plaintiffs were outside the pale of protection, and it was irrelevant that some of their customers were Americans.

In the two cases discussed in the text, however, the plaintiffs were American. *Empagran* should not be read to extend the FTAIA as a shield for defendants, whether they be American or foreign, from anticompetitive behavior that harms American consumers.

94. *See, e.g.*, Animal Science Prods., Inc. v. China Minmetals Corp., 654 F.3d 462 (3d Cir. 2011) (holding that FTAIA adopts an objective standard regarding defendant's intent, so that plaintiff need only show that the adverse effects on domestic commerce were foreseeable to an "objectively reasonable person"), *cert. denied*, 132 S. Ct. 1744 (2012); Precision Assocs., Inc. v. Panalpina World Transp. (Holding) Ltd., 2011 WL 7053807, at *36–37 (E.D.N.Y. Jan 4, 2011) (holding that conspiracy by freight-forwarders, elevating prices for shipment of goods exported from foreign locations into the United States, had a direct effect on the prices of goods themselves and thus were within exception to FTAIA); In re Static Random Access Memory (SRAM) Antitrust Litig., 2010 WL 5477313 (N.D. Cal. Dec. 31, 2010) (holding that direct purchasers of products that were billed to parties in the United States could complain of a price-fixing conspiracy, even if those products were shipped to purchasers outside the United States).

Chapter 9

I would like to give special thanks to Tae-Yong Kim, Young-Joo Sim, and Paul Youm for their kind assistance.

1. ICN, Advocacy and Competition Policy Report, 25 (2002), *available at* http://www.internationalcompetitionnetwork.org/uploads/library/doc358.pdf.

2. *Id.*

3. *See, e.g.*, Hak-KuK Joh, Korea's Experience in Competition Advocacy and Ways to Improve the Effectiveness of the Advocacy, ICN Advocacy Working Group (April 2004), *available at* http://www.internationalcompetitionnetwork.org/uploads/library/doc534.pdf.

4. However, because enactments or amendments that occur through unofficial administrative legislation only refer to procedures such as notifications that have been delegated under the law, soft laws that have no binding force, such as guidelines and policy statements, are not applicable.

5. KFTC, Guidelines for Review of the Competition Restricting Factors under Article 63 of MRFTA enacted on March 17, 2010.

6. This is provided with reference to the competition checklist of the negative effects presented in OECD, The Competition Assessment Toolkit, *available at* http://www.oecd.org/daf/competition/42228385.pdf.

7. *See* Joh, *supra* note 3.

8. KFTC, 30-Year History of Korean Fair Trade Commission 41 (2011).

9. Sung-Guk Cho, *Structure and Enforcement Procedures of Competition Law Authority, in* 30 Years' History of Korean Competition Law, 552-558 (Oh-Seung Kwon ed., 2011). The structure of the KFTC changed from a nonindependent deliberation/resolution body (1st period: 1981–1989), a nonindependent administrative body (2nd period: 1990–1994), and as an independent central administrative authority (3rd period: since 1995).

10. The State Council refers to the highest deliberative body chaired by the president and attended by 16 cabinet-level members who are charged with reviewing major policy decisions.

11. MRFTA, art. 38(2).

12. Hwang Lee, *Globalization and Development of Korean Competition Law, in* Korea Competition Policy 415 (Chang-Ho Yoon et al. eds., 2011).

13. James C. Cooper & William E. Kovacic, *U.S. Convergence with International Competition Norms: Antitrust Law and Public Restraints on Competition*, 90 B.U.L. Rev. 1555 (2010).

14. MRFTA, art. 3.

15. FAAR, art. 2, ¶ 1, § 5.

16. Office of the Prime Minister, Format Suggestions of Regulation Impact Analysis 12 (Dec. 2008).

17. *See supra* note 14.

18. In-Suk Jung, Development of Competition Impact Assessment Methodology and Model with Examples of Developed Nations, Korean Industry Structure Institute, KFTC Committee Service Report 8 (July 2009).

19. The Competition Assessment Toolkit was first published in 2007 and then updated in 2010. The main difference between Versions 1.0 and 2.0 is that Version 2.0 provides additional examples of the benefits of competition and an introduction to the Competition Checklist.

20. *Available at* http://www.oecd.org/general/olis.htm.

21. *See supra* note 8, at 62.

22. Nam-Ki Lee, Advocacy Role of the Korea Fair Trade Commission in Regulatory Reform, OECD Global Forum on Competition 5 (2001).

23. *Id.* at 2 (noting that Recommendation of the Council Concerning Effective Action Against Hard Core Cartels adopted by OECD in April 1998 was the basis of the project).

24. *Id.* at 2.

25. KFTC, 30-Year History, *supra* note 8, at 41.

26. KFTC, 2009 Annual Report (English version) 21–22 (2009), *available at* http://eng.ftc.go.kr/bbs.do?command=getList&type_cd=53&pageId=0301.

27. KFTC, 2011 Annual Report (English version) 174–75 (2011), *available at* http://eng.ftc.go.kr/bbs.do?command=getList&type_cd=53&pageId=0301.

28. Lee, *supra* note 12, at 397.

29. External effects such as natural monopolies, pollution, and public goods are typical examples of the market failures that allow the government to intervene. Robert Baldwin & Martin Cave, Understanding Regulation: Theory, Strategy, and Practice 9–16 (1999).

30. Notably, from April 1997 to March 1998, the Economic Regulation Reform Board of the KFTC has improved 169 policies that existed in areas including IT, auditing industry and factory locations, logistics, transportation, distribution, and construction.

31. Administrative guidance is defined as an administrative action by an administrative agency through which it provides recommendation, advice, or guidance for its subjects (Administrative Procedures Act, art.2, ¶ 3).

32. Administrative Procedures Act, art. 2, ¶ 3.

33. KTFC, KFTC's General Stance on Concerted Acts that Had Complied with Administrative Guidance (October 2002); KFTC, Guidelines for Review of Concerted Acts Involving Administrative Guidance, established on Dec. 27, 2006, amended on Aug. 12, 2009.

34. Korean Supreme Court Decision No. 96*Nu*150, 1997. 5. 16.

35. Ho-Young Lee, Monopoly Regulation and Fair Trade Act 28–29 (3rd ed. 2011).

36. Telecommunications Business Act, art. 39, ¶ 2.

37. Regulation of interconnection in the telecommunications industry does not contradict competition law enforcement but should rather be seen as a complementary involvement that fills the gap that occurs when competition is first introduced and the environment to compete is being fostered. Ho-Young Lee, *Relationship between Industry Regulation and Competition Law*, 20 Mgmt L. 559 (2009).

38. Korean Supreme Court Decision No. 2007*Du*19584, 2008. 12. 24.

39. Broadcasting Act, art. 77.

40. Korean Supreme Court Decision No. 2009*Du*1983, 2010. 5. 27.

41. Korean Supreme Court Decision No. 2002*Du*12052, 2005. 1. 28.

42. Korean Supreme Court Decision No. 2007*Du*26117, 2009. 7. 9.

43. KFTC press release: KFTC and FSS Jointly Introduce a Plan for Efficiently Regulating Financial Institutions (Nov. 2007). KFTC press release: KFTC and KCC Hold Conference for Preventing Duplicative Regulations of Unfair Practices (Feb. 2009).

44. Constitution of the Republic of Korea, art. 52.

45. The KFTC applied provisions regulating the abuse of market dominance in eight cases at the Korean Supreme Court since 2007. Among eight cases, the KFTC won only one case, lost six cases, and partially won one case.

46. By introducing the Ministry of Science, ICT and Future Planning in March 2013, a substantial part of the ex ante regulatory role of the former KCC was transferred to the new ministry even though the establishment of the new ministry intended to help the KCC focus on the regulatory role.

47. Seonghoon Jeon, *Using Competition Policy to Promote Shared Growth in Korea*, Competition Policy International (2012), *available at* http://www.competitionpolicyinternational.com.

Chapter 10

1. Loretta Chao, *China Telecom, China Unicom Face Monopoly Probe*, Wall St. J., Nov. 9, 2011, *available at* http://online.wsj.com/article/SB10001424052970204358004577027283900972206.html.

2. Eleanor M. Fox, *An Anti-Monopoly Law for China—Scaling the Walls of Government Restraints*, 75 Antitrust L.J. 178 (2008).

3. Shiying Xu, *Regulating Abuse of Administrative Monopoly Is an Essential Choice for Anti-Monopoly Enforcement in China, in* Hot Spots of Chinese Antimonopoly Legislation, 112 (Xiaoye Wang ed., 2007); Yong Huang, *Pursuing the Second Best, The History, Momentum and Remaining Issues of China's Anti-Monopoly Law*, 75 Antitrust L.J. 117, 130–31 (2008).

4. Bruce M. Owen et al., *Antitrust in China: The Problem of Incentive Compatibility*, 1 J. Competition L. & Econ. 123–48 (2005).

5. Richard A. Maschmeyer & Yang Ji-Liang, *Results of the Contract Responsibility System in the People's Republic of China: An Analysis of Two Enterprises*, 35 Int'l Bus. Rev. 253, 254 (1993).

6. Peter Nolan & Wang Xiaoqiang, *Beyond Privatization: Institutional Innovation and Growth in China's Large State-Owned Enterprises*, 27 World Dev. 186 (1999).

7. *Id.* at 183.

8. World Bank, China 2030: Structural Reforms for a Modern, Harmonious, Creative High-Income Society 110 (2012).

9. *Id.*

10. Yong Huang et al., *China's Anti-Monopoly Law: Competition and the Chinese Petroleum Industry*, 31 Energy L.J. 361 (2010).

11. Owen et al., *supra* note 4, at 9.

12. *Id.*

13. World Bank, *supra* note 8, at 113.

14. *Id.*

15. In 2011, only 24 of 124 SOEs under SASAC supervision had a board of directors.

16. World Bank, *supra* note 8, at 118.

17. Huang Yong, *Coordination of International Competition Policies: An Anatomy Based on Chinese Reality, in* Cooperation, Comity and Competition Policy 246 (Andrew T. Guzman ed., 2011).

18. Huang et al., Chinese Petroleum Industry, *supra* note 10, at 347.

19. H. Stephen Harris, Jr., et al., Anti-Monopoly Law and Practice in China 196 (2011).

20. *Id.* at 194–95.

21. Fox, *supra* note 2.

22. *Id.*

23. Salil K. Mehra & Meng Yanbei, *Against Antitrust Functionalism: Reconsidering China's Antimonopoly Law*, 49 Va. J. Int'l L. 379, 405 (2009).

24. Huang at al., Chinese Petroleum Industry, *supra* note 10, at 349.

25. *Id.* at 347–48.

26. Chao, *supra* note 1.

27. *Id.*

28. *Id.*

29. David E. M. Sappington & J. Gregory Sidak, *Competition Law for State-Owned Enterprises*, 71 Antitrust L.J. 479, 479–80 (2004); David E. M. Sappington & J. Gregory Sidak, *Incentives for Anticompetitive Behavior by Public Enterprises*, 22 Rev. Indus. Org. 183 (2003).

30. Sappington & Sidak, *Competition Law*, *supra* note 29, at 480.

31. Sappington & Sidak, *Incentives for Anticompetitive Behavior*, *supra* note 29, at 192.

32. R. Richard Geddes, *Case Studies of Anticompetitive SOE Behavior, in* Competing with the Government: Anticompetitive Behavior and Public Enterprises, 32 (R. Richard Geddes ed., 2004).

33. Sappington & Sidak, *Competition Law*, *supra* note 29, at 510–11.

34. Colin Lawson, *The Theory of State-Owned Enterprises in Market Economies*," 8 J. Econ. Surv. 287 (1994).

35. Sappington & Sidak, *Incentives for Anticompetitive Behavior*, *supra* note 29, at 195.

36. Xueguo Wen, *Market Dominance by China's Public Utility Enterprises*, 75 Antitrust L.J. 151, 165 (2008).

37. *Id.*

38. Bing Song, *Competition Policy in a Transitional Economy: The Case of China*, 31 Stan. J. Int'l L. 387, 402–03 (1995).

39. Wen, *supra* note 36, at 157–58.

40. *Id.* at 159–60.

41. *Id.* at 164.

42. Deborah Healey, *Anti-Monopoly Law and Mergers in China: An Early Report Card on Procedural and Substantive Issues*, 3 Tsinghua L. Rev. 29, 30 (2010).

43. Jiawei Zhang, *China Eastern Merger Plan May Be Released Next Week*, China Daily, July 10, 2009, *available at* http://www.chinadaily.com.cn/business/2009-07/10/content_8408248.htm.

44. Centre for Aviation, *China Eastern-Shanghai Airlines "Restructuring" (Merger) Enters Final Phase*, CAPA Aviation Analysis (Oct. 22, 2009), *available at* http://centreforaviation.com/analysis/china-eastern-shanghai-airlines-restructuring-merger-enters-final-phase-13415.

45. Rang-rang Bai, *Dominance of State-Owned Enterprises and Price Collusion Under Abuse of Administrative Monopoly*, 12 China Indus. Econ. 46 (2007).

46. Caijing Magazine, *Telecom Industry in China*, Caijing.com.cn (Jan. 23, 2009), *available at* http://english.caijing.com.cn/2009-01-23/110053429.html.

47. *Id.*

48. Owen et al., *supra* note 4, at 11.

49. Tim Lindsey, *The Proposed Antitrust Law and the Problem of Administrative Monopolies in China*, 12 Trade Prac. L.J. 109 (2004).

50. Yong Huang, The Role of State in Shaping China's Competition Policy—An Analysis in Chinese Context (on file with author), 23.

51. *Id.*

52. Harris et al., *supra* note 19, at 179–80.

53. *Id.*

54. *City Slaps License Ban on Smaller Vehicles*, South China Morning Post, Aug. 20, 2001.

55. *Players Ranks to Thin as Car Sector Surges*, South China Morning Post, Sept. 8, 2001.

56. Wang Zheng, *Beware Picket Fences Are Re-erected—In Some Places, Tangible Regional Protectionism Has Decreased, but Intangible Regional Protectionism Has Increased*, People's Daily, Apr. 15, 2002.

57. Fox, *supra* note 2, at 191; Song, *supra* note 38, at 410.

Chapter 11

1. The United States, Canada, and Australia do not impose such controls on states or provinces. The NAFTA has yet to agree on a subsidy control regime. The WTO rules on subsidies may constrain some forms of subsidization for goods but not services, and their application is far less reaching than the European state aid regime as set down in Articles 107 to 108 TFEU. *See further* A. Sykes, The Questionable Case for Subsidies Regulation: A Comparative Perspective, Stanford University School of Law—Law and Economics (Research Paper Series No. 380, 2009).

2. The enforcement of the state aid regime cannot be discussed within the confines of this short chapter. For this aspect, *see* L. Hancher et al., EU State Aids, pt. v (2012). *See also* E. Szyszczak, Research Handbook on European State Aid Law, ch. 26 (2011).

3. The procedural rules governing notification and clearance are not further discussed here. For a full analysis, *see* Hancher et al., *supra* note 2, at pt. v, ch. 25.

4. *See* Commission Communication "EU State Aid Modernisation (SAM)," COM/2012/0209 final, *available at* http://eur-lex.europa.eu/LexUriServ/LexUriServ.do?uri=COM:2012:0209:FIN:EN:PDF.

5. Article 107(1) states, "Save as otherwise provided in this Treaty, any aid granted by a member state or through state resources in any form whatsoever which distorts or threatens to distort competition by favouring certain undertakings or the production of certain goods shall, in so far as it affects trade between member states, be incompatible with the common market." *See* http://eur-lex.europa.eu/LexUriServ/LexUriServ.do?uri=OJ:C:2010:083:0047:0200:en:PDF.

6. [2000] ECR I-3271; Case C-487/06 P British Aggregates v. Commission [2008] ECR I-10515, ¶ 111. As the AG observed in his Opinion in Case C-290/07 P Scott, at ¶¶ 101–03, and confirmed by the Court at ¶ 66 of its subsequent ruling.

7. For environmental protection, *see* Article 192 TFEU.

8. *See* Joined Cases C-71/09 P, C-73/09 P, and C-76/09, Comitato "Venezia vuole vivere" v. Commission [2011] ECR I-4727¶ 94.

9. Case C-387/92 Banco Exterior de España [1994] ECR I-877, ¶¶ 13–14. *See also* Case T-308/00, Salzgitter v. Commission [2004] ECR II-1933, ¶ 84; and Case 30/59, Steenkolemmijnen v. High Authority [1961] ECR 1, 19.

10. *Ex multis*, Cases 67, 68, 70/85, Van der Kooy v. Commission [1988] ECR 219, ¶¶ 27 *et seq.*

11. Case C-280/00, Altmark Trans GmbH and Regierungspräsidium Magdeburg v. Nahverkehrsgesellschaft Altmark GmbH [2003] ECR I-7747.

12. *See* Hancher et al., *supra* note 2, at ch. 3.

13. The market economy investor principle also applies to investments made by public undertakings inasmuch as the resources of these entities can be deemed to be state resources. For example, in its decision concerning the legality of tariff rebates made by EdF to firms in the paper industry, the Commission considered that EdF had acted in accordance with the MEIP test. The investigation concerned rebates granted between 1990 and 1996—that is, before the adoption of EC Council Directive 96/92 on the internal electricity market, at a time when EdF disposed of overcapacity in nuclear energy. The French authorities demonstrated that EdF covered its variable costs and at least 35 percent, and on average 57 percent, of its fixed costs. In a situation of overcapacity and in the absence of competition, the Commission considered that a private operator would rather sell an additional unit of electricity without covering the total cost for that unit rather than not sell it at all. Hence, EdF's behavior was justified on commercial grounds, and the rebates did not constitute state aid. It is of interest to note that the Commission emphasized that the decision should be seen in the context of the prevailing circumstances on the French market in the past and should not be seen as preventing the Commission from examining the creation of the said overcapacity and its implications in the context of the ongoing liberalization of the electricity market. *See* IP/00/370, Apr. 11, 2000.

14. The bounds of the MEIP test remain perhaps by their very nature vague and uncertain. The mere fact that the state has resources at its disposal that no other private actor can deploy has always

been an important question mark over the reliability of the test. This is not only confirmed in the recent EdF case, but it is also borne out by several of the appeals lodged against Commission decisions relating to recent bank restructuring. *See* Case T-457/09 Westfalisch-Lippischer Sparkassen v. Commission [2010] OJ C11/35; T-33/10 ING v. Commission [2010] OJ C 80/40; Case T-319/11 ABN-Amro Group [2011] OJ C252/35. *See* M. Parish, On the Private Investor Principle, 28 E.L. Rev. 70–89 (2003). *See also* the Opinion of AG Mengozzi in Case C-399/10P Bouygues SA v. Commission, June 28, 2012.

15. [1993] ECR I-887, ¶ 24.

16. *See* L. Hancher, Towards a New Definition of a State Aid under European Law: Is There a New Concept of State Aid Emerging?, 3 EStAL 365, 368 (2003).

17. Case T-196/04, Ryanair Limited v. Commission [2008] ECR II-3643.

18. Commission Decision of December 16, 2003 on the state aid granted by France to EDF and the electricity and gas industries, OJ 2005 L 49/9. In principle, for a measure to fall within the scope of Article 107(1), the measure in question must confer a benefit or advantage, and all of the following cumulative conditions must be met: (1) the aid has been imposed by or can be imputed to a public authority; (2) the measure results in a transfer of resources from the state or the state receiving less resources; (3) the aid distorts competition by favoring certain undertakings or the production of certain goods (selectivity test); and (4) the products or services in question are traded within the EU. *See* H. Lesguillons, *The State as Shareholder and the Private Investor Principle*, 4 Int'l Bus. L.J. 363 (2003).

19. Case T-156/04, EDF v. Commission [2009] ECR II-4503.

20. *See* E. Szyszczak, *The Survival of the Market Economic Investor Principle in Liberalised Markets*, 1 EStAL 35, 36 (2011).

21. Case T-156/04, EDF v. Commission [2009] ECR II-4503, ¶ 283. *See* A. Bartosch, Case Note on EdF v. Commission, 3 EStAL 679, 681 (2010).

22. Case C-124/10 P, Commission v. EDF and others [2012] not yet reported, ¶ 108.

23. B. Slocock, 2002 Competition Pol'y News l. 23, 24 (2002).

24. Case C-124/10 P, Commission v. EDF and others, not yet reported, ¶¶ 82 *et seq.*

25. *See, e.g.*, Case C-482/99, France v. Commission [2002] ECR I-4397, ¶¶ 71–72.

26. The EU Commission stated, "The effects of temporary state aid rules adopted in the context of the financial and economic crisis," SEC (2011) 1126 final, Oct. 2011. This chapter does not deal with the Commission decisions related to the financial crisis due to reasons of space. For a full discussion, *see* Hancher et al., *supra* note 2, at ch. 19. In addition, these Commission decisions represent an *hapax legomenon* in state aid law, since it was the first and only time that the Commission used as a legal basis Article 107(3)(b)—that is, "aid . . . to remedy a serious disturbance in the economy of a member state." Thus, due to their special character where bank restructuring has been chosen for reasons of financial stability rather than for a return on investment, these decisions may not be representative of state aid rules as a whole, although the General Court appears to accept that the application of the private investor test may still be feasible in certain situations. *See* Case T-29/10 and T-33/10 Netherlands and ING Group v. Commission, Mar. 2, 2010, now under appeal (Case C-224/12 P).

27. *See also* W. Bishop, From Trade to Tutelage: State Aid and Public Choice in the European Union, presentation to the Conference of ACE, Dec. 2, 2005.

28. Buendia Sierra, unpublished speech at the Fourth Expert Forum on State Aid, Brussels, May 2006. *See also* Sykes, *supra* note 1. *See also* the Commission Consultation Document entitled Less and Better Targeted State Aid, a Roadmap for State Aid Reform 2005–2009, also known as the State Aid Action Plan (SAAP), where the Commission also observed, "State aid control comes from the need to maintain a level playing field for all undertakings active in the Single European Market, no matter in which member state they are established. There is a particular need to be concerned with those state aid measures, which provide unwarranted selective advantages to some firms, preventing or delaying the market forces from regarding the most competitive firms, thereby decreasing overall European competitiveness. It may also lead to a buildup of market power in the hands of some firms—for instance, when companies that do not receive state aid (e.g., nondomestic firms) have to cut down on their market presence or where state aid is used to erect entry barriers. As a result of such distortions of competition, customers may be faced with higher prices, lower-quality goods and less innovation" (at ¶ 7).

29. Council Regulation (EC) No. 994/98 of May 7, 1998, on the application of Articles 92 and 93 (now 87 and 88, respectively) of the treaty establishing the European Community to certain categories of horizontal state aid (OJ 1998 L 142/1).

30. A key goal of the SAAP was to introduce more predictability into state aid control, but of course the SAAP does not bind either the EU or the national courts. Nor did the SAAP purport to deal with the very definition of a "state aid" but only with issues of compatibility. The number of cases appealed from the General Court to the European Court of Justice confirms the continuing search for a stable definition of the very concept of aid and its constituent elements. This is particularly, but not exclusively, evident in the area of taxation, as the British Aggregates and Dutch Nox cases illustrate. *See* C-487/06 P [2008] ECR. I-10515; and Case C-279/08 P, Netherlands v. Commission, not yet reported.

31. Commission Regulation (EC) No. 800/2008 of Aug. 6, 2008 declaring certain categories of aid compatible with the common market in application of Articles 87 and 88 of the treaty (General Block Exemption Regulation) (OJ 2008 L 214/3)

32. In general, existing guidelines are reviewed and updated at regular intervals following an extensive public consultation process. However, some sets of guidelines are merely prolonged pending a further comprehensive review—a useful tactic to avoid reopening legal and political controversy. Examples include the cinema guidelines ([2001] OJ C43); the export credit insurance ([1997] OJ C281/4.); and perhaps most importantly, the 2004 Rescue and Restructuring Guidelines, which formally expired in December 2011 ([2004] OJ C244/2).

33. For an economic assessment of the new approach, *see* L. Coppi, *The Role of Economics in State Aid Analysis and the Balancing Test, in* Research Handbook on State Aids 64–89 (E. Szyszczak ed., 2011).

34. COM (2011) 356 final, June 22, 2011.

35. COM (2010) 2020.

36. For a detailed explanation, *see* Hancher et al., *supra* note 2, at ch. 21.

37. Press release IP/11/493 of Apr. 19, 2011. *Available at* http://europa.eu/rapid/pressReleasesAction.do?reference=IP/11/493&format=HTML&aged=1&language=EN&guiLanguage=en.

38. Press release IP/10/581.

39. Speech delivered at the 10th Expert Forum on State Aid, Brussels, June 7, 2012, and *available at* http://europa.eu/rapid/pressReleasesAction.do?reference=SPEECH/12/424.

40. *Id.*

41. COM (2012) 209 final, *available at* http://eur-lex.europa.eu/LexUriServ/LexUriServ.do?uri=COM:2012:0209:FIN:en:pdf.

42. *See* ¶ 14. Monitoring progress and ensuring the active involvement of EU countries are key elements of the Europe 2020 strategy. This is done through the European Semester, an annual cycle of macroeconomic, budgetary, and structural policy coordination.

43. For an evaluation of the SAAP on this point, *see* T. Kleiner, *Modernization of State Aid Policy, in* Szyszczak, *supra* note 33, at 1.

44. For a full analysis of the regulations applying to the sector, *see* A. de Streel, *The Current and Future European Regulation of Electronic Communications: A Critical Assessment* 32 Telecomm. Pol'y 722 (2008).

45. *See further* N. Tosics & N. Gaal, *Public Procurement and State Aid Control—The Issue of Economic Advantage*, 13 Competition Pol'y Newsl., 15 (2007). *See also* the 2004 Pyrenees Atlantiques case (N 381/2004—France, Nov. 18, 2004), concerning a broadband infrastructure to be developed and managed by a private entity through a concession contract awarded through a tender. The infrastructure would remain in public ownership. The concessionaire was subject to detailed auditing rules, and, furthermore, it was allowed a fixed rate of return on its investment (approximately 11 percent), and if the revenues exceeded a certain amount, the concessionaire was required to repay the surplus to the authorities. Furthermore, although the operator was selected in a final round on the basis of a negotiated procedure, where criteria other than price were used, the Commission concluded that this type of project could not be awarded on the basis of simple price criteria.

46. [2009] OJ C235/7.

47. *See also* Commission Recommendation of Sept. 20, 2010, on regulated access to Next Generation Access Networks (NGA)—C(2010) 6223, OJ 2010 L 251/35.

48. These terms (white/gray/black) are used to represent different types of market failures in accordance with the State Aid Action Plan (State Aid Action Plan: Less and Better-Targeted State Aid: a Roadmap for State Aid Reform 2005–2009. *Available at* http://eur-lex.europa.eu/LexUriServ/LexUriServ.do?uri=COM:2005:0107:FIN:EN:PDF.

49. *See* ¶¶ 73, 75, and 79 of the guidelines of 2009. In its decision to approve a fiber deployment project in the French department Hauts-de-Seine, the Commission applied the provisions of the

guidelines regarding public service compensation for NGA projects for the first time. This decision, which involves some €55 million of public funding to one of France's most densely populated and wealthiest regions, is currently subject to challenge before the General Court in Case T-79/10. Other important cases in which the Commission applied the 2009 guidelines include an aid scheme to encourage the deployment of NGA networks in very sparsely populated areas in Finland that are not covered by private projects (Case N388/2009) and a German scheme where municipalities will invest in and own specific ducts to encourage broadband deployment in underserved areas. If such dedicated ducts are made available to broadband network operators without appropriate payment, this constitutes state aid. The aid was found compatible, as it concerned multifiber ducts that will allow several broadband operators to deploy their networks, thereby encouraging infrastructure-based competition (N368/2009). In another German case, where the Commission further clarified that where a municipal authority is undertaking general civil works (such as digging up public roads), which can be useful also for the deployment of other utility networks (water, electricity, etc.), and allows the placement of ducts and passive infrastructure by broadband network operators at their own expense, this does not constitute state aid (Case N383/2009; *see* IP/10/141).

50. *Available at* http://ec.europa.eu/competition/consultations/2012_broadband_guidelines/index_en.html.

51. Following the General Court's ruling in Cases T-443/08 and T-445/08, Leipzig Halle, March 2011, nyr, the Commission has concluded that aid for infrastructure projects will often meet the "selectivity" test where certain parties, including operators, benefit from public support measures.

52. *See* in this respect the French decision cited *supra* note 49.

53. Commission Recommendation of Sept. 20, 2010, on regulated access to Next Generation Access Networks (NGA), *supra* note 47.

54. *See* the response of the Board of European Regulators for Electronic Communications (BEREC) to the Commission questionnaire, Oct. 2011, 18–19, *available at* http://berec.europa.eu/doc/berec/bor_11_42.pdf.

55. *See* M. Monti, Report on the Future of the Single Market, May 9, 2010, 73.

56. "The Union recognises and respects access to services of general economic interest as provided for in national laws and practices, in accordance with the Treaty establishing the European Community, in order to promote the social and territorial cohesion of the Union."

57. Case C-280/00, Altmark Trans GmbH and Regierungspräsidium Magdeburg v. Nahverkehrsgesellschaft Altmark GmbH [2003] ECR I-7747.

58. *See* C-280/00, Altmark Trans GmbH and Regierungspräsidium Magdeburg v. Nahverkehrsgesellschaft Altmark GmbH [2003] ECR I-7747, ¶¶ 89–93.

59. The first three texts of the package were adopted on December 20, 2011, while the new *de minimis* regulation was subject to a different procedure and, consequently, adopted on April 25, 2012.

60. The package, which replaced an earlier package from 2005, consists of four texts: (1) communication on the application of state aid rules to compensation granted for the provision of services of economic general interest (the "Communication"), which clarifies, in accordance with the Altmark jurisprudence, the conditions under which public service compensation is to be regarded as state aid (OJ 2012 C 8/4); (2) decision 2012/21/EU on the application of Article 106(2) TFEU to state aid in the form of public service compensation granted to certain undertakings entrusted with the operation of services of general economic interest (the "Decision"), which lays down the conditions under which state aid in the form of compensation for a SGEI is not subject to the prior notification requirement of Article 108(3) TFEU, as it can be deemed compatible with Article 106(2) TFEU (OJ 2012 L 7/3). This decision replaces decision 2005/842/EC of November 28, 2005; (3) communication containing a revised EU Framework for state aid in the form of public service compensation (the "Framework"), which specifies how the Commission will analyze cases that have to be notified to the Commission (OJ 2012 C 8/15); and (4) Regulation 360/2012 on the application of Article 107 and 108 TFEU to the *de minimis* aid granted to undertakings providing series of general economic interest (the "Regulation"), which set out the conditions under which small amounts of public service compensation are not caught by Article 107(1) TFEU—and do not fall under the notification procedure provided for in Article 108(3)—as such compensation is not deemed to affect trade between member states and/or no to distort competition (OJ 2012 L 114/8).

61. Communication from the Commission to the European Parliament, the Council, the European Economic and Social Committee, and the Committee of the Regions: a Quality Framework for

Services of General Interest in Europe, COM(2011) 900 final. *See* A. Sinnaeve, *What's New in SGEI in 2012?—An Overview of the Commission's SGEI Package*, 2 EStAL 347, 348 (2012).

62. That is the communication containing a revised EU Framework for state aid in the form of public service compensation (the "Framework"), which specifies how the Commission will analyze cases that have to be submitted to the Commission (OJ 2012 C 8/15).

63. J. L. Buendia Sierra & M. Munoz de Juan, *Some Legal Reflections on the Almunia Package*, 2 EStAL 63, 75 (2012).

64. The Framework develops a methodology to determine net costs.

65. Framework, ¶¶ 21 *et seq.* and 47 *et seq.* In addition, member states have to prove that (1) the compensation is not discriminatory vis-à-vis providers already entrusted with the same SGEI; (2) they have launched a public consultation to take the interest of users and providers into account; (3) the duration of the entrustment is justified by reference to objective criteria; (4) they have included incentives to achieve efficiency gains in the contract with the provider; and (5) they have complied with the transparency obligations contained in the Framework. Finally, the Commission reserves a right to intervene in case of serious competition distortions—that is, when the above-mentioned compatibility conditions prove not to be sufficient.

66. Communication, ¶ 46. That being said, the Commission points out at ¶ 48 that "it would not be appropriate to attach specific public service obligations to an activity which is already provided or can be provided satisfactorily and under conditions, such as price, objective quality characteristics, continuity, and access to the service, consistent with the public interest, as defined by the state, by undertakings operating under normal market conditions."

67. Social services, such as public housing and hospitals, constituted a serious bone of contention between the Committee of Regions and the European Parliament. *See* Committee of Regions' opinion 155/2004 of September 29, 2004, ¶ 2.4; K.-H. Lambertz & M. Hornung, *State Aid Rules on Services of General Economic Interest: For the Committee of the Regions the Glass Is Half-Full*, 2 EStAL 329, 330 (2012); and A. Sinnaeve, *What's New in SGEI in 2012?—An Overview of the Commission's SGEI Package*, 2 EStAL 347, 349 (2012).

68. For broadcasting, a separate set of guidelines apply, as well as a separate protocol; *see further* Hancher et al., *supra* note 2, at ch. 18.

69. At ¶ 13 of the Framework, the Commission states that member states cannot attach SGEI obligations to services that are already provided or can be provided satisfactorily and under conditions such as price and so on that are consistent with the public interest, as defined by the state, by undertakings operating under normal market conditions.

70. T-490/10 R, Endesa and Endesa Generación v. Commission, OJ 2011 C 152/23.

71. T-490/10 R, Endesa and Endesa Generación v. Commission, OJ 2011 C 152/23, ¶ 99.

72. T-490/10 R, Endesa and Endesa Generación v. Commission, OJ 2011 C 152/23, ¶ 100.

73. T-490/10 R, Endesa and Endesa Generación v. Commission, OJ 2011 C 152/23, ¶ 100.

74. C-242/10, Enel, not yet reported.

75. In this case the EC Directive 2003/55 on the internal market for gas.

76. IP/12/703, 27/06/2012.

77. At this stage of its investigation the Commission does not rule out that the public service compensation received by these undertakings could give them an unfair advantage over their competitors in the internal market in breach of the EU rules on services of general economic interest (SGEI); *see* IP/11/1571.

78. Case C-379/98 *Preussen Elektra* [2001] ECR 1-2099.

79. A fine case in point is Austria's legislation on aid to energy intensive users where, despite all the care Austria put into designing a system that evaded state aid control, the Commission still found that the measure was aid. *See* Case C-24/2009 State Aid for Energy-Intensive Businesses under the Green Electricity Act in Austria, *available at* http://ec.europa.eu/competition/state_aid/cases/232434/232434_1202618_94_3.pdf.

Chapter 12

1. The Australian competition law was the Trade Practices Act 1974 until January 1, 2011, when its name was changed to the Competition and Consumer Act 2010. For avoidance of reader confusion about name changes and because the provisions we are discussing were not changed in 2010, the competition law is referred to as "the Act" throughout this chapter.

2. P. D. Finn, Law and Government in Colonial Australia 2 (1987).

3. *Id.* at 3.

4. Warwick Funnell et al., In God We Trust: Market Failure and the Delusion of Privatisation UNSW 82 (2009).

5. *Id.*

6. *Id.* at 19.

7. *Id.*

8. John Quiggan, *Governance of Public Corporations: Profits and Public Benefits, in* From Bureaucracy to Business Enterprise: Legal and Policy Issues in the Transformation of Government Services 28 (Michael J. Whincop ed., 2003).

9. National Competition Council, Competitive Neutrality Reform: Issues in Implementing Clause 3 of the Competition Principles Agreement 2 (2007).

10. The first annual report of the Industry Commission, for example, stated that productivity growth was low compared to other OECD countries, particularly in areas such as gas, electricity, and water and that reform of other areas such as transport and utilities could increase GDP. Commonwealth of Australia, Industry Commission Annual Report 1989–1990 30 (1990).

11. Rod Sims, Is Competition a Myth?, Speech to Australian Economic Forum, Sept. 23, 2011, *available at* http://www.accc.gov.au/speech/is-competition-a-myth.

12. Stephen P. King, *Corporatisation and the Behaviour of Government-Owned Corporations, in* From Bureaucracy to Business Enterprise: Legal and Policy Issues in the Transformation of Government Services 28 (Michael J. Whincop ed., 2003).

13. *Id.*

14. Mark Aronson & Harry Whitmore, Public Torts and Contracts Law Book 3 (1982).

15. Each body politic in Australia is governed by a written constitution and has perpetual succession. It must act through natural persons but has a legal status independent from the. *See* Nicholas Seddon, Government Contracts Federal State Local 139 (4th ed. 2009).

16. The practice in distinguishing between the various manifestations of the Crown is to refer to "the Crown in right of the commonwealth" or, for example, "the Crown in right ofVictoria" in respect of a state.

17. Seddon, *supra* note 15, at 139.

18. *Id.* at 173.

19. Province of Bombay v. Municipal Corporation of Bombay (1947) AC 58.

20. Bropho v. Western Australia [2005] FCA 941 (July 8, 2005).

21. The Australian Industries Preservation Act 1906 was declared unconstitutional by the High Court under a now-discredited view of constitutional interpretation. The 1965 Trade Practices Act was also declared to be unconstitutional and was replaced by the more limited Trade Practices Act 1971. It was superseded by the Trade Practices Act PA 1974, which was amended and renamed the Competition and Consumer Act (CCA) in 2011 (the Act).

22. Trading, financial, and foreign corporations: Constitution, § 51(xx); Act, § 4(1).

23. Trade and commerce power: Constitution, § 51(i); Act, § 6.

24. Trade or commerce power, Constitution § 51(i); Act, § 6(2). There are some other relevant constitutional provisions, but those mentioned provide the major platform for the law.

25. Under the Act, the Australian Parliament could also enact laws exempting particular conduct and certain bodies from the operation of the Act without giving substantiating reasons: the Act § 51(1)(b), (c), and (d) prior to amendment by the Competition Policy Reform Act 1995.

26. The Act, Section 2A, was inserted on recommendation of the Swanson Committee: Trade Practices Act Review Committee, Report to the Minister for Business and Consumer Affairs 87, 10.25 (1976).

27. Productivity Commission, Review of National Competition Policy, Apr. 14, 2005, at xiv, *available at* http://www.pc.gov.au/projects/inquiry/ncp/docs/finalreport.

28. Report of the Independent Committee of Inquiry into the Trade Practices Act, National Competition Policy, AGPS Canberra (the "Hilmer Report") (1993).

29. For further details and the text of these documents, *see* the National Competition Policy website *at* http://ncp.ncc.gov.au.

30. Hilmer Report, *supra* note 28, at 7.

31. *See* Competition Principles Agreement; Conduct Code Agreement; and Agreement to Implement National Competition Policy and Related Reforms. A National Competition Council was

established as part of these reforms to provide advice about competition policy matters and make various recommendations in relation to the statutory access regime contained in Part IIIA of the Act.

32. While the Competition Code repeats the substantive provisions of Part IV, it applies to "persons" rather than to corporations to address the issue of the limitations on the commonwealth Parliament's power to legislate in this area.

33. Authorization that is an administrative sanction may be granted by the ACCC for most Part IV conduct on the basis of individual application if it can be justified on public benefit grounds. *See* Act, pt.VII.

34. *See* Hilmer Report, *supra* note 28, at xxvii, 343. The Hilmer Report noted that at the time of the review, government-owned business constituted 10 percent of Australia's GDP (at 169).

35. There were also a number of other bodies such as statutory marketing bodies and the professions. Other groups were able to be exempted by the laws of the states and territories in a nontransparent way. Other conduct could be given administrative approval after a more transparent process.

36. Each of these provisions is in a separate part of the Act and makes provision for application of that part to the Crown regardless of whether or not it is conducting business.

37. Section 4(1).

38. Section 2A(2).

39. Sections 2A(3), (3A).

40. This was the extent of agreement under the Hilmer Report reforms; *see supra* note 38.

41. Section 4(1)

42. Sections 2B(2), 2B(3).

43. It does not, however, need to be a trading or financial corporation as defined in Section 4(1) as do private corporations.

44. Seddon, *supra* note 15, at 137.

45. *See, e.g.*, NT Power Generation Pty Ltd v. Power and Water Authority & Anor (2004) 219 CLR 90, where the subsidiary of PAWA, Gasgo, was incorporated under the Corporations Act, not a specific statute.

46. Seddon, *supra* note 15, at 149.

47. The position in Queensland under the Government-Owned Corporations Act 1993 and in Victoria under the State-Owned Enterprises Act 1992 is the same.

48. Seddon, *supra* note 15, at 148.

49. Bropho v. Western Australia, *supra* note 20.

50. *Id.* at 21–22.

51. *See, e.g.*, Province of Bombay v. Municipal Province of Bombay, *supra* note 19.

52. *See* Robertson Wright, *The Future of Derivative Crown Immunity—With a Competition Law Perspective*, 2007 Competition & Consumer L.J. 14.

53. *See* Bropho v. Western Australia, *supra* note 20, at 19.

54. NT Power Generation Pty Ltd v. Power and Water Authority (2001) 184 ALR 481 (Federal Court); NT Power Generation Pty Ltd v. Power and Water Authority (2002) FCR 399 (Full Federal Court).

55. Northern Territory Electricity Commission.

56. *See* S.G. Corones, Competition Law in Australia 232 (5th ed. 2010).

57. Section 2C(2).

58. NT Power v. Power and Water Authority, *supra* note 54.

59. Section 4(1).

60. NT Power Pty Ltd v. Power and Water Authority, *supra* note 54.

61. *See* J. S. McMillan Pty Ltd v. Commonwealth (1997) 77 FCR 337; GEC Marconi Systems Pty Ltd v. BHP Information Technology Pty Ltd (2003) 128 FCR 1.

62. Seddon, *supra* note 15, at 309.

63. *See supra* note 61.

64. Corrections Corporation of Australian Ltd v. Commonwealth of Australia (2000) 104 FCR 448.

65. Easts Van Villages v. Minister Administering the National Parks and Wildlife Act (2001) ATPR (Digest) 46–211.

66. Thomson Publications Pty Ltd v. TPC (1979) 40 FLR 257.

67. ACCC v. Australian Medical Association (WA) Inc. (2003) 199 ALR 423.

68. NT Power Pty Ltd v. Power and Water Authority, *supra* note 54.

69. The High Court overruled the decisions of the Federal Court and the Full Federal Court. Misuse of Market Power is somewhat similar to the EU provisions on Abuse of Dominance and U.S. provisions on Monopolization.

70. ACCC v. Baxter Healthcare Pty Ltd (2007) 232 CLR 1. There the court found that Baxter had engaged in abuse of market power in bundling in its tender winning supply contracts with several state governments who were entitled to Crown immunity.

71. Bradken Consolidated Limited v. Broken Hill Pty Co. Ltd (1979) 145 CLR 107, regarded as the high-water mark of this principle. *See generally* Wright, *supra* note 52.

72. NT Power Generation Pty Ltd v. Power and Water Authority, *supra* note 54, at ¶ 170.

73. The SPAs were acquiring supplies for public hospitals.

74. The bundled products included one product that was in a competitive market and one product that only Baxter could supply—in other words, it was a monopolist in respect of the second product.

75. Bradken Consolidated Ltd v. Broken Hill Pty Co Ltd, *supra* note 71.

76. Bropho v. Western Australia, *supra* note 20.

77. Section 2.

78. *See* Agreement to Implement the National Competition Policy and Related Reforms, *available at* http://ncp.ncc.gov.au/docs/Agreement%20to%20Implement%20the%20NCP%20and%20Related%20Reforms.pdf.

79. Section 51(1)(a).

80. Section 51(1)(b), (c), or (d).

81. Corones, *supra* note 56, at 260.

82. *See* Competition Principles Agreement 1995, cls. 5.1, 5.5. Under the specified test the benefits of the restriction must outweigh the costs, and there must not be a less restrictive alternative. Factors for consideration are set out in clause 1(3).

83. OECD, Reviews of Regulatory Reform, Competition Policy in Australia (2010), at 54, *available at* http://www.oecd.org/documentprint/0,3455,en_2649_34569_46255013_1_1_1_1,00.

84. These included reforms to the dairy industry, shop trading hours, and liquor licensing. Not all commentators agree that this process has worked well. *See* D. Margetts, *National Competition Policy and the Australian Dairy Industry*, 60 J. Australian Pol. Econ. 98 (2007).

85. OECD, *supra* note 83, at 60.

86. Productivity Commission, *supra* note 27, at 14.

87. The Competition Principles Agreement set out commitments for a regime to cover "third party access to services provided by means of significant infrastructure facilities" (cl. 6). The regime has been reviewed and amended several times since its introduction. Productivity Commission, Review of National Access Regime Report No. 17 (Ausinfo, Canberra, 2001); *see also* Trade Practices Amendment (National Access Regime) Act 2006.

88. *See generally* Stephen King & Rodney Maddock, *Competition and Almost Essential Facilities: Making the Right Policy Choices*, 15 Economic Papers 28 (1996).

89. *See* §§ 44B, 44H.

90. The regime is well established with a large number of determinations and court decisions on the record. *See* Corones, *supra* note 56, at ch. 14.

91. Part IIIA of the Act. The regime has been criticized for its complexity.

92. Hilmer Report, *supra* note 28, at 300, recognized that "corporatization" alone would be adequate and that an appropriate model required five basic principles: clarity and consistency of objectives; management authority and accountability; performance monitoring; effective rewards and sanctions; and competitive neutrality.

93. Hilmer Report, *supra* note 28, at 295, noted that distortions relating to government business enterprises are generally "less deliberate and transparent and typically flow from a failure to reform laws, policies, and practices to keep abreast of developments as bureaucratic and monopolistic enterprises move to more commercial and competitive operating environments." *See generally* Ian Hanrahan, *Becoming Competitively Neutral*, Trade Prac. L.J. 19 (2004).

94. Productivity Commission, *supra* note 27, also considered possible ongoing competition policy reform.

95. Productivity Commission, *supra* note 27, at xx.

96. Priorities for reforms going forward included strengthening the national electricity market, building on the national water initiative, developing integrated national strategies on efficient and integrated freight transport services, and an overarching review of the health system.

97. *See* http://ncp.ncc.gov.au/pages/about.

98. The OECD has recommended better regulation to promote efficient use of existing facilities and well-targeted public and private investment decisions. *See* OECD, *supra* note 83.

99. Infrastructure Australia has released a variety of documents, *available at* http://www.infrastructureaustralia.gov.au.

100. Productivity Commission, Potential Benefits of the National Reform Agenda Report to Council of Australian Governments (Research Paper, 2006), *available at* http://www.pc.gov.au/__data/assets/pdf_file/0003/61158/nationalreformagenda.pdf.

101. The current chairman of the ACCC has suggested that in the infrastructure area, incentives may assist in bringing competition to the fore in major reform areas. *See* R. Sims, chairman, ACCC, *supra* note 11, at 6. *Available at* http://www.accc.gov.au/content/index.phtml/itemId/1008823/fromItemId/8973; *see also* R. Sims, ACCC, Some Perspectives on Competition and Regulation, Speech to Melbourne Press Club, October 10, 2011, *available at* http://www.accc.gov.au/speech/some-perspectives-on-competition-and-regulation.

102. Business leaders surveyed for the Global Competitiveness Report have ongoing concerns about the burden of government regulation and rank restrictive labor regulation, inefficient government bureaucracy, tax rates, access to financing, and inadequate supply of infrastructure as the most problematic factors for doing business. K. Schwab (Ed.), World Economic Forum Global Competitiveness Report 2010–2011, World Economic Forum, Geneva (2011), *available at* http://www3.weforum.org/docs/WEF_GlobalCompetitivenessReport_2010-11.pdf.

103. The three streams of government referred to are commonwealth, state, and local government.

104. *See* COAG Reform Council, National Partnership Agreement to Deliver a Seamless National Economy: Performance Report for 2009–2010, December 23, 2010, *available at* http://www.coagreformcouncil.gov.au/reports/competition-and-regulation/national-partnership-agreement-deliver-seamless-national-econom-0.

105. *See* Productivity Commission, Terms of Reference and Framework Report (2011), *available at* http://www.pc.gov.au/projects/study/coag-reporting/framework-report.

106. Seddon, *supra* note 15, at 274. The description "limited" does not acknowledge the many other initiatives affecting government undertaken as part of competition policy in the Hilmer reforms and the significant body of regulation on government tendering and bidding. Seddon does, however, identify a significant omission from the Act.

107. Hilmer Report, *supra* note 28, at 161.

108. Productivity Commission, *supra* note 27, at 332.

109. *Id.*

110. The review is expected to report within the next 12 months. The outcomes will provide a new competition law and policy framework for the next 20 years.

Chapter 13

1. *See* Marina Androulakakis, Public Contracts and Competition Law, *available at* http://www.bernitsaslawoffices.eu/files/PUBLIC%20CONTRACTS%20AND%20COMPETITION%20LAW_Updated_July2012.pdf.

2. *See* http://eur-lex.europa.eu/LexUriServ/LexUriServ.do?uri=consleg:2004l0017:20090807:en:pdf, and http://eur-lex.europa.eu/LexUriServ/LexUriServ.do?uri=OJ:L:2004:134:0114:0240:en:pdf.

3. Jean-Jacques Laffont & Jean Tirole, A Theory of Incentives in Procurement and Regulation (1993) (describing the theory of optimal regulation).

4. Philippe Gagnepain & Marc Ivaldi, *Incentive Regulatory Policies: The Case of Public Transit Systems in France*," 33 Rand J. Econ. 605 (2002) (measuring the impact of different types of contract on the efficiency of urban transport networks).

5. Philippe Gagnepain & Marc Ivaldi, Regulatory Schemes and Political Capture in a Local Public Sector, TSE Working Paper No. 10-15 (2010) (exhibiting the factors that govern the choice of contract types by the transport authorities).

6. This chapter is inspired by a decision of the French competition authority concerning a merger between Veolia and Transdev in the local public transport industry. The decision—in French—is *available at* http://www.autoritedelaconcurrence.fr/pdf/avis/10DCC198decisionoccultee.pdf.

7. William P. Rogerson, *Simple Menus of Contracts in Cost-Based Procurement and Regulation*, 93 Am. Econ. Rev. 919 (2003), suggesting that these two types of contracts could approximate around 75 percent of the welfare gains that could be achieved under a full menu of contracts.

8. The inefficiency is intrinsic. It is due to exogenous factors such as the topology of the network but also to past decisions such as underinvestment.

9. To simplify the exposition, we omit the index that refers to the type of contract.

10. Laffont & Tirole, *supra* note 3.

11. This situation could also be observed in other industries, like water or gas distribution, waste collection and treatment, or intercity transport.

Index

Italic page numbers indicate material in figures and tables.

Global Competition Law and Economics

Thomas K. Cheng, Ioannis Lianos, and D. Daniel Sokol, editors

Competition law and economics—known in the United States as antitrust—is an area of cutting-edge academic work with significant policy implications. Once confined to the United States and a few other countries, antitrust has taken off as an area of study in a relatively short period of time. More than 100 jurisdictions now have competition laws. Increasingly, enforcement activities abroad have far-reaching implications for any antitrust regime. Moreover, developments in economic thinking have helped to reformulate attitudes in both academic and policy circles. This book series is at the forefront of the development of new ideas and approaches within the field.

Competition Law and Development
2013
The Global Limits of Competition Law
2012